What Is Anything?

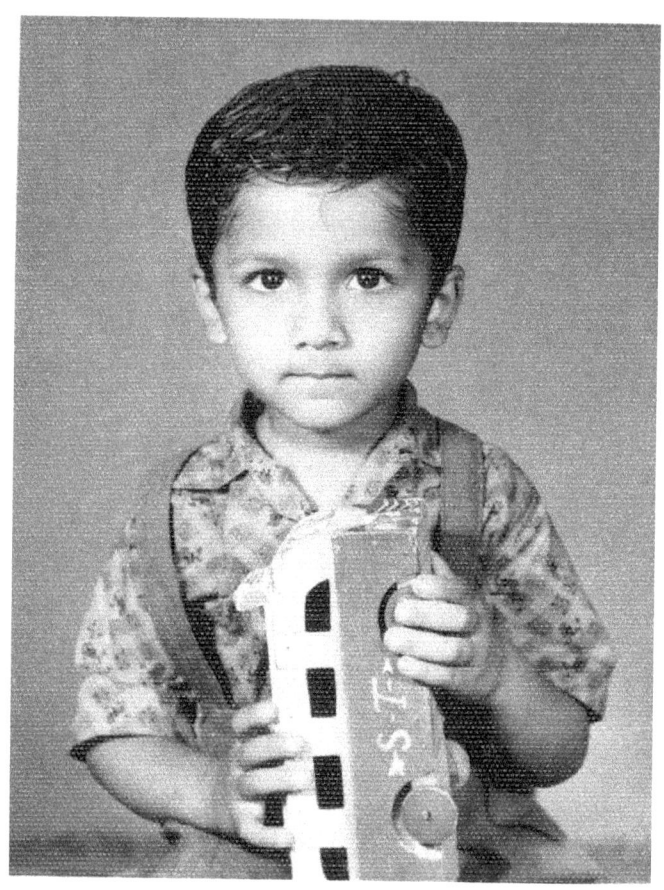

Sunand Tryambak Joshi, age 4 (Poona, India)

WHAT IS ANYTHING?

Memoirs of a Life in Lovecraft

S. T. Joshi

Hippocampus Press
New York

Copyright © 2018, 2023 by S. T. Joshi

Published by Hippocampus Press
P.O. Box 641, New York, NY 10156.
http://www.hippocampuspress.com

All rights reserved. No part of this work may be reproduced in any form or by any means without the written permission of the publisher. The opinions expressed in this publication are those of the author. They do not purport to reflect the opinions or views of the publisher. The author is grateful to Leslie G. Boba, Jason V Brock, Nalini Elkins, Will Hart, and Mary K. Wilson for providing some of the photographs used in this volume.

Cover illustration by Jason C. Eckhardt.
Cover design by Daniel V. Sauer, dansauerdesign.com.
Hippocampus Press logo designed by Anastasia Damianakos.

Library of Congress Cataloging-in-Publication Data

Names: Joshi, S. T., 1958- author.
Title: What is anything? : memoirs of a life in Lovecraft / S. T. Joshi.
Description: First edition. | New York : Hippocampus Press, [2018] |
  Includes index.
Identifiers: LCCN 2018012258 (print) | LCCN 2018019971 (ebook) |
  ISBN 9781614982234 (ebook) | ISBN 9781614982203 |
  ISBN 9781614982203¬q(hardcover ;¬qalk. paper) |
  ISBN 9781614982210¬q(pbk. ;¬qalk. paper)
Subjects: LCSH: Joshi, S. T., 1958- | Critics--United States--Biography. |
  Editors--United States--Biography. | Lovecraft, H. P. (Howard Phillips),
  1890-1937--Criticism and interpretation.
Classification: LCC PS29.J67 (ebook) | LCC PS29.J67 A3 2018 (print) |
DDC 801/.95092 [B] --dc23
LC record available at https://lccn.loc.gov/2018012258

First Paperback Edition
1 3 5 7 9 8 6 4 2

ISBN: 978-1-61498-221-0

To Mary K. Wilson

now and forever

"I have concealed nothing from you, nor do I expect ever to regret of having thus opened my heart."—Samuel Johnson

Contents

Preface 9

1. From India to Illinois (1958–68) 11
2. Indiana I (1968–72) 29
3. Indiana II (1972–76) 47
4. Brown (1976–80) 81
5. Brown and Princeton (1980–84) 113
6. Chelsea House I (1984–90) 135
7. Chelsea House II (1990–95) 157
8. New York (1995–2001) 185
9. Seattle I (2001–05) 213
10. Moravia (2005–08) 241
11. Seattle II (2008–12) 263
12. Seattle III (2012–18) 283
13. Seattle (2018–2022) 321

Epilogue 345

Index 349

Preface

In 1930, H. P. Lovecraft wrote to James F. Morton: "I'd damn well like to come out with a book some day, even though I might never win a place beside Schopenhauer, Nietzsche, or Bertrand Russell. I think I'd call it 'What Is Anything?'—in spite of the popular catchpenny sound of such a title." Lovecraft was referring to a work expressing his philosophy of cosmic indifferentism, and it occurs to me that it is not the most appropriate imaginable title for a memoir—even one whose chief purpose is to outline my own involvement in the study and dissemination of Lovecraft's work. Still, the title is so piquant that I cannot resist using it.

The difficulties in writing about oneself, even at a relatively early age as far as memoirs are concerned (several months shy of my sixtieth birthday), cannot be minimised. Lovecraft himself exhibited a remarkable ability to remember abundant details of his childhood and adolescence, but I cannot claim to duplicate his feat. Moreover, my innate reticence and reserve (a central feature I share with Lovecraft) render me incapable of speaking of intimate personal matters, especially since many other individuals with whom my life has been entwined over the years are still alive, and I do not care to invade their privacy or my own; mercifully, I am confident that few readers would be interested in such matters. Conversely, whether the chronicle of my multitudinous projects and publications over the years holds any genuine interest even to devotees of Lovecraft or of weird fiction is something I shall have to leave to others to determine.

If this account is to be of value as anything other than an exercise in egotism, it might be from the perspective of the remarkable ascendancy of Lovecraft, over the past half-century, to canonical status in American and world literature, as well as an icon in popular culture; and, concurrently, the rise of weird fiction as a whole in both popularity and critical esteem. I like to believe that I have been extensively involved in both phenomena for much of my adult life, and I am hopeful that the particulars of my involvement may be of some interest to scholars and historians.

But in reality, I have written this book because I myself wish to preserve as many memories of my own life as I can, and I have been led to believe that these may be of interest to a select readership. Another of Lovecraft's colleagues, the redoubtable Adolphe de Castro, once expressed the wish to write an autobiography with the title *All I Care to Tell*. Such a title would in fact be a more accurate reflection of what is in this book than the one I have chosen.

The quotations I have affixed to the various chapters are not necessarily intended to reflect the content of the chapters, but are merely piquant statements I have stumbled upon in the course of my reading. But they all embody, to a greater or lesser degree, some facets of my personal philosophy.

Seattle, Washington
December 2017

1. From India to Illinois (1958–68)

"Few men appear sane when their lives are well documented."—Joseph Wood Krutch

Sunand Tryambak Joshi was born on June 22, 1958, in Poona (now Pune), Maharashtra Province, India, to Tryambak Mahadeo Joshi and Padmini Tryambak (Iyengar) Joshi.

My paternal line is quite distinguished: one ancestor, Narayan Malhar Joshi (1879–1955), was a noted labour leader whose image appeared on an Indian stamp, and Vaman Malhar Joshi (1882–1943) was a philosophical novelist of some renown. Indeed, it would appear that the names of my sisters, Ragini (b. 1952) and Nalini (b. 1955), were derived from the titles of novels written by this author; my own first name (meaning "bringer of great joy") was derived from a character in one of his books, although this person's name was not the title of the book.

The first question that may occur to a reader of this book is: *How do you pronounce "Sunand"?* My frank answer is: I don't know. When forced to say my name, I usually enunciate it as: *Soo´-nand*. But occasionally my father would say *Soo-nand´*, and others have said *Soo-nahnd´*, *Soo´-nund*, and other variants. If one relies on the analogy with the name Anand, which is usually pronounced *Ah´-nahnd*, then *Soo´-nahnd* would seem to be correct. I myself never determined what my own preferred pronunciation would be—and during my teenage years, when I decided to be a writer, I threw in the towel and used initials, thereby avoiding the pronunciation problem altogether.

As for my middle name (my father's first name), its pronunciation is somewhat more straightforward. The name is pronounced, not as three-syllables, but as two: TRIM-buk. My friend J. Vernon Shea amusingly noted that, to a Westerner, the name looked as if it read "Try and back up!"

My father (1910–1994) was a distinguished economist and author of several published books on Indian economics (including the notable *Bombay Finance*, 1947). I believe that he had once taught at Nagpur University, but at the time of my birth was a professor at Ferguson College in Poona. That is where he met my mother (b. 1927), who was a graduate student in mathematics. Lest he be accused of cradle-robbing, let it be known that it was my mother who pursued my father and secured his hand in marriage. In 1939 he had married a woman who regrettably went mad and died at about the age of thirty. Indeed, my mother was acquainted with her and tended to her from time to time; it appears this woman was schizophrenic, and in those primitive days there was little knowledge of this ailment and few drugs to treat it. My parents married in 1951.

I am embarrassed to say that I remember almost nothing of my life in India. In large part this is apparently because I (like Einstein) did not utter a word until I was about four years old—and memory is intimately tied to speech. The reasons I was given for this anomalous silence were that (a) a number of languages were spoken in my household, including my native Marahti (which I did indeed learn to speak and can still understand to some degree) but also other Indian languages such as Hindi, Gujarati, and Tamil, as well as English; and (b) I was able to make my desires sufficiently known by gestures and other non-verbal means.

For the plain fact is that I was very spoiled as a baby. Bowing to the inveterate Indian custom (or prejudice) for male offspring, my parents tried twice to have a son and came up empty—but the third time was the charm! My maternal grandmother in particular indulged me in just about any wish that came into my infant mind, carrying me about like a little prince and giving me whatever I wanted after I had merely pointed to it. What need was there of speech?

The end result is that whatever events occurred during the five years of my life in India are only reflected in anecdotes that have been widely current in my family for decades. One particularly amusing tidbit is that, at about the age of three, I was playing in the yard of our bungalow on the edge of the Ferguson College campus, and all of a sudden I took it into my mind to run away as fast as my little legs could carry me. I not only left the yard, but ventured out onto the public sidewalk and then took off down the street like nobody's business. My sister Ragini, who was eight or nine at the time, was horrified at the spectacle and raced after me, followed by my ageing and hefty grandmother, who waddled along as fast as her thick legs could take her. Fortunately, I had the forethought to stop at the corner and did not plunge ahead into traffic, at which point Ragini seized me. Why I ever engaged in this truancy was unfathomable to all concerned, including myself. I

1. From India to Illinois (1958–68)

suspect I merely wanted to exercise my legs and enjoy a bit of joyous freedom from stultifying monotony.

The pictures in this book show me as an incredibly fat little Buddha-baby. Note the one where I am shown overflowing on Ragini's lap! I always seem to have a jovial expression on my face—no doubt the result of getting every one of my wishes fulfilled. This early indulgence has certainly made me a sloth and a wastrel, as is evident in my later career!

I have been told that I was passionately attached to various toys or other objects in the house. The frontispiece shows me clutching a toy truck (or is it a fire engine?) closely to my chest, and I was also immensely fond of a little car that I could sit in and pedal around. (Evidently it did not occur to me to use this vehicle on any extracurricular rampages, probably because my weak legs wouldn't allow me to gain much in the way of speed.) But I can't say that I have any genuine recollections of these possessions.

I was, of course, too young to have had any schooling in India, although my sisters must have. So my time was largely my own, chiefly spent in the company of my grandmother and other relatives (my father was the youngest of five or six sons, and my mother had a brother and sister). There is some reason to think that the two branches of my family didn't get along so well. My father was born and raised in the town of Junagadh, in the northwestern province of Gujarat; my mother and her family originated from southern India, in the area around Mysore, in the province of Karnataka. There are apparently all manner of regional and sectarian conflicts and rivalries in India, not unlike those in the United States; and so my parents' union was regarded as almost a "mixed" marriage. Of course, the fact that both my parents were Brahmins and part of the intellectual elite must have helped matters, but it does not appear that the two sides of my family interacted very much.

I have no recollection of ever visiting Bombay (Mumbai), the enormous megalopolis near Poona, on the other side of the ghats (mountains) that form the backbone of west-central India. Any number of my relatives must have lived there, however. We certainly did not visit the Taj Mahal, the Ganges, or any other of the standard tourist sites in the country. What is more, I (mercifully) failed to gain another important component of "Indianness": the Hindu religion.

My father was a self-proclaimed secularist. I am not sure he was a full-fledged atheist, although probably he would have admitted to being such if he had been pressed. I know that he met Gandhi—the great proponent of

Indian secularism—on at least one occasion; and there is a celebrated photograph of my father, along with all manner of other dignitaries (including four current or future prime ministers of India, among them Nehru and Indira Gandhi), at the founding of a business college. My mother, on the other hand, was for many years a devout Hindu and subscribed to many of the standard dogmas, including reincarnation. But early on my father stated that he did not wish his children to be indoctrinated (i.e., brainwashed) into either Hinduism or any other religion; we should be allowed to determine our own religious sentiments when we were intellectually and emotionally ready to do so. He supposedly said to my mother: "If you wish to pray, please pray in secret." This sane and sensible policy may have contributed to my eventual atheism. It is not, indeed, that my sisters and I were *prevented* from adhering to a religion or learning about other religions; in our various homes in the United States there was always an abundance of books about the religions of the world, and we were (languidly) encouraged to investigate them if we were so inclined. At a later date I did do exactly that—and found all religions so preposterous and contrary to common sense that I was never a believer.

The critical issue of my early life, of course, was my parents' decision to uproot themselves and immigrate to the United States. This decision was clearly spearheaded by my mother, who apparently believed that she was not progressing in her academic career as she wished, perhaps due to ongoing prejudice in Indian society against female professors (or females in general). Both of my parents were well familiar with the United States and spoke English fluently. My mother had received a master's degree from Bryn Mawr, and my father had gained his Ph.D. in 1959 from the University of Pennsylvania. And so my mother began applying to American colleges and universities for a teaching position. The matter was rather more complicated than it would appear, since the immigration restriction laws that had been passed in the 1920s (and enthusiastically endorsed by one H. P. Lovecraft) were still largely in effect. This meant that my mother had to have a "sponsor" at a university who would ensure that she could support herself (and, eventually, her family).

With my mother's excellent academic credentials, she was able to secure such a sponsorship at the University of Illinois in Urbana. (Urbana is part of the twin cities of Champaign-Urbana—although of course the residents of the latter, while far outnumbered in population by the former, refer to the locale as Urbana-Champaign.) The result was that, for the academic year of

1. From India to Illinois (1958–68)

1962–63, my mother left by herself to begin her teaching career there, while also working on a Ph.D. (In most Indian and British universities at the time, a professor was not required to have a Ph.D.; but most American institutions were now insisting on the degree, especially if the professor wished to advance in his or her career.)

The incredible thing was that I do not have the slightest recollection of my mother leaving the household—perhaps because the abundance of other relatives lessened the loss for me. And yet, it appears that I wrote my mother letters even at that tender age—including one letter *in Sanscrit!* I believe she still has this piquant document, although I have not seen it lately. Nowadays, I have forgotten not only the Sanscrit language but the entire Sanscrit alphabet with the absurd exception of exactly one letter (the one corresponding to the letter n).

In any event, the rest of my family—my father, my two sisters, and I—followed my mother the following summer. I set foot on American soil on July 12, 1963 (curiously enough, my parents' anniversary). I do remember the dreadful flight from Bombay to Chicago (with probably a stopover somewhere, maybe London, for refueling). I was dreadfully afflicted with motion sickness and was compelled to use the bag provided for such maladies. So terrified was I at repeating this embarrassing experience that I did not board a plane for another fifteen years.

I also have some dim memory of being driven the 200 or so miles south from Chicago to Urbana, sitting in someone's back seat in the darkness. The car must have been driven by some friend or colleague of my mother's, for she did not have a driver's licence and did not learn how to drive until a good many years later. We resided in what is now called Orchard Downs, at 1841 Orchard Place in Urbana. This is a residential area for graduate students and their families, about a mile southeast of campus. The next year we moved to an apartment (presumably a larger one) at 1107 W. Green Street, just north of campus; still later, perhaps in 1967, we moved to yet another apartment at 901 W. Springfield.

In the fall of 1963, I was enrolled in kindergarten—the first formal education I ever had. I attended Yankee Ridge School for kindergarten and then Leal School, at 312 West Oregon Street (about a half-mile due north of our home), for grades one to four. I imagine my sister Nalini also went to Leal, but Ragini (who was almost eleven) might have gone somewhere else. In any case, I have a distinct remembrance of sitting on the floor with other children in this class, with the (inevitably female) teacher speaking in a language I did not understand. The experience was not frightening, just puzzling. I pondered what exactly I was doing here, and what was expected of me. I also have a delectable recollection of taking wonderful naps on thick plastic mats (presumably provided by the school) in the early afternoons.

Clearly I picked up English pretty quickly, as one does at that age if one is immersed in it as I must have been. And yet, for years thereafter, certain grammatical and syntactical usages of the English language puzzled me terribly, and even at the age of seven or eight I found myself poring through some books on English grammar in the house and trying to figure out what was going on. The problem with English, for a non-native speaker, was that it has *too few rules*—almost anything goes, and the fact that English is a mishmash of German, Latin, Greek, French, and other languages makes it one of the most unsystematic languages on earth. I remember being particularly baffled, even infuriated, at why the past tense of *seek* was *sought*. That made no sense at all and didn't follow any coherent rule for the formation of the past tense that I could ever ascertain.

Once we were settled, my father returned to India. I am not sure when exactly this occurred—it was probably sometime in 1964. And yet, my own recollection (mortifyingly enough) was that my father was absent during the entire period from the summer of 1963 to the summer of 1968. This was certainly a critical time in my own development for my father to be absent, but I have not been able to pinpoint specifically what effect this had on my life, my temperament, or my career. I was never clear on exactly *why* my father did not stay with us; but I was led to understand that he had important work to do in India (or perhaps he had to teach a few more years to secure a full pension). And so he left.

The fact is, however, that my mother was an incredible dynamo of energy and determination, and she worked with unflagging energy not only to do her best for her family but also to foster her career. While teaching a full load of classes, she also was writing her Ph.D. dissertation and taking care of three small children—an heroic task that, I am sure, would have crushed the spirit of many other women (and men). And yet, it is also true that my mother in effect enlisted my oldest sister, Ragini, in the task of looking after Nalini and myself. Perhaps that robbed Ragini of a bit of her childhood by dumping more responsibilities on her than a pre-teen should rightfully bear. In any case, I myself was the beneficiary.

I would not say that I was totally spoiled in my early years in America—not, at any rate, to the extent that I was in India. For one thing, we were

1. From India to Illinois (1958–68)

quite poor, as my mother's salary as an instructor in mathematics was pretty low (possibly my father augmented it with some portion of his earnings), and had to live in cramped apartments for the first five years of our life in this country. For another thing, we naturally did not have any extensive network of relatives on whom we could draw for whatever needs might arise. I recall taking almost no family vacations during those early years—or, for that matter, the entirety of my youth and adolescence. I also never had an allowance. The fact that for many years my mother wasn't able to drive or afford to purchase a car limited our mobility, and I remember riding buses, walking, or riding my bicycle to wherever I wished to go. Nevertheless, I now realise that my family made a concerted effort to shield me from the worst effects of poverty and deprivation by giving me an abundance of toys, books, and other items to keep me amused and intellectually and culturally stimulated.

We did have some benefactors among my mother's friends and colleagues. Chief among them was an elderly professor of mathematics, Josephine Chanler, who at once took us under her wing and became a kind of benevolent aunt to us all. She would often take our entire family to dinner at a nice restaurant (perhaps the Faculty Club) on campus, and would bring us back to her house for further refreshments and socialising. (She had stacks of *Mad* magazine in the house, but somehow they never interested me very much.) She had a Southern accent—her family was from Kentucky, although she was born in St. Louis—and had a tried-and-true sense of Southern hospitality. She was a wonderful, jovial lady with a quick and infectious laugh and innate good breeding. (A friend of hers, Frances Wolever, was also kind to us, but she was a little more stiff and formal—a classic little old lady of the period.)

Other purported benefactors were more problematical. Some American family decided that we heathens needed some instruction in religion—the Christian religion, of course, and specifically the Roman Catholic faith. This family took me *alone* to a Catholic Mass. I was probably about eight years old at the time. I had absolutely no idea what was happening and was rapidly getting bored. This was an unusual church in that the priest would come to each pew and hand out the wafer individually. This piqued my attention: I was rather hungry, and even that little wafer, insubstantial as it was, might be welcome. But the fellow skipped over me! No doubt my hostility to religion comes from that scarring episode.

My family did take a trip to Chicago in 1967—but its purpose was largely utilitarian. In fact, we had an appointment with the immigration office to obtain permanent resident status—in other words, the invaluable green card, which prevents an immigrant from being deported in most circumstances. I guarded that card with my life until I secured U.S. citizenship in 1978. The trip was livened by a visit to the Museum of Science and Industry, where I was mesmerized by a machine that could take a piece of soft plastic and fashion a bust of Lincoln as you watched. I kept that bust for several years, but finally it somehow perished or got lost.

Precisely because my mother was so busy with her academic responsibilities, I myself developed a certain self-sufficiency from an emotional standpoint. As a child (and, indeed, for a good many years thereafter) I was terribly shy and withdrawn. Whether this was a result of my being an immigrant or was an innate facet of my personality, I cannot now determine. I was quite close to my sister Nalini, at times following her around like a puppy; Ragini, being five and a half years older than I, already seemed a kind of "adult" to whom I looked up (literally—I was quite short as a kid and she seemed to me very tall) with awe and reverence.

One very curious type of solitary play I devised for myself involved a set of tiny (about 2 inches high) porcelain figures of all the American presidents from Washington up to Lyndon Johnson. I have no idea how my mother obtained these objects, but they fascinated me from the start. The pedestals gave the dates of each president's term in office, so that to this day I know the entire sequence of all the presidents and the years in which most of them served.

But I went beyond merely absorbing dry information about these august figures. I began concocting *games* in which the presidents figured as players—notably what I called "Presidents' Baseball" and "Presidents' Football." For the former, I used a marble (I played with marbles quite a bit) as a (rather large, proportionately speaking) ball and used the pedestals to propel the ball crazily all across my room. (This was, I suppose, closer to kickball than baseball—but I didn't care about such a trivial detail.) I am astounded that I didn't break mirrors and other delicate objects in my room, but somehow I didn't.

What I did do, however, was leave these objects (whose four-cornered pedestals were rather sharp) all around the floor of my room and maybe elsewhere, with the result that my sisters would often step on them while walking about the house. They were so incensed by this that they once surreptitiously placed a bunch of presidents in my bed, so that I myself (who somehow never managed to step on these figures) would feel their pain. Well, I easily detected their trap and evaded it with a bland chortle. How I

1. From India to Illinois (1958–68)

wish I had that set of presidents! They were all incredibly lifelike, and I gained a keen sense of the presidents' appearance (from the diminutive James Madison to big Bill Taft) that remains with me to this day.

And yet, I also had a fair number of friends (all boys) in school. The five years I spent at Leal School (kindergarten to fourth grade) were a period I look back upon with poignant nostalgic fondness. My best friend was a boy of my age named Glenn Huff (he had a younger brother, but I cannot recall his name). I remember spending a good deal of my time after school at his home, and have distinct memories of his father, a gruff but genial man who welcomed me without any reservations about my race or background. We played all manner of games in their back yard. I also remember other boyhood friends—Mark Sullivan, David Voigtlander, Alfred Walker, and others. They were of course all white Americans, but they treated me with such unaffected friendship that I myself in very short order felt that I was more American than Indian.

For I had adopted American ways and become fascinated with American culture from an early age. It should be noted that the general expectation at the time was that immigrants would indeed shed most of their native cultural heritage and become Americans in word and deed, and my family naturally went along with the practice. Although in India we had naturally been vegetarians, my mother now permitted—indeed, encouraged—us to eat meat. She was (and remains) a fabulous Indian chef, but she now began mixing in American dishes—or interesting fusions of Indian and American dishes—into our diets. I myself became an ardent consumer of bacon, a taste I have yet to renounce. (My father, when he came over to join us in 1968, remained vegetarian for the entirety of his eighty-three and a half years of life.)

I also became rudimentarily aware of political developments in this country. I cannot say that I recall the assassination of President John F. Kennedy, which would have occurred only a few months after I entered kindergarten; but I do recall watching with awe and a bit of terror the stately funeral procession as it was shown on our tiny (probably 12-inch) black-and-white television. I soon became aware of the war in Vietnam, as we watched Walter Cronkite faithfully for many years. To this day—as with so many of our generation—such names as Saigon, Hue, the Mekong Delta, the DMZ, and the Tet Offensive remain etched in my memory as markers of a sad and turbulent chapter in American and world affairs. When I was about eight, Nalini dragged me to a Vietnam War protest rally on the campus of the University of Illinois. I was not entirely clear what was going on, but I knew that a lot of people were mighty upset about *something*.

More wholesomely, I developed an enthusiasm for many forms of American popular culture. I played plenty of sports—mostly football and baseball—with my little friends, and proved to be rather good at them in spite of my slender build. (I never liked, or was much good at, basketball, since my short stature and my unusual clumsiness at handling the big ball mitigated against my thriving at this sport.) And, of course, at school I excelled at such games as kickball and that exquisite exercise in sadism known as dodge ball. I made up all sorts of games with my cadre of friends and followed professional sports ardently. To this day I remain a rabid fan (much to the bafflement and consternation of those colleagues of mine to whom sports represent all that is base and vulgar in American society) of all the Chicago teams: the Bears (football), the Cubs and White Sox (baseball), the Bulls (basketball), and the Blackhawks (ice hockey).

Unfortunately, most of the Chicago teams were rather mediocre at this time, even if they featured the occasional superstar. I was well aware that the Bears had drafted both Gale Sayers and Dick Butkus in the college draft of 1965; and to this day I believe that Sayers is the most electrifying running back in the history of professional football, while Butkus is one of the most fearsome linebackers. Sayers's career was regrettably truncated by a pair of crippling knee injuries; but that did not prevent him from being inducted into the Hall of Fame, as Buktus was. (I was only dimly aware of the true tragedy of Brian Piccolo, Sayers's fellow running back who died of testicular cancer at the age of twenty-six in 1970.)

The Bulls were at that time led by such figures as Bob Love, Jerry Sloan (later a distinguished coach), and the curiously named Tom Boerwinkle (no relation to Rocky & Bullwinkle!). On the Blackhawks were the spectacular pair of Bobby Hull and Stan Mikita, although the team itself won no championship between 1961 and 2010. Of the Cubs I shall speak a bit later.

Another form of popular culture that I found extremely compelling was rock music. The early to mid-1960s remain, to my mind, the acme of this art form, and as early as 1964 I was a Beatles devotee for life. I am not absolutely certain that I recall their appearance that year on *The Ed Sullivan Show*, since I have seen clips of that appearance so often on documentaries and other venues; but I do remember their performance on that show in 1969, as well as on David Frost's show around the same time. I have a distinct recollection of being in Glenn Huff's company when I heard their song "Blackbird" (this must have been 1968, when the *White Album* was released): I broke down crying, thinking it the most poignant thing I had ever heard.

I kept elaborate lists of my personal "Top 10" (I could not really extend the list to the top 40) bands or musicians. The Beatles, of course, were never dethroned from being at the head of the list, but the Monkees, the Byrds, the Hollies, Paul Revere and the Raiders, the Turtles, Peter, Paul, and Mary, and other bands (including, a bit later, Simon & Garfunkel) were constantly vying for supremacy just under the Beatles. I never much cared for the Rolling Stones, since they were just a bit too wild and unruly for my taste; in fact, I rarely even heard many of their songs at the time. Earlier musicians such as Elvis Presley or Little Richard either did not appeal to me or were unknown to me, while my aesthetic taste was insufficiently developed at the time for me to appreciate Bob Dylan.

I did listen to the actual Top 40 radio show, although I had to do it surreptitiously on a large and clumsy portable radio that my mother had acquired: she had a taste only for classical music (for which see below) and did not approve of her children's fondness for these wild-haired bands with their noisy electronic instruments. I have a vivid memory of how, in 1968, the Association's "Windy" vied for No. 1 on the charts for many weeks with a now-obscure song (one of those one-hit wonders) called "Little Bit o' Soul" by a band that I now do not remember. I also remember being fascinated with Jefferson Airplane's "White Rabbit," even though I did not know at the time that this was a perverse retelling of *Alice in Wonderland*. (I did not read that book until I was almost twenty.)

Rock music was, of course, the voice of its generation's social conscience—which in large part gave it its profound meaning to those who absorbed it. The music fueled the anti–Vietnam War protests, and its imperishable songs dealing with that turbulent time—"War," "Abraham, Martin, and John," "Turn, Turn, Turn!" (whose lyrics I thought some of the most profound ever written—unaware that they had largely been taken from the Bible), even such preposterous things as "In the Year 2525"—are searingly etched into the minds of anyone who was conscious during the 1960s. To the extent that I, young as I was, regarded myself as a "child of the 1960s," I gained—and still retain today—a general inclination toward countercultural rebellion against authority (although not extending to such flamboyancies as taking drugs), a cynicism regarding any true progress in social or cultural life, and emphatic liberalism in politics.

But I cannot plausibly maintain that a social conscience was dominant in my makeup at such an early age as I am now writing about. Instead, I relished the offerings of American pop culture as embodied in sports, music, and especially television. Up to the age of fourteen I was an emphatic and unrepentant TV addict, and to this day the sitcoms of this and a slightly later era evoke immense nostalgia in me—*The Dick Van Dyke Show, The Beverly Hillbillies, Mr. Ed, Bewitched, Hogan's Heroes, My Favorite Martian, Petticoat Junction, Green Acres, Get Smart, McHale's Navy, F Troop, The Andy Griffith Show, Gomer Pyle, U.S.M.C.*, and on and on and on. Some of the crime /suspense/espionage dramas of the era were also entertaining: *The Man from U.N.C.L.E., The Wild Wild West* (what a stupendous foreshadowing of steampunk!), *Mission: Impossible*, and so on. I must have watched *The Twilight Zone* (and I'm certain I watched the later *Night Gallery*), but strangely enough it did not leave a significant impression upon me at the time. In the afternoons, after coming home from school, I watched not only game shows (*Password, Truth or Consequences*, etc.) but *The Galloping Gourmet*, where the Australian chef Graham Kerr would go into orgasmic ecstasies upon eating the scrumptious dishes he cooked up. (I did not, however, care for *Dark Shadows*, finding it hokey and contrived.) Curiously, I was also attracted to the many Westerns of that period: *Gunsmoke, Bonanza, Rawhide, Dead or Alive, Branded*. What I could possibly have found appealing about these shows, so remote from my own experience, I can never explain. We all watched these shows simply because they were on TV. Let us remember that there were only four channels in that primitive era—CBS, NBC, ABC, and PBS. But it was the sitcoms that drew me, and to this day I find many of them unaffectedly amusing.

 I did not watch many shows that were specifically aimed for children, although I did take in *Captain Kangaroo* and was inveterately fascinated with his extensive train set—more for the elaborate landscaping than for the train itself. I did not watch *Mister Rogers' Neighborhood* (which, in any case, did not begin until 1968) and was of course too old for *Sesame Street*, which commenced in 1969. But I was addicted to Saturday morning cartoons, my favourite (then and now) being the rather twisted and slyly satirical *Road Runner*. But I watched plenty of others—*Underdog, Rocky and Bullwinkle, Snagglepuss, Popeye*, etc. I never watched "serious" or action comics (*Johnny Quest* and the like) and didn't care for *Scooby Doo* (which began only in 1969).

 The odd thing is that I don't recall much of my actual schooling during these early years. I found schoolwork fairly easy and don't remember doing much in the way of homework: perhaps at that time homework wasn't assigned to children in these grades. I have no recollection of what classes I

1. From India to Illinois (1958–68)

took (if indeed there were separate classes outside of our "home room") or what I was taught. I do recall my mortification when I received a C in penmanship. Imagine! I had otherwise received (and would receive throughout my entire scholastic career through high school) nothing but A's—but here was a teacher who thought I had bad handwriting! I actually thought my cursive handwriting was rather nice-looking, and I enjoyed practising it. Well, there's no accounting for tastes—or for the whims of persnickety teachers.

My schooling was affected by the fact that I early on developed nearsightedness. From a very young age I had become fascinated with maps and geography, and I spent much time tracing countries, continents, and so on from atlases and other reference works. I do not know if this practice affected my eyes, but from as early as the age of seven I had to wear spectacles. Initially I found the whole business of putting glasses on my face so repulsive—and so disfiguring to my beautiful little face—that *I simply refused to wear them*. I had to do this covertly, however: I of course was compelled to wear glasses at home, but when I went to school I simply stuck them in my pocket and tried to carry on as best I could with my blurry vision. But my silly ruse was detected in a few weeks, and I was thereafter forced to wear glasses permanently. Eventually I became used to them—and wore glasses for more than thirty years. (Now I wear contact lenses, a vast improvement in comfort and appearance.)

My devotion to maps did lead me astray on one occasion. About the age of eight I found myself poring over the map of Urbana as found in the telephone book. Somehow I took it into my mind that I had found a clever short cut from Leal School to my house—and one day I acted upon the notion. But what I did not realize is that my new path was taking me far away from home. I may have actually left the city limits (I think I was heading in a southerly direction) and soon found myself in a remote area of farmland. In other words, I was totally lost! Petrified by my inability to return home, I simply trudged along—when a passing jogger passed me by and looked at me curiously. Amidst my tears I was able to mutter to him, "I think I'm lost." He quickly took the situation in hand and brought me back to his own house, where he contacted my mother and effected a rescue. I believe he had to drive me back to my apartment building, since my mother of course didn't have a car of her own. Saved by the kindness of strangers!

In addition to being shy, especially with strangers, I was quite nervous as a child and given to erratic behavior. I recall one time when I was in the school library, or perhaps some other room in Leal School. I found myself on a kind of stage or raised platform and felt that the best way to get down to the desks and tables on the main floor was simply to jump from the stage down to the floor, rather than to take a small flight of steps on one side of the stage. I believe I ended up landing rather efficiently in a chair—but the teacher frowned upon this irregular mode of locomotion and chastised me gently. Another time, as I was walking to school, I was so preoccupied with my thoughts that I crossed the street without looking. This could have been disastrous, but what actually happened was that I walked smack into a car that had come to a stop at a stop sign. I simply didn't see the car in front of me.

One of the several notorious instances of my bad—or, rather, unthinking—behavior occurred when my entire family was being driven in a car by someone or other. In spite of the number of people in the car, the conversation had come to a dead halt. Bothered by this, I piped up with: "When are we going to drink the rest of the Champagne?"

The fact was that my mother, who generally avoided alcohol, had recently been given a bottle of Champagne by some well-meaning friend and had doled out maybe a spoonful of it to me just so I could sample it. So naturally it occurred to me, as a conversation starter, to allude to this harmless event. How was I to know that the lady who was driving us in the car was a teetotaler! She must have had nightmarish visions of my mother plying me and my sisters with alcoholic beverages at every turn—for after all, I had explicitly mentioned "the *rest* of the Champagne"! So as I was sitting in that car, I wondered why my perfectly innocent remark didn't get the conversation going: in fact, the silence became deeper and still more ominous.

Most of my memories of this period focus on play—especially play with my little gang of friends. There was one time when my pals (all male, of course) decided to form an informal club for the purpose of expressing our unremitting hostility to some girls who had apparently formed a similar club. We were of course imbued with the inveterate small-boy prejudice against females, and we were quite literally bouncing off the walls trying to come up with a suitable name for ourselves that would express both our noble manliness and the danger we posed to those disgusting and potentially evil girls. After much futile debate, I came through with what we all agreed was the perfect name: WAR (an acronym for We Are Ready). A brilliant stroke of genius! Quite frankly, in those innocent times, the extent of our "war" was to hide in the bushes and hurl spitballs at the girls as they passed us on the sidewalk. I'm not even sure we pulled their hair or made any other physical contact with them.

1. From India to Illinois (1958–68)

And yet, I was not entirely immune to feminine charms even at that tender age. My first "girlfriend" was a sweet little girl named Marcia Caton, to whom I became mildly attracted at about the age of eight. There was of course no sexual—and perhaps not even any romantic—element in our friendship; she was just a nice girl and I liked spending time with her. But the mere act of being alone with a girl at that age was considered a bit odd. One time I actually went to her house after school—something entirely unheard-of in those far-off days of the mid-1960s. Boys were supposed to fraternize with boys, girls with girls. If I may say so, Marcia seemed more taken with me than I was with her. On this little "date" at her house, she for some reason decided to cut my toenails, doing so with the intense, all-consuming care and precision that only an eight-year-old girl could manage. Were my toenails exceptionally long and untidy? Did they scratch her? I have no idea. But after a while I felt that this "relationship" was somehow wrong. I can't recall whether I was actually teased about it by my male friends—I may well have been. The last thing a boy wanted to be called in those days was a sissy. In any event, I never went over to her house again, and she quickly fell out of my life.

*

For all that I was becoming rapidly indoctrinated in American popular culture, my mother insisted that I begin absorbing elements of higher culture as well. There were always books in the house, although I wasn't much of a reader at that time. I read very few of the standard children's books, either classic or contemporary. I seemed more interested in *facts,* and recall poring over a multi-volume children's encyclopedia called *The Book of Knowledge,* filled with engaging colour illustrations of all sorts. Later my mother purchased the *World Book Encyclopedia,* which I also enjoyed; and she may already have purchased the 14th edition of the *Encyclopaedia Britannica*—the last great edition of that epochal reference work, before it dumbed itself down (with the Macropedia/Micropedia distinction) for the great unwashed.

The only children's book (or series) I read—and this may actually have occurred a few years later—was the Mother West Wind books. At the time I did not pay attention to who their author was, but I now see that these books were written by one Thornton Burgess (1874–1965), an American writer whose first Mother West Wind book was published in 1910. I recall reading these books in their original hardcover editions (from a public library), filled with engaging line drawings. The premise of the books was simply the display of a wide array of talking animals: evidently the books were designed by the author to promote the cause of conservation, but that point escaped me entirely as I simply revelled in the antics of these engaging creatures.

But beyond literature, my mother was keen on conveying to me her own love of (Western) classical music. She purchased many LPs of such music, mostly boxed sets that contained samplings of the more familiar chestnuts. Her own preference was for the Romantic composers of the nineteenth century, mostly Beethoven, Strauss, Chopin, and Liszt. I immediately fell under the sway of this musical feast, although at times I annoyed my mother by declaring that the main theme of *Swan Lake* was "Flash Gordon music" (the theme was used repeatedly at key moments of the old *Flash Gordon* live-action TV show). And, of course, the *William Tell Overture* was "Lone Ranger music."

My mother took yet bolder action. In the summer of 1966 (I had just completed the second grade), she enrolled me—without my knowledge or permission—in a violin class. I have a sense that a part of the motivation for this was simply her desire to get me out of the house (and out of her hair) for a part of the day. In any event, I had to go. (Ragini was taking piano lessons and kept them up for several years. At some point I also took some lessons, but for some reason I threw a tantrum during one such session and was asked not to return.) Evidently I proved to be reasonably proficient at the tiny little instrument I was given, so I kept at it. I never really liked practising very much, but I managed to get by on raw talent. I must have joined the regular children's orchestra when I entered third grade, although curiously enough I don't have any clear recollection of doing so. I kept up the violin regularly for the next ten years, and music has become an immense and central element of my aesthetic life.

Around this time, however, my violin career suffered something of a setback. One day right after school, my friends were playing in the schoolyard, hitting a softball high in the air. I strove to catch the ball—but was doing so with my bare hands, without a mitt. (I think some of my buddies had mitts—perhaps they stocked them in their lockers.) The ball ascended from the bat and came right down—and landed in my hands in an awkward manner. I felt a surge of pain—and when I held up my left hand, I found that the top joint of my left pinkie had been dislocated! The very

1. From India to Illinois (1958–68)

sight of the thing appalled and horrified me; and yet, I bravely struggled to carry on as if nothing had happened. But pretty soon I could no longer hide the fact that I had been injured. I started to cry and showed my friends my horrible injury.

Luckily, the school nurse was still on duty, and I was shepherded into her office. (I later heard that my friend Glenn Huff, who was not permitted to join me and remained outside, kept jumping up as high as he could outside the nurse's office window in order to see what was being done to me.) Unfortunately, the nurse proved utterly ineffectual, and I was transported to the local hospital. I imagine my mother was duly notified.

I was being taken to some examining room or something of the sort when a gruff doctor—who looked strikingly like Sergeant Carter from *Gomer Pyle*—proceeding in the other direction stopped us in the hallway and said, "What's going on here?" I held up my injured hand to his gaze. He said, "I can fix that." He took my hand and, over my weak and feeble protests, simply snapped the joint back into place by brute force. Once again, the agony I felt was beyond anything I had experienced up to that time—but at least my dislocation was remedied! The doctor (or maybe it was just a nurse) who was with me now led me to some office where a splint was attached to my finger, and then I was allowed to go home. The injury was healed in short order.

And yet, the effect on my violin career was not insignificant. The left hand is of course the hand whose fingers are placed on the strings to produce a given note; and the pinkie (what is called the "fourth finger" in violin parlance) is vital in playing certain notes that cannot be played otherwise. For months, perhaps years, my "fourth finger" was so weak from my injury that I simply couldn't play those notes; in fact, I couldn't even bend the top joint to any significant degree. So my career as the next Heifetz or Menuhin was doomed!

I am, however, proud to announce that from that date to this, I have never suffered any more serious injury than that dislocated pinkie. I have never broken a bone and have never spent a night in a hospital. No doubt this is largely a matter of luck, but there it is. I of course did endure the usual array of childhood diseases—measles, mumps (of which I have a vivid recollection—I may even have hallucinated a bit), and chicken pox at the ungodly age of seventeen. Otherwise, in my youth and adolescence I remained quite healthy, even robust—probably more through nervous energy than through actual musculature, as I remained quite slim and short for many years. I was probably continuing to grow into my early college years, until I finally attained my towering height of five feet, seven and a quarter inches. (I of course round that up to five feet eight inches.)

At some point during my stay in Urbana, I ventured upon my first creative utterances—nothing less than my own cartoon or comic book! This is all the more amusing given that I actually read very few comic books at this time or later, and when I began reading actual literature I expressed towering disdain for this humble art form. But at the age of eight or nine, I guess I was not too highbrow to indulge in it. What I designed was a comic book called *Catman and Bobbin*—an obvious parody of Batman and Robin, presumably reflecting my absorption of the campy *Batman* television show, which began airing in 1966. The fact of the matter is that I didn't really know what a "bobbin" actually was: I only chose the word for its parodic similarity to Robin. What I envisioned was simply a ball of yarn that flew through the air, a single strand trailing like a comet's tail. Whether the figure of Catman (a standard figure of a cat with a cape, also capable of flying at will) reflected my lifelong devotion to cats is not clear: at that time I didn't really feel any overwhelming fondness for felines, although I probably still preferred them to dogs (my mother's lifelong phobia of dogs may have influenced me in this regard).

I put quite a lot of care, thought, and effort into writing, drawing, and "publishing" this comic book. I would fold and cut pieces of paper so that the item could actually be read as a book. My art was no doubt quite crude—then as now my artistic skills were of a very low order. The whole cartoon was of course humorous (at least purportedly so), but I must have had some modicum of imagination in depicting an entire sequence of events that would cover 12, 16, 20, or 24 pages (very small pages, of course—about one-quarter of a standard 8½ × 11 page). The "book" was "published" only in an edition of a single copy, which I would circulate among my little friends. It proved quite popular among my buddies, and they looked forward with some minimal enthusiasm to each new "book."

Alas! none of these *Catman and Bobbin* books survive. How I wish they did: they would no doubt shed some light on my nascent fantastic (and comic) imagination. But they have long been consigned to oblivion; indeed, in some cases I don't recall ever getting these items back once they went on their informal rounds among my friends.

2. Indiana I (1968–72)

> "All the Sitwells look at the average man with something akin to bewildered horror, tempered by inordinate pity."—Vivian Mercier

In the summer of 1968 my mother left the University of Illinois and got a position in the mathematics department of Butler University in Indianapolis. In the event, she stayed there only a year, as she found the department and the university variously unsatisfactory; the very next year we moved to Muncie, home of Ball State University, where I remained until 1976, when I left for college. I do not have a great many memories of the one year in Indianapolis—we lived at 4621 Cornelius Avenue, in the northwest quadrant of the city—but I can recall a few things.

I was, of course, terribly saddened to leave my little friends—especially Glenn Huff—in Urbana, and no doubt I shed bitter tears on my departure. Those years in Urbana had been essential both to my general intellectual and social development and to my acclimatisation to American life, and I had gained an immense attachment to my buddies. It didn't help that we stayed in Indianapolis for only a year—my fifth grade. The result was that I have absolutely no recollection of any friends I made at school. Instead, all I can recall was a boy of my age, a Chinese-American named David Lee, and his little brother (name forgotten), who lived about two blocks away from us. I spent much time with them and had all manner of adventures.

The best thing about my year in Indianapolis was the house we lived in—for it was an actual house, of at least two stories (I cannot recall whether there was also a basement—there could well have been), with an impressive white stone façade that made me think it was a kind of fortress. (My later memories of the house misled me, as I thought the entire house was constructed of stone. But when I visited the place early in this millennium, I found that only the front of the house was covered with stone.) Naturally, I gloried in the spaciousness of the house—although, curiously enough, I no longer have any clear recollection of the exact contours of the place, either my own room (if I in fact had a room of my own) or the rest of the house. I do recall that, as you enter the front door, there is a long corridor that leads all the way through the house to the kitchen and, presumably, the back door and back yard.

I went to a public school only a block or two north of our house. (All the Indianapolis public schools were numbered at this time, but I cannot recall the number of my school.) I can no longer find this school on any online maps, so perhaps it has been torn down in the interim. The house was within walking distance to the Butler University campus—it was no doubt chosen to make it easier for my mother, who still didn't drive a car, to reach her office—but I have little recollection of ever venturing onto the campus.

The most momentous personal event of that year, of course, was my father's emigration from India. He now rejoined the family and remained with us until his death more than twenty-five years later. But the dismaying—even horrifying—thing for me was that I had *virtually forgotten him*. I have a distinct recollection of my mother leading me into a bedroom one morning (my father had presumably arrived the night before, after I had gone to bed), and seeing this portly, friendly-looking man lying in bed, still exhausted from his trip. He was introduced to me as my father, but I simply couldn't attach a meaning to that idea. He embraced me warmly as he remained lying on the bed, and I remember the stubble on his face scratching me.

I simply had to accept the fact that this was my father. Naturally there were some difficulties in re-integrating him into the family, and in the end I came to think of him more as a pal or benevolent uncle than my father. We got along splendidly and hardly ever argued, and I came to admire his quiet, dignified bearing. He also had the habit of singing Indian songs in a language I did not understand (of the seventeen or so Indian languages, I only understood Marathi, and these songs were probably in my father's native Gujarati language), but which I found charming and evocative. Perhaps I was also pleased that the male quota in the family had been so significantly augmented: I was already having a time fending off merciless teasing by my two sisters, to say nothing of occasional rebukes from my mother. My father would later teach me the rudiments of tennis. He himself had been a great tennis player and cricketer in his youth (he was now fifty-eight), and he quietly smirked at the absurdities of American baseball. Imagine the players needing to wear *gloves!*

In terms of schooling, all I can remember is that, when I showed up to enrol in the fifth-grade orchestra, the conductor quickly realised that the music we were playing was too elementary for me, and he ordered me to play in the junior high school orchestra. I was initially terrified of the prospect, not at all sure that I would be able to handle the more difficult music; but in fact I did quite well. I wouldn't say I was a prodigy, but evidently I was better than average.

But again, the focus of my life was play—especially with David Lee and his brother, and with other kids of a similar age in the neighbourhood. We had become fixated on an immense hornet's nest that was hanging high on a tree in a lot just across from the Lees' house, and our little gang was determined to bring it down. It was in fact quite a nuisance, as the hornets would buzz around our heads as we tried to play in the vicinity. So one day we decided to make a concerted effort to eliminate it from our midst. We gathered as many rocks as we could and began flinging them in the direction of the nest. It was pretty high up on the tree, maybe twenty feet off the ground, and it took considerable effort to hurl our rocks even close to the nest. But in the end we did bring it down!

However, the hornets were not particularly pleased with our destruction of their home and hearth. All manner of hornets began flying around in a rage, and one of the boys instructed us to lie as low as possible to avoid them. But at an inopportune moment I raised my head to get a glimpse of what was happening—and at that exact moment a hornet stung me just above my left eye. It literally felt as if someone were drilling a nail into my head, and I can to this day hear the angry buzz of that hornet as it punished me for my vandalism.

The upshot was that the sting caused the general area above my eye to swell up to such an extent that I was unable to open my left eye for several days, perhaps a week or more. But I figured this was a well-earned battle scar: we had eliminated the hornet menace and were now free to play in the area without disturbance!

Otherwise, I have very little recollection of that year in Indianapolis. All I can remember is my throwing a temper tantrum when my mother tried to prevent me from going trick-or-treating that Halloween, thinking I was already too old. I was only ten, going on eleven! And I couldn't endure the thought of giving up all that free candy. So she relented, and I quickly fashioned a homemade costume as a hippie—using, I believe, scarves and other attire that belonged to Nalini.

I hardly need add that the year 1968 was an epochal one in American and world history, and I was riveted and appalled at the succession of assassinations—first Martin Luther King, Jr., then Robert F. Kennedy—that rocked the nation. I have a distinct memory of the awesomeness of watching President Lyndon Johnson soberly announcing on television that he was not running for re-election. The Vietnam War had destroyed whatever good will he had gained from the American people (some of them, at any rate) with the Civil Rights Act, Medicare, and other Great Society programs. My family watched Walter Cronkite faithfully every evening, and I remember him actually chuckling when he announced the casualty figures for the day (figures that it was later determined were deliberately cooked up by the Defense Department), something like: "500 Viet Cong killed, 2 Americans killed." I also remember watching on television some of the turbulent events of the Democratic National Convention, although I did not see the celebrated faceoff between Gore Vidal and William F. Buckley, Jr. The election of Richard M. Nixon seemed a sorry culmination to a year of horror and misery.

But as 1968 gave way to 1969, we had to face the prospect of moving again. This move didn't trouble me so much, as I had not developed many close friends or much attachment to the large and rather unimpressive metropolis of Indianapolis. But my mother had secured an associate professorship in mathematics at Ball State University in Muncie, about 50 miles northeast of Indianapolis, and in the summer of 1969 we headed there.

The house we lived in—initially numbered 313 Normandy Drive, later numbered 405 S. Normandy Drive—was in the southwest region of the relatively small city (population at that time about 80,000), and in a good part of town. Other parts of town were not so good. The house was at least a mile, perhaps a bit more, from the Ball State campus, but the university was easily reached by bus, bicycle, or even on foot. It was quite a small house—one story with a partially finished basement and an attic accessible, rather charmingly, by a ladder that one pulled down from the ceiling in a hallway.

The house might have seemed rather crowded but for two countervailing events. First, Ragini, having skipped two grades in junior high or high school, was already heading off to college at the age of sixteen. She would be attending Bryn Mawr, my mother's M.A. alma mater, and would follow her footsteps to some degree by studying mathematics. So there were only my parents, Nalini, and myself to account for, and initially Nalini took possession of the long, low attic, which became her bedroom. But the second event was that, a year or two after we began living in the house, my mother decided to build a true second story—two bedrooms and a bathroom. This counted as a fairly major renovation in that era—indeed, I was staggered by the fact that it would cost us a whopping $8000! (We had purchased the house itself for the sum of $29,000.) The construction of this floor took a good many months and caused considerable inconvenience; but once it was finished, we revelled in the additional space. Naturally, Nalini took one bedroom and I took the other. The walls of the room were only of varnished wood, without plaster, and created a pleasing rustic look, as if we were in a remote lodge. My windows looked out on the driveway at the side of our house (leading to the garage) and the back yard, which was of moderate size.

I immediately became acquainted with other children in the area—but it happened, initially, in an odd way. It was still summer, so I could not develop any friends from school (I would be entering sixth grade in the fall). So I found myself rather bored, and took to hitting a tennis ball against the side of the garage and doing other things in the back yard. Very quickly my activities were noticed by my neighbours to the rear of our property—specifically two brothers, David (age eight) and Tommy (age five) Naumcheff, whose abundant family (they had three or four older sisters in addition to their parents) occupied a modest house behind ours.

So David and Tommy, finding a way through the large hedge that separated our respective properties, introduced themselves. Because I, although three years older than David, was still rather slight of build, he and I were pretty much equal in size, strength, and speed; possibly I was a tad faster than he, but he was a bit stronger than I. We became friends at once and began engaging in all manner of games and sports—not just the standard football, baseball, and basketball, but seemingly countless games we devised out of our own imaginations. (David went on to become quarterback for the Ball State University Cardinals. I wondered whether he might actually be drafted by an NFL team, but that did not happen.) For the next several years, David and Tommy became my best friends.

There were others in the neighbourhood—Scott Parker, Matt King (whose older brother, Mark, I will discuss a bit later), and several others. I don't suppose I need state that all of them were white—but none of them had any problem associating with me, and I never felt the slightest concern that I was a "foreigner" with dark skin. I in effect became white—or at least a true-blue American.

Our towering concern was to find exactly the right field to play football. None of our yards really suited the purpose, because they weren't quite long enough or because they had too many tedious impedimenta such as trees, shrubs, flower beds, and the like. Finally we resolved on a rather small area between Scott Parker's house and the house next to his. This field was long but quite narrow—but it was the best we could do. I don't imagine we used a regulation-size football; we must have used one considerably smaller. David tended to play quarterback, and I played running back or wide receiver. On defence I was a rather formidable tackler, my ferocity making up for my slight build. These roles allowed me to channel (in my fancy) the essence of my two football idols, Gale Sayers and Dick Butkus!

Years later, I actually "suited up" for a game—that is, I put on shoulder pads (extremely uncomfortable!—I couldn't imagine how anyone could throw a pass, let alone move unconstrainedly, while wearing such gear) and helmet. The idea was that our neighbourhood would play a game with another neighbourhood quite a distance away. Technically, this game was to have been restricted to boys aged twelve or younger; but even though I was fifteen, I looked much younger and no one questioned my right to play in the game. Our neighbourhood won by the score of 63–0 (recalling the great 1940 Chicago Bears, who beat the Washington Redskins in the NFL championship game by a score of 73–0). David was of course the quarterback. I did not distinguish myself in this game: I ran the ball only once, for a minimal gain, and caught a few passes—but I do recall making a diving catch on an extra point. (The field did not have goal posts, so a team would have to run or pass the ball after a touchdown for the extra point.) The other team really was rather pathetic, and I suspect they played with less and less enthusiasm as we piled up the points.

There was one amusing sequel to my football mania at this time. My mother had the foresight to obtain insurance for my glasses, which meant that if my glasses were broken (either lenses or frames), I could get a replacement for free. Well, in the summer of 1969 (or maybe it was 1970) I played so much football that *I broke my glasses five times.* After each breakage, I calmly walked over to the optometrist's office and said, "Um, I believe these need to be replaced." The expression of frustration and outrage on my eye doctor's face was not to be believed. He thereafter denied us insurance from that point forward.

In baseball I wasn't so good. Although at this time my mother purchased a mitt for me (no more possibilities of dislocating my finger!), and although I did evolve into a pretty good fielder and a passable pitcher, I was unable to hit for any power—I was the classic "singles hitter." But I did run the bases with some speed and efficiency, so at least I wasn't totally hopeless. After a time I became rather afraid of the ball hitting me (especially given the fact that David had a powerful arm and threw the ball with great velocity), and that didn't help my batting average.

Speaking of baseball, I am forced to recount the searing event of 1969: the spectacular collapse of the Chicago Cubs, who were leading their division by more than eight games in August (or maybe even in September) but ended up losing to the New York Mets, who went on to win the World Series. This was the closest the "lovable losers" (who had not won the World Series since 1908 and had not even been *in* the World Series since 1945) had come to reaching the playoffs in many years, and their loss devastated their fans, including myself. Even a certain recent event has not assuaged my pain and misery. To this day I can remember the Cubs' "all-star infield" of that year—the infectiously cheerful Ernie Banks (first base), the defensive specialists Glenn Beckert (second base) and Don Kessinger (shortstop), the stocky and powerful Ron Santo (third base), and Randy Hundley (catcher). Among the other luminaries of the team were "Sweet-Swinging" Billy Williams in the outfield and the lanky African American pitcher Ferguson Jenkins, whose pitching motion I myself attempted to imitate. (I was actually a reasonably good pitcher, with a strong fastball and even the rudiments of a curve ball.)

I suspect it was at this time that my enthusiasm for miniature golf first manifested itself. David Naumcheff and I actually fashioned a crude golf course (consisting of exactly one hole) in his own back yard; we bought some tees and golf balls, and spent many happy hours knocking the balls here and there. But David's yard was quite uneven, so getting the ball into the hole was largely a matter of luck. There were some actual miniature golf establishments around the city, and we frequented them whenever we got the chance.

I have surprisingly few recollections of the actual school year of 1969–70 (sixth grade). I attended Westview School, quite literally up the street from me—at the head of Normandy Drive (a street that only spanned two or three blocks) at Jackson Street, one of the major east-west thoroughfares in Muncie. I can't even recall what classes I took, although my home room teacher was a gruff elderly man whose name I have forgotten. Incredibly, I don't even remember playing in the school orchestra, although I must have done so, as my expertise in the violin was increasing steadily.

What I do remember is being a member of the patrol staff. There were two sets of students (each with their own adult monitor) who led the other students across the street (Gilbert Street on the north, Jackson Street on the south) at the beginning and the end of each school day. Our intersection was made more complicated by the fact that railroad tracks crossed Jackson Street at an angle, and freight trains would chug down those tracks at a fairly frequent clip. (These trains would continue travelling into the night, and I still find the mournful whine of the train whistle highly evocative of my childhood.) Our adult monitor was an elderly woman named Mrs. McKee, who seemed to take a shine to me. I took my responsibilities with vast seriousness—to such a degree that I was ultimately promoted, first to lieutenant, and then to captain, of the patrol staff. (There were also lieutenants and captains of the patrol staff on the north side of the school.) This allowed me to wear a red (lieutenant) and then blue (captain) badge on my chest. Once a week or thereabouts, both patrol staffs would gather in the hallway for some kind of meeting—I have some vague recollection that my own home room teacher led these meetings. He too seemed proud that I had attained this lofty honour.

I have only the dimmest memories of my actual classmates; but one who sticks in my mind (chiefly because he went on to be my classmate in junior high school and high school) was Mark King, exactly my age and the older brother of Matt. I cannot recall whether Mark at this early date exhibited the imaginative skill in art that distinguished him in later years; but I do remember that he was quite the troublemaker. He was something of an anarchist who chafed at the multitude of rules that constricted his freedom of action, in school and out of it. On one occasion I actually lied on his behalf, so that he escaped some punishment that he no doubt richly deserved. But he was my friend, and I felt no compunction in the act. He was suitably grateful.

Otherwise I remember some females who were now gaining my attention as objects of desire rather than horrible creatures to be shunned. The names Jackie Oxley and Suzanne Federlein stick in my memory—the one slender and dark-haired, the other curvy and blonde. Where are they now, I wonder? Probably they are grandmothers by now. They were probably the first of my "crushes" (my earlier encounter with Marcia Caton hardly counts, for I didn't have particularly tender feelings for her)—but they were certainly not the last.

With the fall of 1970—and junior high school (seventh and eighth grades)—impending, my parents made a momentous decision. I would have had to go to a rather inferior junior high school, Storer, based on the location of our house; but my mother apparently pulled some strings and had me

2. Indiana I (1968–72)

enrol in Burris Laboratory School—a branch of the teachers' college. Ball State University had in fact been founded in 1918 as Ball State Teachers College, and to this day it remains one of the leading teachers' colleges in the nation. Burris was established in 1929 as a public school, but one that would allow students from the teachers' college to gain hands-on instruction at teaching, under the guidance of actual teachers (many of them with Ph.D.'s) who would act as their tutors or mentors. The school was built directly across from one side of the campus, on the south side of University Avenue. The 1929 building, an imposing and highly attractive neo-Georgian structure, is still intact, although the interior has (to my alarm when I saw it some years ago) been radically renovated and modernised.

Given my mother's employment at Ball State, it was natural that she would wish me to enrol there. (My father, incidentally, did teach a few economics courses over the years, but otherwise he was retired from teaching.) And she contrived to bring that about. I won't say that I would not have received a good education elsewhere—but, as this account will demonstrate, Burris truly transformed my life.

Burris was also a K–12 school, and there were some students who had actually attended from kindergarten through high school. I spent six years there and grew so familiar with the building that I could probably find my way about in the dark. The elementary grades (K–6) were on the first floor, the upper grades (7–12) on the second floor. That floor consisted of a hallway that traversed the entire span of the rectangular building, with classrooms leading off of it; in the middle was the expansive library, and of course one could cut through the library to reach classrooms on the other side. The music department (all-important to me) was in the basement. The total enrollment was quite small: my senior class (1976) consisted of 73 students, and the entire high school (grades 9–12) was probably no greater than 250. Including the K–8 students, the number probably came up to about 500. The great majority of us were "professors' brats"—i.e., children of parents who taught at Ball State.

The most significant aspect of my junior high school years involved music. I of course participated in the orchestra, playing second violin (eighth graders played first violin). As a result of my abilities, I became principal second violin—much to the irritation of a girl, Patricia (Patty) Higgins, who had assumed she would get that coveted position. Our friendly rivalry on the violin highlighted much of the subsequent six years at Burris. Patty was in fact the daughter of a math professor at Ball State; and although I myself became somewhat acquainted with him and his wife (along with Patty's younger sister, Betsy), my mother curiously enough did not. There was also an older sister, Kathy, with whom my sister Nalini became good friends.

Playing in this junior high orchestra introduced me to the music of the late Baroque era, an era of music I still find immensely vital and powerful. The Baroque period is roughly dated from the time of Monteverdi's *Vespers* (1610) to the death of J. S. Bach (1750), and the late Baroque era featured the great trilogy of Bach, Handel, and Vivaldi (and their monumental but lesser-known predecessor, Arcangelo Corelli), along with many other interesting figures. We played this music in our orchestra (as well as in the high school orchestra) for the simple reason that it was relatively easy and therefore suited to our level of expertise. One of the first pieces we played were extracts from Handel's *Water Music* and *Fire Music* (more properly, *Musick for the Royal Fireworks*), along with his six *Concerti Grossi* (Opus 3) and even more impressive twelve *Concerti Grossi* (Opus 6). We also played some of the concerti in Vivaldi's great collection *L'Estro Armonico* (Opus 3).

My mother did not have many recordings of Baroque music at home (aside from some of the great organ works of J. S. Bach—especially the famous and demonic *Toccata and Fugue in D Minor*, masterfully and imaginatively played by Virgil Fox), but she allowed me to purchase some inexpensive but excellently rendered recordings issued by a mail-order company, the Musical Heritage Society. To this day its recording of Handel's *Concerti Grossi,* Opus 3 and 6, played by the Jean-François Paillard Orchestra, remains my favourite performance of these works. I don't think I latched on to Corelli quite this early, but in a few years I was overwhelmingly affected by his work: the 48 trio sonatas (Opus 1–4), 12 violin sonatas (Opus 5), and the 12 *Concerti Grossi* (Opus 6), which Handel used as a model. Among the great composers of Western music, Corelli is perhaps the one with the smallest body of work—rather like Poe and Lovecraft in that regard!

The junior high school orchestra was conducted by Marian Cooley, wife of John C. Cooley, who conducted the high school orchestra. Both Cooleys (but particularly John) became hugely important figures in my life during my years at Burris. I was, indeed, encouraged to take private lessons from both Marian (while in junior high school) and then with John (while in high school). These lessons, occurring once a week directly after school, cost a grand total of $3 per hour. I didn't really like the private lessons, because I felt nervous and intimidated with this one-on-one tutorship; indeed, I made up all manner of ridiculous excuses to skip the lessons, especially with Marian. Nevertheless, I guess I did become a better musician with this instruction; and I also began studying scores with some avidity. The Ball State music department was well regarded and presented a fine array of concerts on campus, and the main library had an abundance of music scores. I was allowed to use my mother's library card to check them out, and later I purchased a good many scores for myself, including the complete works of Corelli and the complete symphonies of Beethoven. (I quickly became entranced by Herbert van Karajan's 1963 recordings of the Beethoven symphonies, one of the great recordings of all time. They were included in the mammoth Beethoven Bicentennial Collection, a series of many dozen recordings that my mother purchased at this time.)

Even though I was in the orchestra, I was allowed to join the choir, which met at the same time. Members of the orchestra could sing in the choir one day a week—and that was enough, because our musical knowledge was generally superior to that of the other students and we could thereby learn the parts more quickly. Both the junior high school and the high school choir were conducted by William Wakeland, with his wife Ruth as accompanist on the piano. Wakeland was a genial but highly knowledgeable instructor who could get the best out of his unskilled charges (there were no tryouts to join the choir—anyone who could sing, or couldn't sing, could join). Here too, Baroque music was heavily on the agenda, and I was thrilled to sing such things as Vivaldi's *Gloria,* Pergolesi's *Magnificat,* and Handel's *Messiah* in choir. But we sang contemporary pieces as well: there was a charming rendition of some Simon & Garfunkel songs (including "The Sound of Silence," "Feelin' Groovy," and "Bridge over Troubled Water"), along with a haunting musical setting of Shakespeare's exquisite song that contains the line "Journeys end in lovers meeting" (a line that runs chillingly through Shirley Jackson's *Haunting of Hill House*).

And yet, the most significant thing that happened to me in terms of my future career didn't occur in school. I did, of course, dutifully walk or ride my bicycle to school each weekday. Burris was about a mile from our house, and either mode of transportation was easy. I do not recall that a school bus was even an option at the time; at any rate, I never saw such a vehicle. Sometime in sixth grade I had obtained what I thought was a super-sporty red bicycle, purchased for the princely sum of $10 from a friend (Thad Lindahl) who was my colleague on the patrol staff at Westview. For a while I thought this bike was just the cat's pajamas, but in fact it was not a particularly efficient machine. A year or two later my parents purchased for me a fine ten-speed bicycle that I rode here, there, and everywhere.

I have one vivid memory of riding like mad with David Naumcheff to the new Muncie Mall, far to the northeast of the city, which had a movie theatre—possibly a multiplex. We were desperate to see some recently released horror film—and got there just in time! But the film was dreadful, and we laughed about it all the way home. I should mention that the first film I ever saw in a movie theatre was *Planet of the Apes*. This must have been in the late spring of 1968, since the film was released on April 3. Before that, I had to be content with watching old movies on television, or the "Movies of the Week" on the major network channels. One film that I remember being utterly petrified at was *I Saw What You Did* (1965), a non-supernatural horror/suspense film about teenagers who dial numbers at random and say, "I know who you are and I saw what you did." Well, that gets them into trouble when they encounter an actual individual who has done something criminal. *The Fly* (1958) also terrified me. In fact, during sixth grade I had a sleepover with a friend, David Kelley, who lived directly across the street from Westview (north side). We quite literally clung to each other as we watched—or tried to watch—Hitchcock's *The Birds* on television. In fact, at a critical moment—when the birds invade the cabin in which the hapless Tippi Hedren and her friends find themselves trapped—we had to turn the TV off. I didn't see the ending of *The Birds* for another decade or more.

But this is an aside. The fact is that, although I did well at Burris, I regularly came home and immediately got together with David and Tommy Naumcheff and other local boys to play various games and sports. I remember a game of kick the can that went on for hours, as I lurked behind various natural (a tree) and artificial (a car) objects to approach nearer and nearer that can to free the "prisoners" who were trapped there. Then there was another time when I contracted poison ivy. Man, that was horrible! My arms and perhaps my legs—maybe even portions of my face—were infected, and I was in torment. For some reason, the treatment for my ailment was delayed, so I endured days of itching before a lotion was applied and I was cured.

My sister Nalini, who was by now in tenth or eleventh grade, noticed my relative anti-intellectualism and said sharply to me, "You need to start reading books!" I've mentioned that we had an abundance of books in the house, but they were largely reference works or books that Nalini herself had obtained for her pleasure reading, and they did not appeal to me. So Nalini did the next best thing: she dragged me to the Muncie Public Library and said, "Get some books—I'll check them out for you."

2. Indiana I (1968–72)

This simple act changed the entire course of my life.

There were at that time several branches of the library aside from the main library at 301 E. Jackson Street (probably a good mile and a half to two miles due east of our house), and I recall my first expedition with Nalini as occurring at the John F. Kennedy branch (1700 W. McGalliard Road), about the same distance north of us. As my digression about films indicates, I was already tending toward interest in horror, fantasy, and science fiction, and so that was where I gravitated among the library shelves. Of course, in that era there was no such thing as a "horror" shelf in the public library or in bookstores (and I hardly ever frequented bookstores at this time, both because there were relatively few of them in Muncie and because I had no money to buy books), so such books were heterogeneously shelved among the fantasy/science fiction shelves. I probably read some young adult horror anthologies around this time, such as *Rod Serling's Triple W* (1963) and *Devils and Demons* (1967), and *Alfred Hitchcock's Ghostly Gallery* (1962).

But—amusingly in light of my later atheism—the series of books that really got me addicted to reading was nothing less than C. S. Lewis's Chronicles of Narnia! Remember that I had *absolutely no knowledge* of Christianity at this time, or virtually none; so these seven books delighted me as engaging works of the fantastic imagination. (Less than a decade later, I tried to read them again—and was dismayed and repelled by the heavy Christian symbolism that to my mind crippled their atmosphere of ethereal fantasy.) So in short order I was a diligent and enthusiastic reader! This extracurricular reading was all the more important because my school library was poorly stocked with reading material of this kind, and I rarely made much use of it.

I also became a voracious reader of detective stories and quickly latched onto such writers as Agatha Christie, Margery Allingham, and especially John Dickson Carr, whose incredibly complex "locked-room mysteries" (often laced with strong suggestions of the supernatural, although of course the supernatural never came into play—except in the striking tour de force, *The Burning Court*); and of course, many of the Hitchcock anthologies did contain a considerable amount of mystery and suspense fiction.

The critical issue that everyone will want to know is: *When did I first come upon H. P. Lovecraft?*

I have to confess that I myself am no longer clear on this point. I have long stated in articles and interviews that I stumbled upon the standard three-volume edition of Lovecraft's fiction (published by Arkham House in

1963–65) while roaming the shelves of the Muncie Public Library (main branch); and while this is no doubt true, I have now come to believe that my reading of Lovecraft was anticipated by Betty Owen's anthology *Eleven Great Horror Stories* (1969), which contained "The Dunwich Horror." This paperback volume was published by Scholastic Books, and I believe I purchased it for a grand total of 95¢ (my parents did give me some money to purchase books of this kind). Now I do not have a distinct impression of reading the Lovecraft story (which led off the volume) at that time, but I suspect the name—of which I had not previously heard—stuck in my mind, and that is what led me to explore the Arkham House books when I came upon them in the Muncie Public Library. That probably happened around 1971–72.

I have a list of all the books I read in high school (mostly on my own—not as school exercises), and Lovecraft's *The Dunwich Horror and Others* only shows up as the twenty-fifth book I read during the 1972–73 school year (ninth grade), probably in the fall of 1972. But I believe this already constituted a *re*-reading of the book, for I read those three editions numerous times in high school. I do have a clear recollection of beginning my Lovecraft readings (after the Owen anthology) with *At the Mountains of Madness and Other Novels*. A mistake! That title novel is so stylistically dense, and so chock-full of scientific terms and conceptions (and—as I shall explain presently—my knowledge of science was very poor at this time), that I simply couldn't finish it. In fact, I stopped exactly at page 53 of the Arkham House edition, putting the book aside as "too deep" for me.

Some months later I began *The Dunwich Horror and Others*. Even here, I got off to a bad start. Because the editor, August Derleth, developed a perverse fondness for the mediocre story "In the Vault," this tale led off the volume; and I thought it quite a poor piece of work (which, indeed, it is). The next story, "Pickman's Model," was better, but to my mind no great shakes. Then . . . "The Rats in the Walls"! Omigod! Whether it was that one story that made me a Lovecraft devotee for life, I cannot quite say—but I certainly was by the time I reached the end of that book. I distinctly remember reading the conclusion of "The Whisperer in Darkness" at school one evening—we were there for some kind of orchestra dress rehearsal. During a break I wandered over to some remote corridor of the school and absorbed that ending—and covered my face with my hands (appropriately enough—"the face and hands of Henry Wentworth Akeley"!) in shuddering horror. I also remember my first reading of "The Outsider," where I *almost* guessed the ending—but not quite. In a sense, the ending of that story parallels the ending of Agatha Christie's *The Murder of Roger Ackroyd* (where the first-person narrator proves to be the murderer), a book I imagine I had already read by this time.

I was certainly doing a lot of extracurricular reading (and would do much more during high school), but school was indeed becoming an increasingly central part of my life, especially in regard to personal friendships. And yet, aside from music, I actually have little recollection of what I did during the two years of junior high school. No doubt I took the usual array of classes in English, math, social studies, and so on. (I remember virtually no instruction in any of the sciences.) Our math teacher was a charming woman piquantly named Iris Brashear, evidently from the South; and we mercilessly teased her about her accent, as well as the embarrassing fact that her last name closely resembled the term for a delicate item of female attire. But I and others made it clear that we liked her and thought her an able instructor.

One of the most useful classes I took around this time was *typing*, from an attractive but no-nonsense female teacher whose name I have forgotten. I distinctly recall the array of manual typewriters, with blank keys, and a big chart of the keyboard on the wall to aid one in memorising the layout of the keys. I took another such class in high school, with the result that I eventually developed a typing speed of more than 100 words per minute, although my accuracy wasn't all that it could be. This facility came in very handy in short order, as I shall relate in the next chapter.

I paid relatively little attention to what was going on in the nation and the world. The Vietnam War was dragging on, in spite of Nixon's vow to end it. Indeed, my parents became increasingly concerned that I myself might somehow have to become involved in the conflict. (Although I was not yet a U.S. citizen but only a permanent resident, such persons were indeed eligible for the draft.) We actually watched the televised "draft lottery," in which days of the year were randomly selected, the dates chosen first being the birthdays of those who would be drafted first. It was rare that my own birthday (June 22) was very high on the list; but if the war (and the draft) had lasted longer than it did, there was at least a small chance that I would be drafted. (Probably, as a student heading to college, I would have received an exemption.)

What did affect me deeply was nothing less momentous than the breakup of the Beatles in the spring of 1970 (i.e., toward the end of sixth grade). I had been increasingly fascinated with the Beatles' late work, especially as embodied in such albums as the *White Album* and *Abbey Road;* and I knew nothing of the internal dissension that was tearing the band apart. So the news hit me like a cataclysm; and to add insult to injury, the event was reported in a derisively small paragraph (presumably from a wire service) on a back page of our local paper! I later acquired their final album, *Let It Be* (1970)—although even this was a "cut-out" (i.e., an album that had been remaindered in the shops), so I may not have acquired it until late 1970 or early 1971. I have no idea how I came up with the money to buy it, for I was still receiving no allowance and was not making money in any other fashion.

But junior high school was significant for my development of friendships that, because Burris was a K–12 school, would in many cases last a full six years. It was at this time that I became friendly with such boys as Ed Alexander, Erik Carr, John Hampton, Joe Lauck, Andy and Randy Lykens (twins whom I found it nearly impossible to tell apart, although eventually I managed to detect slight differences in their appearance), Jay Marhoefer, Fred Nay, Jon Nussbaum, Bill Rector, and Jeff Turner. I also liked one Andy Albright, but he departed to some other high school after eighth grade. Mark King, who had come with me from Westview, was also a pungent presence. I see in the class list in the 1971 yearbook (the *Oracle*) another Indian boy, Sonny Chuidian, although I never became particularly close to him. Otherwise, with rare exceptions our class was uniformly white.

I remember hanging out with Ed Alexander quite a bit. We somehow took to going to women's volleyball matches at the Ball State University gymnasium. Ball State had one of the best volleyball teams in the nation at the time. My interest in the performance was, of course, purely aesthetic. In the summer of 1973, a fat, elderly Irish nun (name forgotten) took Ed and me to see our first R-rated movie—nothing less than the gangster film *Dillinger*. I somehow thought that the sexual content of the film was astoundingly daring; many years later, when I saw the film again, it turns out that the only hint of sexuality was a little bit of Michelle Phillips's exposed thigh. That was one cool nun, however—loads of fun to be around, very jovial and not making the slightest attempt to convert such a heathen as myself.

Did I have any crushes on girls in my class? In all honesty I cannot remember—that is, I can't remember if such crushes (undeniably present) occurred so early. One of the most beautiful creatures in our class was Lisa Bowman, and other girls such as Lisa Mansfield, Nancy Marshall, and Jennifer Strother were also quite fetching. One of the few pleasures during obligatory physical education class (during which I was forced to wear that bizarre torture device known as the jockstrap for the first time) was seeing these and other girls in their gym shorts and clingy T-shirts.

At various times, the class would head over to some building on the Ball State campus that had a swimming pool. I was one of the relatively few students who couldn't swim, so we were relegated to the shallow end of the pool doing our best not to look too foolish. I was able to swim with flippers, but the moment the flippers came off I would sink like a stone. Nothing that the instructor said or did could relieve me of my utter incompetence as a swimmer, and to this day I cannot even float in the water. And yet, I still enjoy being in a pool, clinging to the edge and doing random exercises.

My family recently told me that my parents had requested that I be excused from a sex education class during either seventh or eighth grade. Oddly enough, I have no distinct recollection of this event, although I have some memory of sitting alone in a classroom doing not much of anything, so perhaps that was what was happening. However, I did not need formal instruction. A girl named Christy Gossage who lived only a few houses up the street from me had an older brother, Mark. On one occasion David Naumcheff and I congregated in a school bus that for some mysterious reason was parked in the Gossages' driveway, and Mark soberly informed me of the facts of life. David was shooed away as being too young to hear such intimate details of male and female anatomy. So I basically learned all that I needed to know (well, at least the rudiments) in a matter of about half an hour. It would be, however, several years before I would put this knowledge to practical use!

But, as I looked forward to beginning my freshman year of high school in the fall of 1972, I had no idea that that year—and, really, my entire high school career—would prepare me for the long literary career that forms the justification for this memoir.

The Little Prince with father and mother

The Joshi family (c. 1962): Tryambak, Ragini, Nalini, S. T., Padmini

S. T. in Poona, age 4

S. T. at Leal School (Urbana, Ill.)

S. T. at 1107 W. Green Street (Urbana, Ill.)

S. T. at 4621 Cornelius Avenue (Indianapolis, Ind.)

S. T. at 405 S. Normandy Drive (Muncie, Ind.)

3. Indiana II (1972–76)

"Third-rate musicians are a nuisance."—Dorothy L. Sayers

With the beginning of ninth grade, I continued to read voraciously. Indeed, the instructor of my freshman English class—the distinguished Dr. Anthony Tovatt, a Burris legend—had each of his students keep a list of the books they read during the first semester (presumably extending from early September to mid-December). We would write down the authors and titles of the books on large pieces of construction paper that would then be posted all around the walls of the classroom. Needless to say, the students were of varying capacities in regard to literacy (or, more pertinently, literary interest). I believe each was required to read at least three books during the semester. I read *sixty*. Now of course the great majority of these were detective stories—Agatha Christie, John Dickson Carr, Ellery Queen, Harry Kemelman, Erle Stanley Gardner, and so on and so forth. I see some science fiction titles on the list, ranging from the post-apocalyptic novel *Alas, Babylon* (1959) by Pat Frank to Isaac Asimov's *I, Robot* to Ray Bradbury's *Fahrenheit 451*, and not excluding H. G. Wells's *The Time Machine*. Several books about sports—the best of which was Gale Sayers's poignant autobiography, *I Am Third*—appear on the list. I also see that I was beginning to read the great humourist P. G. Wodehouse, not to mention some genuine literature such as John Steinbeck's *Of Mice and Men* (a blessedly short book!) to Evelyn Waugh's *The Loved One* (ditto—but I have indicated on my list that I violently disliked this book) to Erich Maria Remarque's *All Quiet on the Western Front*. But genre literature clearly dominated.

Indeed, so fascinated had I become by horror (less by fantasy and science fiction) that I once stood up in class and read the entirety of Joseph Payne Brennan's short story "Levitation" (contained in an Alfred Hitchcock anthology) to the students. I had, however, underestimated the length of time it would take to read the story, so I had to leave off in the middle of the narrative and only finish the next day; but when I came to the cataclysmic final sentence ("And then it [a person levitated by a hypnotist who unexpectedly died, thereby being unable to reverse his spell] disappeared altogether"), there were both gasps and a few nervous chuckles.

In high school we were required to take three years of English, three years of math, two years of physical education, a year or two of social studies, a year of foreign languages, but only a single year of science. One could of course take more of any of these disciplines as electives. I shall never cease to regret that my lack of knowledge and interest in the sciences impelled me to take only that one year of instruction—and this being an utterly trivial and superficial course called "Environmental Science" about which I retain almost nothing. Clearly, it was English that fascinated me, and I gained immense benefit from the instruction of Tovatt (ninth grade), Peter Goodell (tenth grade), and Robert C. Rose (eleventh and twelfth grade). I felt so grateful to these individuals (although I had my disputes with Goodell, who was a bit unconventional and iconoclastic) that I dedicated my first true book, *H. P. Lovecraft: Four Decades of Criticism* (1980), to them and mailed each of them a copy. They seemed suitably flattered by the tribute.

Some of these classes were most entertaining, and not entirely for reasons that the teachers would have appreciated. Physical education (or "gym class," as we called it) was run by two individuals—the stern and elderly Robert Gordon, and his assistant, Tom DeWitt. It was inevitable that the latter became nicknamed Tom DimWit, for in fact he wasn't the brightest candle in the candelabrum. During tenth grade Jeff Turner (who had by this time become my best friend) and I easily pulled a fast one on him by declaring that we had been diligently playing tennis in the courts across the street from school. (We had been allowed to pursue "independent" gym class.) Of course we were doing nothing of the kind, but were instead just goofing off. But DeWitt readily erased all the absences he had tallied for us, and we received sterling grades for our diligent exercise.

Gym class, when it was a group enterprise, was engaging in its own right. I did rather well in both flag football (chiefly on the defensive side, where I continued to channel Dick Butkus) and soccer. I do not believe we played much if any baseball, because our relatively limited grounds didn't have a formal baseball diamond (and perhaps there was the possibility of injury from playing "hardball"). I do not recall playing softball either. During winter we stayed in the gymnasium, and I became quite good on the uneven bars and certain other gymnastic activities.

For a foreign language, I began taking French and kept it up for three

3. Indiana II (1972–76)

years. Burris actually offered Latin (taught, no doubt ably, by Betty Hinshaw), as well as French and Spanish (both taught, not particularly well, by a rather hefty but jovial female named Mary Wood). I recall reading large chunks of Verne's *Around the World in Eighty Days* in French, although I don't think we actually finished the book. During senior year I did take a course by Mrs. Hinshaw called "Latin Derivatives of English," and that proved of some significance in my college career.

One hilarious episode occurred in a social studies class. A new teacher had just come in: I do not remember his name, but he too (like Iris Brashear) had a Southern accent. On his first day, he was of course genially grilled as to his knowledge of the subject, and one student threw out a question: "Who was the seventeenth president of the United States?" The teacher hemmed and hawed a bit, then tentatively ventured, "Ulysses S. Grant." Without raising my voice in the slightest, I calmly (and somewhat contemptuously) interjected, "Andrew Johnson." The class exploded in laughter as this twerp of a student (and an immigrant, at that) knew something more than the teacher did. Those porcelain presidents that had filled so many hours of my playtime came in handy!

Another social studies teacher, Jim Sargent, recognized that I was quite a bit brighter than most other students in the class. We were reading a textbook in which each chapter contained, as an appendix, numerous documents illuminating the history of the period covered in the chapter. Students would be randomly assigned to study a given document and discuss it the next day; I would be assigned *all* the documents and serve as a kind of backup instructor, correcting any errors a student made in presenting his given document.

A somewhat similar thing happened in math class. During sophomore or junior year, Bill Rector and I were so obviously smarter than everyone else in class that the instructor—a genial fellow named Mr. Kratzner, whose chief distinction was a set of impressive sideburns (sprinkled, alas, with dandruff, as was his hair in general)—allowed us to work far ahead of the other students. Not only that, but we became his informal assistants, helping those less gifted than ourselves. At the end of class, long lines would snake out from our desks, as we calmly and patiently elucidated the mysteries of algebra or geometry to our thick-witted classmates.

But my focus remained primarily on literature and music. For—all apart from what I was doing in the actual English class at school—it was at this time that I developed the determination to become a writer and, more significantly, took active steps in that direction. In other words, I began writing—and writing prolifically.

I am convinced that this happened during ninth grade (1972–73). I cannot say it was specifically Lovecraft who led me in this direction; at this moment he was only one (even if the chief) of the genre authors in the realms of mystery, horror, fantasy, and science fiction who attracted me and whom I wished to emulate. Luckily for me, right from the beginning I kept fanatical records of my readings, writings, and other activities, so that I have a fairly accurate idea of the progress (if such it could be called) of my early work. According to a "Complete Chronology of Writings of and by S. T. Joshi" (what the distinction between "of" and "by" means, I have no idea) that still exists in a pencil draft, the first six works I wrote were:

> Murder
> The Touch of Death
> The Picture
> The Suicide
> Love, Hate, Money and Murder
> The Ordinary People

The first five were short stories; the fifth was *a novel*. I will get to that in a moment; but of the short stories, the first is supernatural, in spite of its title; the second and third are probably supernatural, although at this point I cannot recall; the fourth may be a tale of psychological suspense; the fifth is likely to be a murder mystery.

My first story, "Murder," which I have dated in my chronology to February 1973, actually survives, both in an error-riddled typescript and in "published" form—in a school publication called *Literary Lapses*. This was an ongoing annual publication in which some student or other (probably a senior) was chosen as the editor, under the guidance of another English teacher, Helen Sargent. The student editor would collect all the material submitted to him or her (whether any items were actually rejected is unclear), and it would be issued in a stapled pamphlet of some size (maybe 50 or 60 pages, perhaps more) at the end of the school year (i.e., May). My records indicate that "Murder" appeared in *Literary Lapses* No. 19 (1972–73), published in May 1973. I have reprinted the story in an appendix to my *200 Books by S. T. Joshi* (Hippocampus Press, 2014). It is of course screamingly bad—highly artificial in its narrative framework and written in incredibly bad prose. If there is any influence on the story, it is the tales of horror and suspense in the Alfred Hitchcock anthologies.

The next two stories were also published (after a fashion) in a school publication called *Double Take,* which appears to date to the spring of 1973. I believe this item (which I no longer possess) emerged out of Dr. Tovatt's English class and was reproduced in ditto. Whether I was the actual "editor" or "co-editor" I cannot remember; possibly there was no actual editor. In any case, the publication needs to be located by devoted Joshians, as it contains my two lost stories, "The Touch of Death" and "The Picture"!

Now we turn to *The Ordinary People,* written in the summer of 1973. This was a full-length novel, or at least as close to such as a fourteen-year-old could manage. I remember writing it out by hand and then banging it out on a Smith-Corona manual typewriter that my mother had obtained for me. The final manuscript came to about 175 double-spaced pages, or probably just under 45,000 words. I suppose it is impressive for someone so young to have even written an extended narrative of this length, but that is the most charitable thing one can say of it. Otherwise, it was a mechanical imitation of the "cosy" mysteries of Agatha Christie and others. I devised my own know-it-all amateur detective, Dr. Heinrich Schecter (a German—analogous to the Belgian Hercule Poirot). Whether he had some amiable and dimwitted sidekick, I cannot recall: I actually think not, for the novel was not narrated in the first person by this person, but had third-person narration. I gathered my band of suspects in some remote house or other (location forgotten—probably England, since I was already becoming an Anglophile like Lovecraft), and no doubt I had Schecter reveal the identity of the culprit in typical jack-in-the-box manner at the end.

I did not show this work to anyone—and probably destroyed it almost as soon as it was written. Immediately thereafter I plunged into another detective novel, this one called *At the House of Sebastian.* Aside from involving Schecter again, being set in a mansion or castle in England, and being purportedly complex in plotting after the manner of John Dickson Carr, I can remember nothing about it; I progressed to about 120 double-spaced pages before somehow encountering an obstacle (I do not recall actually planning out the whole work in an outline or synopsis, as I probably should have done) and abandoning it too.

I thereafter resumed the writing of short stories, some of which may have reached novelette or even novella length. I see that one of my early works was called "The Coffin," co-written with Jay Marhoefer. Jay was an exceptionally brilliant classmate who lived in an impressive house near Burris. His family was quite wealthy, as his father was owner of a meat company bearing his name (we always bought Marhoefer bacon at the grocery store). I assume this story was supernatural, but I really have no idea. It could well have been a tale of graveyard humour in the manner of Bierce. I know for a fact that another story (dating to early 1974), entitled "An Error in Calculations," was indeed of that sort.

Were any of these early stories Lovecraftian? I cannot clearly recall. The titles of some of them suggest that they may have been—"The Lost City," "He Who Liveth in the Depths," "The Sixteen Gargoyles," "The Eldritch Tome" (!), and so on. Of course, I can clearly state that one story *was* Lovecraftian: "The Recurring Doom," for it survives to this day. Somehow it survived the holocaust of my other juvenile writings, and I allowed it to be published, first in Ken Neily's *Lovecraftian Ramblings* (15 October 1980), and then in *Crypt of Cthulhu* (Michaelmas 1985), and then in Robert M. Price's anthology *Acolytes of Cthulhu* (2001). The tale was lengthy—the current draft, not all that different from the one I wrote in late 1974, is almost 9000 words—but whether it was worth preserving, I shall leave to others to decide.

Like Lovecraft (who, not long after writing "The Beast in the Cave" when he himself was fourteen, was in the process of assembling a collection of his stories under the title *Tales of Terror*), I began contemplating the gathering my stories into book form. My chronology indicates that I wrote both a preface and an afterword to a volume called *The Monster of Moonlight and Others* (the title story was a supernatural narrative based upon my fascination for Beethoven's *Moonlight Sonata*); and not long after I wrote "The Recurring Doom" I was envisioning a volume called *The Recurring Doom and Others,* which may well have been intended to collect my Lovecraftian tales.

Another opportunity to "publish" my work came in the 1973–74 school year, when I took an English class taught by Pete Goodell. Here we produced two issues of a ditto magazine called *The Cosmic Meld*. In spite of its pretentious title (this was, of course, the tail end of the hippie movement), the issues contained nothing but short book reviews, arranged in two columns on a page. The first issue dates to 1973—probably it came out in the fall of that year. The second issue dates to January 1974. In that first issue I published four book reviews, including three reviews of books by Lovecraft (*The Dunwich Horror and Others, At the Mountains of Madness and Other Novels,* and—oddly—*Collected Poems*). The fourth book I reviewed was Thomas Tryon's recent bestseller *Harvest Home* (1973). Given that these re-

3. Indiana II (1972–76)

views apparently constitute my very first writing about Lovecraft, I will reproduce the first review in its entirety:

> ". . . I turned to the bulky, closely-written letters . . . and for the next three hours was immersed in a gulf of unutterable horrors . . . I found myself faced by names and terms that I had heard elsewhere in the most hideous of connections—Yuggoth, Great Cthulhu, Tsathoggua, Yog-Sothoth . . .—and was drawn back through nameless aeons and inconceivable dimensions to the worlds of elder, outer entity . . ." So says Albert Wilmarth in the famed novelette, *The Whisperer in Darkness*. This is only a fraction of the brilliant horror literature of possibly the greatest horror story writer in history—Howard Phillips Lovecraft. The short stories in this large (432 pp.) collection take you into worlds of fantastic horrors and hideous monsters. The book will lead you into the dreadful Cthulhu Mythos, an entire mythology invented by HPL. You will be pleasantly horrified by the fantasies of this somewhat eccentric author.
>
> Once you begin reading the works of Lovecraft, you will immediately be held spellbound as the author slowly unveils various horrors. Almost from the first page HPL creates an atmosphere of terror. Even the titles of the short stories provoke the imagination: *The Dunwich Horror, The Shadow Over Innsmouth, The Rats in the Walls, The Colour Out of Space,* among others.
>
> The reader who is just beginning to read horror stories should not begin with this book. Save it until you are well-versed into horror literature. For this is undoubtedly tops in the field of horror and the macabre.

Not so hot! This sounds more like a press release than a review. The review of *Collected Poems* also contains some oddities. Even though I state tritely that *Fungi from Yuggoth* "is without a doubt one of the best horror poems in the world," I go on to state: "After reading these poems, you must agree with the many who have said that Lovecraft is the best prose stylist since Poe." How one could determine that Lovecraft is a great *prose* stylist after reading his *poetry* is not very clear. In my other review, I express fondness for the title novel, but with this caveat: "Many times HPL's ideas are hard to understand for he uses many words which even college professors have not heard" [*sic*]. As for the other two novels in the book, *The Case of Charles Dexter Ward* and *The Dream-Quest of Unknown Kadath:* "I recommend you do not read the latter for it is very confusing and tiresome. But the famous former [*sic*] always is superbly fascinating [?], possibly even better than *At the Mountains of Madness.*"

And yet, it is indicative of my reading preferences that the second issue of the *Cosmic Meld* had my reviews of three celebrated detective novels, Agatha Christie's *The Murder of Roger Ackroyd,* John Dickson Carr's *The Case of the Constant Suicides,* and Dorothy L. Sayers's *The Nine Tailors.*

I have no idea whether these reviews somehow led me to shift my literary work from fiction to criticism. In reality, I knew very little about literary criticism; but I seemed to enjoy expressing my dogmatic and magisterial opinions on the books I read, so perhaps I figured that that would be a more promising route to literary stardom. It did not in fact seem very likely that I would attain any immediate celebrity as a fiction writer, whether in the horror or the detective field. I was actually submitting my work to major magazines, dutifully enclosing a self-addressed stamped envelope for the return of the manuscript if it were rejected. Of course, they were all rejected. Could I really have been so deluded as to imagine that such venues as the *Atlantic Monthly* and *Playboy* would actually accept the work of a tyro like myself? Evidently I was. Somewhat more realistically, I also submitted my detective or crime stories to *Alfred Hitchcock's Mystery Magazine* and *Ellery Queen's Mystery Magazine.* I recall writing a virtual novella (maybe 40 or 50 pages) entitled "Foulness Island" (the name of an actual island in the delta of the Thames—but I knew nothing about it otherwise), but of course it promptly came back.

The shift of focus came in July 1974, the summer before I entered eleventh grade. It was at this time that I began a ponderous tome entitled *Mystery and Horror Writers of the Twentieth Century.* The numerous permutations of this book are elucidated in a learned essay that I wrote in 1975 (after I had shelved the book indefinitely) and published in *200 Books by S. T. Joshi.* At its maximum girth, the book came to some 250 pages; but at this point (early 1975), I somehow came to the realisation that the book in its current form was pretty awful, and so I radically reshaped it to bring it more in line with Lovecraft's "Supernatural Horror in Literature" and its condensed analyses of key figures. An outline of the time gives some indication of the kind of authors I wished to cover:

Mystery Writers.
  I. The Sayersian School: Dorothy L. Sayers, Margery Allingham, Ngaio Marsh, and Others.
  II. The Americans: John Dickson Carr, August Derleth, Ellery Queen, Margaret Millar, and Others.
  III. Agatha Christie.
  IV. The English: L. P. Davies, John Creasey, Philip MacDonald, and Others.

3. Indiana II (1972–76)

Horror Writers.
  I. H. P. Lovecraft.
 II. H. P. Lovecraft's Circle.
III. The Horror Novelists: Thomas Tryon, Robert Bloch, Shirley Jackson.
IV. The Anthologists: Alfred Hitchcock, Peter Haining, August Derleth.
 V. The Miniaturists: Roald Dahl, Shirley Jackson, and Others.

Some interesting things are revealed by this outline. Even though I had earlier written essays on Ray Bradbury, Rod Serling, and other weird writers, they appear not to have "made the cut" in terms of inclusion in this draft (unless they were included in the "Miniaturists" chapter). And, in the mystery section, the complete omission of the hard-boiled writers is notable. I don't believe I was even aware of Hammett, Chandler, Ross Macdonald (even though I greatly enjoyed the psychological mysteries of his wife, Margaret Millar), and others—I only read them a good many years later.

I did not entirely abandon the writing of fiction, but during my last two years of high school I wrote very few tales. And yet, I did not give up hope of eventually becoming a published fiction writer. If *Playboy* didn't want my fiction, maybe Arkham House would! I actually sent a full manuscript of my tales to Arkham House around 1974, receiving a polite rejection from Roderic Meng, who was the interim editor after the death of August Derleth and after Donald Wandrei stepped down after a brief tenure. He applauded my youthful enthusiasm (I must have told him how old I was) but delivered the standard boilerplate response that the book "wasn't suitable" for Arkham House. So there went my chance to become the next Ramsey Campbell, who had published his first Arkham House book at the age of eighteen!

*

The other great focal point in my life was music. Once I entered the high school orchestra, I was of course relegated once again to second violin after having played first violin during eighth grade. Patty Higgins and other familiar faces were with me at violin, viola, and cello. (This was exclusively a string orchestra—no brass or woodwinds. I do not even recall a double bass, although perhaps there was one from time to time.) What initially struck me was the extraordinary talent of some of the older musicians, including the concertmaster, one Robert Yeo. To me he seemed pretty much an adult (and, strangely enough, he actually looked a bit like Lovecraft—lean, with short blond hair and a long face that may or may not have had a lantern jaw). He and the next-best violinist, Peggy Cooley (daughter of John C. and Marian Cooley), were so accomplished that at one point I simply found myself marvelling at their entrancing music, and failed to play when I was supposed to. This much amused John Cooley. I cannot find Yeo in a Google search, but I find it hard to imagine he did not pursue the violin as a career.

But beyond playing all manner of great Baroque music (Bach, Handel, Vivaldi, and—at my own recommendation—Corelli) and some works from the Romantic era, I myself ventured into composition. Yes, I was trying to be both a writer and a composer at the same time! My records indicated that this began in November 1973 (in other words, shortly into my sophomore year); and, as with my writing, I started with a grandiose vision of writing a full-length symphony—*and I did so*. I pompously named the work *Symphony No. 1 in C major ("Baroque"), Opus 1*. It was in the standard four movements, and I estimated that it would run to about 23 minutes. It was a "baroque" symphony because, even though I had some elaborate orchestration including trumpets, trombones, and bassoons, the basic themes and harmonies were derived from my study of the later Baroque composers. (The third movement had something of the atmosphere of Renaissance dance music.)

At one point I showed this composition to Mr. Cooley, and he was duly impressed—by my diligence if not at my actual competence in composition. We spent an entire session (which should have been devoted to a private lesson on the violin) in going over this work, and he made numerous suggestions for revision. But the fact is that I really didn't know enough about music theory and composition to undertake a work of this kind. I ended up discarding it and shifting my attention to smaller-scale works. My Opus 2 consisted of some trumpet "sonatas" (really concerti for one or two trumpets and strings), and my Opus 3 was a set of six *Concerti Grossi* in the manner of Handel, although with much infusion of Vivaldian elements. These latter works were quite a bit better than the symphony, and Cooley actually felt that they might be creditably performed. On May 20, 1974 (the end of my sophomore year), the *Concerto Grosso No. 1 in A minor* (now identified as Opus 1, No. 1, since I had presumably repudiated or discarded my symphony and the trumpet sonatas) was performed at Burris, with one Cathy Branam playing solo first violin, I playing solo second violin, and Ann Millard playing solo cello. Needless to say, I had to copy out all the parts for each section of the orchestra, a highly tedious undertaking.

On October 16, 1974, my *Concerto Grosso No. 3 in G major, Opus 1, No.*

3 was performed; I played solo first violin, Leah Wakeland (daughter of the choir director) played solo second, and Lisa Keener played solo cello. On May 22, 1975, my *Trio Sonata No. 1 in D major, Opus 5, No. 1* was performed by myself (first violin), Patty Higgins (second violin), and Ann Millard (cello). This latter work was clearly modelled upon the trio sonatas of Corelli.

I wrote numerous other works, ranging from trumpet concerti to what I called "fanfares for brass" (these were inspired by the splendid Renaissance music I heard on the PBS miniseries *The Six Wives of Henry VIII*). In July 1974 I seem to have begun (and perhaps completed) an elaborate work: *Concerto in D major for 2 Trumpets, 2 Oboes, Strings and Tympani.* This fascination for trumpet music stemmed from my listening to numerous performances of Baroque trumpet music as recorded by the great virtuoso Maurice André and his pupils, which I ordered from the Musical Heritage Society.

It appears that I ceased my attempts to become a composer in November 1974, only a year after I had begun. Even at that time I had come to realise that I really had nothing original to say in music: as with Lovecraft and his predilection for composing verse imitative of the eighteenth century, my musical compositions had as their sole purpose to re-create the harmonies and general ambiance of the Baroque (and, to a lesser degree, Renaissance) music I so loved. But it amused me to dabble in composition.

Meanwhile, I continued to do well at the violin, and by at least my junior year I was concertmaster of the high school orchestra. The result was that I ended up playing a fair number of solos from time to time, and in private lessons I worked on some fairly difficult pieces, among them a violin concerto called the *Adelaide Concerto,* once attributed to Mozart but almost certainly not by him. I also participated in the city's Youth Symphony Orchestra, but here my fortunes were more mixed. This orchestra required try-outs, and I recall one extremely humiliating experience when I played very badly the designated piece (one movement of Handel's *Concerto Grosso No. 5*) and was demoted from concertmaster to fourth chair. To this day I cannot listen to that piece without remembering my catastrophic failure! On another occasion, as principal second violinist I became lost during the playing of the incredible slow movement of Beethoven's *Seventh Symphony,* with the result that the entire second violin section simply stopped playing at a critical juncture. Mr. Cooley, who was conducting, later made some tart comment ("That went well, didn't it?"), to which I replied with suitable embarrassment and self-condemnation.

My devotion to Corelli led me to a signal triumph during my junior year. Every winter, small groups would play chamber music in a competition at Ball State University, and I persuaded Mr. Cooley to let me play one of the Corelli trio sonatas (I chose Opus 3, No. 2 in D major), with Patty Higgins at second violin and Emily Huston at cello. We played splendidly, and as a result we were allowed to participate in a contest in Indianapolis for all such groups throughout the state. We received the highest mark at that event also. This doesn't mean we were the "best" trio in the state (many other groups, no doubt, were also awarded the highest mark), but it was a notable distinction nonetheless.

But I never really worked hard enough on the violin to excel at it. I hated practising and got by on whatever raw talent I had. I did improve in various ways simply by playing in the orchestra, and I think I was a pretty good concertmaster; but the likelihood that I would go on and become a soloist, or even a member of an orchestra, were becoming pretty dim. I simply wasn't interested in making a career of the violin, or of music in general. At this time music (purely classical music—I had ceased to have any interest in rock or other popular music) was so vital to my psychological well-being that making a living from it would have been odious to me: it would have deprived me of all the joy I experienced in the appreciation of music. Mr. Cooley, who (along with my mother) hoped I would become a professional violinist, finally threw in the towel by saying to me early during senior year, "Do you want me to lay off?" I said in relief, "Yes," and our private lessons stopped. I of course continued to play in the orchestra, and I did have an impressive triumph that I will mention later.

Between reading, writing, and music, I didn't have much time for anything else. Indeed, as of the fall of 1972 I abruptly ceased to watch television or pay attention to national or international affairs. This tendency continued throughout my undergraduate years of college, so that the period 1972–80 is largely a blank to me as far as the external world is concerned. The re-election of Nixon in 1972, and the impending scandal of Watergate, so repulsed me that I deliberately paid no attention to politics. I could hardly avoid noting Nixon's resignation in 1974, and I recall in a social studies class discussing the issue of whether President Gerald Ford was right or wrong in pardoning him (I actually determined that he was right, solely because it would be a bad thing for the nation to see a former president go on trial). On another occasion, an earnest young woman from Ball State came to our class to preach the merits of socialism. I found much of what she was saying quite silly, and when I was finally allowed to speak I waged a devastating rebuttal to many of her arguments, saying in essence, "So long as human beings are motivated by greed, socialism cannot work." She was stunned into silence. Although I myself have now been a moderate socialist for many years, I fear that my analysis of the situation is sadly true.

One other unfortunate result of my devotion to reading, writing, and music was my rather brutal casting off of my young friends David and Tommy Naumcheff. By the time I was a sophomore, I felt that it was rather absurd to keep on playing sports and games with these fellows: for Gawd's sake, David was only in junior high, and Tommy was still in grade school! At a time when even a single grade made an enormous difference in one's whole attitude to life and the nature of one's friendships, I felt I had become too much of a brainiac to associate with these once-beloved companions of my youth; so I made increasingly implausible excuses for not coming out to play with them, and eventually they got the message and left me alone. I did not enjoy disappointing them, but I felt I had no choice; in all honesty, I really had little in common with them anymore, as my chief interests had become intellectual and aesthetic, and there was no way they could participate in them.

My readings really had become monumental—I was devouring books at an incredible rate. Whether I was truly understanding what I was reading, even in the area of genre fiction, is another matter. But I have exact records of what and how much I was reading at this time: in the 1972–73 school year (including summer), I read 189 books; in 1973–74, 237 books; in 1974–75 (this may include the entire calendar year of 1975, hence a total of about fifteen months), 258 books; in 1976 (calendar year), 131 books. It is true that a great many of these books were short and frivolous—many, many detective stories, not to mention horror and fantasy (I gradually ceased reading science fiction). I no doubt absorbed (no doubt as a result of devouring Lovecraft's "Supernatural Horror in Literature," which I found at the back of *Dagon and Other Macabre Tales*) such classic weird writers as Bierce, Machen, Dunsany, and Blackwood at this time. Bierce and Dunsany immediately charmed me, for entirely different reasons (Bierce because his sardonic humour appealed to my growing interest in literary satire, as evidenced by my reading of that great trio of twentieth-century British satirists, Evelyn Waugh, Aldous Huxley, and George Orwell, not to mention other such writers as Voltaire and Nathanael West; Dunsany because of the exquisiteness of his prose and his realms of ethereal fantasy); Machen and Blackwood were a bit less appealing to me at this juncture. I of course read as much contemporary horror as I could.

One curious interest that developed around 1975 was a passion for English history, especially as told by some of the great historians of the nineteenth century. I believe this interest was first ignited by Thomas Babington Macaulay, whose *History of England* (covering the years 1685 to 1702; he had meant to carry it up through the reign of Queen Anne [1714], but died before he could finish) I devoured in a splendid edition at the Ball State University Library. (I was allowed to borrow books from this library by checking them out on my mother's card.) I subsequently read multi-volume histories by James Anthony Froude (covering the Tudor monarchs from Henry VIII to Elizabeth) and Samuel Rawson Gardiner (covering the seventeenth century, especially the English Civil War). I was reading these monumental tomes purely for my own amusement—they would certainly not have been assigned in any of my classes.

I also developed an interest in some nineteenth-century novelists, chiefly the Brontës and Thackeray. This interest was in no small part inspired by my delight in reading some sturdy old collected editions of these authors, which I found at the university library. Dickens I loathed then and loathe now. George Eliot I found tiresome and dull. I briefly tried Trollope, but he didn't do much for me. Perhaps it was these authors who led me to absorb the work of the contemporary British writer R. F. Delderfield, whose expansive sagas of English life augmented my ever-growing Anglophilia. I don't believe I had much interest at this time in the eighteenth-century writers: that only came a few years later, when I explored them in order to understand what Lovecraft saw in them. But I did work my way through a good many volumes of a collected edition (in English translation, of course) of Voltaire; and I did the same with a more modest edition (in English) of Molière, whom I found most amusing. Aside from the British and American satirists I've mentioned, I didn't do much reading of twentieth-century novelists.

A countervailing tendency was my perceived need to keep up with bestselling books of the era. For some reason I felt I had to be "up-to-date" in my readings, absorbing books that others were reading. My family had a long-standing subscription to *Time* magazine, and I pored over its list of bestsellers and absorbed as many as I could, both fiction and nonfiction, ranging from Laurence J. Peter's *The Peter Principle* to such fluff as Richard Bach's *Jonathan Livingston Seagull*. It was at this time that I developed a peculiar taste for the flamboyant novels of Irving Wallace, especially *The Word* and *The Seven Minutes*. (A few years ago I reread *The Word*, a book about a supposed ancient fragment that would revolutionise our understanding of

3. Indiana II (1972–76)

Jesus Christ, and found it a surprisingly creditable work for a popular novel.) It was also at this time that I first read some of the novels of Gore Vidal, notably the historical novels *Burr* and *Julian*. I recall reading Alvin Toffler's *Future Shock* (1970) and being highly disturbed by its conclusions. I do not believe I read this when it came out; it may have been assigned in a class around 1974.

All this frenetic activity set the stage for my two final years at Burris. The critical event was my founding of my own "literary" magazine, the *Forum*, which I ran as a monthly magazine during the school year (eleven issues in 1974–75, eight issues in 1975–76) during my junior and senior years. My co-editors were Jeff Turner and Joe Lauck. Our informal supervisor (although in fact he did little but offer helpful advice) was Robert C. Rose, whose English class I took in both those years. He had just shown up at Burris and was keen on promoting "journalism," whether it be in the form of the newspaper (a long-running weekly called the *Vanguard*), the yearbook (the *Oracle*), or independent ventures such as mine.

I had become increasingly dissatisfied with the lack of a venue for creative writing (i.e., my own stories) at school. Since it was becoming obvious that I was not likely to get published in actual professional magazines, I could at least get my work out to my fellow students. In the eighteen issues of the *Forum* (September 1974–May 1976), I published a fearsome array of my own work, especially a sheaf of stories:

"Disposall, Inc." (December 1974)
"The Evil Captain James" (January 1975)
"Philosophical Tale" (February 1975)
"Smith and Jones" (February 1975)
"The Daemoniac Ride: A Fantasy" (March 1975)
"Back from the Dead" (March 1975)
"A Musical Theory" (April 1975)
"The Wells Manuscript" (April 1975)
"'You'll Reach There in Time'" (May 1975)
"The Narrative of a Murderer" (September 1975)
"Scherzo in D-flat" (December 1975)
"Book-World" (January 1976)

While I have copies of each issue of the *Forum* (as well as two issues of *The Best of Forum*), I have not ventured to reread these tales in many years, so their very plots are largely forgotten. I do recall that "The Evil Captain James" was a story of cannibalism on the high seas (manifestly influenced by my reading of Poe's *Narrative of Arthur Gordon Pym*). "Scherzo in D-flat" was a parodic Lovecraftian squib in which the protagonist comes upon that most horrifying of sights—the *Necronomicon* in *paperback*. A slightly revised version appeared a year or so later in a fanzine edited by Edward P. Berglund.

The one item of note may be "You'll Reach There in Time,'" a tale that Rose persuaded me to submit to a Purdue University contest for high school students in the state. The story won an honourable mention, and I figured that was a not insignificant distinction. I subsequently revised it for appearance in Ken Neily's *Lovecraftian Ramblings,* then revised it again (slightly) for Jason V Brock's anthology *A Darke Fantastique;* but even this latest version is largely identical to what I wrote in late 1974.

My writing took a different turn in late 1974, when I began writing . . . poetry. Gawdelpus, I wrote dozens, perhaps hundreds of dreadful little poems, long and short, all in free verse, although I wrote one group of six poems that I titled "The Nothing Verses" that were rhymed. One of my first poems—perhaps my very first one—went like this:

> There was a man
> In a boat
> At the bottom of the sea.
> He was bailing water.

The influence on this poem should be obvious—the poetry of Stephen Crane, which I found at the back of some collected edition that I stumbled upon at the library. The cynicism and perception of the futility of existence that this poem crudely reflects are, I suppose, accurate reflections of my own mental state. Another poem, titled "Motives for Suicide," is a much longer disquisition on the same general subject. I dumped a great many of my poems—many of which were untitled and identified only by Roman numerals—into the *Forum,* in some cases merely to fill out a page. Robert Rose claimed to find one series of three long-winded and bombastic pseudo-philosophical poems, under the general title "Time and Men," impressive enough to submit to some Ball State University contest, but nothing came of this.

I kept on writing poems diligently through 1975, to the point that I felt I had enough (in quantity, at any rate—putting aside the matter of quality) to assemble a collection. The result was *The Nothing Verses and Other Poems,* completed in October. I dutifully typed up this manuscript and sent it out to a poetry publisher I had found somewhere or other—John F. Blair, Publisher. Some hapless editor at that press actually read the book and wrote back: he of course rejected the book, calling the poems "loose," but was otherwise tolerably cordial. Not in the least discouraged, I at once began another collection of poetry titled *A Dismal Paradox and Other Poems*, but mercifully never completed it.

The *Forum* itself was a most engaging enterprise. (Robert Rose should have advised me to find a different title, as he should have pointed out the fact—of which I, somehow, was entirely unaware—that there was already a literary magazine of long standing called *Ball State University Forum*.) Once the magazine appeared, I was inundated with all manner of contributions—poetry, fiction, essays—by other high school students. A good many of these proved fairly respectable, and I was happy to publish them. Some contributions did, however, create controversy.

Bill Rector somehow took it into his mind to write a morbid little poem titled "Death," whose final line read ponderously: "I am Death." One would never have thought that this wholesome, cheerful chap (who subsequently had a distinguished career in the Army) could have produced such a thing, but there it was. The poem came to the attention of the physical education teacher, Robert Gordon, who sternly pulled me aside after gym class one day and said I shouldn't publish such horrible stuff. I formulaically agreed with his criticisms—and went on publishing such stuff (whether written by myself or others) as it came to me.

A somewhat more serious matter came when a poet whose work I highly admired, Matt Bartlett, sent me a long free-verse poem entitled "Blows against the Empire." I thought it brilliant and featured it in the next issue. What was my surprise when another student came up to me and said, "Why are you printing song lyrics by Jefferson Starship?" For indeed, the "poem" was a verbatim transcript of the song! How was I to know? My interest in rock music had plummeted after the dissolution of the Beatles. Robert Rose used this kerfuffle as a teachable moment, urging me to write a solemn and apologetic letter to the record company expressing regret for the inadvertent infringement of the copyright. Needless to say, I never received a reply from the record company. But I continued to stand up for Bartlett, who I was convinced had some genuine poetic talent—if he could just stay away from plagiarism.

Then there was the time when I published some work (a poem or maybe a very short story) by a convicted criminal. During my junior year, the school was stunned when one boy stabbed another with a knife; the boy ended up dying. I have forgotten the names of both the assailant and the victim, but I can remember how we all congregated in whatever classrooms we happened to be in at the time, and some of us saw the boy's father (who was a teacher at Burris) head over to Ball Memorial Hospital with some other staff members to check on the boy's condition. Such horrible things *simply did not happen* at Burris—I don't know that any such event has ever occurred before or since. It was all pretty traumatic. Then, somehow, the assailant, now in prison (or, more likely, some juvenile penitentiary), managed to send me this literary work he had written; it was no great shakes, but I felt it was worth publishing. It created a bit of an uproar for a while, but eventually we all forgot about it—and him.

One of the chief virtues of the *Forum* was its cover and interior art, for it was here that Mark King showed his skill and imagination. His artwork graced every cover, and he also illustrated some items in the issue (including, I believe, that lamentable "Blows against the Empire"!). Given my own interests in weird and fantastic fiction, I seem to have influenced other students to write tales and poems of this sort, and King was happy to exercise his own penchant for the fantastic in his illustrations. The entire first year (1974–75) and the first issue of 1975–76 were on ditto, and I spent many hours in the typing room banging out the pages. The remaining issues of 1975–76 were on mimeograph—theoretically an improvement, but at times the reproduction of some pages was a bit problematical, and large blank spots would appear on the page. I persuaded Rose to let me edit a *Best of Forum* at the end of each school year, and these were actually reproduced by offset printing, so their print quality is much superior.

I may note that, whereas my previous "publications" in things like *Double Take* or the *Cosmic Meld* were signed "Sunand Joshi," for the *Forum* I definitively adopted my literary name of S. T. Joshi.

*

One of the main reasons why I abandoned my *Mystery and Horror Writers of the Twentieth Century* was that I had come to realise that it was really H. P. Lovecraft, and not other writers of mystery or horror, who had become my central literary interest. It was becoming evident to me that there was something in Lovecraft's work—and, indeed, in his life and attitudes, from what little I knew about them—that was exercising an uncanny fasci-

3. Indiana II (1972–76)

nation with me. It was not merely that I was hypnotised by his rich, dense, at times flamboyant prose, or his outré conceptions and imagery, so different from those of other weird writers; it was that I began sensing a remarkable parallelism between my life and beliefs and his:

- He was devoted to the past, as I was;
- He had begun playing the violin at age seven (I had begun at age nine—and of course played a lot longer than he did);
- He and I had a fascination for England—history, literature, culture, etc.;
- He and I were both cat-lovers;
- He and I were both shy, bookish, and withdrawn in youth.

This list could be extended quite a bit, and in some cases I adopted attitudes *because* Lovecraft had them. This isn't quite as slavish as it sounds, for I was heading in those directions anyway and Lovecraft's views just gave me added impetus toward them.

The point about cats is of some interest. My family did not have any pets in my childhood—our various residences were small enough just for the human occupants, and we had little money to spare to take care of an animal—but at some point during my high school years my sister Ragini (who was by this time, I believe, in graduate school at Columbia, where she would eventually get a Ph.D. in mathematics) dumped a cat upon us, because she could no longer take care of it. She had variously named the cat Hamlet or No Trump, but my mother didn't think either name was suitable for a cat, so she bestowed upon this lovely Russian blue female the grandiose name Scheherazade (Sherry for short). The cat really was a regal creature, her dark grey fur being wondrous to the touch. She was quite standoffish and actually arched her back away from you if you tried to pet her; but for all that, we all fell in love with her, and I have been a devoted ailurophile ever since. (Later, Nalini similarly dumped a cat on my parents, by the name of Annabelle, a rambunctious and fluffy long-haired Maine coon. Sherry and Annabelle did not get along at all and regularly engaged in fisticuffs. But I had left for college by the time Annabelle arrived in Muncie.) I found Lovecraft's writings about cats—in stories, poems, and letters—so affecting that it made me feel that much more of a bond with him.

Initially I had some difficulty learning anything about Lovecraft, for back in those palaeolithic days information was hard to come by. My public library did have *The Dark Brotherhood and Other Pieces* (1966), the last of the several "miscellany" volumes that Arkham House issued; this book contained some interesting material, notably Jack L. Chalker's bibliography. The university library had *Beyond the Wall of Sleep* (1943), although, aside from W. Paul Cook's splendid memoir, it didn't offer much *about* Lovecraft that was new; the library also had *Something about Cats and Other Pieces* (1949), and this was much more informative. I believe I had already come upon some critical works on horror literature, ranging from the superficial *Horror!* (1966) by Drake Douglas to more reputable studies, such as Peter Penzoldt's *The Supernatural in Fiction* (1952).

But my downfall came when, strolling in the John F. Kennedy branch of the public library one spring day in 1975, I found a fat volume in the "New Nonfiction" section—nothing less than L. Sprague de Camp's *Lovecraft: A Biography*. Since I was of course not in any way involved in Lovecraft fandom at the time (like so many others then, I felt I was the only one of my friends and acquaintances who had such a passionate devotion to the Providence scribe), I had no idea that such a volume was in the works. I devoured it in no time, and my enthusiasm for Lovecraft was redoubled. At the time I felt that it was a flawless biography—I would learn differently in fairly short order. I don't remember having any particular reaction to the revelation (if, indeed, I didn't know of it already) of Lovecraft's racism; it didn't affect me one way or the other. What the book really did was to confirm my belief that Lovecraft was one of the most *interesting* (even if "eccentric" in the conventional sense) people of his generation; and yet, even then I felt that there was much more work to be done on this enigmatic writer, and in my not-quite-seventeen-year-old arrogance I felt that I might be able to do it.

What I did, therefore, was to sit down in the months of May and June 1975 and write a ponderous, 82-page treatise called *H. P. Lovecraft: A Critical Analysis*. This would probably have come to about 20,000 words. It was a pretty elementary piece of writing: I made no attempt to develop any kind of thematic overview of Lovecraft's fiction (and I believe the work was devoted solely to his fiction—possibly I had a small chapter on his poetry), but merely presented my dogmatic and cocksure opinions on Lovecraft's stories, one after the other. I suppose I studied them more or less chronologically, using the error-sprinkled chronology that August Derleth had printed at the beginning of *Dagon and Other Macabre Tales*.

I was quite proud of this work and thought it might be my ticket to getting published. In the event, I was proved right—after a fashion.

3. Indiana II (1972–76)

Somehow I had learned of the existence of a small-press publisher, Shroud Publishers, now based in North Hollywood, California, and operated by one Ken Krueger. (At the time I had no idea that Krueger had, decades before, issued a shoddy edition of *The Dream-Quest of Unknown Kadath* [1955], borrowing the pages of the serialised reprint of the novel from the *Arkham Sampler*. Krueger was then based in Buffalo, New York.) I wish I could remember how I learned of Krueger; it may have come from a fanzine I somehow secured, the *Spoor Directory*, edited by Fred C. Adams. But if so, how did I ever obtain *that* item?

In any case, I sent the manuscript of *H. P. Lovecraft: A Critical Study* to Krueger. What was my surprise when, in August, he wrote a letter to me, accepting the book!

You could have knocked me over with a feather. The letter stated that Krueger would offer me either a flat fee of $250 (which I thought a staggeringly immense sum) or a royalty arrangement; the latter, he stated, would net me a bit more money, but of course it would probably take longer for that money to show up, as it would be tied to the sales of the book. Well, I wasn't going to say no to an immediate $250, so I wrote back at once, accepting that offer.

The news of my becoming an (almost) published author created something of a stir among my friends, even though we were still on summer vacation. Somehow the leading local paper, the *Muncie Star*, got wind of the event and sent over a reporter to our house. He spent all of a half-hour interviewing me, and a tiny article—of the standard "local boy makes good" sort—duly appeared in the paper. When I came back to school the next month, I was looked upon with awe by all and sundry.

Thankfully for my future reputation, the book was never published. Krueger never sent me a contract and never sent me that $250. Soon thereafter he fled south of the border to Mexico, where he apparently published soft-core pornography. I would hear from him every now and then during my early college years; and I always wrote back, threatening him with legal action if he ever dared to publish my mortifyingly dreadful little book. I suppose he is long dead by now—but I wonder if his heirs and assigns still have my *Critical Study* in their grubby little hands?

As I entered senior year of high school (1975–76), I found myself being pulled in many different directions. I continued to pursue my interest in Lovecraft; but I had many other things to do. I had become involved in *seven* different musical groups, as follows:

1. The high school orchestra
2. The high school choir
3. The high school chamber orchestra
4. An independent chamber orchestra I had established
5. A "madrigal" group (really a kind of chamber choir)
6. A madrigal group made up of Ball State freshmen
7. The Twilights

The madrigal groups were delightful: the English (and to a lesser degree Italian) madrigals of the late sixteenth and early seventeenth centuries are some of the most exquisite fruits of the late Renaissance period, and to this day I find them vividly evocative of their historical and cultural era. Some of the lyrics are quite piquant, and I've never forgotten Orlando Gibbons's "The Silver Swan":

> The silver swan, who living had no note,
> When death approach'd unlock'd her silent throat.
> Leaning her breast against the reedy shore,
> Thus sang her first and last and sang no more:
> "Farewell all joys, O death come close mine eyes;
> More geese than swans now live, more fools than wise."

How true!

I had established that independent chamber orchestra because I wanted to play even more works of Baroque music than we were playing in the orchestra. One of the things I did was to transcribe Bach's *Brandenburg Concerto No. 6*—originally scored in B-flat for certain now-archaic instruments (two viole da braccio, two viole de gamba, and cello)—into G major for two violins, two violas, and cello. I thought I did a pretty effective job of it. I do not know if this group actually performed a concert, but it was entertaining to rehearse.

The Twilights was an independent vocal quartet consisting of Susan Stump (soprano), Patty Higgins (alto), myself (tenor), and Ed Alexander (bass). We had begun in the 1974–75 school year, performing at various local functions here and there—and actually made money in the process. At the end of that school year, we took our hard-earned pay (about $150) and went to a tolerably fancy restaurant in the neighbouring town of Anderson, where I believe I had filet mignon for the first time. I still remember the

3. Indiana II (1972–76)

heavenly taste of that superb cut of beef. The next year Susan left (she was a year ahead of us), and Patty's sister Betsy filled in. Again we made a fair wad of money, but this time we simply distributed it equally among ourselves at the end of the school year.

A new face had shown up in the orchestra at this time—one HolliAnne Jones. Because her family had moved around quite a bit during her adolescence, she was about a year and a half older than others in her class. Not only that, but she had suddenly switched from playing the clarinet to playing the violin; so proficient was she that she quickly became my chief rival as a violinist. I managed to hang on as concertmaster even during my senior year (when I was no longer taking private lessons, as she was); but in fact she was probably better than I at this point.

I was struck by her enthusiasm for music, which went to the extent of studying scores (as I was doing, although I was no longer composing music). We naturally became fast friends, rehearsing music in our spare time, going over to the university library to look up music scores, and so on and so forth. In spite of my residual shyness (especially around girls), I began inviting her to my house so that we could hole up in my bedroom and listen to various recordings (the record player was now stationed in my room). I would also go to her house, a little ways north of school, where her genial parents would greet me cordially.

The inevitable occurred—we fell into a romance. It would seem that this was the first such experience for both of us, and we went about it in the most clumsy manner imaginable; but sure enough a bond developed, and we spent a great deal of time cuddling in my bedroom or hers. Prudence forbids me to expatiate any further on our activities; suffice it to say we were very much in each other's company during that senior year. We had our difficulties and arguments, but somehow we always managed to patch them up.

When it became apparent that my parents (especially my father) didn't approve of our hanging out in my bedroom for hours on end, we decided to do our cuddling elsewhere. Luckily, HolliAnne had a car, so we could go here, there, and everywhere. We wished to find some spot where we could have reasonable privacy in the evenings—and found the perfect site: nothing less than the large parking lot of St. Mary's Catholic Church, about a half-mile east of my house on Jackson Street! The place was practically deserted at night, so we went there often, exploring each other's bodies in the back seat of the car.

I believe it was in the spring of 1976 that the choir took a field trip to

Chicago. (HolliAnne was in the choir also.) This would be for an entire weekend, and during the two nights in whatever hotel we were in there was a certain amount of surreptitious bedswapping, although it went little beyond that. I recall buying some inexpensive classical recording at Marshall Field's, and also seeing a performance of Shaw's *Devil's Disciple* at a theatre.

HolliAnne was also central to my achievement of the pinnacle of my violin-playing career. We both persuaded Mr. Cooley to let us play the solo violin parts to one or the other of Vivaldi's *Four Seasons* (Opus 8, Nos. 1–4). I chose the *Spring Concerto* (Opus 8, No. 1) and performed it reasonably well. HolliAnne chose the much harder *Winter Concerto* (Opus 8, No. 4) and also did very well. Cooley had also noted my interest in conducting (I was conducting my independent chamber orchestra while simultaneously playing first violin) and allowed me to conduct one of the Corelli *Concerti Grossi* (Opus 6, No. 3 in C minor, I think). I recall that that performance went tolerably well.

Work on publications was also taking up a great deal of time. Indeed, by the time I entered senior year I had already accumulated so many credits that I only needed to take two classes each quarter (the school had switched from a semester system to a quarter system); but I was at school the whole day, and beyond. In fact, I was so busy that I had no time for a proper lunch; instead, I would simply bring a piece of French bread and a hunk of cheese from home and eat them as I walked around the school grounds in the five minutes between one class (or rehearsal) to the next. I felt very bohemian—too bad I didn't have a beret and was too young to drink wine!

The publications I worked on were not only my *Forum* but the school weekly newspaper, the *Vanguard,* and most significantly the yearbook, the *Oracle.* I had written some book reviews for the *Vanguard* during junior year, covering books ranging from Bierce's *Devil's Dictionary* to Wilde's *The Picture of Dorian Gray;* and I continued at this task for a short time during senior year until I decided that my time commitments would not let me continue it. Thereafter, all my time was devoted to the *Forum* and the *Oracle.*

Robert Rose took very seriously the editing of the yearbook. In the past, our yearbooks were rather slapdash affairs and were not held in high esteem. During junior year Rose arranged for several of us—who would be working on the next year's yearbook—to go to Indianapolis to learn more formally about yearbook editing and design. This proved to be quite helpful, and we applied our newfound knowledge to the yearbook. I was appointed the "copy editor"; by tradition, the editor-in-chief was a junior, in this case one Barba-

3. Indiana II (1972–76)

ra Schmidt. Barbara and I had a reasonably good working relationship, and we and others got together frequently to prepare the material. We had to get about one-quarter of the book ready every month or two, and sometimes this caused difficulties.

As copy editor I ended up writing *every word of that 1976 yearbook.* This meant writing not only about the little kids (grades K–6), about whom I knew next to nothing (I arranged to pass out questionnaires to some of those classes, and later worked their responses into the copy I wrote), but the sports teams, various organisations, and so on and so forth. It was an immense task. I was also organisations editor, and in this task I dodged a spectacular disaster. We had hired a professional photographer to come to school and take photos of the various groups (choir, orchestra, student council, etc.)—but the fellow came a day early! Either that, or I was misinformed as to when he would show up. Well, he blandly informed me that today was his only free day, so I had to work like a lunatic to get all the different groups set up for their photo shoots a day ahead of schedule. This is why, in some of the photos in which I myself appear, I am glowering with ill-concealed rage and frustration.

Somehow, we managed to get the work done, and the *Oracle* of 1976 (which I still possess) is, if I do say so myself, quite a creditable publication of its kind. (I may add that, during the summer before my senior year, I also secured some of the ads in the back of the issue, going around—with Ed Alexander—to various local establishments and persuading them to purchase the ads in question. I guess I was a bit better than Lovecraft, who was once compelled to undertake a similar activity during his trying days in New York!)

As an aside, I may mention that the photographs of me in that *Oracle* are of interest if only because they display the immense Afro that I was then sporting. From at least the age of six, and no doubt influenced by the mop-headed Beatles and other rock bands, I had been partial to long hair; but because my hair (unusually for an Indian) was curly instead of straight, the result was a luxuriant Afro of which I was vastly proud. Indeed, going to the barber was always a traumatic event for me, and I threw tantrums on several occasions as a child; in later years I simply cut (or, more properly, trimmed) my own hair. My Afro was so impressive that on one occasion in typing class, a girl named Erin Bowman (no relation to Lisa Bowman) came up behind me, seized my head, and held it to her chest. I made no complaint. My formal senior portrait in the 1976 *Oracle,* taken a little later in the year, does not show quite as flamboyant an Afro, but it does show a tentative mustache

I was attempting to sprout—something I kept up through my college years. But, as Lovecraft said of Frank Long, my mustache struggled to have much more than five hairs on one side and six on the other.

It was through Robert Rose's influence that I was assigned to write a monthly article on school happenings in the *Muncie Evening Press* during senior year. The paper had asked to have one report per week from each of the four public schools (Northside, Southside, Central, and Burris), and I had to find something interesting to write about once a month. This kind of reporting was not my cup of tea at all, and I struggled to find anything to write about; when push came to shove, I ended up writing about myself or my friends' activities (e.g., "Eleven Burris String Groups Plan Concert"; "Burris Players into Baroque Tuesday Night"). I would actually walk over to the newspaper office downtown and hand my articles in person to the editor. But I was glad when this assignment was over.

In spite of what seems to be my complete immersion in academic, literary, or aesthetic pursuits, I actually was not merely a bookworm (or music-worm) all the time. Even aside from assignations with HolliAnne, I was quite a popular guy at school and hung out with friends when time permitted. For years (possibly reaching back to junior high school), I would accompany Jay Marhoefer in collecting money from the households he served on his paper route; afterwards, we would head over to the Dairy Queen and he would buy me a root beer float, hot fudge sundae, or whatever else struck my fancy. Not only did I enjoy the treat (which I couldn't have bought for myself, as I had no money), but I enjoyed playing the jukebox in the establishment. This was where I first heard Don McLean's "American Pie" (although it was probably an abridged version—I didn't hear the full version until I secured the album some years later). Burris folks would also hang out at the Ball State student center: our presence was not entirely welcomed by the college students, but they couldn't do anything about it. It was there that I first heard Roberta Flack's "Killing Me Softly," which brought tears to my eyes.

As the end of the school year approached, we had to think of the prom. Naturally, I was obliged to take HolliAnne: no problem there; but whether we would actually do any dancing was another matter. Probably because they thought our awkward romance amusing, our classmates had actually voted us "best couple," so our presence was mandatory. When HolliAnne picked me up at my house, she looked gorgeous in a long gown that reached to her feet: I could rarely recall her ever wearing a skirt or dress of any kind, so this yielding to conventional femininity was most welcome. At the actual

3. Indiana II (1972–76)

prom, we did our best to stay inconspicuous; but at one point the master of ceremonies essentially demanded that we step onto the dance floor, so we had no choice but to trudge out there and shuffle around. Mercifully, the song we were dancing to was a slow one, and it was over quickly. Afterwards, we (strangely enough) parked in front of my house and made out in the back seat.

And yet, it was clear—to me, at any rate—that our romance was coming to an end. We really didn't have much in common, and I was dismayed at what I felt was HolliAnne's insensitivity to literature—at least, to the type of literature I was becoming increasingly devoted to. I remember being mightily offended when, after reading some pages of a book by Lord Dunsany, she declared his prose style "effeminate." The idea! She was presumably intent on pursuing music, and she was also strong in the sciences; whereas by this time I had resolved that music would only be an avocation, and I was eagerly looking forward to giving up the violin and focusing on literature and literary criticism. I assume our romance dragged on through the summer; but since I had already been accepted at Brown (for which see below) and she had decided to go to Reed College in Portland, Oregon, I figured that our relationship would die a natural death as a result of increasing temperamental differences and the 3000-mile distance between us. It turned out that I was not quite accurate in that prediction.

*

It was increasingly clear that I was becoming obsessed with Lovecraft. I was re-reading the Arkham House volumes of his fiction over and over again; indeed, on my third reading, I sat down with the books and a dictionary, so that I could finally figure out what such words as *eldritch, cacodaemoniacal, domdaniel,* and the like meant. Very illuminating! I was seeking out anything by or about him that I could find; I even read the Derleth "posthumous collaborations," not realising how little of Lovecraft there was in them but recognising them as inferior work. He must have written them on a bad day! I also read *Tales of the Cthulhu Mythos* (a bit better but still uneven) and other such volumes, not to mention delving further into the work of Lovecraft's predecessors and influences.

But Lovecraft influenced me in a much profounder way. Through the de Camp biography, I came to understand the importance of Lovecraft's letters, and I made efforts to secure these documents. I had my mother order the first three volumes (all that were available at the time) of *Selected Letters* from interlibrary loan, since the Ball State library did not have them; they duly came, and I appear to have read them in the spring of 1976. Aside from being charmed by his curious eccentricities, I was struck with the cogency of Lovecraft's arguments on behalf of atheism. I had previously been something of a "passive atheist," not ascribing to any religion but not being a particularly vociferous unbeliever. That changed when I read these letters, and they led me to other thinkers of the same sort—notably Bertrand Russell and Friedrich Nietzsche, who influenced my thought significantly over the next several years.

On July 1, 1975 (the summer before my senior year of high school, and even before my *Critical Study* had been accepted by Shroud), I began the work that would become my first true book: *H. P. Lovecraft: Four Decades of Criticism.*

At this juncture the book was blandly titled *A Collection of H. P. Lovecraft Criticism.* My purpose was not necessarily to reprint the "best" criticism that had been written on Lovecraft up to that time, but to depict the history of Lovecraft criticism from the time of his death to the present day. (At that time I was not aware of any significant criticism of Lovecraft during his lifetime, so I began my volume with the reviews of the first Arkham House books of his work in the early 1940s.) Beyond what I could find in de Camp's biography and other sources, I really had little idea of what to include; and some of my early choices were embarrassingly silly. For example, I chose Philip Herrera's review-essay "The Dream Lurker" (*Time,* June 11, 1973), an assessment of the early Ballantine paperback editions of Lovecraft that had been issued over the past few years. Herrera's review was actually written as an engaging parody/homage of Lovecraft's flamboyant prose, and I remember being stunned by its very appearance: here was a clear token of Lovecraft's increasing popular appeal, even if that didn't automatically translate to critical or academic recognition. That's where I would step in.

In the course of researching the book, I had stumbled upon Colin Wilson's extremely hostile attack on Lovecraft in *The Strength to Dream* (1961). This screed so offended me that I wrote a ferocious rebuttal, "Remarks on Colin Wilson's Analysis of H. P. Lovecraft in *The Strength to Dream*" (July 1975). In September, having found his address in the *Spoor Directory,* I wrote to R. Alain Everts, who was then establishing a fanzine entitled *Ozymandias.* He accepted my piece for his journal, although in the end the magazine never appeared, and I have lost my copy of my article. But it was

Everts who urged me to get in touch with Dirk W. Mosig, which I did in October.

This contact with the leading Lovecraft scholar of the day was so influential to my own eventual emergence as an authority on Lovecraft that I could devote an entire book to the subject. For the next four or five years, Dirk became my mentor in Lovecraft (and in other areas as well), writing letter after letter that deepened and broadened my understanding of Lovecraft incalculably. It was also through Dirk that I came in touch with other scholars and fans, ranging from Peter Cannon to David E. Schultz to George T. Wetzel to Barton L. St. Armand to J. Vernon Shea and many others.

When I first heard from Dirk, he was preparing to head to the First World Fantasy Convention in Providence, and he casually asked me if I were planning on attending. I had not even heard of this event, and the idea of my venturing out there all alone was petrifying to me, so I said no. Just as Lovecraft himself had, up to the age of thirty, not stepped outside the states of Rhode Island, Massachusetts, and Connecticut, I had up to this time not set foot in any state except Illinois and Indiana. So I wished Dirk well and hoped the convention would be a success.

I sent Dirk my *Critical Analysis,* and he painstakingly—but always cordially and sympathetically—criticised its deficiencies in analysis and general scholarship. I was not always amenable to his reasoning at this time; in one sense, I correctly perceived that Dirk didn't care to find *any* flaws in Lovecraft's work, but in another sense I was still too wrapped up in my own dogmatism to be open to criticism about my opinions. It took me some time to reform in this regard.

Knowing that I was a senior in high school, Dirk was keen on my applying to Brown, since he had made it clear that if I were truly to pursue research on Lovecraft I would have to spend months if not years poring over the Lovecraft materials housed in the John Hay Library there. I believe I had already come to realise the importance of Brown's holdings—probably through reading de Camp's biography. Dirk himself, a professor at Georgia Southwestern College in Americus (later he moved to Kearney State College in Kearney, Nebraska), knew that he could never be in such a position himself, so he was probably hoping that, if I got to Brown, I could help him with his own research.

My mother would let me apply only to Harvard, Yale, and Brown. She figured that I would get into at least one of these schools, based on my reasonably impressive school record and the fact that I was the author of a (soon-to-be-)published book. I was accepted at Yale and Brown and was placed on Harvard's waiting-list. This latter decision was probably a result of my less-than-stellar SAT scores: 740 (out of 800) in English and only 650 in math. (The days when I had long lines of students seeking help in math were long over, and I took no math classes during senior year.) Well, I'd never wanted to go to a snooty school like Harvard anyway. My mother pleaded with me to go to Yale, since she assumed that Yale was a more impressive institution than Brown; but I put my foot down and said I'd go to Brown, salivating at the thought of spending years essentially getting a degree in Lovecraft studies. And so it happened. Dirk was, needless to say, thrilled at my acceptance.

I continued to work on my anthology of criticism. I also worked on a revision of my *Critical Analysis*. Whether this work was inspired by Dirk's criticism or my own growing understanding of the shoddiness of the original version of that work, I cannot now recall. I in fact wrote a scathing review of my book in the *Forum* (March 1976), in which I condemned it as being superficial and opinionated. I have no recollection what the revised version was like, and cannot remember if I had promised to send it to Ken Krueger in lieu of the first version; in any case, I was no longer hearing from Krueger. I actually breathed a sigh of relief at this, as I was already becoming mortified at the prospect of this work seeing print.

Late in 1975 I began soliciting publishers for the anthology. I immediately went right to academic publishers, because I was convinced that Lovecraft needed to find greater recognition in that arena rather than in the fan press. I was already aware that Lovecraft fandom was in full swing and was familiar with some of the small-press publishers of that era—Silver Scarab Press, Mirage Press, and so on. Indeed, my records indicate that I sent a letter to Mirage Press in September 1975: I believe I sent some minimal corrections to *The Revised H. P. Lovecraft Bibliography* by Mark Owings and Jack L. Chalker (Mirage Press, 1973), which I found in the university library. I never heard back from anyone in reply.

Why is this of any importance? Well, you may recall that at this time Chalker had achieved surprising popularity with various fantasy novels. Imagine my surprise when I (or maybe it was someone else) browsed through a copy of Chalker's *Quest for the Well of Souls* (Ballantine, 1978) and found a fairly significant character named Joshi! Is it possible that Chalker saw my letter to Mirage and that my name stuck in his memory as an appropriately outré one to use in a novel of fantastic adventure? I suppose the possibility should at least be considered.

In any case, I felt that my anthology would accomplish little if it was merely published by one of these small presses in the horror/fantasy/science fiction field: what was needed was to bring Lovecraft to the attention of a more academic audience. So I bombarded university presses, pretty much at random. Over the next three years I queried a total of thirty-three such publishers. Some of them—Cornell University Press and the University of Pittsburgh Press—did look at some parts of the manuscript as it existed at the time, but ultimately declined. I will record the book's acceptance in a later chapter.

One publisher I queried in the spring of 1976 was Kent State University Press. I have no idea why I approached this publisher, but I was astounded to receive a reply in which an editor stated that, although he was not interested in the anthology, his firm did have a long-running series, the Serif Series of Bibliographies and Checklists. He noted that, to his knowledge, there was no comprehensive bibliography of Lovecraft available. Would I consider compiling one for the series?

After I had come out of my faint, I wrote back saying, "You bet!" I expatiated at the inadequacies of the relatively recent Owings/Chalker bibliography and said that I would be happy to try to do better. Now you must understand that I really had no idea how to compile a bibliography at this time, certainly not the sort of "descriptive" bibliography that Kent State was publishing in the Serif Series; moreover, I felt that I would merely act as a kind of compiler of information provided by others. David E. Schultz, for example, was already assembling what looked like a fairly exhaustive listing of anthologies in which Lovecraft's work appeared, and I figured I'd use that and other information provided by Dirk Mosig and others. Indeed, for quite a long time I was considering merely referring to myself as the "editor" of the bibliography.

It is transparently evident that Kent State did not realise I had not quite graduated from high school when it wrote to me about this project. I cannot recall if the editor actually called me "Professor"; he may well have. I made no attempt to disabuse him of his error. But the result was that I was now able to write to other academic publishers about the anthology, stating that "I am compiling a bibliography of Lovecraft for Kent State University Press's Serif Series." I felt this was only a slight exaggeration: Kent State had of course not given me a contract, and it was conceivable that it would reject the bibliography if it proved inadequate; but I felt rather clever in conjuring up a phantom "publishing credit" while seeking to land my anthology.

With the coming of summer and my awareness that I would be heading both to a prestigious Ivy League institution as well as to Lovecraft's hometown for at least four years, I made a momentous decision: I would conduct a preliminary trip there to get my feet wet in Lovecraft scholarship. I am amazed that I managed to persuade my mother to go along with this plan, but she clearly sensed that I was a studious lad and would fare well enough, assuming I didn't get lost in transit. Transportation was indeed a problem: I was still terrified of flying, remembering my horrible experience coming to the U.S. from India at the age of five; and expense was also a factor. So it was decided that I would take a train to Providence. At some point in late June I boarded a train in Indianapolis for the *twenty-hour train ride* that loomed ahead.

That trip was far worse than any plane ride could have been, for I did not purchase any kind of sleeping compartment but instead had to get by dozing in a standard cushioned seat on the Amtrak train. Still more foolishly, I had somehow decided to take my typewriter along (I think this was a Smith-Corona electric), meaning that I was burdened with a huge suitcase and the typewriter. Further adding to the confusion, I seemed to have jotted down the wrong address for Brown's housing office, where I was supposed to go to pick up keys for the room I had presumably reserved. So when the taxi driver, flummoxed at where I wanted to be dropped off, simply left me at what I later learned was the John D. Rockefeller Library (across the street from the John Hay Library), in a light, misty rain, you might think I was petrified at being all alone and essentially lost in a city (certainly the biggest I had ever been in, aside from my year-long residence in Indianapolis and two brief visits to Chicago) whose geography was utterly unknown to me.

And yet, as I took cover under an awning with my clumsy suitcase and typewriter, I felt a strange elation: *I was in Lovecraft's Providence!* It did not matter what happened to me; my presence in this place was euphoria enough. Somehow I managed to find the housing office (only a block or two away)—and then encountered a further difficulty, in that the office had apparently not received my reservation. Well, the campus was fairly empty, so I was lodged in a room in the same building as the housing office. It was not much better than a monk's cell, but it would do for the purpose.

The next day, I was on the doorstep of the John Hay Library close to the time it opened—9 A.M. Even though I was not then fully aware of the massive extent of the Lovecraft Collection (both printed matter and manu-

3. Indiana II (1972–76)

scripts), I did have some idea of the kinds of research I wished to do. First, I was looking for more material for my critical anthology. Second, I had been in close consultation with David E. Schultz, and we were attempting to establish a complete and accurate chronology of Lovecraft's fiction. We were well aware that the chronology that Derleth had slapped together and included in his introduction to *Dagon and Other Macabre Tales* was quite inaccurate—especially given that, when several tales were written in a single year, he had *alphabetised* the stories! So I wished to check manuscript letters to see if I could find discussions of the writing of any given story.

I was shown the register of the Lovecraft manuscripts—a sheaf of bound pages that probably spanned about 300 or 400 pages. (It is much larger now.) The manuscript collection existed in an array of forty-one boxes, each containing many folders. Being unaware of library protocol (especially that of rare book libraries), I blandly filled out a call slip stating that I wished to consult Boxes 1–41 of the Lovecraft Collection!

The assistant librarian and curator of the Lovecraft Collection, John H. Stanley, approached me and said, "You're freaking out the librarians; let me show you how things are done." He calmly explained that I would be allowed to look at only one box at a time (nowadays one is only allowed to look at a single *folder* at a time), and that I should focus on those boxes that contained Lovecraft letters as opposed to other documents (manuscripts of stories, poems, and essays; letters and other documents by persons other than Lovecraft; etc., etc.). I grudgingly accepted this limitation on my research and set to work.

In the course of the week, I did indeed unearth some nuggets of information on the date of writing of some stories. How much progress I made in my anthology I cannot quite recall; there was such an immensity of criticism (even at that time) that I had trouble taking it all in. And that ridiculous typewriter I had brought along proved to be all but useless; all that I used it for was to type up Clark Ashton Smith's superb elegy "To Howard Phillips Lovecraft," which I hand-copied from Smith's *Selected Poems* and then typed up when I got back to my humble little room.

I don't recall doing much exploration of the city—even of the immediate Brown University area—during that week, although I assume I frequented various cheap eateries on Thayer Street and elsewhere. I had really not come prepared with any kind of list of sites to look up: probably I did take a gander at Lovecraft's last residence, 66 College Street (now moved to 65 Prospect Street), and I may have looked up the house at 10 Barnes Street; but that is probably all. I was still a bit frightened at being in this unfamiliar city all by myself, and, after the library was closed, I did little but take a quick meal and retreat to my cubbyhole of a room to read and prepare for the next day.

The week passed all too quickly, and I was sorry to leave the city, even though I knew I would be returning in less than two months. The visit, in which I had not accomplished nearly as much as I had hoped, was nonetheless useful in giving me a foretaste of what it would be like to be a Lovecraft scholar. The question was whether I could manage to do that while also taking a full load of classes at this intimidating institution of higher learning.

4. Brown (1976–80)

"There is a point beyond which researches are only for curiosity."—Voltaire

I believe my mother drove me the 1000 or so miles from Muncie to Providence. She had acquired a driver's licence a few years earlier, and our first vehicle was a Chevrolet Caprice—an unwieldy boat of a car that my mother had difficulty handling. I myself had taken driver's education with Mr. Gordon during my senior year, and at that time one could get an Indiana driver's licence by merely taking the written test if one had passed driver's education. So I got my licence; but since I never drove or had access to a car, I let the licence expire.

The school year (Brown was on a semester system at this time) started unusually late, on September 19, so we probably arrived in Providence around mid-September. I was given a room (#315) in a dorm, North Caswell, just off the main green; its rear faced Thayer Street, although there was no exit in that direction. I was also assigned a roommate, as all freshmen were—one Douglas Edwards. I had exchanged some brief letters with him over the summer, but really didn't get much of an idea of the kind of person he was. The room itself was pretty austere—merely two beds and two desks and chairs. The room did have its own telephone. I do not believe there was even a bookshelf, so what few books I had were dumped unceremoniously on the floor or perhaps placed in a closet. I had also brought along some of my favourite classical recordings and my stereo system—a clunky solid-state machine that was pretty much on its last legs.

Having never lived with a roommate (not at all the same thing as living with one's sisters, since I never shared a room with them), I naturally had some difficulty getting along with Doug. Even though we perforce spent a lot of time in the library studying, we eventually worked out a system whereby I would stay in the room and he would be elsewhere. The one thing for which I remain eternally in his debt was his introducing me to the music of Bruce Springsteen, who has come to rank second only to the Beatles in my regard as far as popular music is concerned.

Caswell was a coed dorm, men and women living on alternate floors. I got to know several fellow students tolerably well, but I can't say I was particularly sociable. I don't believe I went to a party of any kind during my entire stay at Brown, aside from occasional gatherings at professors' houses. I also never once went on a date with a female, although the reasons for that will become apparent presently.

The fact that I had been accepted by Yale and Brown did not mean that I was at all confident of my ability to handle what I figured would be radically higher expectations for intellectual achievement here. I quickly realised that, admirable as my Burris schooling had been in certain directions, it was painfully deficient in others. In particular, my understanding of history—especially the course of Western history from the Greeks to the present—was very poor. That is why I enrolled, in my freshman year, in year-long courses in Greek history and European history (from the Renaissance through World War II). The latter course in particular was immensely beneficial, and I could almost literally feel my mind being reshaped by the facts I was learning. The Greek history course was also incredibly stimulating, and the next year I took a year-long Roman history course so that I could have a firm grasp of the whole trend of classical antiquity.

One thing I didn't do was to pursue my musical career. By this time I was heartily sick of the violin, so I gave it up without regret and made no attempt to join the college orchestra or any other group. I did not give up my instrument (it was a reasonably good piece of work, valued at about $750), but I buried it away in my closet so that I didn't even have to look at it. I did try out for the college choir, but after a mediocre audition I was unsurprised—and not particularly disappointed—to learn that I had not been selected. Curiously enough, at the very end of the school year I was seized with inspiration and wrote a violin concerto, more or less in the Vivaldian manner; but a later examination convinced me that it was a poor piece of work, so I discarded it.

I did not entirely give up the thought of writing fiction. I had essentially run out of ideas for new tales, but I felt that some of the stories I had written in high school might be rewritten in such a way as to be a bit more respectable. I rewrote one of my *Forum* stories, "The Narrative of a Murderer" (a psychological horror tale), retitling it "I Am a Murderer." This was readily accepted by *Issues,* the student-run literary magazine, where it appeared in the December 1976 issue. A purportedly humorous squib, "A Musical Theory" (also a rewriting of an earlier tale), appeared in *Issues* for March 1977. But that was the extent to which I tried to write fiction.

Naturally, the bulk of my time was devoted to actual classwork. I was so petrified of failure during that first year that I took nearly all courses pass/fail—something that was permitted but not recommended, since one would eventually need to secure actual grades if one were to go on to graduate school. The one course I took for a grade was an English class in which we read a batch of twentieth-century novels and wrote critiques of them. I assumed this would be right up my alley; but as a matter of fact, I found most of the novels quite dull (with the exception of Nathanael West's *Day of the Locust,* which I had read already), and the young female professor teaching the class was not exactly very inspiring.

The very fact that this English class proved so unstimulating produced a kind of existential crisis in me. I had always assumed—based on my relative success as a writer in high school—that I would be an English major. But this lacklustre class made me wonder if I really wanted to do that. English departments throughout the country were at this time becoming very theoretical, as such fashionable methodologies as poststructuralism, deconstruction, and the like were making headway. Brown was a hotbed of semiotics, and from what little I learned of it I came to the conclusion that this was not how I wished to approach literature. But if I wasn't an English major, what the blazes was I going to do?

As in so many other situations, Lovecraft came to my rescue.

Robert Bloch once stated that "Lovecraft was my university." By this he meant that, because he himself did not go to college, and because he had engaged in a four-year correspondence with Lovecraft at just the time when he would have been attending college, and—most relevantly of all—because Lovecraft's letters had opened up so many interesting avenues of intellectual and aesthetic pursuit that might not have occurred to him on his own, he felt as if he was being tutored by a college professor. I myself, though obviously in a college (and a prestigious one at that—one that Lovecraft himself had wished to attend but had been unable to), felt the need to investigate some of his own interests in order to understand him better. Lovecraft was my intellectual superior in so many different areas of study (except, perhaps, music) that I felt woefully ignorant in comparison; so I sensed that I had to remedy that deficiency.

One of the first ways I sought to do so was to probe further into his fascination with the classical world. Certainly, I was learning Greek (and later Roman) history; but that was not enough. Was not Lovecraft thoroughly versed in the Latin language, to the point that—as I discovered a bit later—he had actually translated the first 88 lines of Ovid's *Metamorphoses* into English at the age of about ten? Why not study the Latin language and see why Lovecraft enjoyed it so much?

So, during second semester of freshman year, I took an introductory Latin class. This class would concentrate solely on grammar; in a single semester one would learn the fundamentals of the language so that, the very next semester, one would be able to read actual Latin texts, whether in prose or in poetry. I was actually thankful that I didn't take high school Latin, because (as I learned from discussions with others who had done so) the progress of one's learning of grammar in high school is so slow that many students lose interest. Here, in this concentrated course, one was fully prepared to plunge into the ancient texts after a single semester.

And so I did. The next semester, I actually took a course in Ovid's *Metamorphoses,* reading large chunks of it. Later I took classes in Virgil (with Michael C. J. Putnam, one of the world's leading authorities on that poet), Latin prose of the late Republic (where we read huge chunks of Caesar, Cicero, and others), and so on. Since I had already become interested in English satire, I absorbed the Roman satirists—Horace, Persius, and especially the supremely mordant Juvenal. And my eventual interest in ancient philosophy led me to do a profound study of Lucretius, whose *De Rerum Natura* I probably read about fifty times in the course of my six years at Brown.

In "The Case for Classicism" (1919) Lovecraft wrote: "The literary genius of Greece and Rome, developed under peculiarly favourable circumstances, may fairly be said to have completed the art and science of expression. Unhurried and profound, the classical author achieved a standard of simplicity, moderation, and elegance of taste, which all succeeding time has been powerless to excel or even to equal." This sounds flamboyant, but only someone who has actually read the ancient authors in the original languages can grasp the fundamental truth of this utterance. There is a kind of compressed perfection in the greatest of the classical authors that makes even the most towering writers in English seem tepid indeed. (Of course, there are plenty of mediocre classical authors, but even they are of some historical interest.)

So it was not long before I determined to major in classics—Latin, Greek, and ancient history. By the end of my sophomore year, as this tendency was becoming increasingly evident in me, Professor Putnam pulled me aside and urged me to begin reading Greek, for a mastery of both languages was required to achieve a major in classics. I promptly enrolled in beginning Greek during the first semester of my junior year, and I subsequently read bits of Homer and Herodotus, some of the Greek tragedians (immensely difficult!), random dialogues of Plato, and other Greek authors. But like Lovecraft, I found Latin much more to my taste than Greek; I mastered Greek far better than he ever did (note his wildly erroneous derivation of the word *Necronomicon!*), but Latin remained my first love.

But all this was in the future. During freshman year, I was still trying to become accustomed to living in what I felt was a big city (where one could actually encounter homeless people on the street) and feeling my way through classes where I was no longer the most intelligent student in the room. I took all my meals in the main student cafeteria, Sharpe Refectory (charmingly nicknamed "the Ratty"), although I occasionally frequented the less expensive eateries near the campus.

My finances during that first year were pretty tight—my parents only gave me $25 a month for miscellaneous expenses. During subsequent years of my undergraduate career, I received $100 from Social Security: as a full-time student, I received this sum as an adjunct to my father's Social Security payments. But I augmented my income in another way. Almost from the time I got to Brown, I hired myself out to type papers for fellow students who struggled with the typewriter. I charged only 50¢ a page; and in my naïve chivalry I charged female clients only 25¢ a page—until so many of them took advantage of me that I upped the rate to 50¢. I was particularly busy toward the end of semesters, when lengthy papers were due. Since I myself generally had little difficulty keeping up with my own course work, I took on quite a load of typing. And with the proceeds I went out to local record stores and purchased recordings of my favourite classical composers. This was a splendid era for the securing of classical LPs, especially of Baroque music, which was then experiencing a vigorous revival. I ended up purchasing immense numbers of recordings of Vivaldi's works, especially as recorded by the superb Italian chamber orchestra, I Musici; later I was thrilled to hear Vivaldi's sacred choral music. Handel's oratorios also thrilled me—especially things like *Israel in Egypt, Judas Maccabaeus, Saul, Samson,* and others. Eventually my collection of classical LPs extended to nearly 1000.

Then there was my Lovecraft research. Now that I had essentially unlimited access to the resources of the John Hay Library, I went about exploring its treasures in a rather unsystematic way. Certainly, I was still working on my critical anthology, sending out letter after letter to academic publishers and getting few positive responses. But I was also working on the bibliography for Kent State, and I soon came to realise that I would end up having to do a great deal of the work myself. Early during my freshman year, John Stanley came up to me and made mention of the unfortunate fate of Kenneth W. Faig, Jr., who a few years earlier had come to Brown (he had been in a graduate program in mathematics, I believe) and became so fascinated with Lovecraft that he all but stopped going to classes and did nothing but Lovecraft work—and pioneering work at that. He was kicked out of Brown two years later for his troubles. Stanley wanted to make sure I didn't meet the same fate, but I assured him that I was not slacking off in my classes. But whenever I wasn't in class or studying for class, I was at the Hay poring over Lovecraft materials.

In those pre-computer days, I was compiling the bibliography on what eventually became an immense array of index cards. This was actually a fairly efficient system, and I kept it up with some precision. In the course of that first year's work I already made some interesting discoveries. For example, I was browsing through the *Providence Evening News* looking for something or other when, in the December 18, 1914, issue I found a previously unknown poem, "New England." Wow! Perhaps not the most earth-shaking find in the world; but given that there is no surviving manuscript of that poem, it is likely that it would not have been discovered for many years, if at all, had I not then stumbled upon it. I proudly wrote a letter to my parents on the matter, and they duly congratulated me.

The fact of the matter is that the previous bibliographies of Lovecraft—by George Wetzel, Jack L. Chalker, and Mark Owings, not to mention smaller-scale bibliographies by numerous others—had been compiled by fans who really had no training whatever in bibliographical method. I can't say that I had any training at the start either, but I learned quickly. I remember being astounded that Wetzel, even though he had done impressive work with Lovecraft's publications in amateur journals, had failed to find a long article called "Lucubrations Lovecraftian" in the *United Co-operative* (April 1921). Who else could have written an article with such a title? Wetzel had clearly consulted this issue, since it contained the collaboration "The Crawling Chaos," which he had noted in his bibliography. There were other things of this sort.

One of the things that Dirk Mosig was exercised about in terms of the bibliography was the status of the Lovecraft-Derleth "posthumous collaborations." I had initially concluded that we were forced to list these works in some fashion or other, since they did bear Lovecraft's name; but Dirk convinced me that they actually contained very little of Lovecraft (most of them had no Lovecraft prose at all, but were written entirely by Derleth based upon plot-germs in the commonplace book) and should therefore be segregated from actual Lovecraft work. And so I listed these works in a catch-all chapter I entitled "Apocrypha and Other Miscellany."

My haunting of the John Hay Library was incessant—it irked me that the rare book library was only open from 9 A.M. to 5 P.M. on weekdays, but I managed what I could. So far as I could tell, no one—not other students nor researchers from outside the university—were doing any Lovecraft research, so I came to regard the Hay collection as something of my own private domain. The card catalogue (paper, of course, not computerised) was growing exponentially through the diligence and zeal of John Stanley in securing the increasing array of Lovecraft-related publications, and I got to know those long wooden drawers full of entries typed on stiff paper and arranged in a complex manner according to orthodox library practice. It was this sense of possessiveness that led to an amusing encounter.

Only a few weeks after I had entered Brown, I found to my astonishment—and irritation—that *someone else* had appropriated the main Lovecraft card catalogue drawer. In fact, there were two individuals, both male, one seemingly about my age and the other slightly older. Once I ascertained that they were indeed looking at the drawer I wished to consult, I said rather snidely, "That's my Lovecraft drawer." The older man replied in gentle reproof, "It's everyone's Lovecraft drawer."

This was my introduction to Paul R. and Marc A. Michaud.

It is possible that I was already aware of Marc's Necronomicon Press at this time. I remember being astounded when, browsing through the university bookstore, I stumbled upon a humble publication, *H. P. Lovecraft: First Writings: Pawtuxet Valley Gleaner 1906*. I snatched up the book immediately, later doing the same thing for other early Necronomicon Press publications, such as *Writings in The United Amateur* and *The Conservative: Complete*. Crude as these publications were (merely photocopies of the original appearances or laboriously typed out on a typewriter, the pages fastened with heavy staples), they nonetheless suggested that the growing fan interest in Lovecraft was leading to the publication of rare and obscure materials by and about him.

I became fast friends with Marc, who was then a senior in high school (although he was applying to Brown and was accepted for entry the next fall), and the rest of his family, then living in West Warwick. I'm pretty sure they invited me to have Thanksgiving dinner with them, since of course I had nowhere else to go and was certainly not going home for that occasion. Paul eventually returned to Paris, where he had been living off and on for years, and I saw little of him thereafter.

I was also continuing to keep in touch by correspondence with an ever-growing array of Lovecraft scholars and devotees. One of these was a young man (maybe a year older than I), Scott Connors. Scott was at this time living in western Pennsylvania, and he proposed a visit to Providence for various research, since he figured he could save money by holing up with me and my roommate to avoid hotel bills. And so he arrived in late December, staying until mid-January.

Our prime goal was to locate the articles on astrology that Lovecraft had written against J. F. Hartmann, who had incurred Lovecraft's ire by writing several columns making either mundane or bizarre predictions in the very paper—the *Providence Evening News*—that was publishing Lovecraft's own monthly astronomy columns. This paper was not available at Brown, but microfilms could be found in the library of the Rhode Island Historical Society on Hope Street, just east of the Brown campus. So we headed there.

The location of the articles proved simple enough: we found not only those that Lovecraft had signed under his own name, but those that appeared under the "Isaac Bickerstaff, Jun." pseudonym. We also found several more articles by Hartmann, and Scott did good work on Hartmann's life and career, such as it was (it turned out that one source of the fellow's employment was as a Santa Claus for various department stores). This work led eventually to my second book, *Science versus Charlatanry: Essays on Astrology*, published in 1979 by R. Alain Everts's Strange Company.

Scott and Dirk Mosig urged me to investigate Lovecraft's manuscripts and early published appearances to gauge the accuracy of the texts printed by Arkham House. Over the years, a number of minor errors had been detected in the Arkham House editions, and there was a suspicion that the texts were not very sound. Dirk clearly sensed that it would require sustained investigation of original sources—something that no scholar who was not based at Brown or in Providence could manage—to come to grips with the situation; but not even he could at that time have grasped the full scope of this undertaking.

4. Brown (1976–80)

My initial textual comparison—of "The Dunwich Horror"—proved to be rather disappointing, in the sense that this text (as I later ascertained) was actually printed fairly accurately in the Arkham House texts, because Derleth had followed Lovecraft's typescript. But then, in early 1977, I moved on to *At the Mountains of Madness*—and was flabbergasted at the results.

It must have taken me several weeks to do a thorough comparison of the text, and I became increasingly appalled at the degree and nature of the divergences I was finding: countless errors in paragraphing and punctuation, and two short passages omitted in an early chapter. By the time I was finished with a preliminary examination, I had identified *1500* apparent errors in the Arkham House edition.

But this, I realised, was only the beginning of the process. I had to ascertain not only *what* the errors were, but *how* they had occurred. I knew that Lovecraft had complained loudly about the butchery of the story in its serialisation in *Astounding Stories* (February–April 1936), so I knew that the printed text was unreliable. But I also knew that Lovecraft had "corrected" the printed text (in fact, three separate copies of it), so presumably that version might be more reliable. Well, it wasn't; even though I was fascinated to see Lovecraft's actual corrections (made in pencil, but also with a razor blade as he scraped off excess punctuation in the *Astounding* text) on the one copy of the serialisation that the Hay possessed, I quickly sensed that Lovecraft simply couldn't be bothered to fix all the alterations that the *Astounding* editors had made—Anglicisation of his British spellings, changes in paragraphing and punctuation, and so on. I therefore concluded that Lovecraft's own typescript was by and large to be followed, except in cases where he seems to have made a deliberate change.

The matter is much more complex than this, and indeed the whole field of textual studies is a highly specialised discipline in the humanities. And this is where my burgeoning classical studies fortuitously came in handy. The establishment of the text of the ancient authors is an immensely difficult task because we are reliant on a succession of handwritten copies made mostly by monks and other scribes throughout the Middle Ages. As such, it is important for almost any classical scholar to have some knowledge of textual studies and the transmission of texts. The knowledge that I gained in the study of classical texts was directly applicable to my investigation of Lovecraft's texts—although I also augmented that knowledge with general discussions of the subject, such as James Thorpe's *Principles of Textual Criticism* (1972). I also examined critical editions of various authors, notably the

University of Virginia edition of Stephen Crane, edited by Fredson Bowers, one of the leading textual critics of the era.

It would take me the better part of six years to prepare corrected editions of Lovecraft's fiction, poetry, and essays. Once the research on the bibliography was done, I turned the great bulk of my attention to this task. There was one time when I compared *five* different texts of *At the Mountains of Madness* simultaneously: 1) the autograph manuscript; 2) the typescript; 3) the *Astounding* serialisation (annotated by Lovecraft); 4) the first book appearance, in *The Outsider and Others* (1939); and 5) the later Arkham House edition, in *At the Mountains of Madness and Other Novels* (1964). I had to commandeer virtually an entire table in the reading room of the Hay for this task, but the librarians didn't seem to mind.

It was in early 1977 that I began actually appearing in print with some of the initial fruits of my Lovecraft research. Marc Michaud had asked me to write a foreword to his edition of *Writings in The Tryout* (February 1977), and I was happy to oblige. Almost at the same time, my article "Lovecraft Criticism: A Study" appeared in Dirk Mosig's *Miskatonic,* his journal for the Esoteric Order of Dagon (EOD) amateur press association. This was in fact a version of my introduction to my anthology of Lovecraft criticism. Quite frankly, it is not a particularly distinguished piece of work, but I suppose it was adequate for the time. I was astounded when, a few months later, the Dutch fanzine *Rigel* asked my permission to translate the piece; I was happy to oblige, and it appeared in the November 1977 issue. My first appearance in a foreign language!

In March 1977 I acceded to Randy Everts's request to join his Necronomicon amateur press association. This was purportedly a more scholarly organ than the EOD, and at the time I held the EOD in lofty disdain as the work of tyros and fans (a term I regarded as pejorative), although as a matter of fact the EOD was a dynamic organisation that was doing good work in promoting cutting-edge Lovecraft scholarship; the mere presence of Dirk Mosig in its midst should have been enough of a recommendation, but I did not join the EOD until 1980. The first issue of my Necronomicon journal, *The Cynick,* featured what I still regard as one of the finest portraits of Lovecraft I have ever seen. It was a line drawing by my old Burris pal Mark King, and I was thrilled to see it printed (Randy printed all my journals at no cost). I continued issuing *The Cynick* periodically until around 1983, when the a.p.a. collapsed; most of my contributions were merely vast listings of Lovecraft-related publications as I was assembling them for my bibliography, although I do recall translating a French piece on Lovecraft by Jacques Bergier and writing a learned commentary on it.

I was also promoting Lovecraft locally. On March 15, 1977 (the fortieth anniversary of Lovecraft's death), I gave a half-hour talk on Lovecraft over Brown's radio station, WBRU. Then, in the evening, Marc and I gathered a small band of devotees (which also included Henry L. P. Beckwith, a professor at the Rhode Island School of Design who would soon write a guidebook to Lovecraft's Providence) to commemorate the occasion. We ended up at St. John's churchyard (i.e., the churchyard of St. John's Episcopal Church on North Main Street, where Poe had courted Sarah Helen Whitman and where Lovecraft frequently took his out-of-town guests), and I read "The Outsider" under an eerie floodlight. The event was captured by a student photographer, and I was portrayed (with my still-luxuriant Afro, but without my name in the caption) on the front page of the *Brown Daily Herald* of March 17.

While all this was going on, I was not slacking in my schoolwork. I believe I took an intermediate French course during the second semester of my freshman year. But even this decision was Lovecraft-inspired: I wished to brush up on my French so that I could translate Maurice Lévy's *Lovecraft ou du fantastique* (1972), which struck me as an outstanding and even pioneering study. The book was relatively short, so I figured I could do the job. Mercifully, Lévy's treatise eschewed obfuscatory lit-crit jargon and was a pleasure to read in French.

As I headed home to Muncie at the end of freshman year, I had numerous tasks to perform. I did indeed spend a full month preparing a preliminary translation of the Lévy book. Where it was to be published, I did not yet know; but I figured some academic publisher might be interested. But a more urgent task was the Lovecraft bibliography, which was approaching a critical stage.

There was, even then, an immense amount of material by and about Lovecraft in foreign languages, and the Hay had only some of it. Dirk Mosig had made a specialty of collecting this work, having established contacts with scholars, editors, publishers, and fans in several countries. Dirk didn't have the time to catalogue all these items for the bibliography, so he urged me to come down and visit him in southern Georgia. I readily accepted the offer—why wouldn't I want to meet my revered mentor in Lovecraft studies?

Transportation was a bit of a problem, but I received providential help from an old friend. Patty Higgins's family was planning a trip to the South that summer, and they allowed me to tag along. We hit the road in mid-July, and I recall a splendid drive through the Shenandoah Valley before we headed west. The Higgins family dropped me off at the bus station in Chattanooga, Tennessee, where I first caught a bus for Atlanta, and then another bus to Americus. This was in the southern part of Georgia, nearly at the border with Florida. I stepped off the bus around 11 P.M. and found Dirk awaiting me.

He was an easily recognisable figure—a tall, barrel-chested, jovial man with a quick smile and a dry sense of humour. He still had a very thick German accent. Also in the greeting committee was Joe Moudry, who was then Official Editor of the EOD; and there were one or two others whose names I forget. We drove the short distance back to Dirk's house, where we were welcomed by Dirk's charming wife; he also had three small children, but I imagine they must have been in bed by this time.

What ensued was a non-stop talkfest that probably didn't end until about 4 A.M. This was really the first time I had congregated with a group of Lovecraftians, and the experience was electrifying. What a thrill it was to find people who, as it were, all spoke the same language! I doubt that I got much sleep that night, as I was so energised by the Lovecraftian confabulation.

Over the next week, I did indeed systematically go through Dirk's entire collection, foreign and otherwise. Dirk was attempting to collect not merely every publication relating to Lovecraft, but every *mention* of Lovecraft, wherever it might appear—on a dust jacket, a fanzine, whatever. At that time one could probably have accomplished such a thing, although even then it was becoming difficult (and expensive). Dirk's array of foreign materials was indeed impressive. In fact, some months earlier he had attended a conference on Lovecraft in the Italian city of Trieste, where he had met Alfred Galpin. I was thrilled when Dirk played a tape of Galpin performing his own "Lament for H.P.L." on the piano. It was a rather modernistic piece, but it was still a highly moving experience.

In the evenings, I passed on to Dirk some of my findings in regard to the textual errors infesting Lovecraft's fiction. Over several days he painstakingly recorded the 1500 corrections to the text of *At the Mountains of Madness*, writing them directly into his own copy of *At the Mountains of Madness and Other Novels*, as I myself had done. After the tiresome job was over, Dirk said, with only slight exaggeration, "I now have a new novel by Lovecraft to read."

Dirk made sure that I got some actual enjoyment out of the trip (although the research I was doing was enjoyment enough for me). He drove me around to visit some of the historical sites in the area, most of them pertaining to the Civil War. Awkwardly enough, on one occasion Dirk advised me to slide down the passenger seat and remain out of sight—because there was a Ku Klux Klan rally nearby! More pleasantly, I was utterly enraptured by the *four kittens* that were gambolling in Dirk's house. He was as much a cat-lover as HPL (and as I was becoming). At night, they would frolic all over my recumbent body as I rested on the sofabed in the living room, and they seemed particularly to enjoy being flung gently in the air as they wrestled with my feet over the blanket. Dirk's children were also delightful, and I believe the eldest one, Leila (probably about eight years old at the time), soberly proposed marriage to me—or, rather, exacted a promise that I would marry her when she came of age. (She did not hold me to that promise.)

The trip was over all too fast, and I caught a series of buses back to Muncie. But my research work was not done. I think I came back to Brown early. In part this was to get away from HolliAnne and other high school folks with whom I no longer had much in common. We tried to revive our vocal quartet, the Twilights, but after a few mediocre performances we gave it up. I myself, not having sung for a full year, was not in good voice at all, and anyway my heart was not in it.

I had been lucky enough to be selected by lottery to take a room in the graduate center, a series of four towers that took up the entire block at Thayer, Charlesfield, and Power Streets. Every year, a limited number of undergraduates were allowed to occupy single rooms in this complex, and I luckily got in. Once there, I could remain there for the remainder of my undergraduate career—and did so. The room was quite small, but adequate to the purpose; and I was able to house my growing library of weird books on the bookshelf attached to the wall, while my burgeoning record collection had to be housed wherever there was space.

My urgent task, however, was not to get back to the John Hay Library, but to venture forth again for research—not quite as far as Georgia, but to a perhaps even more forbidding place, namely, New York City.

I had learned of the existence of a large collection of amateur journals housed in the New York Public Library. I believe this collection had largely been assembled by the prominent amateur Edwin Hadley Smith, with additions from other amateurs' collections. The Hay did have a fair number of Lovecraft's amateur appearances, but not nearly all. The problem was that the NYPL collection was not catalogued; there existed only a typed alphabetical list of the journals, and the journals themselves were not housed in the main library (Fifth Avenue and 42nd Street) but in an annex at Tenth Avenue and 43rd Street.

I figured it might take me a full week to pore through the collection. I now cannot recall where I stayed, but I suppose I must have found some inexpensive lodging somewhere. The library annex was in a very bad part of town. I was petrified enough at merely being in this megalopolis, so different from the small Midwestern towns I was used to; but venturing over to the annex day after day was almost too much for me to bear. Once I got there, everything was fine, and I buckled down to work. I had brought along a large drawer full of file cards containing information on Lovecraft's magazine appearances (fiction, poetry, essays, miscellany); and I systematically filled in whatever information I needed.

I finished my work in such haste that I dashed back to Providence after about four days. Indeed, I had been scheduled to meet T. E. D. Klein (with whom Marc was acquainted) and other Lovecraftians in the area; but I was so eager to get away from this frightening city, and so unaccustomed to socialising, that I called Ted to explain that I was heading back early and could not meet him and others for the dinner they had planned. How gauche of me! But truly, New York City terrified me as badly as anything out of Lovecraft's own stories!

Another reason for coming back to Providence early that summer was to help Marc and his brother Paul with an intriguing project—nothing less than a full-length documentary film on Lovecraft. They had already interviewed Frank Belknap Long in New York, and now they planned to talk with Lovecraft's second cousin, Ethel Phillips Morrish, who was about ninety years old but still quite sharp and vigorous. Marc and I had already become acquainted with her grandson, Robert C. Harrall, a lawyer at the Rhode Island Supreme Court who in 1974 had established himself as the administrator of the Estate of H. P. Lovecraft, with a view to challenging Arkham House's control of the Lovecraft copyrights. We met Harrall a number of times in his office to discuss various Lovecraftian matters.

The interview with Ethel took place, I believe, somewhere in Cranston, a western suburb of Providence. It was a fascinating experience. I had primed Paul (who was officially conducting the interview) on what to ask, but even so I found some of her comments surprising and revealing—such as the fact that Lovecraft didn't seem to know how to use a swing! The very idea that here was a woman who could remember Lovecraft when he was four years old was strikingly akin to Lovecraft's own notions of *defeating time*. He himself had, when a child, spoken with a woman born in 1796 who could remember the presidency of George Washington! I believe I saw the footage of Paul's interview with Frank Long, but cannot remember many details of it now. Of course, the film was not completed, and the footage (shot on film, not videotape) remains in Paul's possession. Let us hope it is eventually released.

As I settled into my sophomore year (1977–78), I was of course delighted to strengthen my friendship and association with Marc, who had been accepted into Brown and was starting his freshman year. In all honesty, Marc wasn't exactly the most diligent student one could imagine, and he had probably secured entry by appealing to a certain well-connected family friend who had donated much money to the university. During his rather undistinguished career, I ended up writing several papers for Marc; I was happy to do that, as they didn't take much effort.

We now saw each other on an almost daily basis, and we worked out a schedule whereby we would basically get up late and get to the Sharpe Refectory as soon as it opened for *lunch* (11 A.M.), then have dinner early (around 5 P.M.), and then have a late-night meal at one of several off-campus eateries around 11 P.M. The one we frequented most often was called the East Campus Dining Center (ECDC), where excellent burgers could be had. We would then retire around 2 A.M. and begin the cycle all over again. Naturally, we did all we could to avoid taking early-morning classes!

Sometime during that school year, we made acquaintance with none other than Jason C. Eckhardt, the great Lovecraftian artist. I was advising Marc on his ongoing publications, although I did not contribute much to them as yet. At one point he decided that, rather than merely continue his reproductions of Lovecraftian material in facsimile on 8½ × 11 paper, he would retype them (as, indeed, he had already done in part with his *Conservative* edition, although the result was rather ungainly) and publish them in a saddle-stitched 8½ × 7 format (i.e., an 8½ × 14 sheet folded in half). And, instead of merely block type on the cover, we would actually have cover art. But since neither of us could draw, where to find an artist? Well, why not try the Rhode Island School of Design, an art school that was at the foot of College Hill, just below Brown? Marc put an ad in the RISD school newspaper, and I believe that one of the only responses he got was from Jason.

I recall heading down the hill to visit Jason in his cubbyhole of a room at RISD, and very soon thereafter Marc and Jason had come to an agreement: Jason would do a wraparound cover illustration for an upcoming book—

nothing less than my first official published book, Lovecraft's *Uncollected Prose and Poetry* (Necronomicon Press, 1978).

In the course of my bibliographical work I had discovered dozens of pieces by Lovecraft that had never been reprinted. To be sure, a good many of them were scraps of no particular interest (such as random letters to the editor in *Driftwind*); but some were more significant. Accordingly, Marc and I gathered the most interesting of these in a booklet of 80 pages, with windy and pompous commentary by me. The chief item in the book was "The Night Ocean" (1936), a story that Lovecraft had revised for R. H. Barlow. This was not my discovery: Dirk Mosig had learned of Lovecraft's involvement in the story in letters to Hyman Bradofsky (Dirk had obtained copies of these letters directly from Bradofsky), and Dirk had arranged for a reprint of the story in an Italian translation in 1976. But our reprint was the first in English.

I myself typed the camera-ready pages: I believe that by this time I had acquired an IBM Selectric, and it was a splendid machine. Alas! My typing skills weren't quite what they should have been, and my proofreading skills were even worse; the book was littered with typos, forcing Marc to add an errata sheet at the last minute at the end of the book. Aside from that, though, the book was a pretty good piece of work for its day; and its superb Eckhardt cover (he had illustrated a scene from *At the Mountains of Madness*, even though this had nothing to do with anything in the book) was worth the price of admission all by itself.

Marc, Jason, and I quickly formed a triumvirate—not only of Lovecraft devotees, but of close friends. We were augmented by other fans in the area, among them Ron Marshall, Herb Marshall (apparently not related), and Ken Neily. Ken was then in his mid-thirties, I believe, but his boyish enthusiasm caused him to fit right into our youthful circle. He then lived in Barrington and was a collector of Lovecraftiana along the lines of Dirk Mosig, although somewhat less inclined toward the academic side. He had amassed so much material that he tore out some walls in his house to make room for his exponentially growing collection (rather like Wilbur Whateley accommodating the presence of his twin brother). At that point, his wife bid him an unsurprising goodbye, and he assumed a bachelor existence. We gathered at ECDC frequently late in the evenings to shoot the bull on all matters Lovecraftian, and we also did considerable exploration of the area to glimpse Lovecraft-related sites. Naturally, we gazed reverently at Lovecraft's surviving houses—598 Angell Street, 10 Barnes Street, and 65 Prospect Street (formerly 66 College Street). The latter two were very close to the Brown campus. But we hunted out much more obscure locales as I continued to read Lovecraft's letters and came upon places in his hometown that were of significance to him.

Marc did me a huge favour early in my sophomore year. I had been plagued by a low-grade headache that had lasted for several *weeks* without cessation, so finally he dragged me to the university health services to have me checked over. At first, a doctor assigned me some pills and urged me to try them for a week. I did so—and they worked like magic! I came back to the clinic and said, "Oh, boy! I want more of these!" But the sober, elderly doctor said to me, "That was Valium. We cannot give you anymore, as they are addictive." He compelled me to see the university psychiatrist. I had a few sessions with her, and she felt I was already working too hard, what with both my course work and my outside Lovecraft work. But I refused to budge, saying to her, "If I continue to work this hard and end up dying at forty, I'd prefer that than working less hard and living to eighty." At that point she cast me away.

But she did suggest that I give up coffee. For you see, I had gradually been increasing my dosage of coffee until I was drinking *eight cups a day*. (I had illegally snuck in a little hotpot for the purpose of heating water; it was confiscated once, but I promptly bought another one and this time hid it more securely in my little dorm room.) I heeded the psychiatrist's advice and switched from coffee to tea. There was no immediate result, but gradually the headaches did subside. And over the course of years—actually decades—I reduced my intake of tea from eight to five to the current three (with one additional cup of peppermint tea). I figure that is an acceptable amount. I once did try going cold turkey and giving up tea altogether, but the resultant caffeine-deprivation headache was so horrible that I couldn't endure it more than two days before resuming my intake.

While I still snobbishly refused to join the EOD, I did enjoy helping Ken Neily prepare issues of his EOD journal, *Lovecraftian Ramblings;* on a few occasions I even ghostwrote some articles (chiefly just some reports of recent publications in the field) under his name. This venue proved to be of use when a contretemps in the Lovecraft fan world consumed us for the better part of two years.

In 1977 Tom Collins, a Lovecraft devotee in New York, had launched a lawsuit against Marc for "theft of intellectual property" in regard to Marc's edition of Lovecraft's *Conservative.* Collins's argument was that he had discovered that original copies of the *Conservative* (all except the first issue) existed in the New York Public Library collection of amateur journalism, and that Marc had somehow "stolen his research" by issuing his edition. The absurdity of this claim should have been evident to all: I myself had seen these issues of the *Conservative* during my trip to the library, and I am not likely to have been the only one to have done so. But Collins was determined to pursue the matter by litigation, forcing Marc to defend himself. I can't recall if the matter actually went to court; eventually the suit was dropped, but not after a great deal of infighting and backbiting had occurred within the Lovecraft fan community.

I myself, being friends with Marc, naturally sought to defend him—and an opportunity conveniently emerged when, in late 1977, Collins published an edition of Lovecraft's uncollected poetry, *A Winter Wish,* from Stuart David Schiff's Whispers Press. I secured a copy of the book (or might even have been given one by Collins, with whom I was in touch discussing general Lovecraftian matters) and began investigating the textual soundness of the book. I was appalled to discover a mountain of errors—some simple typos, but in other cases some serious textual errors—peppering the book. In one particularly egregious instance, Collins had found a clipping of a Lovecraft poem as it had appeared in a Providence newspaper; the poem (in rhymed couplets) had been printed with a line inadvertently dropped, so Collins took it into his mind to *write his own line* and stick it into the text without notifying the reader to that effect! Unfortunately for him, a clipping of the poem existed in the John Hay Library—*but Lovecraft had written in the missing line himself.* Collins was evidently unaware of this fact; and needless to say, his fabricated line was quite different from Lovecraft's.

I first prepared a commentary and errata list to *A Winter Wish* (it came to at least 12 single-spaced pages) and issued it to selected colleagues as a set of photocopied pages. Dirk Mosig then published the document in the *Miskatonic* (May 1978). All hell broke loose. Collins's supporters (and he had many) attempted to come to his defence—chiefly by attacking me and also Marc, who had said some pungent words about the matter himself. Ben Indick, an elderly fan and critic in Teaneck, New Jersey, referred to Marc and myself as those "snits from Brown." (Ben and I later put aside our differences and became the best of friends when I moved to the New York area.) Dirk of course stood up for us and sharply criticised Collins for his carelessness. Collins himself was stunned by the revelation of his manifold blunders, writing in his own EOD journal, *Unquiet,* a meandering *mea culpa* and trying to excuse his rewriting of the Lovecraft poem with the hoary "the dog ate my homework" excuse. But his reputation as an editor and Lovecraftian was destroyed, and he drifted away from the field soon thereafter.

As my sophomore year ended, I resolved to stay in Providence for the summer: there was simply too much work to do on Lovecraft, and anyway my life—and my friends—in Muncie had come to seem increasingly remote from my present concerns. For the next several years I spent every summer in Providence, staying in a succession of fleabag sublets that were quite adequate for the purpose. It was in that summer of 1978 that, in a matter of six weeks, I compiled the *Index to the Selected Letters of H. P. Lovecraft*. Some time before I had written to James Turner, who had taken over the editorship of Arkham House and had issued the final two volumes of the *Selected Letters* in 1976, whether there were any plans to publish an index. He claimed that he was working on such a project, but I doubted whether he actually was. After I finished the index, Marc and I sat on it for quite a while, then decided to issue it in 1980: by then it was becoming obvious (as it was all along) that Turner would never get around to the job himself. The book was cordially received in the fan world. A charming review by Richard Lupoff in *Starship* (Summer-Fall 1981) marvelled at the very existence of the index and speculated on the identity of the unknown compiler. "Mr. Joshi (Ms. Joshi? Colonel Joshi? Dr. Joshi? Thing Joshi?) is to be congratulated. And thanked." Thank you in return, Dick!

I must have returned to Indiana for at least a brief time in the summer of 1978, for this was when I finally became a U.S. citizen. My application for citizenship had begun in high school; but because it had to be carried out in Indiana, the process was unusually prolonged. However, on August 15, 1978, I did receive my certificate of citizenship. I believe a few of my old Burris friends—Ed Alexander, Jon Nussbaum (now in the Army, and hence a good character reference!), and others—showed up for the event. My physical dimensions on the certificate were given as 5′ 8″ and 110 pounds—not too far from the gaunt Lovecraft's purportedly ideal dimensions of 5′ 11″ and 140 pounds!

Back in Providence, other projects fortuitously emerged around this time. Both Marc and I knew that the Hay owned a complete run of *Weird Tales*; indeed, most of the issues during Lovecraft's lifetime were his own copies, the rest supplied by R. H. Barlow (who had also microfilmed the first several issues, as they were apparently in a rather fragile state). These copies were uncatalogued, but by this time Marc and I had clearly proven our bona fides as Lovecraft scholars and publishers, so we were allowed access to these issues. What we wanted to do was to publish not only Lovecraft's own letters published in the letter column of the magazine, "The Eyrie," but any and all comments about Lovecraft from the time his first story appeared ("Dagon" in the October 1923 issue) till the end of the magazine in 1954. Well we did so; but because the issues were so fragile, we were obliged to *copy out all the letters by hand.* In the course of several weeks we filled whole notebooks with our scribbling, spending hour upon hour in the library (not in the reading room but in an area usually reserved only for library staff), with the issues being placed in a special device to minimise damage to the brittle pages. The result was *H. P. Lovecraft in "The Eyrie"* (Necronomicon Press, 1979), a book that in some ways has still not been superseded, although the letters about Lovecraft were reprinted in my later compilation, *A Weird Writer in Our Midst* (Hippocampus Press, 2010).

The other project that dropped in our laps came about when someone—possibly John Stanley—notified us that there existed a rather rough listing of Lovecraft's personal library, compiled a few years after his death by one Mary Spink. Spink was a friend of Lovecraft's surviving aunt, Annie E. P. Gamwell, and Annie was contemplating selling the collection in order to bring in some needed revenue. Marc and I were first shown a typescript that somebody (evidently not Spink herself) had made; this was clearly inaccurate in parts, as the person had not been able to read Spink's handwriting very well and was, moreover, apparently not of literary bent. One title came out as "Master Chuzzlewut"—which we easily figured out was Dickens's *Martin Chuzzlewit. Dracula* was written, in the opinion of the typist, by "B. Stokie." Luckily, at some later point Spink's actual handwritten list (contained in a sort of ledger, as I recall) surfaced, so that we were able to get a better idea of what she had actually written.

We now set about fleshing out Spink's extremely skeletal entries—usually just author, title, publisher, and date, although sometimes she would omit one or more of these elements seemingly at random. She was clearly not a bibliographer. I was becoming one, and I knew that an important reference work that would help us in our task was the *National Union Catalog of Pre-1956 Imprints,* a titanic series of about 750 bound volumes that listed every holding of every book contained in every library in the U.S. and Canada. Even this massive work proved insufficient at times, and we also had to consult the British Library Catalog, the catalogue of the Bibliothèque Nationale, and many other reference works.

The result was a listing of just under 1000 titles, which I also annotated

4. Brown (1976–80)

in terms of Lovecraft's use of the books in his fiction or their possible influence on his work. It was here that I first discovered Lovecraft's ownership of such books as Henri Béraud's *Lazarus* (1925), Barry Pain's *An Exchange of Souls* (1911), and many other works that clearly found their way into his fiction and other writing. It was a fascinating exercise; and although the resulting book—*Lovecraft's Library: A Catalogue* (Necronomicon Press, 1980)—didn't create very much of a splash, I still feel that this is one of the most important reference books for the serious Lovecraftian. It has undergone several revisions, and by the time of the fourth edition (Hippocampus Press, 2017) I (with significant help from David E. Schultz) have found nearly 100 more titles, usually mentioned in Lovecraft's letters.

Although I was allowed unprecedented access to the Lovecraft materials at the Hay, I realised that I might have to take some irregular measures if I were to complete certain aspects of the work in a reasonable period of time. I had found large numbers of unpublished essays and poetry among the manuscripts (there were, of course, thousands of unpublished letters—or, at any rate, letters that had been published only in highly truncated form in the *Selected Letters*—but I was not quite masochistic enough to envision doing anything with these items aside from taking extensive notes). The task of transcribing this material seemed overwhelming, especially since, because of legal disputes as to who actually owned the copyrights to the Lovecraft material, the library refused to make photocopies of any of the unpublished manuscripts.

However, in those prehistoric days security at the library was rather lax, and so I was able to sneak a good many manuscripts out of the library, usually hiding them in a folder or under the all-weather coat that I habitually wore, like a trenchcoated spy; I would then take them around the corner to a conveniently located copy store, make photocopies of the material, and then return the manuscripts to their proper folders. Lest anyone think that I risked damaging these invaluable documents, I should note that the library had photocopied the entire Lovecraft collection and allowed scholars to look only at the photocopies; only in rare instances, and after much haranguing, was anyone able to look at the original manuscripts, which were consigned to a "vault" (very much like a bank vault) in the basement of the library. So there was no possibility of my damaging anything. But as a result, I only had second-generation Xerox copies to work from; even so, these were generally good enough for me to take home and make typed transcripts.

I in fact ended typing up the entirety of Lovecraft's fiction, poetry, and essays on my sturdy electric typewriter, marking textual notes with asterisks and writing out the textual variants on separate pieces of paper in pencil or pen. The task of comparing the texts was not a simple matter, and I frequently checked the texts three or four times against manuscripts, early publications (such as appearances in amateur journals or *Weird Tales*), book appearances, and so on. I did not type out every one of his "revisions" or ghostwritten stories, but I still have my typed transcripts of all the other work—a matter of thousands of pages generated over four or five years.

At some point during my junior or senior year, I gave a formal lecture on Lovecraft to a class on fantasy fiction being taught by George P. Landow, a widely published professor at Brown. I was not actually taking the class, but Marc was—and he suggested to Landow that I be allowed to lecture on the Lovecraft text they were reading, *The Dream-Quest of Unknown Kadath*. In my lecture (given, as I recall, in the List Art Building—the site of Lovecraft's last residence, 66 College Street) I focused on the autobiographical elements in the novel, noting how it was a reflection of his ecstatic return from the hated New York to Providence. I gave a rather flamboyant recitation of portions of Lovecraft's famous letter to Frank Long in which he recorded his homecoming ("HOME—UNION STATION—PROVIDENCE!!!!"). I think the class was a bit stupefied by how much information I was throwing out at them, but I hope I got some essential points across.

Let it not be thought that I was doing nothing but work—schoolwork and Lovecraft work—at this time. It is true that I didn't have much of a social life, but my frequent meetings with Marc, Jason, Ken, and other Lovecraftians—and our expeditions to Lovecraftian sites, bookstores, and other places of interest—made me anything but a recluse. It was around this time—i.e., early 1978—that I probably attended my first convention: the Boskone, a science fiction convention in Boston. (This probably took place just after the great blizzard of February 1978, when over the course of a day and a half Providence received 36 inches of snow; some inland areas received 54 inches. Later the snow turned to ice, coating trees, shrubs, and buildings in a glittering glaze out of some fantasy realm. Brown was closed for an unprecedented four days.)

Even though I wasn't greatly interested in science fiction, I found plenty of things to interest me at the convention. This was a time when the dealers' room was still dominated by actual books, magazines, and other print items, as opposed to media, T-shirts, jewellery, and the like, as happened in later years in many genre-related conventions. While I had already begun amassing a library of weird fiction from the bookstores in Providence, I found a great number of tempting items in the Boskone dealers' room—all for prices that would now be regarded as astoundingly low.

I can't recall whether I actually saw much of the programming—panel discussions, art show, and the like. It was thrilling enough just to be in an environment where so many people roughly shared my interests. Most of our gang could not afford a hotel room, so I think we must have commuted back and forth from the convention by bus, which was pretty inexpensive. But by Sunday, I was becoming so fatigued by the non-stop activity that I had to take a few hours' rest in a hotel room that Herb Marshall secured. I felt immeasurably refreshed by my nap and resumed what little activity there was before the convention ended.

But this was only a foretaste to a much more impressive convention that I attended just before the start of my junior year: the World Science Fiction Convention (Iguanacon), held in Phoenix around Labour Day weekend of 1978. Dirk Mosig was asked to assemble a panel discussion on Lovecraft, and I was amazed that he invited me to participate—especially when the other panelists would be J. Vernon Shea, Donald R. Burleson, Fritz Leiber, and Dirk himself. Talk about a pygmy amongst giants! I had very few publishing credits to my name; I am not even sure that my edition of *Uncollected Prose and Poetry* had emerged by the time of the convention. But I couldn't say no to participating in such an important event, so I went.

Like Lovecraft, I had never been west of the Mississippi up to that point; and Phoenix in early September was a furnace, with temperatures exceeding 100° every day of the convention. I was thrilled to meet Dirk again, and even more thrilled to meet Don Burleson, a lively math professor then living in New Hampshire whose well-trimmed beard and sparkling eyes argued for both keen intelligence and a pungent sense of humour. I had been corresponding with Vernon Shea since 1976 and felt I knew him quite well: he too was full of good humour and genial friendliness. I met Fritz Leiber (who happened to be exactly the age of my father) only during the panel, but that was enough for me to gain a sense of his imposing physique and immense literary gifts.

The panel itself was a remarkable event. Dirk had summoned me partially because he knew that I was doing significant work in Lovecraft studies in regard to the bibliography, the anthology of criticism, and most of all my work on restoring Lovecraft's texts. So I suppose I held my own. But a remarkable thing happened when the panel actually got underway. It was supposed to last one hour; but after the hour passed, no one came to evict us, as there seemed to be no other event planned for that room. So, at the urging of the audience, we stayed in that room for *an additional two hours* in a wide-ranging discussion of all things Lovecraftian. It was one of the most stirring events of my young existence, as both panelists and audience seemed fully engaged in the topic and sensing that a new era in the understanding of Lovecraft was approaching.

The rest of the convention was also engaging. The dealers' room was in an immense hall the size of a gymnasium, and I secured many tempting items (including the plays of Lord Dunsany). Don Burleson and I frequently went out of our way to gawk at a luscious female who was dressed in some kind of fantastic costume that left very little to the imagination. I was flattered that Dirk invited me to have dinner with the elderly Jack Williamson. The Lovecraftian talk continued in various attendees' rooms after hours. Will Hart took many photographs of the event, and some of these have recently been made available on the Internet.

We Lovecraftians wished to make our presence emphatically known in a venue—the world of science fiction—that did not always respect or pay much attention to Lovecraft. Didn't Isaac Asimov refer outrageously to Lovecraft as a "sick juvenile"? So what we would do is to take the elevator to a high floor of the hotel, take our places all around the vast atrium, and then, upon a signal, yell *"Yog-Sothoth!"* at the top of our lungs. The first time we did this, the attendees in the lobby were so stupefied that there was a dead silence for several seconds; subsequent repetitions of the cry didn't evoke quite as impressive a reaction.

But Dirk took his Lovecraftian evangelising to still greater lengths. We once found ourselves wandering outside the convention—and what did we come upon but a church service being held a few blocks away? This service seemed to be of a fundamentalist or Pentecostal sort, with all manner of crying and shrieking amongst the parishioners. As we—Dirk, Don Burleson, I, and several others—made our way dubiously into the front hall of the church, we were approached by some functionary who inquired what we wished. Dirk got into a bantering argument with this person, who seemed astounded that we were not fundamentalists like himself. In a thick Southern accent this poor fellow asked, "Ain't you ever read the Bible?" Dirk instantly replied, in his rich German accent, "Haven't you ever read the *Necronomicon?*" At one point the chap placed a hand on my shoulder; after he had removed it, I quickly brushed my shoulder, as if feeling the urgent need to rid myself of his unclean touch. Don later told me he almost exploded in laughter at my gesture. I suppose we were playing with fire, twitting this pious gent in this manner; but we escaped unscathed.

Getting back to Providence after the convention, I entered my junior year, continuing to do my best to balance my ongoing classical studies with my ongoing work on Lovecraft. It was in November of that year, however, that I received an unexpected boost to my self-esteem: my anthology of criticism was finally accepted by an academic publisher.

After having queried more than thirty publishers over the course of several years, I had begun to wonder if the book would ever land anywhere; maybe I would have to settle for a specialty press, which in fact would have defeated the whole purpose of the volume. But then I received an expression of interest from Ohio University Press (I wonder if I queried them because I could point to the fact that I was doing a book—the bibliography—for their cross-state rival, Kent State University Press); after a month or two, Ohio reported that it wished to publish the book.

The book had, indeed, undergone fairly extensive revisions since I had initially conceived it in 1975, and I believe I had removed the inessential and trivial items and done a good job of selecting significant pieces to reprint. I had also been privileged to receive unpublished pieces by Peter Cannon, R. Boerem, and others. Indeed, a last-minute contribution was J. Vernon Shea's "On the Literary Influences Which Shaped Lovecraft's Works," a lengthy piece that I felt could have been improved, but which the publisher seemed to like well enough. I had also stumbled upon a fascinating sociological piece, "Dystopia as Utopia: Howard Phillips Lovecraft and the Unknown Content of American Horror Literature," published in the Spring 1976 issue of the *Minnesota Review* and written by Paul Buhle, a young scholar who lived in Providence and edited the leftist periodical *Cultural Correspondence*. I spoke to Buhle a few times while securing his permission to reprint his article. Of course, the best parts of the book were legendary articles by Fritz Leiber ("A Literary Copernicus"), George T. Wetzel ("The Cthulhu Mythos: A Study"), Winfield Townley Scott ("A Parenthesis on Lovecraft as Poet"), and others. For historical reasons, I felt the need to reprint Edmund Wilson's hostile essay-review from 1945, "Tales of the Marvellous and the Ridiculous."

In one sense I went a little overboard in my scholarship. I peppered many of the articles with needless footnotes debating the opinions or conclusions of the author or offering alternate interpretations. This really exceeded the bounds of what an editor of such a book should do; indeed, one of the expert readers of the book, who was evaluating it for the publisher, felt that my scholarship was "overdone."

Naturally, the publisher assumed I was a professor. I had fostered that impression by writing to Ohio on fake Brown University stationery—that is, stationery that I purchased at the university bookstore that merely had "Brown University" written in fancy type on the top. It was only when I signed the contract that I notified my editor, "There's no need to refer to me as Professor Joshi; I am a humble undergraduate." There appears to have been some consternation at Ohio at this revelation, but I calmly pointed out that I assumed they had accepted the book on its merits and not on what position I happened to hold. In any event, the reception of the book (which I shall discuss a bit later) did more to reassure them than anything I could have said.

Various delays with the publisher caused the book to undergo a very prolonged production schedule, and it did not appear until the summer of 1980. But I could now say that I had a true academic publishing credential. I was still not entirely certain that my bibliography would be accepted by Kent State: although it had attained a substantial size by this time, I was still not sure I was doing the job in the manner they had recommended, and I also wondered whether they were really convinced that Lovecraft was worth such treatment. Luckily, I was later reassured on that score.

It was around this time that I myself began venturing into the critical analysis of Lovecraft. My ongoing studies in ancient and modern philosophy, in the history of weird fiction, and in Lovecraft's own life and work led me to sense that I could contribute to Lovecraft studies as a critic as well as an editor and bibliographer. I had actually written a minor philological article, "Who Wrote 'The Mound'?," as early as 1977. I had sent a draft of it to Frank Long, because Long, although not actually involved in the writing of the tale, had been acting as Zealia Bishop's agent ("The Mound" was ghostwritten for her) and she herself had once stated that Long had had a hand in the story. Long, although he couldn't remember the details surrounding the story, generally accepted my reconstruction of how the story was written and marketed. The article appeared in *Nyctalops* (March 1978).

My first true critical article was "'Reality' and Knowledge: Some Notes on the Aesthetic Thought of H. P. Lovecraft," followed by "Autobiography in Lovecraft." I remember being proud of myself for having written "Lovecraft's Alien Civilisations: A Political Study," a piece that came in at a full

10,000 words. I would circulate these articles—just as Lovecraft circulated his stories among his friends and colleagues—to such individuals as Dirk Mosig, Don Burleson, and also David A. Drake, who was at that time in the EOD and offered perspicacious comments on the pieces I sent him.

But as I was writing these articles and reading those by Don Burleson and others, I felt that there was no true venue for them. Dirk Mosig had published a few of his Lovecraft articles in Stuart Schiff's *Whispers*, but that magazine was transforming itself into a professional fiction magazine, and articles were no longer appearing there in any great quantity; and *Nyctalops*, the superlative fanzine edited by Harry O. Morris, Jr., was becoming increasingly irregular in its publication schedule. So it was that, during a late-night session at ECDC, I announced to Marc, "We need a *Lovecraft Studies* journal. Why don't we publish it ourselves?"

The incredible thing was that, sometime earlier, Marc and I had actually proposed such a thing to officials at Brown. We had become acquainted with one Jon Keates, who worked in some capacity in the Brown administration, and had suggested that Brown issue such a journal. Jon seemed interested in the idea, but our discussions with him ultimately came to nothing. I was secretly relieved at this: much as I would have been thrilled at having the imprimatur of Brown on such a journal, I felt it very unlikely that the university would be prepared to entrust its editorship to undergraduates, however knowledgeable in the subject. The only real option was for the journal to be published by Necronomicon Press.

And so I began assembling the issue. This proved to be surprisingly difficult, as my various colleagues didn't seem to have anything readily available. In the event, I did manage to get a nice piece by Peter Cannon that led off the first issue; and I included Lovecraft's (rather lacklustre) preface to John Ravenor Bullen's *White Fire* (1927), which had never been reprinted before. But otherwise I had to fill it up with my own contributions, a grand total of *four:* my editorial; my "Autobiography in Lovecraft" piece; "A Style Sheet for Lovecraftian Studies," a rather dry item in which I outlined preferred methods of citation of works by Lovecraft; and a review of Jack Sullivan's *Elegant Nightmares: The English Ghost Story from Le Fanu to Blackwood*, which Ohio University Press had published in 1978. There were other reviews (including one of my *Uncollected Prose and Poetry*) by J. Vernon Shea, Donald R. Burleson, and William Fulwiler.

Marc had felt so unsure of the success—or, rather, of the marketability—of the new journal that he only printed 250 copies. In fact, the journal (dated Fall 1979) sold very quickly, and many readers were left lamenting their slowness in ordering a copy. In only a few years, we saw used copies selling for as high as $25. I of course hoped that academic libraries would purchase the item, but I didn't know how well Necronomicon Press could reach that market; I think Marc may have sent out a flyer specifically to major university libraries, but I believe only Harvard purchased *Lovecraft Studies* from the first issue. I myself typed that issue—and in fact typed the first fifteen issues on my trusty IBM Selectric and, later, on the much superior IBM Wheelwriter, where I could print italic type and other special characters. Thereafter, Marc set the type on a computer.

I do think that *Lovecraft Studies,* over its long tenure (1979–2005), fostered a significant amount of important Lovecraft scholarship that could not have seen print anywhere else. For the first twenty years, it came out like clockwork twice a year, in spring and fall; thereafter, because of some difficulties that Marc faced, it became quite irregular and finally gave up the ghost. But it had served its purpose.

That first issue of *Lovecraft Studies* came out around the time of the Fifth World Fantasy Convention, which returned to Providence that fall. The most notable—or at least the most notorious—event of that convention was a panel discussion on Lovecraft in which I participated. I cannot even remember the other participants, but I imagine Don Burleson was there; I'm not sure Dirk Mosig came out for that event. When it was my turn to talk, I began a disquisition on the textual work I was doing on Lovecraft's stories, and I naturally segued into a discussion of the lamentable errors in Tom Collins's edition of *A Winter Wish.* I in fact held up a copy of the book.

Why would that be of any note? Well, as a matter of fact, I had found the book so worthless that I had begun using it as a coaster for my frequent cups of tea in my little dorm room, to the point that tea stains had soaked through the dust jacket so that the jacket had all but fused with the hardcover binding. On top of that, Marc still harboured such ill feelings toward Collins that, on random visits to my room, he used his cigarette lighter (he had regrettably taken up smoking) to set several pages of the book on fire! So the book was a bit of a mess. What I didn't realise until later was that, as I was delivering my excoriation of the book, Tom Collins was sitting stone-faced in the audience! Thankfully, I never encountered him in person during the convention.

Even with all this Lovecraftian activity, I had still not given up the hope of becoming a fiction writer—and, in the summer of 1979, I undertook to write a full-length detective novel. I finished it in a matter of three weeks, writing it out in longhand (as I habitually did with all my work—essays, school papers, and the like), and then typing it up. The result—*Tragedy at Sarsfield Manor*—was a very short novel indeed, only about 140 double-spaced pages, or under 45,000 words.

What I was attempting to do with this book was to elevate the detective story to a higher aesthetic level; but the way I went about it proved, as I later concluded, a failure. The plot was evidently based on a story I had written in high school (about which I remember nothing); but I peppered the text with all manner of ruminations on literature, music, philosophy, and the like that slowed down the action to a crawl. I actually sent the text to my sisters (Ragini in particular was and remains a great devotee of the detective story); but they reported that, while the mystery element was riveting, the philosophical asides were dull and tedious. Amazingly, I managed to pique the interest of an editor at a major publishing house (Scribner's, I think); although rejecting the work, she did make some nice comments about certain aspects of it. This proved to be my last major work of fiction for more than twenty years.

I was by no means neglecting my schoolwork, and as I continued to take more and more challenging classes I wrote what I felt were some reasonably impressive papers for those classes. I took a thrilling course on colonial American history (again inspired by Lovecraft's own devotion to that era) from one of the premier scholars on that subject, Gordon S. Wood. My final paper was on "Dr. Johnson and the Colonies," a study of Samuel Johnson's views on America, notably his fiery broadside *Taxation No Tyranny* (1775), in which he demolished the fallacious "no taxation without representation" canard being promoted by the rebellious Americans. (I have never forgotten Johnson's pungent remark, "I am willing to love all mankind, *except an American*.") This paper required an enormous amount of research, and I was quite proud of it. It received the highest marks—but the teaching assistant never returned it to me! Maybe she later passed it off as her own work! I also took a Baroque music course (in which, frankly, I didn't learn much that I didn't know already) and wrote a paper on Bach's transcriptions for keyboard of various Vivaldi violin concerti.

But of course it was my papers on classical subjects that most engaged me. By this time I was quite fluent in Latin, coming along in Greek, learning a great deal about ancient history, and becoming increasingly interested in ancient philosophy. A new professor, Kurt Raaflaub, had come to the department: he was a brilliant Swiss scholar who had written a pioneering study of the Roman civil war (*Dignitatis Contentio*)—unfortunately, it was written in a dense and (to me) impenetrable German! But I learned a great deal from Raaflaub, and he and Michael Putnam became my favourite professors in the department.

Among the papers I wrote at this time (which I still possess) are:

"The Three Stages of Man in Lucretius: *De Rerum Natura* 5.821–1457"
"Catullus and Lucretius on Cybele: A Comparison of Catullus 63 and *De Rerum Natura* 2.600–660"
"Tragedy as History: The *Persae* of Aeschylus"
"Satire as History: The *Apocolocyntosis* of Seneca"
"Rome's Treaties with Carthage Before the First Punic War"

All very impressive and learned! That second paper, no doubt, was inspired by Lovecraft's mention of "Atys" (with a direct citation of Catullus) in "The Rats in the Walls."

As my senior year (1979–80) came around, I not only had to think about graduating but what I would do after graduation. For the former, I began work on an honours thesis (meaning that, if it was approved, I would graduate *magna cum laude*—the highest ranking Brown allowed, as it did not have a *summa cum laude* ranking). So I turned to my favourite author of the ancient world, Juvenal; but I put into practice my increasing interest in philosophy by writing a 50-page thesis on "Juvenal and Ancient Philosophy." This was written for John Rowe Workman, a veteran classicist who had taught me Latin grammar all the way back in freshman year. It was indeed approved, and I did graduate *magna cum laude*.

Then there was the matter of my post-undergraduate life. I was reluctant to leave Brown (and Providence), because I had come to love the city and also because I was not in any way finished with my Lovecraft work. So I applied for a master's degree, and of course had little difficulty being accepted. But the Brown professors made it clear that, if my interest in ancient philosophy continued, I would have to go elsewhere, because Brown did not in fact have anyone specialising in that discipline in the classics faculty. I put off that decision for a while, knowing that I would have as much as two years more in Providence.

For my graduation in June 1980, my parents trudged all the way out from Muncie, my mother driving the entire way. I found the entire ceremony so dull that I brought along a copy of W. K. C. Guthrie's slim book *The Greek Philosophers from Thales to Aristotle* (1975)—not to be confused with his mammoth and definitive *History of Greek Philosophy* in six volumes (1962–81), several volumes of which I had already obtained and digested. The ceremony traditionally took place in the First Baptist Church (1775), beloved by Lovecraft, even though that church no longer had any connexion with the university (Brown had, of course, been founded in 1764 as a Baptist institution). Much to my amusement, a photograph of me, clearly reading my little book, was later published in a picture book about Brown that came out the next year! I accompanied my parents up to Boston, where they looked at the tall ships in Boston Harbour, and then returned by bus to Brown.

It was only a few weeks after my graduation that *H. P. Lovecraft: Four Decades of Criticism* emerged from Ohio University Press. I was mortified at the incredibly amateurish art on the front cover (the artist is mercifully unidentified); but nevertheless, I was proud to have a real-live hardcover book appear. This was in fact the first book about Lovecraft published by an academic press, unless one counts Philip A. Shreffler's *H. P. Lovecraft Companion* (Greenwood Press, 1977), which is really more of a popular book. My book received a great many reviews in the academic and specialty press—at least fifteen, ranging from Don Burleson in *Lovecraft Studies* to Darrell Schweitzer in *Science Fiction Review*. The academic reviews were on the whole positive.

But the most striking review came out a full year after the book's publication. Marc called me up one day in June 1981 and said, "You'd better head over to the library and check out the *Times Literary Supplement*." I did so—and was flabbergasted to see, in its June 19, 1981 issue a review that covered the first two pages of the issue. It was entitled "Allurements of the Abyss" and was by one S. S. Prawer, a professor of German at Oxford who wrote a good many books; the closest to our field was *Caligari's Children: The Film as Tale of Terror* (1980), which is not really very close. Although Prawer did point out some deficiencies in the book, he praised it overall; stating at the end, in reference to Edmund Wilson's hostile review:

> I venture to prophesy that *The Case of Charles Dexter Ward, The Colour out of Space, The Haunter of the Dark* and other fictions discussed in the volume under review will remain in print, and be read with fascinated appreciation, longer than that famous essay in *Classics and Commercials* which has induced many a literary jury to return a negative verdict in the case of Howard Phillips Lovecraft.

Not a terribly bold prophecy, all things considered, but one that has certainly been vindicated.

5. Brown and Princeton (1980–84)

"I was never anxious to please the mob."—Epicurus

The year 1980 was certainly a good year for me, in terms of publications. The second volume of Lovecraft's *Uncollected Prose and Poetry* emerged, the chief item being Henry S. Whitehead's "The Trap," which Lovecraft revised. The story was of course not unknown, having appeared in Whitehead's second Arkham House book, *West India Lights* (1946); but I had discovered Lovecraft's hand in the story as discussed in a letter to R. H. Barlow, so Marc and I felt it worth reprinting on that account. Both my *Index to the Selected Letters* and my listing of *Lovecraft's Library* came out in 1980, giving me four books for the year.

That summer I stayed in another wretched sublet, then moved into an off-campus apartment just before beginning graduate school that fall. By this time I was a bit tired of my tiny room in the Graduate Center, and I luckily found a quite spacious apartment—or, rather, the third floor of a house—at 15 Keene Street, just north of the Brown campus. The house was owned by a genial Jewish family, the Levs; it was a double house (15–17 Keene Street), and the other half of the house was occupied, by an interesting coincidence, by James Schevill, a Brown professor who some years earlier had written an eccentric and avant-garde play, *Lovecraft's Follies* (1971). I only met Schevill briefly during my two-year stay in this house, as he no longer had much interest in Lovecraft.

One of the people who helped me move into the house was . . . HolliAnne. In fact, she had visited me on several occasions over the years, as she seemed unwilling to let our relationship dissipate. I was too shy to confront her with the plain fact that we weren't terribly well suited to each other and that we should just go our separate ways, so I made the best of things, even when she showed up and lodged in my cubbyhole of a room at the Graduate Center, whose bed was so narrow that the idea of two people occupying it (for the purpose of sleeping, at any rate) was ludicrous; but, although she had brought a sleeping bag along, I magnanimously didn't ask her to use it, and we managed well enough. But this visit in 1980 did indeed prove to be the last, as she finally got the message that I wasn't very keen on pursuing a relationship with her. I have seen her only once since then. I have now heard that she lives on a farm outside of Muncie, alone as far as other human beings are concerned—*but with twenty-one cats.* How I envy her those cats!

My new home at 15 Keene Street was a very large space, austerely but adequately furnished. I finally had space to house my growing book and record collection, along with my increasing masses of papers (mostly photocopies) relating to Lovecraft. The house was also one block south of Barnes Street; indeed, some years later Jason Eckhardt and his wife at that time, Victoria, actually rented an apartment in Lovecraft's own house at 10 Barnes (that was also a double house—10–12 Barnes—and I think Jason was actually in the 12 Barnes side). The Lovecraft gang—now including Mollie Burleson, who had married Don a year or so before (both had divorced their spouses—Don's had suddenly become a fundamentalist Christian, and as he was an atheist he was well rid of her)—tended to gather in Providence around March 15 (Lovecraft's deathday) and August 20 (Lovecraft's birthday). Given how much room I had, I was able to put several of them up in my place on one March 15 gathering; but the weather was so unseasonably cold, and I was so deficient in spare blankets, that we all nearly froze to death. (Why I didn't ask the Lev family for some additional blankets, I'll never know.)

The gang also would venture up to Marblehead, Massachusetts, every Yuletide (usually December 21), to celebrate the winter solstice and to walk the streets that Lovecraft's narrator in "The Festival" walked on that same occasion. We would usually end up at the summit of Old Burial Hill, where we could still see the "black gravestones stuck ghoulishly through the snow like the decayed fingernails of a gigantic corpse," exactly as Lovecraft describes in the story. Once we had achieved the summit, we would gather under a gazebo and shout *"Yog-Sothoth!"* at the top of our lungs, just as we had done in Phoenix. I can't imagine what the townspeople—assuming they heard our ululations—thought of this. ("Those pesky Lovecraftians!")

It was sometime around this time when one of the relatively few incidents in which I experienced overt racism occurred—and that was only because of mistaken identity. At some point during the Iran hostage crisis (November 1979–January 1981), I found myself wandering around downtown Providence—on foot, of course. A car drove by me, and a boy of probably about the age of twelve stuck his head out the window and yelled at me, "Iranians suck!" Initially I was not even aware that he was addressing me (for of course I was not an Iranian); only after the car drove away did the realisation dawn upon me. Had I been more alert, I might have waved cheerfully at the boy or blown him kisses or something of the sort.

My new residence unexpectedly came in handy on another unusual venture I blundered into at this time. Sometime in 1979, the Estate of Clark Ashton Smith proposed to donate Smith's papers and manuscripts to the John Hay Library. The library, chronically short of staff and knowing that the papers were likely to be voluminous (although not as large as the Lovecraft papers), agreed to accept the material—*on condition that Marc and I catalogue the papers for free.* The library staff knew that, though we were undergraduates, we had a fair knowledge of Smith, and all that was required was that we learn about manuscript cataloguing.

Accordingly, we both took an independent studies course on the subject under the direction of the veteran Stuart Sherman, the university bibliographer, and other members of the library staff. I believe this occurred during the first semester of my senior year. Then, over the next year and a half, Marc and I holed up periodically in a tiny basement office at the library and began sorting out the papers. This process was made more difficult because Richard Kuhn (one of Smith's stepsons), then the administrator of the Estate, customarily threw material—manuscripts, letters, and other documents—into boxes without the slightest order or organisation, with the result that we had no idea what a given box would contain. These boxes did not come all at once, but over the course of many months. This is why the process of cataloguing took so long. It did not help that a certain number of the documents were either burned or water-damaged as a result of a fire that had occurred in Smith's cabin sometime in the 1950s. In the end I believe we did a pretty good job of cataloguing; we sorted through mountains of story manuscripts, poetry manuscripts, letters to Smith (including hundreds by August Derleth and a few by Robert E. Howard), and so on.

How does my off-campus apartment figure in this equation? Well, one of the items that most fascinated me was what appeared to be a juvenile manuscript called *The Black Diamonds*. This was a very long story, possibly of novel length, that was written in pen on legal-size sheets; but there were also various typed copies. Because the material had come to us in such a confused state, I felt I had no option but to sneak it out under my trusty all-weather coat, take it back to my spacious apartment, and lay out all the sheets on the floor of my bedroom. Only in this way was I able to restore the full version (minus two sheets) of the original handwritten manuscript, followed by at least four or five partial typed drafts. I then made a photocopy of the handwritten manuscript, with the idea to transcribing it and eventually getting it published. I had no idea that that process would take more than twenty years.

In terms of my own projects, I imagine that I must have submitted the final version of the Lovecraft bibliography to Kent State University Press sometime around late 1979 or early 1980. Thankfully, it was accepted, although the editor had to make a number of revisions to fix some formatting errors I had made. The book duly appeared in the summer of 1981 (my only book to be published that year); at xxiv + 473 pp., I believe it was the largest book ever published in the Serif Series (a bibliography of C. S. Lewis was a mere 389 pp.). This book also received fairly cordial reviews, including those by Neil Barron, Roger Schlobin, and A. Langley Searles. Of course, the book was outdated even before it was published. Indeed, the irony is that these two books—the *Four Decades of Criticism* and the bibliography—soon became outdated in a more profound sense, but perhaps that was because they in fact helped (along with *Lovecraft Studies,* in its more humble way) trigger a renewed interest in Lovecraft from all directions—among academics, fans, and general readers. The Lovecraft renaissance was decidedly underway!

And yet, we would be forced to do without the chief figure in that renaissance—Dirk W. Mosig. Because of a variety of personal and professional difficulties, Dirk was forced to bow out of the field abruptly around 1980. His absence was startling to many, and I in particular felt as if my mentor had suddenly been taken away from me. It was evidently up to me to become the new face of Lovecraft studies, and I wasn't sure I was up to the job. After all, I was only twenty-three when the bibliography was published. But because I had spent so many years poring through the Lovecraft material at Brown, and because I myself was now in touch with many of the leading scholars—David E. Schultz, Ken Faig, Don Burleson, Peter Cannon, and others who would soon emerge—I felt I had no choice but to carry the torch as best I could.

Dirk's departure left two major projects unfinished, and perhaps not even begun. He had been commissioned by Starmont House (a specialty press located in Mercer Island, Washington, and operated by Thaddeus Dikty, a longtime devotee of science fiction) to write a monograph on Lovecraft for the Starmont Reader's Guide series. And Dirk had received a contract to write a similar but lengthier monograph for the prestigious Twayne's United States Authors Series (Twayne was now controlled by G. K. Hall in Boston). It was probably for the best that these two books were not written by the same person. In any case, Dirk appointed me to write the Starmont book, and I did so in a matter of two or three weeks in the summer of 1981. It was a smallish book of about 80 pages, a fair proportion of which was devoted to an annotated primary and secondary bibliography. I rather liked the way I had integrated Lovecraft's life, work, and thought in this small treatise, and it appeared in 1982. It did fairly well, going through three printings.

Dirk had requested that the Twayne book be assigned to Don Burleson, who struck me as a thoroughly well-informed critic who, in spite of his mathematical background, had a comprehensive knowledge of general literature and had already written several keen articles on Lovecraft, which had appeared in *Lovecraft Studies* and elsewhere. But Twayne decided to award the book to Barton L. St. Armand; I daresay he would have done an outstanding job, but St. Armand had by this time lost interest in Lovecraft (his chief area of scholarship was now Emily Dickinson), and after several years of inactivity he finally conceded to Twayne that he would not be able to write the book. It was later awarded to Peter Cannon, who did a most creditable job; his book came out in 1989.

The Lovecraft gang in Providence—Marc, Jason, and some others—decided to attend the World Fantasy Convention in Baltimore in the fall of 1980. We took the long (eight-hour) train ride from Providence to Baltimore, then had to wend our way to the convention site, which was located a bit outside the Baltimore city limits. Along the way we stopped off at the museum of Johns Hopkins University, where there is one of the three original casts of Rodin's "The Thinker." Very impressive!

The convention was engaging enough. J. Vernon Shea was in attendance, and his rollicking good-humour was always welcome. I believe it was at this convention that I met George T. Wetzel, to whom I had dedicated my bibliography, since I felt that Jack Chalker had essentially stolen Wetzel's research when publishing his own bibliography in *The Dark Brotherhood*. I'm sure I sent Wetzel a copy when the book came out the next year.

Since Baltimore was one of the homes of Edgar Allan Poe, the convention arranged for a bus to take interested guests there. But this was done in the evening—and because the house was in a rather bad part of town, we had to have a police escort accompany us along the way. I don't remember much about the house (which I believe is now closed, because the city cannot afford to keep it open), aside from the fact that it was pretty cramped. (I'm reasonably sure I had by this time already visited the Poe cottage in the Bronx, which Lovecraft saw on many occasions.)

Only a few months after the convention, however, in February 1981, I was grieved to learn of Vernon Shea's passing. He had died alone in his crowded apartment in Cleveland; evidently the body had not been discovered for days. Poor fellow! I had been corresponding with him since 1976, but of late I had let my correspondence become rather irregular; nevertheless, I felt quite close to him and, after Marc told me the news in a phone call, I spent the evening rereading my letters from him. A few weeks earlier, H. Warner Munn had died, but I had never known him.

At some point around this time, the Providence Lovecraft gang welcomed some notable out-of-town visitors—namely, Ted Klein, Kirby McCauley, and Joseph Payne Brennan, who drove up from New York. Brennan was living in New Haven (where he had long worked at the Yale University Library), and the arrival of the trio was somewhat delayed because Brennan's wife apparently engaged in a nonstop talking session that the others had difficulty curtailing. But they finally showed up in Providence; I think they stayed a day or two. It was all great fun, and we were sorry to see them go.

A remarkable development during my two years of graduate school at Brown was the resumption of my musical career. I had assumed that I would be nothing but an appreciator of music, and my collection of classical recordings continued to grow. But somehow, a friend (name forgotten) who was an oboist had somehow learned that I had once played the violin. This fellow collared me and said that a friend of his, one Michael Hurshell, was forming an independent chamber orchestra—would I join? I said, "Omigawd! I haven't touched the violin in four years. I probably sound awful. Assuming I can play at all, you can just stick me in the back of the second violin section, where I can remain inconspicuous." But he wheedled me into attending the first rehearsal.

As it happened, at this rehearsal there were only *two* second violinists—myself and a freshman lad. The latter, knowing that I was a graduate student, deferred to my supposedly superior rank and insisted that I sit as principal second violin. As it happened, my ten or so years of violin playing did not go for naught, and I got back into the swing of things reasonably quickly; I won't say that I was nearly as good as I was at the height of my expertise (such as that was), but I was passable. In the end, I actually ended up

5. Brown and Princeton (1980–84)

playing a solo of sorts: of the several pieces that Hurshell scheduled for performance was a Bach orchestral concerto that had intermittent solos for first violin, second violin, and cello. Hurshell also played one of Bach's keyboard concerti, conducting from the piano (the piece should probably have been played on a harpsichord, but none was available). The performance went rather well.

Hurshell graduated at the end of the 1980–81 school year. What would happen to this orchestra the next year? We all wished to continue, and I confessed to my oboist friend that I had always wished to conduct such a group. Everyone seemed amenable to this idea, so as the school year of 1981–82 began, I trotted out a piece I had always wished to play (and in fact had played in rehearsals back at Burris): Vivaldi's spectacular *Concerto in F major for 3 Violins and Strings.* It is a virtuoso piece that demands high skill from the three soloists, and luckily we secured the services of three fine violinists (all women) who agreed to take on the task. As I did not have the means to purchase parts, I photocopied the full score and cut and pasted each instrument's parts.

The performance—on October 17, 1981 (my mother's birthday)—was quite successful. We started off a bit shakily, but we grew in confidence (and competence) as we went along. There was thunderous applause, and I took three curtain calls. Sometime later our group (we called ourselves the Brown Student Chamber Players) were asked to perform for a reception for the celebrated cellist Mstislav Rostropovich, who was coming to Brown to perform with the regular university orchestra. I dug out one of Handel's orchestral suites as being something suitably pleasant and non-taxing for the occasion. This performance, like the previous one, took place in Sayles Hall (where Lovecraft had given an astronomy lecture in 1907), but this time we were in the organ loft rather than on the main stage. It went well enough—except when, at one point, we actually got lost and had to stop and start over again. But there was so much talking at the reception that no one seemed to notice. I later heard that Rostropovich laid on some formulaic praise of our little group, although I doubt he could have heard much of what we played.

We also played a Christmas concert in December, where I finally fulfilled my long-held dream of performing Corelli's *Christmas Concerto.* I believe we also played Vivaldi's *Concerto in D major for 4 Violins and Strings* (Opus 3, No. 1) and some other works. After that, however, the group disbanded by common consent.

During my first year of graduate school I cemented my friendships with two delightful people at Brown. The first was John Gailey. I had known him for some years, and we were united by a love of classical music. He had an impressive collection of LPs of twentieth-century British music, and he lent me many of them—not only Ralph Vaughan Williams, but such lesser-known composers as Frederick Delius, Gerald Finzi, George Butterworth, and others. I found this music a revelation; to this day I think Vaughan Williams's *Fantasia on a Theme of Thomas Tallis* one of the greatest pieces for strings written in the twentieth century, and I always weep when I hear it. In turn, I lent John some of my extensive holdings in Baroque music.

John was a history major, but he had a strong interest in Latin literature. We both struggled through a course with Professor Raaflaub in which we read immense quantities of Latin prose. John was working on an honours thesis involving a very little-known period—the "Dark Ages" of Britain, following the collapse of Roman rule in the early fifth century C.E. and spanning the next two or three centuries. I felt privileged in typing his thesis, which I felt was a brilliant work of history. I mostly lost touch with John after he left Brown, but did see him once or twice in the years to come.

The other person I became close to at this time was Linda Aro, who remains the only Brown student with whom I am still in touch to this day. She was a year behind me, hence a senior (undergraduate) during my first year of graduate school. I had first met her at a dinner at someone's house, and once we learned of our mutual love of the classical world we talked about Julius Caesar during the entire dinner, ignoring the other guests. We met again when John Gailey married a fellow student named Cassandra, in a ceremony at Brown's Manning Chapel. Thereafter we became good friends, and I also typed her honours thesis. I cannot recall its subject; but I do recall that she had gotten a little behind in her work, so on one occasion as the school year was approaching its end she holed up in my Keene Street apartment, scribbling away desperately on her thesis and bringing me sheet after sheet, whereupon I would calmly type it up. In the end she did finish her work on time.

My work in classics and my musical interests coincided in a curious way at this time, for it turned out that a number of other graduate students (and maybe one or two undergraduates) were also musicians, as were some professors. Accordingly, we decided to get together periodically to play music. What we worked on was nothing less than the *Brandenburg Concerto No. 5*, by J. S. Bach, which had a fiendishly difficult keyboard part. This was played masterfully by Michael Putnam on the piano; meanwhile, Kurt Raaflaub played the flute, his younger brother Hans (who was visiting from

Switzerland) and I played the violin, and we managed to round up a viola and cello to fill out the ensemble. We performed this work quite ably at Raaflaub's house one evening, with many of the classics faculty and graduate students in the audience. We also played at the graduation ceremony for the classics department in the late spring of 1981.

I was still doing a lot of work typing papers for other students and had secured the substantial sum of $300 for my work. I asked Linda to go to Boston with me to help spend that money, chiefly at the Harvard Coop, which had an excellent selection of classical recordings. At my urging, she picked out several items for herself. Then we had dinner and concluded the evening by seeing one of Rex Harrison's last live performances of *My Fair Lady*. A splendid day! I came home with about $4 in my pocket.

And yet, the curious thing was that I myself was, in that summer and fall of 1981, feeling a bit low about various matters, personal and professional. I had suffered some setbacks in my scholarly work, both in classics and in weird fiction. I had queried Marshall Tymn, who was establishing a series (Contributions to the Study of Science Fiction and Fantasy) with Greenwood Press, about an annotated edition of "Supernatural Horror in Literature." Tymn had casually given approval to the project, and I plunged into the work; but late that summer I received what I thought was a rather insulting postcard in which Tymn stated that he was no longer interested in the book. I was rather crestfallen, since I had virtually finished my work. The book would not come out for another nineteen years; and I also learned from this experience never to undertake a project (unless I just wished to write it for my own interest) without a signed contract in hand.

In the spring of 1982 I took a much-needed break and visited John and Cassandra Gailey, who were now living in the Chicago area. We had a wonderful time, and I was able to put many of my worries to rest. John took me to the Wisconsin Dells, where we did a bit of hill-climbing. I was much inspired by seeing the recently released film *Chariots of Fire*, which not only nurtured my fervent Anglophilia but, in its basic motif of triumph over adversity, gave me the courage to carry on against all obstacles. When I returned to Providence, I saw the film at least seven more times in a theatre, as it was frequently playing at the Avon Cinema. (I should note that, throughout my years at Brown, my knowledge of films was vastly augmented by the Brown Film Society, which showed all manner of classic and contemporary movies with which I was unfamiliar. I believe I saw *Casablanca, Psycho,* and many other films in this manner.)

Otherwise, I forged ahead with my work in classical studies. I spent a semester on an independent study project (supervised by Raaflaub) where I read many orations of Cicero in an effort to gauge their historical significance. Aside from writing an extensive paper on the subject, I also came to gain an immense admiration for Cicero's chief foil, Julius Caesar, and a disdain for the snivelling and weak-willed Cicero himself, whose life ended ignominiously only a year after Caesar himself had been assassinated on the Ides of March, 44 B.C.E. I long envisioned writing an historical novel about Caesar (the framework would be his trip from his house to the Senate on that fateful Ides of March, with flashbacks recounting various phases of his earlier life and career); but I've now forgotten so much of what I once knew of him, and of the historical period, that I suspect I will never write such a work.

For my master's thesis I focused on my chief philosophical and literary interest, Lucretius. In a kind of mirror-image of my honours thesis on Juvenal, I wrote a 150-page thesis entitled "*Lucretius Satiricus:* Satiric Elements in the *De Rerum Natura.*" I believe this is a reasonably creditable piece of work. Michael Putnam was my advisor. This thesis can, I think, be obtained through interlibrary loan or other means, assuming there are any who would care to read it.

By this point, of course, I had come to the realisation that my career at Brown was over. I was still assuming that I would become a professor of classics (while doing my Lovecraft work on the side), and that meant getting a Ph.D.; but Brown had no one who was an authority on ancient philosophy (especially the philosophy of Epicurus, which was becoming my specialty), so I had to go elsewhere. (Ironically, only a few years later the renowned Martha Nussbaum came to Brown from Harvard.) So in the fall of 1981 I applied to Yale, Cornell, and Princeton. I was accepted by all three. I once again turned Yale down, as I had done for undergraduate studies. A young professor at Cornell called me up and begged me to come there; but I felt that Cornell was in such an isolated environment, stuck out in the middle of nowhere in upstate New York, that I would be bored out of my mind if I went there. In the end, I came to believe I had no option but to go to Princeton, chiefly because it had a thriving classical philosophy program led by David Furley, a leading authority on Epicurus. I assumed I would be working closely with him, so I accepted Princeton's offer—especially given the fact that I was awarded the prestigious Paul Elmer More Fellowship in Classical Philosophy.

My departure from Brown, and Providence, was certainly a bittersweet experience. I had felt entirely at home both at the university and in the

5. Brown and Princeton (1980–84)

city—a city just large enough to have all manner of interesting features (all apart from its Lovecraftian connexions), but not so intimidatingly large as to be terrifying to someone who was essentially a small-town boy from the Midwest. And it would be difficult to leave the close friends I had gained there—Marc Michaud, Jason Eckhardt, Ken Neily, Don Burleson (living in New Hampshire, although he would eventually move to New Mexico), and others—although I was not so far away that I couldn't return to Providence or New England from time to time.

Conveniently, however, my sister Ragini was working at the RCA Space Center and living in Cranbury, quite close to Princeton. She helped me move into my tiny room at Princeton's Graduate Center in the fall of 1982. I was, however, disheartened to learn that my M.A. from Brown counted for virtually nothing in regard to the classical philosophy program: I would still have to work there for five full years (one more than usual, since I was in an interdisciplinary program, working in both the classics and the philosophy departments), and that prospect seemed increasingly daunting to me.

But as I plunged into the extremely difficult classwork at Princeton, events in the Lovecraftian world were moving in an interesting direction. I believe it was in the summer of 1980 that the first NECON (Northeastern Regional Fantasy Convention) was held at the campus of Roger Williams College in Bristol, Rhode Island. I think it was at the NECON convention of the following year that I met none other than Robert M. Price. Price was a professor of religious studies, teaching at various colleges in New Jersey, but he was also an enthusiast of Lovecraft, Robert E. Howard, and other weird writers. He handed me a paper, "Higher Criticism and the *Necronomicon*," that fused his two interests in a felicitous manner. I thought the piece a brilliant work of scholarship and published it in the Spring 1982 issue of *Lovecraft Studies*. This jovial, bearded young man (he was four years older than myself) was immediately incorporated into our circle of Lovecraftians. More significantly, he fostered Lovecraft scholarship himself by establishing the lively journal *Crypt of Cthulhu*, the first issue of which dated to Hallowmass 1981. That first issue was actually meant as a submission to the EOD amateur press association, but very quickly thereafter Price began selling the item outside the EOD. In short order he was publishing an incredible eight issues a year, using his tireless and genial mother to type up the camera-ready pages.

Bob Price's engaging good-humour and disinclination to take either Lovecraft or himself too seriously made *Crypt of Cthulhu* the perfect companion—or foil—for *Lovecraft Studies* (which he once pungently parodied as *Lovecraft Stuffies*). I still felt that, for the sake of Lovecraft's reputation, I had to keep *Lovecraft Studies* to the austere level of an academic journal, although I detested the bombastic and jargon-laden work of most academics just as much as Bob did. He felt no such compunction, and featured such amusing columns in his journal as "Fun Guys from Yuggoth" and "Advice for the Lovecraft-Lorn." But at the same time he published quite substantial articles. He had an uncanny ability to coax scholars such as Don Burleson, David E. Schultz, and myself to write articles for various "theme" issues he envisioned, with the result that both *Crypt* and *Lovecraft Studies* became flagship journals in their own distinctive ways, producing a mass of scholarship in the 1980s the like of which we have not seen before or since. Bob published several of my own substantial pieces, including my "Alien Civilisations" article as well as such things as "Lovecraft's Other Planets" and "The Structure of Lovecraft's Longer Narratives."

My move to Princeton allowed me to fraternise more readily with Bob and also with another Lovecraftian who was emerging at this time—Steven J. Mariconda. Steve was three years younger than I, but was already a devoted Lovecraftian. He had come into contact with David E. Schultz around 1981; and when I moved to New Jersey, Steve (who was a New Jersey native, having been born in Paterson) dropped me a line. Steve's interests were largely focused on Lovecraft's prose, and he was working on a major piece called "H. P. Lovecraft: Consummate Prose Stylist." This was first published in abridged form in *Crypt of Cthulhu* (Eastertide 1982) and unabridged in *Lovecraft Studies* (Fall 1984). A follow-up piece, "Notes on the Prose Realism of H. P. Lovecraft," appeared in *Lovecraft Studies* in Spring 1985. Many other pieces, long and short, followed.

It was chiefly by virtue of the fact that Bob Price, Steve Mariconda, and I all now lived in New Jersey that (and I hope I can say this without immodesty) the nexus of the Lovecraftian fan and scholarly community shifted from Providence to the New York/New Jersey area. We can throw in Connecticut as well, for it was around 1982 when I first met Sam Gafford, who was then living in Darien. This was when I was still living in Providence, and I recall showing him the usual Lovecraftian sites just as Lovecraft himself would show visiting guests the colonial antiquities of his beloved city.

I suppose it must have been around this time that we formed the New Kalem Club, a gang that included not only the people mentioned above but also Peter Cannon, occasionally T. E. D. Klein, and, a bit later, Stefan

5. Brown and Princeton (1980–84)

Dziemianowicz, whose perspicacious reviews were one of the highlights of *Crypt of Cthulhu*. Later, others joined us, including Miroslaw Lipinski (who became an authority on the Polish weird writer Stefan Grabinski), Gabriel Mesa, and others. Initially we would congregate around noon at the Forbidden Planet bookshop in lower Manhattan, which at that time stocked a fair amount of publications relating to weird fiction, including British imports (this was where I secured my copies of the Panther paperback reprints of Clark Ashton Smith's Arkham House volumes, among other items), then head over to Silver Spurs, a superb burger joint with a western theme (I would always order the Stagecoach, which featured mushrooms, green peppers, and mozzarella cheese). Scott Briggs, who was only a teenager at the time, joined us around 1984, initially in the company of his father.

The problem was that Bob Price took it into his head to invite two devotees of Robert E. Howard, Marc A. Cerasini and Charles Hoffman (they would later write the Starmont Reader's Guide volume on Howard). The others—I especially—did not welcome their company, because they tended to be very conservative politically and also tended to be a bit vociferous in expressing their views. So we were forced to change our schedule and meet for dinner; I made it clear that these gatherings would be by invitation only. Our chosen venue became O'Reilly's, an Irish pub on 31st Street between Broadway and Sixth Avenue, which had superb Irish fare (served by comely Irish waitresses). Later, however, O'Reilly's felt the need to revise their cuisine to a more upscale audience, and it began eliminating the specifically Irish dishes (such as its magnificent lamb stew) for things like pasta primavera. We all lamented this change but continued meeting there out of inertia. I believe the gang still meets there to this day, and whenever I venture back to New York a gang meeting always reconvenes.

At some point in the mid-1980s we took to going over to Lin Carter's apartment on the Upper East Side to shoot the bull. I was flabbergasted by the valuable artwork (much of it by Hannes Bok) he had on the walls, along with an immense number of rare books. Carter was engagingly humble, recognising that he was simply a kind of overgrown fan who had luckily made it as a writer and editor. He always received us cordially. But then he got evicted from his apartment for owing $19,000 in back rent. He ended up in a cramped apartment in Bloomfield, near where Bob Price (who would become his literary executor) lived. He developed some kind of cancer on his face, and my last meeting with him was a spooky episode where he sat in a dark corner like the Whisperer in Darkness because he did not wish his disfigurement to be seen. He died in 1988.

The year 1982 was significant in Lovecraft studies, and in my own personal history, for a single event that occurred in the fall of that year: my attendance of the World Fantasy Convention in New Haven. It was at this event that I met James Turner, the managing editor of Arkham House. I had written to him earlier, outlining my textual work on Lovecraft's stories and querying whether Arkham House would be interested in issuing new editions of the Lovecraft volumes incorporating my corrections. In all honesty, Arkham House was not my first choice; influenced by my discussions with Robert C. Harrall, administrator of the Estate of H. P. Lovecraft, I had come to the conclusion that Arkham House's ownership of the Lovecraft copyrights was highly suspect, and I hoped that the material could somehow appear under some other imprint. Indeed, as early as 1980 I had established contact with an editor at Viking Penguin, who was tentatively interested in a *Portable Lovecraft* that would have used my corrected texts. But Viking had to back out of the plan because it discovered that Arkham House had licensed an exclusive arrangement with Ballantine Books for the issuance of Lovecraft stories in paperback, and Viking was not prepared to undertake any kind of legal challenge on this point.

So I felt my only option was Arkham House, if I were to get my corrected texts in print in anything like the near future. Initially, Turner merely wanted me to turn over my research without compensation, but I made it clear to him that this work was my intellectual property and that, at a minimum, I required some kind of explicit acknowledgement of the fact. It took close to a year of discussions with Turner to work out a mutually satisfactory arrangement, which basically came to this: I would receive $800 for my work in preparing new versions of the standard three-volume edition of the fiction (*The Dunwich Horror and Others, At the Mountains of Madness and Other Novels,* and *Dagon and Other Macabre Tales*), and I would be listed as "editor" of the texts. I wished to scrap the arrangement of the three volumes altogether for some more logical sequence, but Turner said that was legally impossible: because these volumes were jointly copyrighted by August Derleth and Donald Wandrei, any attempt to produce new arrangements would have triggered a suit by Wandrei, who had fallen out with Derleth (or, more specifically, with Derleth's literary executor, Forrest Hartman) and Arkham House. This is why, when the three volumes appeared in 1984, 1985, and 1986, they were declared to be "corrected printings" rather than new editions; indeed, no new copyright was issued for these editions. Derleth still had to be listed as the one who "selected" the texts, but my credit appeared on the title page as "Texts Edited by S. T. Joshi." That was satisfactory to me.

So the work began. Turner sent me new copies of the three volumes, and I was to tear the pages out of the hardcover bindings, scribble in the corrections in pen, and send the pages back to Turner. This process, as can be imagined, took quite a long time, and Turner and I exchanged mounds of correspondence in regard to exactly how the various elements of the new books were to be set up. He also was exceptionally keen in pointing out apparent inconsistencies in Lovecraft's texts; I actually think he went a little overboard on the matter, persuading me to iron out some inconsistencies that probably didn't need to be altered, and when I came to prepare my variorum edition twenty years later I reversed my decisions on some points.

But Turner was nonetheless enormously helpful in getting these editions ready for the press with a minimum of new errors (some, alas, did appear, but were corrected in subsequent printings through the 1990s). My marked-up copies of the books were sent to Arkham House's typesetter, who of course had to set the books all over again manually. I received actual galley proofs—long sheets, sometimes three or four feet in length, that I would go over painstakingly to make sure that my corrections had been correctly inputted. I'm not sure that I ever saw actual page proofs at a later stage, but I was confident that Turner could do the job of looking these over without my involvement.

The first volume, *The Dunwich Horror and Others,* came out in late 1984 and appeared to make something of a sensation. It did not get reviewed in the *New York Times Book Review* until May 19, 1985, and even then it was a capsule review written by one Edna Stumpf. I believe this is the only book of mine, with one exception many years later, ever reviewed in this august venue. Other reviews appeared in the *Village Voice,* the *San Francisco Chronicle,* and of course throughout the fan press. The other two volumes came out in late 1985 and late 1986, respectively. It amazed me that, less than fifteen years after I had initially read these books from the Muncie Public Library, I had now prepared new editions of them!

Aside from the Lovecraft edition, however, I had little time at Princeton to do much more Lovecraftian work. My graduate classes were so onerous that my productivity in outside work was radically diminished. The year 1983 was, aside from 1987, the only one in my career (if we date the beginning of that career to 1978, when my first book was published), when no book of mine appeared. I was of course continuing *Lovecraft Studies* and contributing to *Crypt;* but *Lovecraft Studies* itself went on hiatus, as no issue appeared between Fall 1982 and Spring 1984. After graduating from Brown in 1981, Marc Michaud underwent some difficulties and took something of an involuntary break from Necronomicon Press; indeed, it was Jason Eckhardt who shepherded that Spring 1984 issue into print. But soon thereafter Marc got back into the swing of things, and Necronomicon Press publications resumed. Among the new items we produced were slim editions of Lovecraft's *Juvenilia: 1897–1905* (1984) and *In Defence of Dagon* (1985), both of which contained unpublished material. I also collaborated with the Australian scholar Leigh Blackmore to issue a substantial supplement to my bibliography (1985). For Bob Price's *Crypt of Cthulhu*, I compiled special issues containing Lovecraft's unpublished (*Saturnalia and Other Poems*, 1984) and uncollected poetry (*Medusa and Other Poems*, 1985).

It was not exactly a matter of all play, no work for me. While wandering through the Princeton student union in the spring of 1983, I noticed a flyer for a summer school course for American students to be held at the University of Warwick in Coventry, England. I had by this time become an Anglophile perhaps even surpassing Lovecraft: as I've mentioned, I had read enormous quantities of English history in high school, purely for my own edification; I had, through Lovecraft's influence, plunged deeply into the eighteenth-century writers, much preferring the poets (Pope, Johnson, Gray) and essayists (Addison, Steele, Swift, Johnson, Gibbon) to the novelists (Fielding, Smollett, Richardson, Sterne), just as Lovecraft did. Here now was a chance to experience England at first hand—something that Lovecraft had never been able to do. So I persuaded my mother to foot the bill for the trip, which would span about six weeks from late June to early August. I had no idea how this trip would affect the rest of my life.

The University of Warwick offered about half-a-dozen different courses, and I enrolled in the one on Roman Britain—both because of Lovecraft's interest in that subject as well as Arthur Machen's. I could not be troubled to take the course for credit, since I merely wished to enjoy myself. So I set out on the trip, catching a red-eye flight from one of the New York airports (probably Newark) and landing in London the next morning. I then managed to make my way by train to Coventry, where I was picked up, along with other students, in a van provided by the university.

The trip was all I could have hoped for, and more. I had been vaguely afraid that my actual sight of England would not be commensurate with the possibly extravagant and romantic ideas I had formed of that "blessèd isle," but in fact my six-week visit exceeded my expectations. It was not merely that I managed to cover quite a bit of ground; it was that the mere sight of England's rolling hills and archaic structures, stretching back not merely centuries but millennia, was an incredible tonic to my spirit. I felt *at home* there as I had not felt anywhere except in Providence.

The university arranged for day trips to various locales outside of Coventry, including London and Oxford. We also went to Stratford-upon-Avon to see the Shakespeare sites; the day concluded with a performance of *Henry VIII* at the Globe Theatre by the Royal Shakespeare Company, but I was so fatigued by sightseeing earlier in the day that I nodded off to sleep during much of the performance (not one of Shakespeare's most scintillating plays in any event). I myself decided to head to Cambridge on a solo trip, since my devotion to Bertrand Russell demanded that I visit the university where he had done some of his early philosophical work. My first entry into the exquisite Gothic chapel of King's College, with an organist playing idly in the background and the sun's rays pouring in through the windows, was an aesthetic experience that I do not think has been surpassed in my lifetime.

Incredibly, I managed to persuade my instructor (a professor at Warwick—name forgotten) to take our class on a field trip to none other than Caerleon-on-Usk, Wales, the former Isca Silurum, home of the Second Augustan Legion beloved of Arthur Machen. The length of the trip necessitated at least one overnight stay somewhere, and the visit to the celebrated amphitheatre at Isca Silurum was another highlight of the trip. I also managed a solo trip to Manchester, where I met the family of Barry Bender, a British Lovecraftian who had written a capable thesis on Lovecraft's racism that I published in two parts in *Lovecraft Studies*. I still recall the graciousness with which he, his wife, and his little daughter served me tea in their humble flat.

But it was the other students, all Americans, with whom I spent the great majority of my time. Even though the students—perhaps fifty in all—were taking different classes, we generally met for breakfast and dinner, provided by the university. I recall some half-joking debates with a young fundamentalist Christian in the group, and discussions on music with several others. One woman named Nell actually came from Princeton; she was an undergraduate (as most of the other students were), and I saw her at least once upon my return, as we looked at some of the photographs she had taken. (I took no photographs at all, since I wished to store my memories in my mind.)

There was one woman named Leslie G. Boba who had come from Seattle, Washington, along with her friend, Diana Blumberg. Diana was in my class; Leslie was taking a class on mediaeval Britain, as I recall, but they were both studying classics at the University of Washington. Evidently Leslie had been informed that I was a formidable classicist. I recall one occasion, when we were taken to visit the partially bombed cathedral in Coventry, when Leslie was staring at me with incredible intensity. I would have stared back at her if I had not been quite so shy—because I thought that she was perhaps the most beautiful woman I had ever seen in my life. Blondhaired, with a heartrendingly lovely face and fine figure, she was the very ideal of young womanhood. (She proved to be only six months younger than myself, but she was taking her time finishing her undergraduate degree.)

I then had no idea that I would marry her eighteen years later.

I did speak to her over dinner a day or two later, and we exchanged accounts of what it was to be a classics major. The University of Washington did not require classics majors to study both Latin and Greek, and Leslie was specialising in Latin. I found her utterly captivating; she was a "girly girl" of the sort that I found entrancing. I confess that HolliAnne's relentless pursuit of me over several years after high school had rendered me somewhat gun-shy as far as getting involved with women was concerned; but as the weeks of this summer school passed, I found myself becoming more and more bewitched by Leslie. I even confided my feelings to another woman in the group, Suzanne Stuttman, who came from Connecticut and was living in New York. Toward the end of the course I actually avoided Leslie as much as possible, since the mere sight of her was acutely painful. I had no reason to think she reciprocated my feelings.

My trip to England did result in my departure from Lovecraftian sensibility in one important regard—teetotalism. I don't know that I had any strong feelings on the matter, but as it happened I had rarely had much opportunity to imbibe alcoholic beverages up to this time; but England, with its plethora of charming pubs, led me to experiment tentatively. I didn't drink any actual beer, ale, or wine, but did manage to gain a taste for brandy of various sorts. It was all enjoyable enough, but I never drank enough to become actually intoxicated.

After the various courses were over, students were offered a week-long trip to the Continent. The cost of this trip was not inconsiderable, coming on top of the expenses for the courses themselves; and only two of the students went along, aside from myself. This trip was part of a tour run by some company or other, and most of the participants were (as is common in cruises of this sort) rather elderly. So the three of us hung out together, along with the youthful male tour guide. The trip was truly a whirlwind: within a week we visited Amsterdam (two days), Brussels, Ghent, Bruges, Paris (about a day and a half), and other locales. It was here that I finally shrugged off my fears of solitary voyaging: the moment we hit a given destination, I would secure a map and head out on my own, ignoring the tour group and covering as much territory on foot as possible. In Amsterdam I accompanied two of the (female) students into the vast and celebrated red-light district, actually asking a prostitute how much she charged and regretting that I didn't have quite enough cash on hand to partake of her services. In Paris I strolled by the Bibliothèque Nationale (wondering if the *Necronomicon* was available for consultation), Notre Dame, Montmartre, and other sites—deliberately avoiding the Louvre because I knew I would be able to see little else if I ventured there. The whole trip was thrilling, and I stored up an immense number of impressions; indeed, to date I have still not returned to any of the sites in question.

As I began my second year at Princeton (1983–84), I had to come to an important decision about my future. My English and European trip had significantly bolstered my sense of independence and self-sufficiency, and my ongoing literary and publishing activity was making it increasingly untenable that I could truly lead the academic double life that I had envisioned for myself—i.e., being a professor of classics while doing Lovecraftian work on the side. But I was so unworldly that I couldn't imagine any other career for myself than that of a professor. At long last it dawned upon me that there was a field called publishing in which I might find a foothold. And where was the capital of publishing in the United States? Was it not New York, a city that I was becoming increasingly familiar with through almost weekly day-trips by bus and train? Princeton was such a boring town that I felt the need to escape its stifling atmosphere by visits to the nearby megalopolis that lay less than an hour away; and my gradual acclimation to the hectic pace of New York allowed me to overcome the fears I had had of that place from that terrifying first visit in 1977.

Accordingly, in late 1983 I notified my department that I was going to take a leave of absence for a year. The department did not welcome this development, since it had bestowed upon me its most prestigious fellowship, but it could do little to stop me. I was now determined to leave Princeton—and leave academic life altogether, at least in the sense of making a career in it—unless I failed spectacularly to secure a job in publishing. The fact is that

Princeton itself had convinced me that the academic arena was not where I belonged. The contrast with Brown couldn't have been more stark: whereas at Brown I felt a sense of collegiality and a shared interest in learning for the sake of learning, at Princeton the focus was all on becoming a professional in one's field, and there was a constant tension between the graduate students and the faculty, who seemed at times to regard us with contempt and at other times (absurdly enough) as rivals to their positions. We also had nothing at all to do with the undergraduates in our department, which made us feel isolated and alone. Moreover, I had come to feel that universities in general were artificial environments cut off from the real world; and with my growing interest in political and social issues, I felt that I needed to get out.

That school year (1983–84) was largely spent in studying for what Princeton called the "general examinations"—very rigorous written exams testing one's ability in all phases of one's discipline; it was necessary to pass these examinations in order to proceed with the rest of one's Ph.D. programme. Given that, even if I passed the exam, I would still be facing three more years of study, part of it involving being a teaching assistant (which I did not wish to do), I felt that this was a good time to leave. But I did study very hard and passed the generals. At this time I was living in a somewhat barracks-like off-campus residence for graduate students north of the university; I had purchased a bicycle to ride to and from campus. I was sharing living space with a fellow graduate student, Joseph de Filippo, who I believe went on to become a professor of classics at Grinnell College. After our generals were over, we were so exhausted that we abandoned studies for a time and did little but watch movies. There was a cheap second-run movie theatre nearby that offered 10 A.M. matinee showings for $1; we watched fifteen movies in two weeks after our exams.

Meanwhile, I had to see about getting a publishing job. In addition to poring over ads in the *New York Times,* I signed on with several agencies who placed applicants in the publishing industry. I was becoming a bit nervous as the weeks of the summer went on and no job—and not even any job prospects—appeared on the horizon. I actually interviewed with Dover Publications, whose reprints of classic horror and science fiction books I had long enjoyed; I was in the running for a position working in its library. I did not get the job, but, just as the summer was coming to an end, one of the agencies notified me that I was to interview with a small firm in lower Manhattan called Chelsea House. I showed up at the place, and within days I was offered an entry-level position. Naturally, I accepted, although the pay

5. Brown and Princeton (1980–84)

was quite poor; but my mother promised to help with expenses. By this time I had already found a small apartment in Jersey City. I was happy to announce this turn of events to Ragini, who was just then getting married to David Gieseker, an old friend from graduate school who was now a professor of mathematics at UCLA.

So, as she took off for Los Angeles, in late August I bid goodbye to Princeton—and to the academic world in general—and became a wage slave. This proved to be the only salaried position I would ever hold in my life.

6. Chelsea House I (1984–90)

> "All genuine historical work is philosophy, unless it is mere ant-industry."—Oswald Spengler, *The Decline of the West*

Chelsea House Publishers was founded in 1964 by Harold Steinberg. The story goes that he was living at the Chelsea Hotel on 23rd Street and named his firm Chelsea House because the hotel receptionist would simply say, "Chelsea," to incoming calls, thereby creating the illusion that she was Steinberg's own receptionist. The firm was later bought from Steinberg by Philip Cohen, although Steinberg still showed up at the office from time to time as a kind of informal consultant. I myself already knew dimly of Chelsea House from its reprint of Tony Goodstone's anthology *The Pulps* (1970), which included some pieces by Lovecraft.

Some years before I joined the staff, the firm had moved its office to 133 Christopher Street in Greenwich Village—conveniently for me, because it was right next to the entrance of the Christopher Street PATH station (the PATH trains chug back and forth under the Hudson River between Jersey City, Hoboken, and Newark to various points in lower and midtown Manhattan). My commute, therefore, was all of about 20 minutes.

At this time, Chelsea House was split into two broad divisions: one focusing on young adult nonfiction books, and the other on literary criticism for the high school and college market. I was, of course, chosen to be an associate editor in the latter division. We were preparing several large series of reference works reprinting previously published criticism on all manner of authors in American, English, and world literature, nominally under the general editorship of the prominent critic Harold Bloom; but Bloom had relatively little to do with the project, only lending his name to the venture for a substantial fee. One of the series was the *New Moulton's Library of Literary Criticism*, reprinting criticism up to 1900 (and therefore all in the public domain). This was a major revision of the *Library of Literary Criticism* (1902f.) compiled by Charles Wells Moulton—which, amusingly enough,

Lovecraft mentions in passing in "Suggestions for a Reading Guide" ("An excellent encyclopaedia covering this ground is Moulton's *Library of Literary Criticism*").

So the idea was to go to the library and hunt up worthy criticism on a given author and prepare it for reprinting. For some of the series we were doing, we were receiving assistance from a legion of researchers (presumably graduate students) at Yale under Bloom's direct supervision, but in all honesty we ended up having to augment their material fairly extensively. My immediate supervisor was one Sally Stepanek, a young woman (younger than I, I believe) who was the managing editor of the literary criticism division.

I plunged into the work, as it was so congenial to me. We actually received library cards to New York University Library, which was a short walk away. Later I insisted that we also get library cards for Columbia University, and we also did work at the New York Public Library. At the moment, there were only about two or three other staff members in the literary criticism division (I remember one named Frank Menchaca, with whom I became good friends), but it was becoming evident that we would have to hire more staff soon if we were to finish these gargantuan projects in anything like the near future.

My work at Chelsea House—I stayed there for the next eleven years—was immensely beneficial to me. Given my focus on classical studies, I had been quite unsystematic in my reading of English and American literature aside from whatever happened to interest me for casual reading. Now I was compelled to become familiar not only with the leading (and many of the lesser) figures in these fields but also with the significant critics who discussed them, past and present. Presumably I had been hired because I was already a published literary critic.

I did not rest on my laurels; and when Stepanek resigned a year after I arrived (I believe she wanted to go to graduate school), I was chosen to be managing editor. By this time I was managing a staff of about four or five full-time workers, with a small army of proofreaders and other part-time staff. One of the projects I worked on at this time was an enormous selection of criticism of Shakespeare from the 1590s to 1900 (this comprises Volume 2 of the *Major Authors Edition of the New Moulton's Library of Literary Criticism* and dates to 1985). I spent about six weeks on this project, doing all the work myself; and was fascinated to discover the array of criticism of the Bard, ranging from Ben Jonson in Shakespeare's own day to John Dryden to Samuel Johnson to Edward Dowden and many others, including

Oscar Wilde's piquant short story "The Portrait of Mr. W. H." (about Shakespeare's sonnets). I also included a section on the ridiculous authorship controversy, beginning with Delia Bacon's venture into fatuity, *The Philosophy of the Plays of Shakspere Unfolded* (1857), through the equally insane work of Ignatius Donnelly, Mark Twain, and others.

In all honesty, I think this is a pretty impressive work of scholarship. I did not include it (or any of the works I worked on at Chelsea House) in the published bibliography of my work, but I suppose there is a good argument for citing it and a few other titles as authentically my own work.

In effect, I supervised a kind of self-contained fiefdom at Chelsea House, since my division had almost nothing to do with the other (and much larger) branch of the company. My own supervisor, once I became managing editor (I later ascended to the titles of senior editor and senior managing editor—these titles being given to me only as an excuse to give me moderate raises in my salary) was Karyn Browne, the managing editor of the entire company—whose husband was, curiously enough, a leading spokesman for the NFL. But Karyn wisely gave me a free hand, given that I was managing my staff with efficiency and turning in volume after volume on or ahead of schedule. At one point I hired both Linda Aro and Peter Cannon as associate editors or freelance researchers. Later Scott Briggs worked for the young adult division.

Once I became managing editor, I did meet with Harold Bloom on occasion, either on the rare instances when he would come to the Chelsea House offices or, more commonly, in an apartment that New York University had given him (he was nominally on the faculty, perhaps teaching a course or two in addition to his work at Yale). My task was to prepare lists of authors to be covered in the various volumes and the number of pages to be given them depending on their relative significance. The whole process truly strengthened my grasp of the totality of Anglophone literature and gave my own critical work on Lovecraft and other writers great depth and breadth. Once Bloom recognised that the project was in good hands, he allowed me pretty free rein to assemble the volumes as I wished. He never even looked at the books until they were published (and perhaps not even then).

One of my closest colleagues at Chelsea House was Richard Fumosa, a gay man who was head of proofreading for my division. He was a remarkably genial and open individual, and I came to feel a strong friendship with him. And it is no accident that his very presence persuaded me to reassess my attitude toward gays and lesbians. I will frankly admit that, growing up in the Midwest in the 1960s and 1970s, I had unconsciously absorbed an unthinking prejudice against gay people; but Richard and others showed me how foolish and cruel this was, and I soon became ardent in my support of gay rights. I spent much time with Richard and his partner, Jim, and we got along splendidly.

As for my residence—I had secured a one-bedroom apartment at 281 Fourth Street in Jersey City, where I occupied the entire third floor of the smallish building. In all honesty, this was something of a dive—as was the city in general; but beggars can't be choosers! I remained in this place for the next six years and managed well enough. I secured lumber and cinderblocks to house my growing library (and also used the same materials to house my record collection), and even purchased a file cabinet or two so that I could organise the masses of papers that I needed for research. I was still diligently banging away on my IBM Wheelwriter, although by around 1987 Chelsea House began switching slowly to computers, and I eventually became proficient in WordPerfect.

As I was not exactly a whiz in the kitchen, I tended to get a fair amount of take-out food or other meals that were easily prepared. I latched on to a fine Chinese establishment not far from my apartment and on Sundays, as a treat, regularly indulged in their scrumptious "half fried chicken and shrimp fried rice," eating every morsel. I entertained myself not only with my books but with a television set. This had been, in late 1983, one of my first purchases from the money I had gotten from Arkham House, and the television immediately became a magnet for the other graduate students (men and women) at Princeton. It was at this time that I rediscovered my love of football—and just in time, for the Chicago Bears (who, like the other Chicago sports teams, had done very little of note since I had stopped following them in 1972) had suddenly become a formidable team. They did well in the 1984 season and even better in 1985. In fact, in January 1986 they beat the New England Patriots, 46–10, in the Super Bowl—the largest margin of victory in that game since its inception in 1967. The game was such a rout that at one point I found myself rolling on the floor in laughter as a result of some particularly clumsy blunder by the Patriots. Alas, the Bears did not return to the Super Bowl for another twenty years—and then they lost!

One of the first visitors in my new place was Leslie. I myself had visited her in Seattle in March 1984, as I obviously wished to renew my acquaintance with her. I don't recall a great many details of that first visit to Seattle, but I do remember meeting Leslie's family (her parents and her sister, two

6. Chelsea House I (1984–90)

years older than herself) and some of her friends, and being led around to the various tourist sites the city had to offer. (We did not ascend the Space Needle, however.)

After that trip, I was convinced that I was in love with her, and I wrote her a long letter to that effect. I suspect she had expected such a thing, and she replied diplomatically that, although she did not reciprocate my feelings, there was nothing better than having a friend. I had predicted such a response, so we continued writing to each other occasionally and speaking on the phone.

That fall she had entered a graduate program in English at the University of Virginia in Charlottesville, and a student was planning a road trip up to the New York area; so she chose this opportunity to visit the city, since she now had a place to stay. I believe she stayed several days, and I took her to the usual sites, including a concert at Carnegie Hall. I also took her to New Jersey, where I had been asked by Sam Moskowitz to speak at a local group of science fiction fans. I don't have much of a recollection of meeting Moskowitz, although we were friendly enough. I saw him again on only a few occasions before his death in 1997.

Leslie maintains that I actually proposed marriage to her on the visit; but oddly enough I don't recall such a thing. No doubt I was being whimsical—or, rather, I was convinced she would not accept. She genially laughed off the proposal.

Shortly after the completion of my big anthology of Shakespeare criticism, I took a well-deserved vacation—and where else would I go but back to England? Much as I had enjoyed my six-week visit of 1983, I knew there was more to see. And, what's more, it was at this time that the British pound was at an all-time low against the dollar: the pound was valued at only $1.10. Suspecting that I would purchase a great many books (and perhaps other things) on my trip, I left New York with one entirely empty suitcase; and, sure enough, I filled it to the rim with books. I not only scoured the bookshops in London—especially the incredible array of used bookstores at Charing Cross and Leicester Square—but also went to Blackwell's in Oxford and Heffer's in Cambridge. Otherwise, I stayed mostly in London—where, incidentally, I went by foot or by underground to every single one of Arthur Machen's residences in that city, which numbered more than twenty. In Oxford I looked up the noted Machenian Roger Dobson, who cordially welcomed me in his small flat.

Otherwise, I did little travelling during my early Chelsea House years.

This period of the mid- to late 1980s was really the heyday of the New Kalem Club. Peter Cannon, Ted Klein, Stefan Dziemianowicz, and I formed the core of the group, and at times we would meet separately for dinner to talk about all things relating to weird fiction. Our busy schedules did not make for frequent gatherings, however; there was one time when it took us about three months to find a mutually convenient time to get together. I was becoming increasingly impressed with Stefan's encyclopaedic knowledge of weird fiction, especially contemporary figures in the field; I may have known a bit more about Bierce, Machen, Dunsany, and Lovecraft than he, but he had it all over me where Stephen King, Peter Straub, the new sensation Clive Barker, and other writers were concerned.

I have not spoken much about the "horror boom" that began in the 1970s (or perhaps really in the late 1960s, when Ira Levin's *Rosemary's Baby* [1967] was made into a blockbuster film in 1968). I did read Blatty's *Exorcist* in high school and thought it a creditable piece of work; but I was not particularly enthused about King. Straub's *Ghost Story* (1979) was to my mind a sensational novel, but I was disappointed with his next two novels, *Shadowlands* (1980) and *Floating Dragon* (1983). I was highly sceptical of the flashy Clive Barker and did not at all think well of the "splatterpunk" movement he seemed to embody. But my admiration for Ted Klein (his full name is Theodore Donald Klein—the E. stands for nothing) was unremitting, and I devoured his novel *The Ceremonies* (1984) and his collection of four long stories, *Dark Gods* (1985), with avidity. Indeed, in 1987 I wrote an essay on "The Events at Poroth Farm"—the short story that had inspired the novel—for an issue of the British fanzine *Dagon*. This may be the first piece I wrote on contemporary weird fiction. Of course, Ramsey Campbell was in a class by himself. I had reviewed his *The Face That Must Die* (the first, and expurgated, edition of 1979)—as early as *Lovecraftian Ramblings* for October 31, 1981, and I continued to read his novels and tales as they appeared.

It may well have been Stefan's influence that led me to conceive of the founding of a journal—analogous to *Lovecraft Studies*—for the serious study of weird fiction, old and new. Marc Michaud was fully in agreement, and we began publishing *Studies in Weird Fiction* with the Summer 1986 issue. Whereas *Lovecraft Studies* bore delightful cover illustrations (many times featuring prominent Lovecraftians, including myself) by Jason C. Eckhardt, each issue of *Studies in Weird Fiction* had vivid cover art by Robert H. Knox, a splendid artist living in a remote area of New Hampshire. As with *Love-*

craft Studies, I typed the first three issues on my typewriter; thereafter, Marc used a computer. Those first three issues appeared only annually, as I had trouble securing contributions. The third issue (Fall 1988) is devoted to Donald Wandrei, who had died in October 1987. I've forgotten to mention that I had been in touch with Wandrei since the late 1970s; he would call me at random, talking nonstop on all manner of subjects without cessation. He had an incredibly sharp intellect, but he was also given to paranoia. I was rather relieved that he did not seem to object to my working with Arkham House in the preparation of my corrected edition of Lovecraft.

The friendship that both Marc and I had developed with Wandrei led to my edition of Wandrei's *Collected Poems,* issued by Necronomicon Press in 1988. I actually did not own any of Wandrei's three poetry volumes—*Ecstasy and Other Poems* (1928), *Dark Odyssey* (1931), and *Poems for Midnight* (1964), but I secured photocopies of all these books and also scoured through other books and magazines to locate uncollected poems (including several items of the *Sonnets of the Midnight Hours* sequence that Wandrei chose not to include in *Poems for Midnight*). What is more, I had been on the mailing list to receive various materials—usually broadsides against his perceived enemies, but also some recent instances of his poetry and prose—that Wandrei sent out periodically, and I culled the poems from these mailings and published them.

If my connexion to Wandrei gave me two degrees of separation from Lovecraft, my move to New York—and my friendship with Peter Cannon and Ted Klein—gave me access to someone who had known Lovecraft even better: Frank Belknap Long. We met Long, individually and collectively, frequently at this time. Frank was living with his insane wife Lyda in a cramped apartment on West 21st Street, so full of his own accumulated possessions (and probably hers as well) that it was difficult even to set foot in the place. Indeed, on one occasion Peter and I had dinner with the Longs—but we never got further than the front hallway, as they had set up a little table there and Lyda brought in the meagre meal from the kitchen. Frank was by this time in his early eighties, and his shock of white hair and high-pitched voice were unforgettable. I would try to lure him out of his claustrophobic apartment and treat him to coffee and dessert at a nearby café that he enjoyed. Every so often, after babbling on about all manner of things, he would let out some little tidbit about Lovecraft that he hadn't recorded before. Jim Turner told me that Long had written his memoir, *Howard Phillips Lovecraft: Dreamer on the Nightside* (1975), in a blinding hurry, trying to counter the negative impression of Lovecraft that was emerging in de Camp's biography, which he had read in manuscript. Turner had to do major revision and reworking of the memoir to get it into printable shape.

Now, Marc Michaud asked Long to write his own autobiography. He had submitted the first half, but I waited many months for him to turn in the second half. He at last did so, handing me a sheaf of erasable paper in which he had written (or, more properly, printed) the memoir in slanting handwriting with a pen. The result was highly disappointing, but we duly paid for and published his *Autobiographical Memoir* in 1985.

At this time several of the New York Lovecraftians got married in quick succession, and I was happy to attend their weddings—Bob Price, Peter Cannon (although his wedding was held in Lincoln, Massachusetts, where his wife's family was located), and Steve Mariconda. Steve's wedding, in New Jersey, was for me the most significant, not only for the ceremony itself but because it constituted my first face-to-face meeting with a friend and colleague who already bulked large in my horizon and would continue to do so in the decades to come—David E. Schultz.

I had been corresponding with David for a decade, and our sheaf of letters was reaching gargantuan proportions. Remember, this is long before emails and even computers! The thrill of meeting David in person was electrifying. His poor wife, Gail, had to suffer through endless hours of shoptalk as we pored over David's various ongoing projects—his annotated edition of the *Fungi from Yuggoth* and his annotated edition of the *Commonplace Book*. The latter appeared in two slim volumes from Necronomicon Press in 1987, but the former dragged on for many years, finally appearing—splendidly illustrated by Jason Eckhardt and superbly produced by Hippocampus Press—in 2017.

David tended to be a homebody, disinclined to stray from his home in Milwaukee; and aside from a few of the NecronomiCon conventions in the early 1990s, I only met him in future years whenever I found myself in the Milwaukee area. Nonetheless, he is now my closest colleague and one of my dearest friends, and it is rare that a day passes without communication from him in some form or other.

I did return to Providence whenever I needed to do research at the Hay. And of course I knew I would have to attend the World Fantasy Convention of 1986, which was again returning to Providence. I was glad to meet my old friends Marc Michaud, Jason Eckhardt, and others. Although I had tried to visit them as often as I could—and attend the annual Yuletide gatherings in Marblehead—I was inevitably drawing apart from them, given the amount of work I had to do in New York. The 1986 convention was lively for a multitude of reasons. I was happy to moderate a panel discussion, "What Is the Cthulhu Mythos?" in which Don Burleson, Bob Price, Will Murray, and David E. Schultz participated. I felt the panel was so lively and substantial that it was worth transcribing. Luckily it had been taped, and I did transcribe the thing and published it in the Spring 1987 issue of *Lovecraft Studies*. It amused me to see that a French small press became interested in translating the discussion, and it duly appeared in a little booklet (which went through several editions) under the title *Qu'est-ce-que le mythe de Cthulhu?*

Other events of that convention were a bit more problematical. Right after our panel, Randy Everts came up to me and wished me to autograph his copies of my three corrected editions of Lovecraft's fiction. Unfortunately, I did not recognise him (I think I had met him once or twice at previous events, but that had been a long time ago), and he neglected to introduce himself by name, assuming that I knew who he was. I somehow thought he was one of the organisers of the convention, one Bob Plante. So I inscribed the first two books as "To Bob"! Imagine my consternation when I saw that the third volume had already been inscribed (perhaps by the artist) "To Randy." Enlightenment dawned, so at least I signed the third volume correctly.

This was also the occasion when, at a party one evening, Randy and L. Sprague de Camp nearly got into a fistfight and had to be separated by Elliot Shorter, an immense black man who, with Faye Ringel, operated the Merlin's Closet bookstore in Providence. Randy and Sprague had bad blood on all manner of issues, and they were hurling insults right and left and almost coming to blows before the imposing Elliot made it clear that such behaviour would not be tolerated. (De Camp was almost eighty at this time, but he was still in very good physical shape.)

I think it was during this convention that some of us strolled over to St. John's Catholic Church on Atwells Avenue in Federal Hill—the site of Lovecraft's "The Haunter of the Dark." A service was in progress, and by some incredible turn of events we managed to clamber our way into the belfry of the church, where the "avatar of Nyarlathotep" was supposed to have resided. Not only that, but once we entered the cramped space we saw a very long ladder leading up to some dark chamber far above our heads. I was yearning to climb that ladder and see what lay in that night-black region, but others wisely prevented me, noting that the rather rickety ladder was unlikely to bear even my relatively light weight.

I was spending quite a lot of time with Will Murray, a multifaceted writer in the Boston area. He was becoming interested in Lovecraft from various perspectives, and I published his first article, "The Dunwich Chimera and Others" (*Lovecraft Studies,* Spring 1984). Will went on to suggest an intriguing revision of our understanding of "Arkham country"—that is, the exact real-life locales on which Lovecraft based his imaginary cities of Arkham, Dunwich, Innsmouth, and Kingsport. Will hypothesised that Lovecraft had initially placed Arkham far inland, in the central part of the state; once, while we were looking at a map of Massachusetts, we actually found a tiny village named Oakham that Will thought might have been the original Arkham. (We went to this village at some later date, although we didn't find much of interest there.) Will wrote two long articles on the subject, published in *Lovecraft Studies* for Fall 1986 and Fall 1989. I was initially persuaded by his arguments, but further research by Robert Marten has led me to feel that Will was barking up the wrong tree. Nevertheless, Will did substantial work on Lovecraft in many articles, short and long, published mostly in *Crypt of Cthulhu.*

It was around this time that Will, Bob Price, and I, in the company of others, made a trip to Boston to look up some Lovecraft sites. We of course had to head over to the North End, where "Pickman's Model" was set. We know that the actual locale for that story was long gone: Lovecraft himself had been disappointed when, a year after writing the tale, he took Donald Wandrei there and found much of the area razed. But there was still the ancient Copps Hill Burying Ground, and we made our way there. What did we find but an actual open grave! That is, there was a gravesite in the form of a rectangular box, one side of which had been pried open. As we shone a flashlight down there, we saw a short set of steps leading downward into the impenetrable abyss. Shades of "The Statement of Randolph Carter"! Bob, who had been bothered by a bad headache all day, immediately ventured down into the area—and, upon his return, claimed that the unwholesome air of the tomb had instantly relieved him of his headache. Moreover, he had come up with a prize—a piece of bone from one of the two bodies (a married couple) buried there. I was not to be outdone, so I clambered down the steps—and managed to snare a piece of vertebra from one of the remains. I had wanted a skull, but graverobbers had already pilfered both the skulls from the unfortunate tenants. Just as I was emerging from the crypt, a resident of the area strode boldly in our direction, worrying that we were out to vandalise the cemetery. (Clearly, others had done so before us.) Luckily, Bob had a paperback copy of a Lovecraft volume that contained "Pickman's

Model," and we showed the resident that we were serious scholars doing a bit of fieldwork. Meanwhile, I made sure to hide my piece of bone in my back pocket. The fellow's concerns were mollified and he left us in peace.

I was also working with Bob Price on various projects. His mother was diligently typing issue after issue of *Crypt* (which was now coming out a remarkable eight times a year, always full of lively material), but Bob wasn't satisfied. He started various spinoff magazines and enlisted me to type them: I had figured out a way whereby my trusty IBM Wheelwriter could not only print text justified on both margins but also in two columns, which was exactly the format Bob wished for his magazines. So I ended up typing the camera-ready pages for *Risqué Stories* (six issues, 1984–88), *Astro-Adventures* (seven issues, 1987–89), and random other things. Bob paid me for all this work. It amused me that I was paid for *typing* these issues but not for *writing* articles for *Crypt* or other of his magazines.

I was of course continuing to do work for Necronomicon Press. In 1985 Marc published my unabridged edition of Sonia Davis's memoir of Lovecraft, titled (by her) *The Private Life of H. P. Lovecraft*. The typescript is at the John Hay Library. Sonia wasn't much of a writer, but I felt it important to print her text as she had originally written it, rather than as it was revised and recast by Winfield Townley Scott and August Derleth. The next year we put out a slim edition of Lovecraft's *Uncollected Letters*, mostly containing letters that had been published in various magazines or newspapers during or just after his lifetime. In 1989 I persuaded Marc to issue my *Selected Papers on Lovecraft*, containing five long essays that had appeared in abridged form in *Crypt*. I arrogantly borrowed the title from the Modern Library edition of *The Selected Papers of Bertrand Russell* (1927).

March 15, 1987, was the fiftieth anniversary of Lovecraft's death. Marc and I and others of course wished to celebrate the occasion with proper obsequies, but we figured it would be a largely private affair, with as many local fans as possible. I made the trip up to Providence—but was startled to discover that the media were interested in covering the event. A local TV station (I can't recall which) interviewed me that morning on a little bench in front of the John Hay Library. I told the reporter that there would be a ceremony at the gravesite later in the day, and sure enough various camera crews showed up there also. I read Clark Ashton Smith's poignant elegy "To Howard Phillips Lovecraft"—something I can never read without choking up. A small bit of that, along with a bit of my interview earlier in the day, showed up on the local news that evening.

At the graveside event, Paul Buhle—who had retained his interest in Lovecraft—approached me and made a strong plea for a major academic or scholarly conference to commemorate the centennial of Lovecraft's birth. I agreed in principle with the idea, but wasn't certain I either wanted or was able to put together such a conference; but I would lend a hand as best I could. It was three years until 1990, so I felt we had plenty of time to decide what to do.

It was in 1987 that Robert H. Waugh and others established the H. P. Lovecraft Forum in New Paltz, New York. Initially, this event—usually held the Thursday before Hallowe'en—was simply a kind of extra session for Waugh's English students—he was a professor at the State University of New York at New Paltz—but eventually it expanded into a fairly impressive gathering. I met John Langan at an early gathering: he was then a graduate student, and I (and perhaps he) had no idea then that he would later evolve into one of the most accomplished weird fiction writers of our time. I would do my best to attend these meetings if I were in the area, and was often accompanied by Peter Cannon, Steve Mariconda, Stefan Dziemianowicz, and others.

It was in 1987 that I made a momentous decision: I would throw my hat in the ring as Official Editor of the Esoteric Order of Dagon. I had reluctantly joined the EOD in 1980 with a journal entitled *Life Is a Hideous Thing*. I carried on sporadically until 1983, when I dropped out again. In 1985 I rejoined, with the journal *What Is Anything?*, which I have kept up to the present day (usually three or four issues a year). But in 1987 Mollie Burleson was wishing to step down as Official Editor, and I figured I might capably take over the job. I won the election—but had no idea that I would continue being the Official Editor *for the next thirty years*, right up to today. At times I would get Scott Briggs to help me assemble the mailings—either in the conference room at Chelsea House or (after 1993) at my Manhattan co-op, where we would spread the various magazines on the floor and collate them. It is a tedious but vital function, as much sound scholarship still emerges out of the EOD.

By the mid-1980s I was rapidly becoming interested in weird fiction beyond (or, rather, before) Lovecraft, although in many ways my interest was restricted to those who had influenced Lovecraft directly or indirectly. In particular, the "modern masters" whom he had identified in "Supernatural Horror in Literature" (Arthur Machen, Lord Dunsany, Algernon Blackwood, and M. R. James) were of consuming interest—well, at least the first three. The difficulty was actually finding their books. I secured a fair number of Machen titles either at conventions or from the Strand Bookstore at Broadway and 12th Street, which at the time still had a fair number of used copies of the old yellow-bound Knopf editions of Machen that had appeared in the 1920s. Indeed, for a long time the most notable book in my library was Machen's *Ornaments in Jade* (Knopf, 1924), all 1000 copies of which were autographed by Machen and which I obtained somewhere for $60. I had a fair Dunsany collection, consisting of the standard American editions of his early works (mostly published by John W. Luce) and some of his novels and plays. Of Blackwood I had very little. For James, all one needed was the *Collected Ghost Stories* and a few other ancillary volumes.

But now, by a felicitous bit of timing, I was in a position to augment my collection substantially. I had somehow gotten in touch with a British book dealer, Ben Bass, who worked out of Bristol. Bass now began offering me first dibs on any copies of books by Machen, Dunsany, and Blackwood that I did not have. I leapt at his offer, given that the prices he was offering were remarkably low. I usually would wait until I had accumulated a certain quantity of titles; then I would head over to Rockefeller Center, where a money exchange establishment would cut a check in British pounds for a small fee (about $7.50). I would mail the check to Bass, and in due course of time the books would come. After about a year or two, I had a nearly complete collection of the writers in question.

The chance to write about these figures providentially emerged at this time. Darrell Schweitzer was compiling anthologies of criticism on classic and contemporary horror and fantasy writers for Starmont House, and I readily accepted his invitation to write long pieces on Arthur Machen and Lord Dunsany. I believe I wrote these articles in 1987 or 1988, but the anthologies were delayed, so I published my Machen piece in *Studies in Weird Fiction* (Summer 1987). It finally appeared in *Discovering Classic Horror Fiction I* in 1992. Schweitzer's other anthology—*Discovering Classic Fantasy Fiction*—was delayed even longer, not appearing until 1996. But by then, both these chapters had appeared in one of my books, as I shall recount shortly.

I of course couldn't get away from Lovecraft, and in the late 1980s David E. Schultz persuaded me to tackle a project that I had put off for years because of the sheer scale of the undertaking: the transcription of Lovecraft's letters. At this point there wasn't even any thought of actually publishing these documents; but it was already evident that there was a gold mine of largely untapped information about Lovecraft in the letters, and that to obtain and transcribe them was a vital mission.

The project began almost accidentally. David had acquired a microfilm of Lovecraft's letters to August Derleth, housed at the State Historical Society of Wisconsin (now the Wisconsin Historical Society) in Madison. But what to do with a microfilm? David of course didn't have his own microfilm reader, although for a time we seriously thought about purchasing one for ourselves. David eventually sent the microfilm to me: since I was going to libraries frequently, I might be able to print out the entire microfilm little by little over the course of time, although the expense of doing so would be considerable. Quite frankly, I was already doing quite a lot of my own research and even writing on company time, but no one at Chelsea House seemed to care so long as I turned in my projects on time.

Once I got the microfilm, I headed over to New York University Library, as the closest library to both my home and my office. And here was another providential event: by some quirk, the particular microfilm reader I chose was malfunctioning to the extent of *allowing me to print an unlimited number of copies without putting any money in the machine!* Holy mackerel! The result was that I printed out more than 1000 pages of the microfilm (containing not only letters to Derleth but letters to his mother and other random individuals) for a fraction of what it would have cost.

I mailed the printouts to David, and he began typing them up. Of course, this was long before scanners—and even a scanner would not have been very helpful in deciphering Lovecraft's handwriting. The only solution was brute manual typing. Meanwhile, I had requested copies of other batches of Lovecraft letters from the John Hay Library, including his voluminous letters to his two aunts, Lillian D. Clark and Annie E. P. Gamwell. Over the course of many months, I typed these letters—which came to more than 400,000 words (the letters just from his New York period—1924–26—were themselves about 250,000 words). Of course, some batches of letters were in other institutions: the library of Indiana University had the five letters to Vincent Starrett; the New York Public Library had the letters to Richard Ely Morse and perhaps some others; and so on.

An immense treasure-trove of Lovecraft letters of course resided in the so-called Arkham House Transcripts (AHT)—a set of about 100 bound typescripts (ranging anywhere from 30 pages to more than 100 pages) that Arkham House's secretary, Alice Conger, had prepared as letters by Lovecraft came in over the years and decades from all manner of correspondents. It is only here, for example, that the original letters to Robert E. Howard survive; Dr. I. M. Howard had unwittingly destroyed the letters in the

1940s. AHT is also the only place where letters to such correspondents as Woodburn Harris, Bernard Austin Dwyer, and others could be found; even some letters to Lillian D. Clark (including the letter of March 9, 1924, announcing his marriage to Sonia), which should have been returned to the Hay after Derleth had borrowed them, can be found only in AHT. And of course AHT habitually abridged the letters, and at times the transcripts did not seem entirely accurate. Nevertheless, they were all we had in some cases.

The John Hay Library luckily acquired Donald Wandrei's set of AHT after his death, and so we finally had access to these invaluable documents. I cannot recall when this occurred—it was either in the late 1980s or early 1990s. Anyway, David and I made repeated trips to the Hay to pore over these and other items. For the time being, however, this research was not designed for publication; but that would change in a few years.

In 1988 my translation of Maurice Lévy's book finally appeared as *Lovecraft: A Study in the Fantastic*. As I've mentioned, I had finished the basic translation as early as the summer of 1977, but made few efforts to find a publisher. Then, around 1980, Frederick Ungar Publishing Company seemed seriously interested—but something happened at the last minute, and they had to decline the book. I felt rather crestfallen at this turn of events and simply set the book aside. Then, around 1987, I made a renewed effort to find a suitable academic publisher—and within weeks Wayne State University Press in Detroit had accepted the book. I was concerned that my English translation was a bit stiff and wooden, and I hoped that Wayne State had a good copy editor to iron out any awkwardnesses in my prose; sure enough, some person whose name I have forgotten did exactly that, and the book came out and was welcomed by both the academic and the specialty press.

In 1988 I went to England for the third time in five years, this time in the company of Will Murray. We were planning on attending the World Fantasy Convention in London; but it made no sense to make such a long trip for only a few days, so we spent at least a week in England. I looked forward to renewing my acquaintance with England's great museums in London (British Museum, Wallace Collection), Oxford (Ashmolean), and elsewhere. Will, however, became a bit fatigued by this museum-hopping and eventually went off on his own. The convention itself was unremarkable. I remember a kind of weird fiction contest between some Americans (including Will, myself, and others) and some Englishmen, with Mike Ashley as the moderator. I made some embarrassing blunders that may have cost our side the victory, but I don't imagine anyone really cared.

Jim Turner commissioned me to prepare a new edition of *The Horror in the Museum and Other Revisions* (1970), which would mean that the great bulk of Lovecraft's fiction—original and ghostwritten—would now be available in corrected editions. With Wandrei now dead, we decided to abandon the charade that we were preparing merely a "corrected printing" (although in fact my edition still bears this designation), and we recast the whole volume to distinguish between those stories that Lovecraft ghostwrote entirely or nearly entirely (which we called "primary revisions") and those where he merely touched up—even if extensively—a pre-existing draft (which we called "secondary revisions"). We also took note of several "new" revisions that had emerged through research by myself and others, including "The Trap," "The Night Ocean," two stories by Duane W. Rimel, and others.

The result was a splendid new edition of *The Horror in the Museum* that came out in 1989. It was here that "The Mound" and "Medusa's Coil"—which Derleth had extensively rewritten after Lovecraft's death in an attempt to make them acceptable to pulp markets—were at last printed in unadulterated form. I don't know that the book made any great splash, but I figured the Lovecraft community was suitably appreciative.

Meanwhile, things were not going so well at my office. Following the stock market's mini-crash in October 1987, I was summoned to the office of the president of Chelsea House, Philip Cohen, and given the unfortunate news that my division was being all but liquidated: only Richard Fumosa and I would be retained, and my entire staff would be let go. This staff now included Patrick and Teresa Nielsen Hayden, who had a formidable knowledge of science fiction and who have now gone on to do distinguished work in that field; Patrick has long been an editor at Tor. I was profoundly shaken by this turn of events, but at least I still had a job. As it happened, our immense series of volumes of reprinted literary criticism were coming to an end, and I spent months preparing the final volumes—which comprised an index and also a "bibliographical supplement" in which I presented huge lists of the book publications by the various authors we had covered in the series. This is actually a rather impressive work of scholarship, if I do say so myself, even though no one has apparently paid the slightest attention to it.

Richard and I carried on bravely. A new, smaller-scale literary criticism series called *Major Literary Characters* was begun, still under the nominal general editorship of Harold Bloom. This was an innovative conception, and I recall having a pretty free hand in compiling an interesting volume on the various treatments of Cleopatra in literature, from antiquity to the present day.

6. Chelsea House I (1984–90)

A bit later, my personal life would undergo similar turmoil. I had been maintaining sporadic contact with Leslie via letter and telephone, but I decided to come out to Seattle to visit her again in March of 1989—and I coincidentally arranged to appear on a panel at Norwescon, a long-running science fiction convention in the area. This panel was, in fact, a kind of pro- and anti-Lovecraft discussion, with me as the "pro" and the redoubtable and venerable L. Sprague de Camp as the "anti." By this time I had come to recognise the deficiencies of his biography, although I was not vociferous in condemning it as Dirk Mosig and others were. So we were on reasonably cordial terms. The panel was a lively affair—made a bit more lively by my having imprudently drunk a large cup of coffee earlier in the day, making me a bit wired. If I may say so, I mopped the floor with de Camp—but did so without offending him, and we remained friends.

I also forced Leslie to accept several presents, including a CD player: she had never before sampled this still new technology, and I bought her one and also a few CDs to go with it (including my favourite recording of Handel's *Messiah* [Colin Davis conducting the London Symphony] and the first album of the rock band Boston). She chided me for my excessive generosity, but accepted my gifts with good grace. Remember that we were still "just friends," with no idea of anything more being (openly) contemplated.

Then something odd seemed to happen. Almost as soon as I came home, we both began writing to each other *every day*. In those days of snail-mail communication, we had to experience the cognitive dissonance of writing replies to letters written several days earlier, but we managed. I poured out my life story in letter after letter, and she did something similar on a rather lesser scale. Over the course of months we essentially became engaged by correspondence, although nothing explicit was ever stated (or written) on the matter. Leslie, who was now in a library science program at the University of Washington, agreed to come and visit me in the middle of June for a week, to see if we could be compatible in an actual living situation.

The time for her arrival finally came, and we had a splendid time. I of course took that week off from work, although on one occasion I brought Leslie to the office to show her off and also to have a big lunch with many of my office mates. I can't even remember what else we did during that week, but our time was full with innumerable activities. (Mercifully, I had eliminated the pestiferous cockroaches that for years had plagued my wretched apartment in Jersey City by the use of Combat, which solved the problem in short order.)

Leslie returned to Seattle, with a promise to return for a six-week period later in the summer. She had managed to secure an internship at the New York Public Library, and this visit would more accurately replicate what it would be like to live together, since we would both be working at our respective jobs. Unfortunately, this visit proved to be an unmitigated disaster. Because I had spent so much time writing letters to Leslie, I had neglected some pressing literary work that I had to finish (for which see below); so, after a hard day's work at the office, I came home and spent most of the evening scribbling away on these projects without paying her the slightest attention. She later admitted that she had been too shy to make any objections, and so she suffered in silence. (I'm not sure I could have accommodated any pleas to be more solicitous of her, since I really did have to finish these projects in short order.) The end result was that, at the end of the six-week fiasco, we had all but decided we were no longer engaged.

But the matter was not definitive. I was now set to come out to Seattle in late October to attend the World Fantasy Convention to be held there. That trip was also pretty much of a disaster, and we formally decided what had long been evident—it would be best if we were to go our separate ways. I think the chief difficulty for Leslie was her reluctance to be torn away from the comfort of her hometown and her family for a part of the country that did not truly suit her—she was never comfortable with the pace of life in New York, and my dreadful little apartment in Jersey City was not exactly a place one could truly call home. On my side, I seemed pretty wedded to remaining in the New York area—in any case, I did not then have any genuine idea of what other kind of job I could hold down except one in publishing.

But really speaking, I at least was not emotionally prepared for marriage—or for any kind of intimate relationship. I was too devoted to my work, too intolerant of others' opinions or ways of living that diverged from my own, and in many other ways was unfit for cohabitation even with a roommate, let alone with a spouse. So our parting of the ways was surely for the best.

Nevertheless, I felt very bitter at this turn of events, and I ceased all communication with Leslie. I retreated into myself and plunged even more vigorously into work. Is that the reason why I had three major books and three lesser titles come out in 1990?

The first of the major books was nothing less than a return to my first literary love—the detective story. I had long wished to write a critical study of my favourite detective writer, John Dickson Carr, and to that end I had secured every one of his published books, which ranged more than eighty in number (one of these I had to obtain as a photocopy from a library). I even acquired some unreprinted stories that Carr had published in the *Haverfordian,* the literary magazine at Haverford College. I queried the Bowling Green State University Popular Press, which published many books on this subject, if they were interested, and they were. I spent about five months in 1988 reading the entirety of Carr's works and then a month in early 1989 in writing the book. It came out as *John Dickson Carr: A Critical Study* (1990). It was, of course, the first true book on Carr, although some minor pamphlets had appeared earlier. Some years later, when Douglas G. Greene published his lengthy biography of Carr, he cited me frequently—including my startling assertion that *The Arabian Nights Murder* (1936) was "the greatest pure detective story ever written"!

A project more in line with the dominant trend of my literary work was *The Weird Tale.* Having written lengthy essays on Machen and Dunsany, I felt it incumbent upon me to write essays on Lovecraft's two other "modern masters," Algernon Blackwood and M. R. James. Then I added an essay on Ambrose Bierce and one on Lovecraft himself. An introduction outlined what I felt to be an innovative theory about weird fiction: that it was *"the consequence of a worldview."* In other words, by studying the philosophical thought of the writers in question, it was possible to read their fiction as direct instantiations of their worldviews—for Machen, a hostility to science and a need to preserve a sense of mystery in the universe; for Dunsany, a sense of the primacy of the natural world; for Blackwood, a mystical desire to expand one's consciousness; for Bierce, a satirical display of human foibles in the face of war or terror; for Lovecraft, an exposition of a mechanistic and atheistic universe.

I still believe my theory works well for the authors in question—and perhaps for some others—but it does not truly hold up as a general theory of weird fiction. This may in part be because we don't have much information on the philosophical thought of other weird writers, but even if we had that information my theory may not hold up. Still, I think the book came out rather well. Mike Ashley, the leading authority on Blackwood whose biobibliography (Greenwood Press, 1987) I extensively used for my chapter on that writer, flattered me by saying that my long chapter on Blackwood was the best analysis written up to that time. (Regrettably, not much more about Blackwood—one of the true giants of weird fiction—has appeared since then, aside from Ashley's splendid 2001 biography.) My chapter on Bierce was rather workmanlike, focusing on how he revised his two major collections of weird fiction, *Tales of Soldiers and Civilians* (1891) and *Can Such Things Be?* (1893), to reflect the critical distinction between supernatural and psychological horror. My Lovecraft chapter was my first attempt to portray the full range of Lovecraft's philosophical views and the infusion of those ideas in his fiction.

I was pleased that the book was readily accepted by the University of Texas Press. It came out in 1990 and, I believe, garnered fairly good reviews (with a few annoying exceptions) in both the academic and the specialty press. Mary Elizabeth Grenander, a leading authority on Bierce, reviewed the book charitably in the prestigious academic journal *American Literature,* although criticising some aspects of my chapter on Bierce. It also got nice reviews in *Locus, Interzone,* and other fantasy and science fiction journals. It was also nominated for a World Fantasy Award ("Special Award: Professional"), but did not win the award. I like to think this book has stood the test of time, as it continues to be cited by other scholars on the authors in question.

My third major book was an expansion of the Lovecraft chapter into a full-length book. Ted Dikty of Starmont House had wished me to write some new book about Lovecraft to commemorate the centennial of his birth, and I could think of no better subject than a full-scale philosophical analysis of Lovecraft. By this time I felt I had learned enough about philosophy in general and Lovecraft's philosophy in particular to write such a book adequately; but I ended up doing considerable additional background research in such areas as aesthetics, the history of racism in America, and the like. The result was *H. P. Lovecraft: The Decline of the West.* It was this book that I was breaking my back writing during that sad time that Leslie was sharing living space with me in Jersey City. I was actually typing up the book on a primitive computer that Leslie had lent me; and by the time I finished (I handed the disks to Dikty in person at the World Fantasy Convention), I stated confidently that the book had come in at about 75,000 words. After I'd returned home, Dikty called me, complaining that the book was, in fact, about 125,000 words. Yikes! He agreed to publish the book as it was, but had to publish it in an oversize paperback edition in two columns—which Steve Mariconda, in a review in *Lovecraft Studies,* rightly says "reminds us of a workbook." Because of its rather technical subject-matter, the book was not widely reviewed; but I trust the Lovecraft community appreciated the effort that went into it.

The lesser books I published in 1990 don't deserve much attention: they were all slim editions of Lovecraft that came out from Necronomicon Press and were clearly meant to capitalise on the impending centennial celebrations. The first was a selection of Lovecraft's own articles from the *Conservative,* as a way of replacing Marc's cumbersome and crudely printed complete editions of 1976 and 1977 (but a complete facsimile reprint of this amateur journal would still be a welcome publication). The second was a reasonably definitive edition of Lovecraft's *Fantastic Poetry* (the revised edition of 1993 added an unreprinted poem, "The Unknown," which Lovecraft had published in the *Conservative* under Winifred V. Jackson's pseudonym, Elizabeth Berkeley). The third was a very short (32 pp.) edition of Lovecraft's *Letters to Henry Kuttner.* David E. Schultz had obtained copies of these letters from the August Derleth Papers (all were transcripts from AHT except for one original letter). This humble volume set the stage for the many other editions of Lovecraft's letters that David and I were to assemble in the coming years and decades.

But issuing publications was not the only or even the most important thing the Lovecraft community was focused on. Rather, we were looking forward to no less auspicious event than the H. P. Lovecraft Centennial Conference.

S. T. and Fritz Leiber at Lovecraft panel, Iguanacon (Phoenix), September 1978

Crispin Burnham, Keith Daniels (standing), Donald R. Burleson, Bob Eber, Will Hart (standing), S. T., and Dirk W. Mosig at Iguanacon

S. T., Ken Neily, Donald R. Burleson, Marc A. Michaud, and Jason Eckhardt at H. P. Lovecraft's gravesite, c. 1979

Charles Hoffman, Robert M. Price, [unidentified], Marc A. Cerasini, S. T., Sam Gafford, and Peter Cannon in New York, c. 1983

Will Murray, Jennifer B. Lee, Jon Cooke, and S. T. at H. P. Lovecraft Memorial Plaque, John Hay Library, Brown University, August 20, 1990

Gail Schultz, David E. Schultz, S. T., Scott Briggs, and Hubert Van Calenbergh at NecronomiCon, Providence, R.I., 1993

Ramsey Campbell and S. T., NecronomiCon (Providence, R.I.), 1995

T. E. D. Klein and S. T. in New York, April 2003

7. Chelsea House II (1990–95)

> ". . . neither the caucus, nor the newspaper, nor the Congress, nor the mob, nor the guillotine, nor fire, nor all together, can avail to outlaw, cut out, burn or destroy the offence of superiority in persons."—Ralph Waldo Emerson

The commemoration of Lovecraft's centennial was in full swing well before 1990. Peter Cannon, who had been chosen to write the Lovecraft volume for Twayne's United States Authors series, produced a fine monograph in 1989. Don Burleson—who had already written what was in effect his own Twayne book, *H. P. Lovecraft: A Critical Study* (Greenwood Press, 1983), which to my mind remains one of the best introductory guides to Lovecraft—came out with a challenging deconstructionist study, *Lovecraft: Disturbing the Universe* (University Press of Kentucky, 1990). And, of course, from a popular perspective there was Robert E. Weinberg's anthology of Lovecraftian stories, *Lovecraft's Legacy* (Tor, 1990), and other such volumes. Perhaps we can even include James Turner's revision of August Derleth's *Tales of the Cthulhu Mythos* (1989), although this was in fact designed to commemorate the fiftieth anniversary of the establishment of Arkham House.

But we Lovecraftians recognised that a formal conference, preferably with academic support, would be vital to the augmentation of Lovecraft's recognition. Unsurprisingly, Brown University agreed to hold the conference, so all that was needed was to arrange the event. That was, of course, more easily said than done, especially as I was living 200 miles from Providence. I frankly used a great many of the resources of Chelsea House—their mail service as well as their phones to make long-distance calls—in the course of the onerous work to set up the conference.

Matters were not aided by the fact that, sometime that summer, I finally moved from the Jersey City apartment I had occupied for six years to a rather smaller but nicer apartment at 607 First Street in the neighbouring city of Hoboken. I persuaded Richard Fumosa, his partner Jim, and a freelance proofreader, Jerry Aliotta, to help me with moving my books, records, furniture, and other possessions into the place. Afterward, as a reward, I treated them to a nice dinner at an Italian restaurant only two doors down the street—which had all the charming earmarks of a Mafia hangout.

I believe it was in June that I was asked to participate in an Italian Lovecraft conference. Actually, this was only a part of a film convention on what the Italians call *giallo* (film noir), sponsored by Italy's leading publisher, Arnoldo Mondadori. Even though I was to speak only on one three-hour panel discussion on Lovecraft, Mondadori paid my expenses to stay for the entire six days of the convention. It was held in Cattolica, a beach resort on the Adriatic. I managed to take day-trips to Florence (where I canvassed the Uffizi thoroughly) and Venice (where the Lovecraft scholar Claudio De Nardi led me to some of the obscurer byways of the city that most tourists would not have known about). I also met Sebastiano Fusco, another leading Lovecraft scholar; he did not speak English and my Italian was pretty poor, so we managed to communicate after a fashion in French. Giuseppe Lippi was there also; he was in the process of publishing my corrected texts of Lovecraft in a four-volume Italian translation, *Tutti i racconti* (Mondadori, 1989–92), for which I received a fee almost four times what Arkham House had paid me.

But the centennial conference was the prime event of that summer. I worked closely with Jennifer B. Lee, a librarian at the John Hay Library, to plan the various panels and other events that would occur during the weekend of August 17–19. I laid out a series of six panels, filling them with those whom I considered most suitable for the given topic. But at this point, Jennifer intervened by maintaining that the panels were insufficiently filled with academicians. She then went to the extent of disinviting some of the non-academic participants I had chosen (including people like Steve Mariconda and Peter Cannon) and adding some professors. At this point I nearly revolted, stating that I would back out of the whole enterprise if my chosen participants were not re-invited. After some tense moments, Jennifer relented and let the participants back in; but she wished to retain the academic guests. This proved to be rather a mixed blessing, for one of them—John L. McInnis III, who had written a Ph.D. dissertation on Lovecraft (the first in English) and was a professor somewhere in Louisiana—was a rather odd individual whose long, droning presentation took far longer than it should have and robbed other panelists of their rightful amount of time.

Otherwise, all the panels were lively and provocative, and we created

7. Chelsea House II (1990–95)

something of a sensation by presenting a surprise guest at the end of the "Lovecraft's Life and Times" panel—none other than the ancient Frank Belknap Long, now a full eighty-nine years old. The unenviable task of ferrying him and his wife Lyda up from New York was bestowed upon Stefan Dziemianowicz (with assistance from Scott Briggs), who loaded them into a minivan and had to endure Lyda's customary insanity all the way along the drive to Providence. But the presence of the frail, white-haired, wheelchair-bound Long was a touching moment.

Overall, the conference went splendidly. I also arranged for walking tours of Lovecraft's Providence and led at least one of the tours myself. A reporter later noted that I basically sprinted through the tour, leaving some of the slower or older members in the lurch. Well, I had a lot of ground to cover in a single hour! Anyway, I was by then so used to a New Yorker's rapid pace that I did not feel I was doing anything particularly out of the ordinary. A special treat was the premiere of Brian Yuzna's film *Bride of Re-Animator,* which was shown at the Avon Cinema. I found it a scream and enjoyed it hugely. It was not commercially released until the following year.

I myself did not appear on a panel as such, although I moderated the final one, "A Reassessment of Lovecraft's Legacy." I reserved my presentation for the concluding address. I had written a part of this at home, stressing the long line of individuals—beginning with R. H. Barlow and proceeding through August Derleth, Dirk Mosig, and others—who had been instrumental in Lovecraft's attainment of his worldwide fame. But I wished to begin the address by a kind of summary of the panels we had heard over the past two days, and I found myself scribbling this in the stifling heat of an un-airconditioned Brown University dorm room that Sunday morning. Providence in August is never pleasant, and the heat that descended upon us all weekend was insufferable; the best that Brown could do was to provide us with some fans for meagre and inadequate relief. I believe I wrote much of my address in my underwear. But my delivery seemed to go across pretty well; Don Burleson later told me he choked up at the end of it.

On Monday, August 20—the actual day of Lovecraft's centennial—there was a quaint ceremony to set up a plaque commemorating Lovecraft. This was the result of a several-month campaign to raise funds (about $6000) for the purchase of a headstone and the plaque itself. A local weird fiction fan named Jon Cooke led the venture, with assistance from Will Murray and myself. We called ourselves the Friends of H. P. Lovecraft. Incredibly, we raised the money in a matter of months, gathering contributions from all manner of notables in our field, including Robert Bloch, Ramsey Campbell, Hugh B. Cave, Fred Chappell, Les Daniels, L. Sprague de Camp, Harlan Ellison, Ted Klein, Giuseppe Lippi, Sam Moskowitz, Wilum Pugmire, Barton L. St. Armand, Darrell Schweitzer, Peter Straub, Richard L. Tierney, Chet Williamson, Douglas E. Winter, and many others. I say this is incredible because, more than a decade earlier, Dirk Mosig had attempted to raise a far smaller sum (about $1200) for the erection of headstones for Lovecraft and his mother at his plot in Swan Point Cemetery, and that effort took several years (I contributed all of $10 to that venture).

We had hoped that the plaque would be set up in some public place in Providence, but our negotiations with city officials proved somewhat frustrating. Thankfully, Brown University came to the rescue and agreed to have the plaque set up in the front garden of the John Hay Library. I chose the quotation from the octet of Lovecraft's "Background" (*Fungi from Yuggoth* XXX), which specifically notes his devotion to his native city. The ceremony was widely attended and covered in the press, and numerous photographs of the event are now available online.

I knew that I wanted to preserve the more significant elements of the centennial conference in a more permanent form, especially the panels. We had taped every panel, and I secured these tapes and began the thankless job of transcribing them. Naturally, the translation of the spoken word to the written word is not a simple task, and I did my best to smooth out the various presentations without losing their character as extemporaneous, free-flowing discussions. (I had specifically asked the panelists not to write out their presentations ahead of time, although I believe McInnis and a few others did so anyway.) I also transcribed some of the more interesting discussions that occurred after each panel. This whole job took months, and it took additional time to send the transcripts to the panelists so that they could check them over and make revisions where necessary. But in the end we produced a nice and rather substantial booklet, *The H. P. Lovecraft Centennial Conference: Proceedings* (Necronomicon Press, 1991).

Books at Brown, the distinguished occasional periodical produced by the Brown University Library, then decided to present a selection of the presentations in a special issue. John H. Stanley was in charge of this process, and he did a fine job—but, in the midst of all his other work, the issue did not come out until 1995, even though it was dated 1991–92. This may have been, in fact, the very last issue of *Books at Brown,* as the magazine was simply too expensive to continue with the limited budget that the library received.

7. Chelsea House II (1990–95)

Aside from my own publications, I had been collaborating with David E. Schultz on a *festschrift* that would present cutting-edge scholarship on Lovecraft. This book was also a bit delayed, but when it finally appeared it was well worth the wait: *An Epicure in the Terrible: A Centennial Anthology of Essays in Honor of H. P. Lovecraft* (Fairleigh Dickinson University Press, 1991). Every one of the thirteen contributors (not counting my lengthy biocritical introduction) did a splendid job. I was particularly taken with Jason Eckhardt's essay "The Cosmic Yankee," a brilliant analysis of Lovecraft's use of his New England heritage in his stories. I frequently urged Jason to write a full-scale monograph on the subject; and although he seemed to take extensive notes for such a project, he never generated the monograph. A great shame! Don Burleson's "On Lovecraft's Themes: Touching the Glass" rivals Fritz Leiber's "A Literary Copernicus" as the single most perspicacious overview of the central motifs in Lovecraft's fiction. And David's essay introduces the provocative notion that the Cthulhu Mythos is an "anti-mythology"—a concept I have cited frequently in my own work (so frequently, indeed, that some scholars have attributed the idea to me, even though I have always acknowledged David's origination of the idea).

One paper, Kenneth W. Faig, Jr.'s "The Parents of Howard Phillips Lovecraft," is of interest. When we invited Ken to write the piece, he eventually obliged—by producing a mammoth, 100-page (single-spaced) document! Naturally, we couldn't possibly publish such a lengthy piece; so David sent it to me to whittle down to size. After waking up from my faint, I undertook the task—going through at least five stages of revision and pruning until I got it down to a manageable length. It was a brilliant piece of writing, although with a certain repetitiveness that would need to have been pruned in any event. We felt bad about having to cut out so much interesting but not strictly essential material, but Marc Michaud came to our rescue and published the document more or less in full. This actually came out ahead of our book, as *The Parents of Howard Phillips Lovecraft* (Necronomicon Press, 1990).

After the conference, I think the Lovecraft community collectively suffered a certain amount of exhaustion. The decade and a half from 1975 to 1990 had been an unprecedented period in the history of Lovecraft studies, and the work by many fans and scholars had revolutionised our understanding of the dreamer from Providence. Not only had we overturned numerous myths about Lovecraft's life and work (notably the incredibly erroneous views of the Cthulhu Mythos spouted over a lifetime by August Derleth), but there had been a marked accession in Lovecraft's general reputation. A single indication, among many, of this development was a capsule review in *American Literature* of Burleson's *Disturbing the Universe:* "It's getting to where those who still ignore Lovecraft will have to go on the defensive." (This was the entire review.) No more was Lovecraft regarded (and scorned) as a pulp hack; his ascension into the canon of American literature was looking more and more likely, while his popular appeal had never ceased to increase since the time of the Ballantine paperback editions of the late 1960s.

The question was: where do we go from here? In the short term, David and I focused on our ongoing work on Lovecraft's letters, which we correctly recognised was something of a "final frontier" in Lovecraft studies. The dissemination of these letters was vital to a full understanding of Lovecraft, and we realised that the only feasible way to issue them was to publish all the surviving letters to a given correspondent. (One of the many reasons why it took nearly forty years for Arkham House to publish the five-volume *Selected Letters*, which were arranged chronologically, was that the editors kept receiving new batches of letters that disturbed the chronological sequence, forcing them to revise the volumes over and over again.) David and I issued the *Letters to Richard F. Searight* (1992), *Letters to Robert Bloch* (1993), and *Letters to Samuel Loveman and Vincent Starrett* (1994) with Necronomicon Press. These volumes were sound enough in their way, although the Bloch volume was a bit of an embarrassment. The manuscripts of these letters had been sold to a book dealer, Erik Kramer of Fantasy Archives, who then sold them individually (in some instances selling only random sheets of a particularly long letter to different purchasers). Luckily, he (or someone) had made photocopies of the entire batch before the letters were sold. We acquired these photocopies and proceeded with our edition; but we noticed that some letters appeared to be missing. We figured they had been lost—but were dismayed when Bob Price came up to us at a convention and said, "Oh, yeah, I have those missing letters!" David and I were forced to issue an absurd little "supplement" to the letters containing these additional documents. To add insult to injury, the print shop where Marc was storing copies of the edition was flooded and many copies were damaged. For years we hoped to publish a complete edition of the letters, with the formerly missing ones in their proper place; but that opportunity did not arise until 2016.

The letters to Samuel Loveman (only a small fraction of what had once existed) were provided by Mara Kirk Hart, one of the two daughters of Lovecraft's friend George W. Kirk and his wife, Lucile Dvorak. Mara got in touch with me sometime in 1993, and we have remained in sporadic touch ever since. She and her sister made frequent trips to New York during my stay there, and it was always a pleasure to meet them.

But my attention was turning toward other weird writers, both old and new. Almost immediately after I had finished *The Weird Tale*, I had begun planning a follow-up volume, *The Modern Weird Tale*. The central issue was: which authors would I cover? Who were the most significant writers of weird fiction after Lovecraft? I knew I would devote major space to such figures as Shirley Jackson and Ramsey Campbell, and I knew that there was no avoiding discussion of such bestselling writers as Stephen King, Peter Straub, Clive Barker, and Anne Rice; but beyond that, my understanding of contemporary horror fiction was weak at best.

It was at this point that Stefan Dziemianowicz stepped in. He had already been writing numerous articles and reviews on recent weird writers in *Studies in Weird Fiction*, and through frequent meetings of the New Kalem Club and elsewhere he undertook to tutor me on the leading figures in the field. It was Stefan who, to his eternal praise, led me to Thomas Ligotti. The funny thing was that I had received a review copy of Ligotti's first book, *Songs of a Dead Dreamer* (Silver Scarab Press, 1986); but I had passed off this rather shoddily printed book as merely an instance of the "fan fiction" I so despised. I had in fact casually given my copy to Steve Mariconda. But Stefan made it clear to me that Ligotti was the real thing—and I came to that realisation myself when I read the revised *Songs of a Dead Dreamer* (Robinson, 1989). This was the first book of weird fiction in many years that gave me a true *frisson*, and I became convinced that Ligotti, with Campbell and Ted Klein, comprised a triumvirate of supremely talented littérateurs in contrast to the bestselling trio of King, Barker, and Rice (Straub, while also a bestseller, was a cut above that level).

Stefan may also have turned me on to Robert Aickman. At that time Aickman's work was pretty hard to find, and I was immensely grateful to a mutual friend, Jay Gregory (who had known Aickman), who lent me copies of some British editions of his books. I had to read some books—including his curious but delicate novel of lesbianism, *The Late Breakfasters* (1964)—at the New York Public Library. I suspect it was Stefan who alerted me to the work of Dennis Etchison and David J. Schow. I also wrote chapters on William Peter Blatty, Les Daniels, Thomas Tryon, Thomas Harris, and a few others.

The end result, however, was that *The Modern Weird Tale* ended up being in excess of 600 double-spaced pages (150,000 words or more). The book was basically finished by 1992, and so I began the thankless task of finding a publisher. You would think that the University of Texas Press, which had published *The Weird Tale,* would be interested; but evidently the publisher was not satisfied with the sales of that book, although I thought that they were respectable (it went through both a hardcover and a paperback edition). At this point I cannot recall if my editor actually read the book and rejected it or didn't even ask to read the book; I believe it was the latter.

So who else was there? Somehow I stumbled upon Southern Illinois University Press. The publisher did ask to see the manuscript, and after several months an editor reported that, although he was impressed with the book, it was much too long. He required that I cut it down by some percentage that I have forgotten; but when I asked whether, after doing so, I would be guaranteed acceptance, the editor said no: the book would still have to go through the usual review process, including evaluation by outside experts. I was not prepared to spend the time and effort to make major cuts (which would have required cutting whole chapters, along with portions of other chapters) for so tenuous a result. So I pulled the book from the publisher's consideration.

Some years later, Robert Reginald, who was operating Borgo Press—which had taken over Starmont House's line of critical studies of fantasy and science fiction authors—accepted the book and actually set it up in type (I have retained a photocopy of the proofs); but just at this time (around 1996 or 1997), Reginald experienced some financial difficulties and had to back out of the project. And so *The Modern Weird Tale* languished unpublished.

One significant effect of my working on contemporary weird writers was my realisation that a venue was needed to cover the increasing number of weird books coming out. I had already been devoting more and more space in *Studies in Weird Fiction* to reviews of these titles, but that space was rapidly proving inadequate. So Stefan Dziemianowicz and I proposed to Marc to publish a separate review journal to cover contemporary weird fiction. This is how *Necrofile* was born. Once the idea of the journal was determined, we had to come up with a name; and I recall a long drive through New England in which Stefan, Marc, I, and others threw out all manner of plausible and absurd names for the journal—including things like *Dead on Arrival*—until, after several hours, we somehow came up with *Necrofile.*

The thirty-two issues of *Necrofile* over the course of its life (1991–99) were, I think, a fairly impressive achievement. The issues were pure text—

nothing but reviews and a few columns. We were immensely lucky in persuading Ramsey Campbell to write a column for each issue, and we livened up the journal in other ways. But the focus remained on reviews. This was the time when, in my judgment, I came into my own as a reviewer. At times I wrote reviews of several titles, which proved to be miniature (or not so miniature) essays that broached important theoretical issues. Michael A. Morrison, a professor and a close colleague of Stefan's, was our third editor, and we generally worked in harmony.

But not always. When my Lovecraft biography came out in 1996, Stefan, without consulting me, assigned the book to Neil Barron. Not only was Barron not any particular authority on Lovecraft, but he and I had had some bad blood because I had given a less than charitable review of his reference work *Horror Literature* in the very first issue of *Necrofile* (Summer 1991). For these and other reasons, I felt that Barron had an axe to grind where I was concerned; and sure enough, his review was one of the few negative (and even hostile) reviews the book received—aside from the fact that the overwhelming bulk of the review covered only the period *after* Lovecraft's death! I was incensed with the unfairness of the review and demanded that I be allowed to append a rebuttal to it; but Stefan (rightly, perhaps) felt that such a rebuttal should only appear in the letters column in the next issue. We both came close to giving up the editorship of *Necrofile* over this point, but we managed to make peace among ourselves; and my pungent rebuttal did in fact appear in the next issue.

My reviews soon gained notoriety for their severity. Ellen Datlow, in the introduction to one of her *Year's Best Fantasy and Horror* volumes (around 1993, I think), bluntly referred to me as "the *nastiest* reviewer in the field" (her emphasis). I took that as a compliment. I had great fun lampooning the work of Dean R. Koontz and other hacks, wrote a blistering review of Brad Leithauser's incompetent anthology *The Norton Book of Ghost Stories* (1995), and was less than charitable to Ligotti's third collection, *Noctuary* (1994), although I very much liked his next book, *My Work Is Not Yet Done* (my review appeared in *Necropsy*, an online continuation of *Necrofile* operated by June Pulliam and Tony Fonseca). Eventually I collected these and other reviews in my volume *Classics and Contemporaries* (Hippocampus Press, 2007).

One of the authors whom I consistently praised in reviews was Ramsey Campbell. I had long been convinced that his second short story collection, *Demons by Daylight* (1973), was a seminal volume, all but singlehandedly ushering in the modern era of literate weird fiction with its scintillating prose, the subtlety and ambiguity of its supernatural manifestations, the bold treatment of sexual themes, and in general a sensitivity to human character and human psychology unparalleled in much prior work in weird fiction. Subsequent volumes, both novels and tales, confirmed my impression that Campbell was far and away the leading weird writer of our time—and perhaps of all time.

So I was looking forward to meeting him, once I learned that he would be the guest of honour at the NECON, now held at Bryant College (Smithfield, Rhode Island) in the summer of 1991. It felt good to be back in New England after nearly a decade away from it (although of course I had visited frequently for research and other purposes). As Marc, Jason Eckhardt, I, and others strolled into the dealer's room of the convention that Friday, we unexpectedly saw Campbell standing by himself examining a book at a dealer's table. I cannot now recall if I had ever met him before, but in any case we all introduced ourselves. Then we hesitantly wondered if he had any dinner plans. We had assumed that he would be wined and dined by the convention committee—but in fact he blandly stated that he had no plans at all. Thrilled, we took him to dinner at a nearby tavern, where he could indulge his taste for unusual beers and ales. The food proved adequate as well. The next night, he was again free for dinner, and we took him out again somewhere.

I do not know if it was this personal encounter that triggered my desire to do yet more work on Campbell. I had already written a lengthy chapter on him for *The Modern Weird Tale,* placing it in the exact centre of the book to suggest his centrality to the whole modern weird tradition; but of course that book was not yet published. In any event, some Campbell-related projects quickly emerged. I felt the need to promote criticism of his work, so I assembled a little anthology of criticism, *The Count of Thirty: A Tribute to Ramsey Campbell* (Necronomicon Press, 1993), containing splendid essays by Simon MacCulloch, Joel Lane, and others, as well as Stefan's lengthy interview of Campbell. An even more significant project followed. Campbell had been keeping a meticulous bibliography of his own writings and publications from the very beginning (and that goes back to 1957, when he began his juvenile volume *Ghostly Tales*). Receiving a copy of this document, I put it into proper bibliographical format, and Stefan wrote plot synopses of every single Campbell work from 1957 up to about 1993. This book was published as *The Core of Ramsey Campbell: A Bibliography and Reader's Guide* (Necronomicon Press, 1995), with a moving preface by Peter Straub.

7. Chelsea House II (1990–95)

Almost immediately after finishing *The Weird Tale*, I sensed that several of the authors I had discussed there really required full-length treatment. The first I chose for such a task was Lord Dunsany, whom I had been reading since high school and who in some ways (e.g., in terms of his extraordinarily mellifluous prose) I felt was superior to Lovecraft. But before I could tackle a critical study, I felt the need to assemble a proper bibliography of his work. I got in touch with Darrell Schweitzer, who had recently published the first critical study of Dunsany, *Pathways to Elfland* (1989), and asked if he wished to team up on the project. He did. I suspect that neither of us realised how much effort it would take, but we plunged in heedlessly.

Much of our work was done at the University of Pennsylvania library, which at that time anyone could enter and use. It had an immense number of bound copies of all manner of old periodicals on its shelves, and at times we simply pored through them issue by issue on the off chance that something by Dunsany might appear there. This procedure wasn't quite as random as it sounds, as we had some ideas as to where Dunsany might plausibly have appeared. We were initially stunned to discover that there were any number of uncollected pieces in the London *Saturday Review*, which had published Dunsany's work as early as 1908. We lugged these large bound copies over to the photocopy machine and made numerous copies.

Book publications were less troublesome, as I had by this time had a nearly complete collection of Dunsany's books (the exception was the rare play *Mr. Faithful*—I still have only a photocopy of this item); but of course there were numerous different editions that neither of us had. At that time, not a great deal of Dunsany had appeared in foreign translation, and there was not a very large amount of criticism; but many of Dunsany's books, especially beginning in the 1920s, had been reviewed widely; and, using the *Book Review Digest* and other resources, I was startled to find reviews of his later books by such figures as Evelyn Waugh, Graham Greene, Elizabeth Bowen, Robert Penn Warren, and others. We at last finished our work, and it appeared as *Lord Dunsany: A Bibliography* (Scarecrow Press, 1993).

Now that I had a better understanding of the full scope of Dunsany's writing, I began my critical study in earnest. I read the entirety of Dunsany's work from beginning to end—short stories, plays, novels, essays, poetry, miscellany. Somehow I felt I had suddenly gained an uncanny insight into Dunsany's mind—or, at least, the basic thrust of his work. The need for reunification with the natural world seemed to tie all his writings together, however superficially disparate they appeared. Drawing upon my recent work on the anthropology of religion (which I had used in my *Decline of the West* study), I saw Dunsany's early fantastic writings as instances of "aesthetic animism"—a use of gods and demigods as embodiments of the natural world. In his later writings Dunsany boldly used a "non-human perspective" (tales, lays, and sometimes entire novels told from the point of view of animals ranging from butterflies to dogs) to point out how artificial civilised human life had become.

In the course of this work, I found many later works by Dunsany—ranging from the charming play *The Old Folk of the Centuries* (1930) to the late novel *The Strange Journeys of Colonel Polders* (1950) to be lost masterworks of fantasy fiction. (I may note here that, although I had read and enjoyed Tolkien well enough in high school and college, I never developed much of a taste for pure fantasy. I disliked David Lindsay's *Voyage to Arcturus* for its pompous and meandering philosophising, and a recent reading of the first volume of Mervyn Peake's Gormenghast trilogy left me entirely underwhelmed.) I developed an increasing irritation at Lovecraft for his view that Dunsany's early work was all that was worth reading. In the end, I found *The Curse of the Wise Woman* (1933) to be his most powerful and richly textured novel, superior even to *The King of Elfland's Daughter*; but several others were nearly as good. Dunsany's poetry, however, was on the whole even worse than Lovecraft's.

The end result was *Lord Dunsany: Master of the Anglo-Irish Imagination*, which came out in 1995 from Greenwood Press—in the very series (Contributions to the Study of Science Fiction and Fantasy) where my annotated edition of "Supernatural Horror in Literature" had been so summarily rejected a decade and a half earlier. The book sold well enough for an academic book, although its high price restricted sales almost exclusively to libraries. But I do regard this book as one of my triumphs of critical analysis.

I need to backtrack a bit to throw in some developments on the personal front. In 1991 I fell into a relationship with a Jewish woman, Judy Klass. She came from a literarily distinguished family: her uncle, Philip Klass, attained celebrity as the science fiction writer William Tenn; her older sister, Perri Klass, is a novelist; her brother, David Klass, is a screenwriter; and her father, Morton Klass, was a noted anthropologist. Judy herself had published a *Star Trek* novel that briefly appeared on the bestseller lists. She was nine years younger than I, but at times it seemed as if we were almost of different generations: perhaps because my own tastes in popular music had become frozen in the 1960s and 1970s, I did not respond much to the music she en-

7. Chelsea House II (1990–95)

joyed (I briefly took an interest in one of her favourite bands, the Pet Shop Boys, but that has since lapsed); and when I chided her for her relative lack of interest in classical music, she shot back that I had made her insensitivity sound like a moral failing. One time, after we saw a grim film of urban violence, I had to rush home and put on some Mozart to cleanse my mind.

So our relationship was a bit on the turbulent side. It lasted about a year, after which time we decided it was best to part. But one interesting result of it was that I tentatively re-established contact with Leslie. Judy was the first woman I had become romantically involved with since my breakup with Leslie two years earlier (although I imagine there were any number of blind dates with women, none of which led anywhere), and I felt confident enough to break the silly silent treatment I had been giving her. I left a message on her phone one day, and she called back that evening. We were nothing but "friends" at this moment, and our subsequent relationship was pretty sporadic; but that was fine for the time being.

Some more socialising occurred when some local fans decided to put on a convention they called the NecronomiCon. This began in 1993 and continued every two years until 2001, and I attended every one of them except the last. The first two were held in Danvers (a suburb of Salem), Massachusetts, the others in Providence. They were all thoroughly enjoyable. I have especially vivid memories of one (perhaps the first) in which David E. Schultz, Steve Mariconda, and I were all present—a jolly time was had by all! I was of course on numerous panel discussions, as by this time I could recite many arcane facts about Lovecraft off the top of my head—even things like the current address of the Nicholas Roerich Museum in Manhattan, which Lovecraft had visited (but it had been in a different location in his day). I believe Ramsey and Jenny Campbell (and maybe his two children also) came to at least one of these gatherings.

I think it was at one of the NecronomiCons in Providence that a number of us went to the John Hay Library to consult some documents. There was one postcard whose text David and I had not fully deciphered, and we badgered the librarians to dig out the original from the "vault" so that we could look at it more carefully. Even so, we found some words hard to make out. One word in particular was covered by the stamp. What to do? Well, scholarship sometimes requires unorthodox methods; so I asked all the assembled scholars (at least five or six of us) to gather around me as I examined the postcard on a raised table, and I surreptitiously applied some of my own spittle to lift up a corner of the stamp. Success! I was now able to read the word, and it is preserved for all eternity!

It was in early 1991 that I bought my first personal computer—a clumsy Compaq machine that worked well until the hard drive crashed a few years later. I was typing out a lot of Lovecraft letters on that machine, using WordPerfect. Up to this time, I was still composing all my writings in longhand—except letters, which I typed directly on the typewriter. Even after getting the computer, I continued to write in longhand for a while, but very gradually I began composing directly on the computer—and now I have reached the stage where I can barely write more than a paragraph by hand without suffering horrible cramps. But I still take voluminous handwritten notes on books I am planning to review or otherwise write about; and I have filled dozens of steno pads with jottings of one kind or another.

The early 1990s was the period when David E. Schultz and I were making regular trips to Providence to conduct various research on Lovecraft. Our task of transcribing Lovecraft's letters was gathering steam, and we needed to consult original documents to fill in gaps in our transcripts.

Our research was vastly facilitated by the kind hospitality of M. Eileen McNamara, a distinguished academic (she was both a Ph.D. and an M.D.) who worked at Rhode Island Hospital, and who apparently saw it as her mission to aid Lovecraft studies by putting David and me up in her house in Providence. The two houses she successively occupied at this time were a healthy walk from the John Hay Library, but we had no difficulty in making the hike every morning and returning at the end of the day. There was one awkward occasion when Eileen left for work before we did: she had made it clear to us that her cat was not to be let out of the house, and we did our best to make sure that didn't happen. We then left for the library and came back before she had returned home. But we didn't see the cat anywhere. Good God! had we in fact let the creature escape? We looked high and low for that feline—and found it trapped in the sofabed, which we had folded up as we had left! The cat was not at all injured—there was plenty of room within the sofabed for her to rest comfortably, even if she was unable to get out of her unexpected prison—but we somehow felt that the cat was never quite the same, psychologically speaking, after that experience.

Several other amusing incidents occurred during these visits with Eileen. Once, we were examining one of Lovecraft's letters to R. H. Barlow, and David had been puzzled by a phrase that I had transcribed (based on a photocopy) that he didn't think was correct. Consulting the original document, he clarified the phrase: *"Retro me, Sathanas!"* ("Get thee behind me, Satan!").

7. Chelsea House II (1990–95)

In spite of my knowledge of Latin, my ignorance of the Vulgate had led me to render this absurdly as *"Ratso me, Sathanas!"* But David's Catholic education saved me from a ridiculous error. Another time (in 1994, as it happened), we had come home after a hard day's work at the library and were looking forward to watching the NBA finals, as both of us were basketball devotees. Imagine our irritation when the game, having reached a critical moment, was interrupted—for nothing less than the slow-motion "chase" of O. J. Simpson by the police! Mildly interesting as this was, we wanted to watch the game—and the station never returned to it, much to our annoyance.

Our research led not only to the publication of small batches of Lovecraft letters from Necronomicon Press, as I have already related, but to our annotated edition of *The Shadow over Innsmouth* (1994; revised in 1997). Was this in fact the first time that a Lovecraft story had been annotated? I believe it was: my bombastic "commentary" in the *Uncollected Prose and Poetry* volumes hardly counted as such; L. Sprague de Camp had provided some annotations in *To Quebec and the Stars* (1976), but that book contained no fiction. We did a pretty good job, I believe, and the book had a fine and evocative cover by Jason C. Eckhardt.

A more ambitious project was now thrust upon me by Jim Turner. As early as the 1970s—or perhaps even before August Derleth's death in 1971—Arkham House had announced a volume of Lovecraft's *Miscellaneous Writings*. My understanding is that, at the outset, this project would merely have reprinted various Lovecraft items that had appeared in the several "miscellany" volumes—from *Marginalia* (1944) to *The Dark Brotherhood* (1966)—that Arkham House had published over the years. Jim Turner had been talking about compiling such a book for many years, but by the early 1990s I think he realised that he was simply not up to the job, given all the other work he had to do for Arkham House. So he thrust the book into my lap.

By this time, of course, I had accumulated virtually the totality of Lovecraft's nonfiction writings, and I felt there were a number of pieces—uncollected or unpublished—that needed to be brought to the attention of Lovecraft devotees. I persuaded Jim to let me have as free a hand with the book as possible, and in the end I assembled a volume that not only included the remaining bits of Lovecraft fiction that had not appeared in the four volumes I had previously edited, but a substantial mass of essays divided topically into seven different categories—essays on weird fiction, philosophy, literary criticism, politics, travel, amateur journalism, and autobiography—as well as a small group of letters published in Lovecraft's lifetime. I wrote both a general introduction and introductions to each of the nine sections of the book. The result was a book of 568 pages—and one that I still think constitutes a pretty good selection of the best of Lovecraft's essays.

I included several unpublished pieces, the most notable (or at least the lengthiest) of which were two long travel essays, "Travels in the Provinces of America" (1929) and "An Account of Charleston" (1930). These items actually got me into a bit of difficulty with the John Hay Library. I had pleaded with Jim Turner to seek permission from the library to publish these documents, since the library had "proprietary" rights by virtue of their ownership of the manuscripts; but Turner (who naturally enough rejected Robert C. Harrall's claim of ownership of the Lovecraft copyrights) maintained that Arkham House had some kind of long-standing agreement that allowed it to publish any works of this kind. On my first trip to the library after the book appeared in 1995, I was collared by John Stanley, who lectured me seriously on the potential illegality of this use of library resources. He reminded me that L. Sprague de Camp had been essentially banned from the library for failing to secure the library's permission to print Lovecraft's Quebec travelogue in *To Quebec and the Stars*. But when I explained the situation, and (rightly) attributed the whole imbroglio to Jim Turner's intransigence, John Stanley relented and did not make me *persona non grata* at the library.

Miscellaneous Writings proved to be the last edition of Lovecraft that I did for Arkham House, although I did do one more book of another sort a few years later. That would give me six Arkham House books that bore my name on them—more, I believe, than any other writer except Lovecraft, Derleth, and Clark Ashton Smith.

Things were quite literally moving on the personal front also. In the summer of 1993 my mother advised me to look into purchasing an apartment in Manhattan. It was foolish to continue in rented quarters, since I was apparently establishing myself as a lifelong New Yorker and had a stable job; and the task of commuting on the PATH trains every weekday for nine years was becoming a bit of a strain. My mother, of course, would need to help me financially in such a venture, but she was prepared to do that. So I began house-hunting.

I signed up with a realtor and began scouring apartments in the company of an elderly but seemingly tireless agent who showed me apartment after apartment in the Chelsea or Murray Hill districts of New York. (Chelsea House had by this time moved to an office at 23rd Street and Park Avenue

7. Chelsea House II (1990–95)

South.) What I didn't realise at the time was that, for mysterious reasons, this very period was one in which housing prices had suffered a spectacular collapse; it was truly a buyer's market. So in the end I managed to snag a place at 10 West 15th Street (Apartment 312), just to the west of Fifth Avenue. Technically this was in Chelsea, but I was only a block away from Greenwich Village; and the other side of Fifth Avenue was Murray Hill.

My apartment was quite spacious—a two-bedroom place of 1200 square feet. Basically there were three long rooms, a living/dining area flanked on either side by bedrooms. One I would use as such, the other would be my study; and of course books would fill both the living/dining area and the study. My mother also gave me some extra money to purchase some genuine wooden bookshelves, although I still retained my cinderblock-and-lumber arrangement for my collection of LPs. I also splurged on a lavish bedroom set, with a king-size four-poster bed, a huge and heavy dresser, and matching end tables.

The move was made on the very last day of 1993—quite dissimilar to the move into the wretched 169 Clinton Street that Lovecraft had had to make on the last day of 1924! I had hired a small moving company, and they were highly efficient; but I was not aware that they were orthodox Jews, and they politely but firmly refused my suggestion to supply them with submarine sandwiches for lunch, since these would inevitably come from a non-kosher venue. I purchased some furniture—including a fine dining table (but no chairs)—from the previous owners, who were moving to a house in Westchester County.

This was a co-op, meaning that there was a co-op board that would have to approve my tenancy. Somehow I felt a great deal of trepidation when I came up—dressed in my best suit—in front of the co-op board, but I was accepted as a matter of course. The place was actually two buildings—one facing 15th Street (my building) and the other facing 14th Street—with a courtyard in between. I use the term courtyard a bit flatteringly, for this was simply an area where the buildings' air conditioning and heating units were placed, and few tenants had any reason to go there. My kitchen was a narrow galley kitchen, but that suited me just fine—I wasn't exactly the world's greatest chef!

I was now able to walk to work, and that certainly made things easier as far as commuting was concerned. I could even have come home for lunch, but figured that was too much bother; anyway, I enjoyed going out to lunch with various other Chelsea House people. At times, however, I went directly to NYU library from home, or came back home directly from the library without returning to the office.

Only days after I moved into my apartment, I received some sad news from Peter Cannon: Frank Belknap Long had died of pneumonia in St. Vincent's Hospital. This had occurred on January 3, although I didn't hear the news until a few days later. It was Peter who, consulting city records, had definitively ascertained that Frank had been born on April 27, 1901: Long himself had, over the years, given 1902 or 1903 as his year of birth, and Lovecraft himself had thought it was 1902. So Frank was approaching his ninety-third birthday when he died.

But the aftermath was still worse. His wife, Lyda, herself in her eighties and not very stable mentally, essentially went into serious denial regarding the fact of his death. For months she did nothing to arrange for Frank's funeral, and eventually we heard that the hospital, no longer able to keep Frank's body in its morgue, had sent it to Hart Island in Long Island Sound to be buried in the potter's field.

Well, we couldn't let this stand, so we—Peter Cannon, Ted Klein, I, and perhaps some others—quickly raised funds for Frank to be interred in his own grave (there was one available to him) in the Long family plot in Woodlawn Cemetery in the Bronx. The matter was duly accomplished, and we held a simple but dignified service at his gravesite. Flying in for the occasion was young Perry Grayson, a Californian who had become interested in Long and counted as the leading authority on his work.

In late January or early February 1994, I received some stunning news from John Stanley: the original autograph manuscript of "The Shadow out of Time" had surfaced. This itself was a "weird tale" almost more bizarre than anything Lovecraft had ever written. We knew that Lovecraft had given the manuscript to R. H. Barlow as a reward for typing the text; Lovecraft had claimed that the text had been accurately typed and that it had been printed reasonably accurately in *Astounding Stories* for June 1936 (at least, it had not been butchered the way *At the Mountains of Madness* had been); but I for one was highly sceptical of these claims. In particular, the paragraphing of the story as printed in *Astounding* seemed entirely uncharacteristic of Lovecraft—and exactly similar to the chopping up of his long, leisurely paragraphs in the *Astounding* version of the Antarctic novel. A good many years earlier I had even attempted a conjectural restoration of the paragraphing, sending it around to Don Burleson and other scholars for their opinion. But of course I could not use this conjectural version as the basis for the text as printed in my corrected edition of *The Dunwich Horror and Others*, so I had to print the text pretty much as it had appeared in *Astounding*, with the usual restoration of Lovecraft's British spellings and other such small details.

We all figured that the original handwritten manuscript had long been destroyed. Surely it would have surfaced by this time, if it had still existed! Jim Turner had even taken a trip to Mexico to examine Barlow's papers at the college in Mexico City where he had been a professor of anthropology, but had turned up nothing.

It was in January 1994 when John Stanley got a fax from a woman in Hawaii saying in essence, "I have a handwritten manuscript by H. P. Lovecraft called 'The Shadow out of Time.' Do you want it?" After Stanley had awoken from his faint, he had said, "Yes, I want it." The woman was the sister of a woman who had studied with Barlow in Mexico City; for some unknown reason he had given her the manuscript as a keepsake, and she had taken it with her when she had retired to Hawaii. Now she had died, and her sister, in looking through her effects, had found it.

When Stanley notified me, I made immediate plans to consult it. Taking the train up to Providence, I spent about two days writing in the corrections to the story—and, as I had surmised, there were many, many corrections (about 400), including those paragraph divisions that I had long suspected—into my copy of *The Dunwich Horror and Others*. It was truly a thrilling experience to see that manuscript—written in an old school composition book, probably from Lovecraft's Hope Street High School days. The paper was lined, but Lovecraft had not followed the lines in writing his story. And, as was habitual with his story manuscripts, there were all manner of revisions, cross-outs, additions written in the margins (sometimes vertically), and so on and so forth. This was a pencil draft, and one had to be careful not to smudge the faded writing.

Now that I had the corrected text, the question remained: what to do with it? When I told Jim Turner of the find, he was highly excited; in fact, he wished to publish the story as a separate booklet. I sent him my corrected text, and he actually generated long galley proofs of the story, which I painstakingly corrected. But the corrected version of the story never appeared from Arkham House—and Jim Turner soon left the company, forming his own small press, Golden Gryphon Press. Although I remained in touch with Turner's successor at Arkham House, Peter Ruber, we somehow never managed to prepare a new edition of *The Dunwich Horror and Others* that incorporated the corrections to "The Shadow out of Time." (Turner had, in subsequent printings of the first three volumes of Lovecraft's fiction, managed to make some minor corrections in the text, including some significant revisions to "Hypnos" based on a typescript that had surfaced, bearing a dedication to Samuel Loveman.)

So my corrected "Shadow out of Time" lay in limbo, although I did circulate it to various scholars privately.

Only weeks after I returned from this Providence trip, I was shaken by the news that my father had died. He was eighty-three and a half years old, but for the last six or seven years he had been struggling with various ailments and had essentially become incapacitated. Indeed, around 1991 my sisters and I had been hastily summoned back to Muncie because my mother believed he was on the verge of passing then; I was picked up at the Indianapolis airport by HolliAnne—the first time I had seen her since her last visit to me at Brown, in 1980. But my father had managed to survive on that occasion. He had suffered a succession of strokes that, while not greatly affecting his mind, had left him physically immobile. Moreover, his diabetes and other problems had resulted in very bad blood circulation, to the point that there was concern that one of his feet might have to be amputated. He flatly stated that he would prefer to die rather than to suffer such a fate; and so my mother spent forty minutes twice a day in massaging his feet to ensure better circulation—all this while she was still teaching full-time at Ball State. Essentially, she was compelling him to stay alive by the sheer force of her will. It was an heroic effort on her part.

I didn't return to Muncie as often as I should have, largely because I hated to see my father in that condition. Here was a man who, in his younger days, was a vigorous athlete, and who even in his fifties and sixties would take long walks—always with his patented cane, although the cane was largely for show and not as an aid to his walking. And much as I found it engaging to see him leaning back on his recliner, with a cat resting placidly on his expansive stomach, I did not relish the sight of him in this physically shattered condition.

Naturally, I returned to Muncie for the funeral, a simple and dignified service. My father was cremated, of course, in accordance with his wishes. What to do with his ashes was another matter. My mother presently announced her desire to scatter his ashes in one of the holy rivers of India (not necessarily the Ganges, which has become a tourist trap for this kind of thing). I, as the only son, would have to participate in the ceremony.

So the result was that, toward the end of 1994, I had to plan for an ex-

7. Chelsea House II (1990–95)

tensive visit to India—my first since leaving there in 1963. Given the long distance one had to travel, it made no sense to go for a short visit, so I arranged to go for about three weeks. My mother would precede me, staying in all about five weeks. But the idea of spending all that time with my mother (even in the company of others, especially the numerous relatives we had in India) was not an especially welcome thought, so I persuaded Richard Fumosa to come with me for about two weeks to act as a buffer.

I left first, sometime in late December. Arriving in Bombay (I can't recall if it had officially been renamed Mumbai at this time; to me it will always be Bombay), I was overwhelmed by the heat, humidity, and congestion of the place. I managed to link up with my mother, who had come with some relatives to fetch me from the airport. We went back to her brother Murthy's house in an exclusive gated community north of Bombay, where we stayed for some days. I met his son (my cousin), whose name I have already forgotten; he operated a shrimp boat in Bombay harbour. His wife was a skilled painter, and she specialised in making copies of classic paintings, which she did quite well. Presently we drove over the Western Ghats (the long, narrow range of mountains that separates the western coast of India from the inland regions) and arrived at Poona. I was shown the bungalow where I had spent the first five years of my life—but, alas! the site evoked absolutely no memories in me.

At a fairly early date, my mother and I carried out the task that was the nominal purpose of the whole visit: the scattering of my father's ashes. We eventually chose a secluded area on the banks of the Trimbakeshwar river, somewhat to the northeast of Bombay. This was a holy river by Indian tradition, and we were pleased with its similarity to my father's first name (Tryambak—pronounced, as I have mentioned, TRIM-buck). We hired a Hindu priest for the purpose, but I had my part to play as well. As we approached the river's edge, I went behind a large boulder, stripped to my underwear, and (with the help of the priest) put on an Indian garment (really just a rectangular piece of cloth that had to be folded and draped around my body in a specific fashion) called a dhoti. Wearing this item, I repeated a prayer that the priest spoke in what I assume was Sanscrit, then scattered the ashes. I confess to feeling a bit bemused by the whole experience, since I had no idea what I was actually saying; but my mother was moved by the event, and I felt I had done my filial duty to my father's memory.

Later my mother, Richard, and I headed south to Mysore, the region where my mother's family originated and where she was born. We took an

Air India flight to the incredibly congested city of Madras (Chennai), then an eight-hour ride on a rattletrap train that seemed to have been unchanged since the 1940s. We passed through Bangalore (the nexus of India's Silicon Valley) to Mysore. At one point we hired a private tour guide to take us to the numerous spectacular Hindu temples in the general vicinity. The decision to head south from Bombay instead of north (or, more specifically, northeast) meant that we could not take in the Taj Mahal in Agra, which I have still not seen. And, of course, such locales as Delhi, New Delhi, Calcutta, and numerous others had to be bypassed also.

The trip was bizarre in more than one sense. I was appalled at the grinding poverty that still plagued the nation. There were beggars everywhere, many of them seriously disabled; and, of course, child beggars were ubiquitous. At one point, as we were skirting some of Bombay's worst slums, my relatives noticed how depressed I was becoming, and they simply said, "Just put it out of your mind." Well, that's all one could do to remain sane, isn't it? Too much focus on this intractable problem could easily drive you crazy. But there is also tremendous wealth and extravagance in India, and a stark distinction between rich and poor far beyond what we find in this country.

Wild dogs run rampant in the cities, and of course cows are everywhere. In Madras, we at one point were driven in a motorised rickshaw down the main street of Madras, and as we came to a stop a cow stuck its enormous head curiously into our vehicle. The cow knew that it was quite literally untouchable—it had no fear of marching right down the street in the midst of traffic, for it knew no harm could come to it. My mother, Richard, and I understood that we could not drink ordinary tap water, as we had not developed immunity to the bacteria that infested it; I recalled that Randy Everts had developed a serious case of dysentery while on a trip to India some years before. So we drank bottled water the whole time. And, of course, we had to bring our own supply of toilet paper, since Indians do not use it.

I felt simultaneously Indian and non-Indian, American and non-American. People came up to me and spoke in Hindi or Marahti or some other language and expected me to reply, but of course I couldn't. But because I had been raised in the United States for most of my life, I was substantially taller than most Indian men. My mother claimed that some young women were admiring my physique, saying things like "Who is that god standing there?" Well, that was all very flattering. I, in turn, did find some Indian women highly attractive. When I expressed my feelings to my cousin as we were passing through Ferguson College in Poona, he replied promptly, "I can

7. Chelsea House II (1990–95)

arrange a marriage for you in half an hour." I quickly said, "I'm not really interested in *marrying* any of these women, only in . . ." Well, you know.

But I was glad to leave. India had been such a sensory overload that I yearned to return to familiar locales. My mother and I flew out of Bombay and landed in Zürich (we were flying on Swiss Air), where I had my first bacon-and-egg breakfast in three weeks. The native food in India was a bit hard to take. Especially in the south, it was so spicy as to be almost inedible for both me and my mother. Then, toward the end of my stay, I did become ill from something I ate—perhaps some of the shrimp from my cousin's boat (he himself, a vegetarian, did not eat any of the shrimp he caught). So I spent the last few days largely in bed, trying to sleep off my illness. I didn't fully recover for several weeks.

I am not entirely sure that I ever want to return to India, although I suppose I will. I have many relatives there, although I can't say that I am close to any of them. And really, how can one die without seeing the Taj Mahal in person?

By this time, of course, I had embarked on a project of some significance—a full-length biography of Lovecraft.

In the fifteen years or so since the publication of de Camp's biography in 1976, I had been hoping against hope that someone else would undertake the job—maybe Randy Everts, who had spent years crisscrossing the country and interviewing all manner of people (many of whom were now dead) who had known or been somehow involved with Lovecraft; or perhaps Ken Faig, who to my mind knew more about Lovecraft's life than anyone. I myself didn't think I was even much interested in his life except as it bore some relationship to his work and thought. But with the passing of years, I developed the sinking feeling that I was really the only one in a viable position to write a full-length biography that would replace de Camp's. And so, sometime in 1993, I began the work.

The initial phase would simply be the assembling of research materials. I had by this time acquired random documents that pertained to Lovecraft's life—his will, made out in 1912; a copy of his marriage certificate; his death certificate; and so on—but I knew that, for large stretches of his life, we had only his testimony as found in various comments scattered throughout his letters. It was here that David E. Schultz's and my years-long effort to transcribe his letters proved immensely beneficial. I was able to arrange all his mentions of his childhood and adolescence into some kind of order, supplementing them with accounts from his friends and family. Lovecraft is singular in the fact that so many of his associates wrote memoirs of him, and these provided invaluable corroborative evidence to supplement what he said in letters and what could be found in the public record.

I was determined not only to avoid some mistakes I felt de Camp had made—being overly judgmental in regard to some of Lovecraft's attitudes (especially his status as an "amateur" and his racism); failing to integrate Lovecraft's life and views with the culture of his time; being insufficiently attuned to the vital qualities of his work (as when de Camp felt that, in writing the chase scene in "The Shadow over Innsmouth," Lovecraft had made the "blunder of putting the climax in the middle," unaware that the true climax was the narrator's realisation that he is, by heredity, one of the Innsmouth denizens himself). I also was determined to come up with a better method of citation, as de Camp's method resulted in incredible confusion as to what source was being cited for a given fact.

But more broadly, I knew that I had to do much background reading in history, philosophy, and general culture to put Lovecraft's whole life and work into proper historical perspective. I read books ranging from studies of Antarctic exploration (Walker Chapman's *The Loneliest Continent* [1964], which in fact had been purchased by my mother and had been in our family library since our time in Illinois) to Thomas F. Gossett's *Race: The History of an Idea in America* (1963), which I still believe is one of the most illuminating studies of the subject. It is not surprising, then, that the whole project took a full two years of my life, from 1993 to 1995.

I was not giving any particular notice to how long the book was going to be. I suspected it would be a bit longer than de Camp's (which I believe runs to about 150,000 to 200,000 words), but didn't think it would exceed 250,000 words. Early on in the process I actually placed an "Author's Query" in the *New York Times Book Review,* requesting that anyone who had documents pertaining to the project contact me and perhaps provide copies. This query didn't result in anything in particular, but I did get a letter from my editor at the University of Texas Press. Ignoring the fact that she had summarily rejected *The Modern Weird Tale* because of its length, she claimed she was interested in the book and was even prepared to offer an advance contract. But I replied with some tartness that I suspected the book would be rather too long for her taste, and I rejected her offer.

What I failed to realise is that, as one progresses in Lovecraft's life, the documentary evidence—especially letters—becomes exponentially larger. I ended up covering the first thirty-five years of Lovecraft's life in about

7. Chelsea House II (1990–95)   181

250,000 words, which I felt was already a bit on the long side; but surely the remaining eleven and a half years couldn't take up all that much space? Well, it did; by the time I struggled to an exhausted finish in the summer of 1995, the book had ballooned to 508,000 words—or 550,000 words if one added the notes. This meant the book was exactly the length of *War and Peace.*

There was a time in early 1995 when I simply had to take a break of a month or two, as I was overdosing on Lovecraft and couldn't stomach doing any more work on the book. I can't remember what I did during that period, but I did return to the biography with renewed energy. I like to think I did a good job in portraying the complex network of friends and colleagues Lovecraft had, especially late in life. I also feel that my portrayal of Lovecraft's life in New York (1924–26)—drawing heavily on his letters to his aunts—is pretty fair. It helped that I myself was so familiar with the New York area. In the course of my work I made some forays to Lovecraft sites I hadn't seen before, such as the site of the apartment that he had occupied with Sonia for a few weeks in the summer of 1928 and the location of the hat shop nearby that she was attempting to establish. Some years before I began the biography, I had taken a trip to Butler Hospital in Providence to see the actual handwritten medical records for Lovecraft's father. I had provided a full transcript of these records to Eileen McNamara, who then wrote an interesting brief article on the subject for *Lovecraft Studies* (Spring 1991). And at some point I was struck when reading the telegram that Annie Gamwell had written to R. H. Barlow after Lovecraft had died at Jane Brown Memorial Hospital: "HOWARD DIED THIS MORNING NOTHING TO DO THANKS." That is how I ended the penultimate chapter; it never fails to bring tears to my eyes.

I also sought to gain some familiarity with the various locales up and down the Eastern Seaboard that Lovecraft had visited in the final decade or so of his life; but in this regard I was a bit less successful. During my years in New England (1976–82), I had canvassed such sites as Salem, Marblehead, and Newburyport in Massachusetts along with Portsmouth, N.H.; I had also once visited Jason Eckhardt and his wife in Portland, Maine, although we did not in fact explore the places Lovecraft had seen. I did spend two wonderful and congested days in Charleston, using Lovecraft's own walking tour to cover all the sites (it took me a full seven hours of walking, with several pauses in between); but I never got to Richmond, Fredericksburg, any of the sites in Florida (St. Augustine, DeLand, Dunedin, Key West), or Quebec. Steve Mariconda and I had once taken a trip up to Kingston, N.Y. (home of

Bernard Austin Dwyer), but didn't find much of relevance there. And I was of course familiar with the New Paltz/Hurley area from my frequent attendance of Robert H. Waugh's Lovecraft Forum.

The prospect of the book's publication, of course, was a ticklish one. Who was going to publish a biography of Lovecraft that spanned half a million words? Even as I was writing the book, I was querying some commercial and academic publishers. Harvard University Press had expressed some mild interest, but after reading one of the early chapters it said no. W. W. Norton also showed some interest, but nothing came of this. Perhaps if I had had an agent, I might have been able to persuade a major commercial firm to issue the book; but as it was, when the book was finished all I had was a mound of paper gathering dust in my closet.

Marc Michaud came to my rescue. At some point in late 1995 or early 1996, he offered to publish the book. Having no other prospects, and feeling that Necronomicon Press could at least get the book out to the devotees who would be most interested in it, I agreed. But even Marc said that he couldn't publish a book of that length—could I cut it down to, say, 350,000 words? I readily agreed and began the task of abridgement. This did not prove to be quite as difficult as I had imagined, for some whole sections (for example, my discussion of Lovecraft's writing of the "Zoilus" column for the *Vivisector* in the early 1920s) could simply be jettisoned. But the bulk of the pruning involved the elimination or truncation of lengthy quotations or some details that didn't seem entirely essential. The job must have been done by late spring, and the book was put into production. We knew we would want to publish a limited hardcover edition—the first, I believe, that Necronomicon Press ever issued—and then, a paperback edition that could be kept in print so long as there was demand.

As the book was in production that summer, we were stunned to receive a laconic request from Joyce Carol Oates for an advance review copy. She did not say why she wanted the copy, but I quickly surmised that it would be for a review-essay in the *New York Review of Books*. I had had a subscription to that magazine for years and saw such articles by her appear there regularly. Now Necronomicon Press was not in the habit of making advance review copies, but in this case we decided it would be beneficial to do so. So we ran off some sets of uncorrected proofs and bound them in a spiral binder. There were several sets, and I still have one. We sent one to Oates and hoped for the best.

Sure enough, soon after the book—*H. P. Lovecraft: A Life*—had ap-

7. Chelsea House II (1990–95)

peared in the fall, a long review by Oates entitled "The King of Weird" appeared in the *New York Review of Books* (October 31, 1996). It was of course largely an occasion for Oates to express her views on Lovecraft; but in the concluding pages of the review she did write some nice things about my book, calling it "definitive," among other things. Other reviews were quite charitable, including those in the *Providence Journal* (by James A. Anderson), *Extrapolation* (Donald M. Hassler), *Deathrealm* (Brian McNaughton), and others. And, to counteract the fiasco of Neil Barron's tepid review in *Necrofile,* I persuaded Stefan to let Steve Mariconda write a much more ample review that appeared in the Spring 1997 issue. Peter Cannon wrote a nice review in *Crypt of Cthulhu* (Lammas 1997), and Ken Faig stressed the book's discussion of amateur journalism in a review in the *National Amateur* (March 1997).

The publication of the hardcover edition, however, was something of a mess. Marc had been unduly cautious in his expectations of the sales of the 700-page book, for which he charged $40; he decided to print only 250 copies. When he began accepting advance orders for the book, it sold out in a week, leaving many readers frustrated at being unable to secure the hardcover edition. We could easily have sold twice as many. A simultaneous paperback edition didn't do much to mollify readers. I myself, when the hardcover edition came out, came up to West Warwick to sign all the copies. Some years later I saw one copy being sold for $825 by a used book dealer. (Whether anyone actually paid that price, I have no idea.)

But at least my book was out, and I believe it did set the record straight on many aspects of Lovecraft's life and thought.

While I was working on the biography, I was also involved in other Lovecraftian projects. One rather frivolous undertaking was the *New Lovecraft Collector,* a four-page magazine (basically an 8½ × 14 sheet folded in half) issued by Necronomicon Press, with the purpose of reporting new publications or other noteworthy events in the Lovecraft world. I contributed brief essays on bibliographical matters, as did some others. In these days before the Internet took off, I think the magazine served a useful purpose. The venture lasted for twenty-six issues (1993–99).

But, incredibly, I also wrote an entire separate critical work. Robert Reginald had asked me to expand my little Starmont Reader's Guide of 1982 into a full-scale treatise, and I was happy to oblige. Indeed, I ended up writing that book—to which Reginald affixed the rather ungainly title *A Subtler Magick: The Writings and Philosophy of H. P. Lovecraft*—entirely at my Chelsea House office. I would bring in a given volume of Lovecraft's stories and simply write, pretty much off the top of my head, my analysis of it. This book, which came to about 120,000 words, emerged just after the biography. I think it has some good analysis, expanding on what I had said in the biography (where I focused on the biographical elements in Lovecraft's stories, essays, and poems).

But the fall of 1995 was momentous in my personal life for reasons other than the completion of the Lovecraft biography. In October of that year, as I came back to the Chelsea House office from a morning spent at NYU library conducting research, I was startled to learn that the company had just gone bust.

8. New York (1995–2001)

"'Lord, how one's women do add up!'"—James Branch Cabell, *Jurgen*

Chelsea House had been struggling for some years, but its troubles were augmented by president Philip Cohen's bizarre decision, sometime in 1993 or 1994, to open a *restaurant* in the Philadelphia area. (The company's business offices were in that area.) This restaurant purported to cater to African Americans, and our art director, who was African American, was heavily involved in the establishment of the venture. But it quickly became an enormous money drain, with the result that in the fall of 1995 the entire New York editorial office was shut down. For some years the company still continued to operate after a fashion out of its Philadelphia office, and now it has returned to publishing books of various sorts, including anthologies of criticism bearing Harold Bloom's name. But, after I finished some projects that had been in progress, I had nothing more to do with the company.

The question was: what exactly was I to do now? I of course applied for various jobs in publishing; but given that I had reached the level of senior managing editor when Chelsea House went bust, it was difficult for me to find openings on even an approximate level elsewhere. I dutifully filled out job applications from the *New York Times* and elsewhere (feeling a bit like Lovecraft when he was forced to do so in 1924–25, although I wasn't exactly in as desperate financial straits as he was), and even went on a few job interviews; but nothing eventuated.

So my mother, not wishing to lose the potentially lucrative investment we had made in purchasing my co-op (of which she was actually co-owner), promised to support me while I attempted to establish myself as a full-time freelance writer. It was really the opportunity I had been waiting for. During all my years at Chelsea House, I struggled to fit in my work as a scholar, critic, and editor of Lovecraft and weird fiction with my office duties; as I've mentioned, I did a good deal of personal work at the office. But the effect was pretty debilitating, and as soon as I came home every workday I had to take a little nap before dinner to rejuvenate myself to do further work for the rest of the evening.

It of course took some years for me to establish myself as a freelance writer, but in the end I managed it. I was nowhere near doing so by the time my unemployment insurance ran out in the spring of 1996, but my mother's infusion of cash tided me over. And my record of publications speaks for itself. In the nineteen years from 1978 to 1996, I published only (!) 51 books, and many of these were relatively small booklets published by Necronomicon Press; in the twenty years from 1997 to 2016, I published 185. In the years 2000 and 2001 combined, I published 21 books.

One of the projects I began working on just before Chelsea House collapsed was the poetry of George Sterling (1869–1926). I had been casually interested in Sterling for years, knowing that he had been a mentor of Clark Ashton Smith; but now, I somehow became inflamed by a passion for his work. Securing photocopies or actual copies of his published books of poetry—from *The Testimony of the Suns* (1903) to the posthumous *After Sunset* (1939), edited (by a curious coincidence) by R. H. Barlow—was easy enough; but I knew that many of Sterling's poems and other writings were unpublished, and so I wrote (using Chelsea House stationery) to many libraries around the country, asking for copies of whatever manuscripts by Sterling they possessed. I received a good many responses, although the major repositories (chiefly the Bancroft Library, the rare book library of the University of California at Berkeley) had so many documents that photocopying would have been impracticable.

David E. Schultz was collaborating with me on this venture, and we quickly obtained some interesting texts. We got a microfilm from the New York Public Library of the joint correspondence between Smith and Sterling, which Smith's widow Carol Dorman Smith had sold to the library. The letters between Ambrose Bierce and Sterling (also at the New York Public Library) were also obtained. We transcribed all these texts (David tackled the published poetry, working with incredible rapidity), but for the time being we didn't have a publisher in mind to issue them.

The Bierce-Sterling letters led us to explore that saturnine journalist himself. We both sensed that more work needed to be done on Bierce, although of course he was more established in the American canon than Sterling was. But as we began our investigations, we realised that we could make contributions ourselves with sufficient diligence. I have always felt that it is

8. New York (1995–2001)

advisable to get a grasp of the full scope of a writer's work before plunging into the criticism or analysis of his work (or even of his life). This is why I compiled bibliographies of Lovecraft and Lord Dunsany before undertaking full-scale critical studies of them. The bibliography of Bierce would be a much more complicated enterprise, since he had published a great deal of material in newspapers, mostly in California. But since his chief venue, at least late in life (from 1887 to 1906), was the *San Francisco Examiner* (a paper that William Randolph Hearst had been given by his father to manage), we felt that the task was at least within reach.

The problem was that the *Examiner* was not readily available in libraries; most libraries had the *Chronicle* as the default San Francisco newspaper of that era. It turned out that only about four libraries outside of California had extensive runs of the *Examiner* for the period in question. One of them was Yale University (Beinecke Rare Book and Manuscript Library), and I'm pretty sure I went up there for Bierce work at some point during this period. But by a curious turn of events, David discovered that an extensive run resided in the library of St. Cloud State University in St. Cloud, Minnesota, in the northern part of the state. This wasn't all that far from David's home in Milwaukee, so we scheduled a visit there.

In fact, I believe we went to St. Cloud at least twice—once in the dead of winter. What could possibly have led us to spend a week or more in Minnesota in early December is beyond my understanding, but somehow we managed. Sure enough, we found enormous quantities of Bierce material—much of it unknown—in the pages of the *Examiner*, and we made masses of microfilm copies and mailed them back to ourselves. I believe we made so many that we broke one of the microfilm printers in the process. But at least we had the documents! We also visited Purdue University, which contained the papers of Paul Fatout (a Bierce biographer). This trip was also made in winter, and David had to drive hundreds of miles in the snow and ice to get there. What struck me, when we examined the papers, was the set of daguerreotypes of Bierce's relatives that Fatout had managed to collect—all of whom looked ferociously ugly and formidable! No wonder Bierce had little to do with his many siblings!

We also scoured the other papers (usually weeklies in San Francisco) where Bierce had published extensively—the *San Francisco News Letter and California Advertiser*, the *Argonaut*, and the *Wasp*. The way we acquired these documents was interesting. These papers were also pretty scarce, but David had discovered that most of them had, like the *Examiner*, been microfilmed—for libraries, of course, not for general readers or even for scholars. But David—who is something of a homebody and doesn't care to travel if he can help it—decided to invest in runs of the papers for those years that Bierce was contributing to them, and in this way we could consult the relevant items in the comfort of our own homes. I myself acquired a good many also. I felt like something of a spy in accumulating all these microfilms, consulting them (at the library, of course, as I had no microfilm reader or printer at home) when the need arose.

The problem with some of these papers is that Bierce appears to have published some—perhaps much—material anonymously in them. We were able to identify some material, but probably not all. Indeed, we got in touch with one Bierce scholar at this time, Elken Osher, who had long been working on a Bierce bibliography and maintained that a truly complete one was impossible. Agreeing in principle with this claim, we nevertheless felt that getting something like an extensive bibliography would be of some use. To date, only an inadequate checklist by Vincent Starrett (1929) and a scarcely less inadequate one by Joseph Gaer (1935) existed; we could certainly do better than that.

Our work culminated in *Ambrose Bierce: An Annotated Bibliography of Primary Sources* (Greenwood Press, 1999), and we rightly took pride in it. Even more than most bibliographies, it represented a monumental amount of research. Maybe we did miss some items (indeed, we inserted into the bibliography itself a hasty appendix containing more material that we had missed from one of the weekly newspapers), but it represented the first comprehensive work of its kind—and, more importantly, the first time that the first appearances of Bierce's fiction had been definitively identified. We learned that much of the material appearing in *Tales of Soldiers and Civilians* (1891) and *Can Such Things Be?* (1893) had been published in a very short period of time during Bierce's first years at the *Examiner* (about 1887–93). We also worked hard to identify the first appearances of the various material that had appeared in Bierce's twelve-volume *Collected Works* (1909–12).

Naturally, we located a great deal of material that had never been reprinted, either in the *Collected Works* or in subsequent collections. And so we undertook to present some of this material to a new readership. I had always been interested in Bierce's "Bits of Autobiography," a series of essays he had included in the first volume of his *Collected Works* but that had never been subsequently reprinted. In the course of our work we found other autobiographical pieces—either separate articles or sections buried in his masses of

8. New York (1995–2001)

newspaper journalism—that could be used to fill out the volume. And so we produced *A Sole Survivor: Bits of Autobiography* (1998), our first book with the University of Tennessee Press. I think the book came out well, although the very small typeface the publisher used was noted—and criticised—in several reviews. Two years later Tennessee published *The Fall of the Republic and Other Political Satires*. This also contained material that Bierce had included in the first volume of his *Collected Works*, notably two long political satires, "Ashes of the Beacon" and "The Land Beyond the Blow." (These were two of the more notable omissions in Ernest Jerome Hopkins's unfortunately titled *Complete Short Stories of Ambrose Bierce* [1970].) These stories had also been of interest to me from an early period, possibly from my high school days. I even persuaded Marc Michaud to issue a short story, "For the Ahkoond," as a separate edition from Necronomicon Press (1980), with piquant illustrations by Jason Eckhardt. We filled out the volume with essays by Bierce ruminating on some of the same issues discussed in the satires—and we persuaded the publisher to have Jason Eckhardt to draw the cover illustration!

That same year, 2000, I published *The Collected Fables of Ambrose Bierce* with Ohio State University Press. It turned out that the two batches of fables most commonly known to have been written by Bierce—"The Fables of Zambri, the Parsee" (included in the early volume *Cobwebs from an Empty Skull* [1874]—surely one of the greatest titles ever devised for a book!) and *Fantastic Fables* (1899)—were only the tip of the iceberg of Bierce's output of fables. In the end, by scouring his newspaper contributions I found a total of 846 fables, and also wrote a learned commentary on them. I had to do some research in the history of the fable, for which my Loeb Classical Library volume of the fables of Aesop and Phaedrus came in very handy.

A final Bierce project of this period was perhaps the most impressive, although it was the one on which I had the least input. David and I had discovered that Bierce's celebrated *Devil's Dictionary* (1906/1911) had first appeared as a succession of newspaper columns under various titles beginning as far back as 1875; what is more, we learned that many entries were not included in either of the two editions (the second and theoretically definitive one being in the seventh volume of his *Collected Works*) that appeared in Bierce's lifetime. Indeed, the first edition, published as *The Cynic's Word-Book* (1906), only covered the letters A–L; the publisher was envisioning a second volume, but poor sales dynamited the plan. Even in the *Collected Works* Bierce was restricted by space limitations: the volume could only be

400 pages (with, on average, only about 200 words a page), meaning that many interesting definitions had to be left out.

You would think that Ernest Jerome Hopkins's *The Enlarged Devil's Dictionary* (1967) would have rectified the situation; but, as with his *Complete Short Stories* edition, Hopkins failed to include numerous definitions from the newspaper columns; moreover, he included some definitions *that were not by Bierce!* This had happened because the editor of the *Wasp*, one Salmi Morse, had begun a column in 1880 called "Wasp's Improved Webster," which Bierce then took over when he became editor in 1881. Bierce had specifically noted this fact in an unpublished letter that Hopkins had clearly not read, so that he threw in the Morse definitions as if they were Bierce's.

We also thoroughly annotated the edition—or, rather, David did. This was one collaborative endeavour in which I contributed no more than about 10%—about the same as Lovecraft had contributed to Barlow's "Night Ocean." David devoted an enormous amount of effort to the task of editing and annotating this important text, which we called *The Unabridged Devil's Dictionary*. After a certain number of sharp disagreements with our publisher, the University of Georgia Press, about formatting and other matters, the book finally came out in 2000.

By this time I was coming to sense the truth of the old adage that "Everything is connected." Lovecraft had led me to Smith, who had led me to Sterling, who had led me to Bierce. Now, in figuring out some way of trying to put Sterling back on the literary map, I stumbled upon H. L. Mencken. I found that Mencken had had a lengthy correspondence with Sterling, and that it was possible to locate these letters without too much difficulty. Mencken had donated the letters he had received from various colleagues to the New York Public Library, where they were available on microfilm. So getting Sterling's side of the correspondence was easy. Getting Mencken's side proved a bit more difficult, as these letters were scattered in various libraries; but in the end I got all the material and produced an edition entitled *From Baltimore to Bohemia: The Letters of H. L. Mencken and George Sterling* (Fairleigh Dickinson University Press, 2001). This edition appears to have made not the slightest difference in the advancement of Sterling's reputation, but it did lead me into a new scholarly direction, as I shall relate later.

David and I also became interested in Bierce's letters. To date, there had only been a volume published long ago, Bertha Clark Pope's edition of *The Letters of Ambrose Bierce* (Book Club of California, 1922), which had some interesting material but, like Lovecraft's *Selected Letters,* presented many of

8. New York (1995–2001)

Bierce's letters in truncated form. I again began a letter-writing campaign to various libraries that owned Bierce's letters, and received a good many—most of them written in Bierce's characteristic flourish with a fountain pen. But there was no substitute for hands-on research, so in the summer of 1998 I spent about three weeks going up and down California, hitting the major repositories that had Bierce material of various sorts (Bancroft Library, San Francisco Public Library, California Historical Society, Huntington Library, UCLA). I had by this time gotten in touch with Mary Elizabeth Grenander, a leading Bierce authority (she had published a fine Twayne book on Bierce in 1971). She herself had been working on an edition of Bierce's letters (or at least on securing texts of all letters by and to Bierce), but she died in 1998 without finishing her project. But her papers were at the library of the State University of New York at Albany, where she had taught for many years. It was an easy trip from New York to Albany, and I spent several days poring through her papers. She had typed out all the letters on small sheets of paper and put them in a succession of spiral-bound notebooks. By this time I had already obtained many Bierce letters on my own, but her collection did alert me to some letters I had not been able to find (including some that are apparently still in private hands).

But it was not all work and no play for me. Only a few weeks after I had been laid off from Chelsea House, I came in touch with a Jewish woman named Mindi Rayner. I was on the mailing lists of several agencies that published personal ads, and her ad struck me chiefly because she declared that she wished to meet someone who "didn't want to start a family." (That was just as well, since Mindi was at this time about six years older than I, or forty-three.) Well, this sounded promising! I had never been particularly interested in producing offspring; in all honesty, I was so devoted to my literary work that I did not wish to spare any time for rearing children—much to my mother's disappointment. (She was somewhat mollified when Ragini bore two children and Nalini one; but she still considered me a failure for not producing any, as the only son in the family. Indeed, when my engagement with Leslie blew up in 1989, my mother expressed satisfaction, since she thought Leslie—then not quite thirty-one—was already too old for childbearing, and she hoped I'd find a younger, more fertile woman to spawn little Joshis in the future.)

Mindi and I hit it off immediately, and we quickly established a relationship. I felt a little awkward in the sudden shift of my economic status from gainfully employed person to unemployed; but I managed to hold up my financial end on dates well enough. Mindi was a publicist for various musicians and composers, including the spectacular mezzo-soprano Jennifer Larmore and the equally spectacular tenor Marcello Giordani. The end result was that, in the five and a half years I was with Mindi, I was taken to any number of opera performances at Lincoln Center and elsewhere, following which we would head backstage and meet the artists. Once or twice we went to the Kennedy Center in Washington, staying at the Watergate Hotel (which was connected to the Kennedy Center). Mindi was also a great devotee of film, and we saw any number of films that came out during this period.

Because Mindi worked from home and also lived with her elderly mother, cohabitation would be difficult. I myself needed absolute silence for my own work, and there was no way that Mindi—who had to be on the phone constantly during the workday—could share space with me. So we settled upon an arrangement whereby she would stay for the weekend in my spacious apartment (Friday night to Monday morning), and we would call twice a week (on Tuesdays and Thursdays) late in the evening, after our work was over. Occasionally I would venture to her apartment in Brooklyn, where her mother greeted me cordially. For several consecutive years Mindi took me to her family's Passover seders, usually held at her brother's house in Westchester County. Mindi herself, like most of her family, was not particularly religious, but they treasured their Jewish heritage. One particular seder was a bit peculiar. Somehow it had become known that I was an atheist, and one earnest young female member of the family looked at me solemnly and asked, "Why don't you believe in God?" I replied calmly, "It doesn't seem to me that there is sufficient evidence to support belief in a deity." The woman had nothing further to say on the subject, and the seder proceeded uneventfully.

I didn't take Mindi very often to meet my Lovecraftian friends, especially the meetings of the New Kalem Club, since she would not have been interested in the shoptalk that would dominate these events. But I did introduce her to my friend Linda Aro, who had been in New York since about 1985, when she had enrolled in Columbia Law School (I had helped her move into her dorm room). Linda had subsequently become a lawyer for a prestigious New York firm, eventually rising to become a partner of the firm; she had also married Chris Pfaff, an engaging and outgoing man whom I couldn't help liking.

But of course work dominated my life. It took some time for me to develop a schedule for my freelance work: there is always the danger that, if one has

8. New York (1995–2001)

all the time in the world to work, one will actually not get much work done. So discipline and self-motivation were vital. I would begin every morning by typing newspaper columns by Bierce for an hour or two. I did not have a scanner at this time; and even if I had had one, it might not have worked so well, because the microfilm printouts of the columns were often of poor quality, and much time would have been spent in correcting scanning errors. So it was a matter of brute typing. David was of course doing his share as well. In the end, we ended up typing the totality of Bierce's published output, which came to about 6 million words. I typed up the entirety of Bierce's surviving correspondence, which came to just under half a million words.

Projects began coming at me thick and fast. Sometime in 1996 or 1997, Dover Publications got in touch with me about doing more books in their already distinguished series of reprints of horror, fantasy, and science fiction texts, many of them assembled by E. F. Bleiler. But Bleiler was no longer with the firm, so they tapped me. I now recall that I had sent them a long list of books that might be worth reprinting, either novels or collections. Dover initially wanted to do a volume of Bram Stoker's best weird tales, and I brought in Stefan Dziemianowicz and Richard Dalby, both of whom knew a lot more about Stoker than I did; the book came out as *Best Ghost Stories* (1997). I then assembled Blackwood's *Complete John Silence Stories* (1998), which included the complete text of *John Silence—Physician Extraordinary* (1908) along with a later John Silence story; and an anthology, *Great Weird Tales* (1999), which included some of my personal favourites in weird fiction (Fiona Macleod's "The Sin-Eater," Algernon Blackwood's "The Man Whom the Trees Loved," Lord Dunsany's "The Unhappy Body," and R. H. Barlow's "A Dim-Remembered Story"). The title of the book got us into trouble, however, because we were unaware that the magazine *Weird Tales* was trademarked; the magazine complained, and I believe Dover paid some kind of fee, but otherwise the book remained in print.

One of the best books (from a personal perspective) that I did for Dover was a collection of Rudyard Kipling's weird tales, entitled *The Mark of the Beast and Other Horror Tales* (2000). There had been various other compilations of this sort, but I felt that mine isolated just the weird tales (as opposed to tales of fantasy or proto-science-fiction), including such masterworks as the title story and "'They.'" I prepared another volume for Dover, a complete reprint of Machen's *The Three Impostors* (1895)—the paperback edition in Lin Carter's Adult Fantasy series (1972) had omitted one story—but this book was cancelled because Rita Tait had prepared an annotated edition in

1995, so another edition was deemed unmarketable.

Around this time, Peter Ruber asked me to compile a history and bibliography of Arkham House to commemorate the publishing company's sixtieth anniversary. The result was *Sixty Years of Arkham House*. Naturally, I used Derleth's *Thirty Years of Arkham House* (1970) as a basis, since I myself did not have access to many earlier Arkham House titles. I provided not only complete tables of contents of each volume (including the magazines *Arkham Sampler* and *Arkham Collector*) but also plot synopses of novel-length works and some notes about each book, including any reprints it might have had. The plot synopses got me into a bit of trouble, as I did not actually read some of the science fiction books published under Jim Turner's regime, and my synopses (taken from secondary sources) proved to be a bit off the mark. But my great point of pride in this book is the indexes—names and especially titles. Of course, the computer did the work for me, but the book does contain a complete index to every single work that ever appeared in an Arkham House volume (as well as in books from its other imprints, Mycroft & Moran and Stanton & Lee) down to 1999. And since only a small number of titles appeared before Arkham House went into abeyance (it has published no titles since 2006 aside from a reprint of the *Arkham Sampler*), I think it is a pretty sound compilation. It avoids the irritating chattiness of Sheldon Jaffery's *Arkham House Companion*. One of the best features of the book was its superbly evocative cover by Allen Koszowski.

Shortly after the book appeared, I got into a bit of hot water with Arkham House. Ruber had sent me proofs of his anthology *Arkham's Masters of Horror* (2000), in which he reprinted selected works by leading Arkham House authors, also writing essays about each one. I found a number of these essays (especially the one on Lovecraft) to be quite inaccurate and in other ways ill-advised—to say nothing of the fact that the whole book was riddled with typographical errors. I pointed out some of the most obvious ones, but Ruber said the book was too far along in production for any corrections to appear. As a result, we have such things as E. Hoffmann Price's life dates given as "1998–1988." (In fact, they should have been 1898–1988.) This led me to write jokingly in a review in *Weird Tales* that Price must have embodied Algernon Blackwood's "The Man Who Lived Backwards"! I had been writing pungent reviews for *Weird Tales* since 1995 (when it was titled *Worlds of Fantasy & Horror*), and the editor, Darrell Schweitzer, later told me that he had frequently been called upon to defend me to his superiors when a particular review caused an author, editor, or publisher to complain.

8. New York (1995–2001)

But the Ruber review, published in *Weird Tales* for Summer 2000, struck a particular nerve.

After just completing my sixth book for Arkham House, I was declared *persona non grata* by April Derleth, August Derleth's daughter and the chief owner. I didn't cry too much: I doubted that I would have had much more to do with Arkham House in any case, and by this time I had found another publisher to issue my Lovecraftian work.

Speaking of Lovecraftian work, it was in 1996 (I think) that I was contacted by one Leigh Grossman, a book packager, to produce an annotated edition of Lovecraft, which would be lavishly illustrated along the lines of *The Annotated Alice* and other such volumes. I of course leapt at the opportunity. I initially generated an annotated version of "The Rats in the Walls," which particularly lent itself to annotation of this sort, because one could reprint such things as the poem (found in Baring-Gould's *Curious Myths of the Middle Ages*) that had inspired one phase of the story, and the Gaelic cries from Fiona Macleod's "The Sin-Eater" that Lovecraft had borrowed for Delapore's concluding utterance. Grossman liked what I had done, and he formally commissioned me to undertake the project, which would also include three other stories, "The Colour out of Space," "The Dunwich Horror," and *At the Mountains of Madness*.

The book—*The Annotated H. P. Lovecraft* (Dell)—came out in 1997 in a paperback edition. It could probably have been illustrated a bit more than it was (most of the illustrative matter was actually in my introduction), but on the whole I think the book was reasonably well assembled. And it sold well—I understood that after a few years it had sold at least 22,000 copies. Douglas E. Winter wrote a flattering review of it in both the *Magazine of Fantasy and Science Fiction* and the *Washington Post*.

This book indirectly led to a still more momentous volume, or series of volumes. In 1998, in the full vigour of my work on Bierce, I had queried the London office of Penguin (where I thought the Penguin Classics series was produced) about a Bierce volume for that prestigious series. The letter eventually got forwarded to the New York office, where the books were in fact produced. I received a letter from the Penguin Classics editor, Michael Millman, who said that he had long been trying to get in touch with me—not to do Bierce, but to prepare a volume of the stories of one H. P. Lovecraft!

Well, you could have knocked me over with a feather. I had no reason to believe that Penguin had any interest in such a thing, but naturally I jumped at the chance. The first volume would include what I believed to be the best of Lovecraft's stories. I made a selection, but Millman insisted that, because of the popularity of the Stuart Gordon films, I had to include "Herbert West—Reanimator." I repressed the inclination to retch and went along. Otherwise, Millman gave me a free hand with the annotations. (I had to dance delicately around the issue of the already published *Annotated H. P. Lovecraft* and had to reword my notes to "The Rats in the Walls" and "The Colour out of Space" to avoid infringing on Dell's copyright.) The book came out in 1999 as *The Call of Cthulhu and Other Weird Stories* (stung by the Dover fiasco, I had sternly warned Millman not to use . . . *and Other Weird Tales* in the title). On my recommendation, it included a spectacular cover painting by John Martin, the early nineteenth-century painter whom Lovecraft had particularly relished for his cosmic *Paradise Lost* illustrations.

The book sold incredibly well over the years: by around 2010 it had already gone through twenty-five printings. (I suspect these printings were fairly modest, perhaps 3000 copies each.) The book did not in fact garner very many reviews, as Penguin is generally not in the habit of sending out Penguin Classics books to reviewers; but Nicholas Lezard did choose it as a "Pick of the Week" in the London *Guardian*.

The awkward thing was that Leigh Grossman had already commissioned me to do a second annotated Lovecraft volume around this time. I tried to back out of the project, but was contractually unable to do so. I did manage to get Peter Cannon to take over the project, but my name had to appear—and get top billing—on the book. I only annotated "Herbert West—Reanimator"; Peter did the rest of the stories, and quite ably. *More Annotated H. P. Lovecraft* came out just before *The Call of Cthulhu*, but I do not believe it did quite as well as its predecessor.

Shortly after *The Call of Cthulhu* came out, Penguin summoned me to its offices at 375 Hudson Street in lower Manhattan. They had received an irate letter from Arkham House's agent, Joshua Bilmes, demanding that the book be withdrawn because it was not authorised by Arkham House, which still had its "exclusive" paperback arrangement with Ballantine/Del Rey. Penguin had of course (on my recommendation) secured permission from Robert C. Harrall. So I spent much of that morning explaining to the Penguin legal department the complex copyright status of Lovecraft's stories. One lawyer flabbergasted me by saying that, in his opinion, the true owner of Lovecraft's copyrights was . . . myself! That is to say, my corrected editions of Lovecraft were my intellectual property, as they could not truly be regarded as "work-for-hire" for Arkham House (in which case the texts would have been Arkham House's property). So Penguin wrote back to Bilmes saying, in effect, "Go jump in the lake." No legal action followed, of course; Arkham House was not in any legal or financial position to do so.

A second Penguin Classics book followed in 2001, *The Thing on the Doorstep and Other Weird Stories*, although I was disappointed that Millman chose a lacklustre illustration by Gustave Doré (from an edition of Poe's *The Raven*, of all things) for the cover art. But I was allowed pretty much unlimited space for annotations—which was just as well, as the notes for *The Case of Charles Dexter Ward* and *At the Mountains of Madness* covered many pages. In the end, my notes came to 60 pages of small type (out of a book of 443 pages). I had properly (and over Millman's objections) kept "The Dunwich Horror," which I held in low esteem, out of *The Call of Cthulhu*, but grudgingly included it in this book.

Another volume that appeared around this time was Lovecraft's *Lord of a Visible World: An Autobiography in Letters* (Ohio University Press, 2000). Perhaps inspired by our cobbling together Bierce's autobiography by way of essays, journalism, and other documents, David E. Schultz and I decided to do the same for Lovecraft—and, of course, we would do so by mining his mountainous correspondence. Indeed, we faced an embarrassment of riches in the task, because the extent to which Lovecraft revealed fascinating tidbits about himself in his letters was all but inexhaustible—and, as with Bierce, we extended the idea of the autobiography by incorporating Lovecraft's views and beliefs, from atheism to amateur journalism to contemporary literature to politics. The result was, I think, a stimulating book—in effect, a kind of one-volume *Selected Letters*. And I was pleased that Ohio University Press, which had published my first true book twenty years earlier, agreed to issue this one. The book did reasonably well in both hardcover and paperback.

The only drawback was the title. I'm not sure who came up with it, but it struck me as a bit opaque. The phrase of course comes from a Lovecraft letter—"There was a kind of intoxication in being lord of a visible world (albeit a miniature one) and determining the flow of its events"—referring to his habit of setting up historical scenarios during his youth with toy soldiers and such; but its broader application to Lovecraft's life and work (not to mention the opacity of the phrase itself) was troubling. We are now planning to reissue the volume as an ebook with a superior title, *The Colour and Mystery of Things*.

One other Lovecraftian project that David and I worked on was the *H. P. Lovecraft Encyclopedia*. I had long been dissatisfied with Shreffler's *H. P. Love-

craft Companion, which attempted to be a sort of encyclopaedia of this sort, although rather limited in scope; and I felt that, with all the research that had now accumulated about Lovecraft's life and work, it was time for a new volume that would be truly comprehensive. So we not only wrote plot synopses (with some critical analysis) of every one of Lovecraft's stories, but also had similar synopses for important essays and poems, entries (sometimes quite lengthy ones) on his family, friends, colleagues, and correspondents, and entries on major characters in his fiction. We also included citations to critical books or articles on the various topics in question. I think this book turned out quite well, and Greenwood Press published the book in 2001.

Then there is the saga of *The Ancient Track: Complete Poetical Works of H. P. Lovecraft.* I had prepared this volume as early as the mid-1990s, probably soon after I finished *Miscellaneous Writings.* Jim Turner of Arkham House was seriously interested in publishing the book; but after he left the company, the project was dropped. A few years later Marc Michaud offered to publish the book through Necronomicon Press, and he generated a fine set of page proofs; but it was just at this time (around 1999) when Marc suffered some personal setbacks that essentially caused him to drop out of publishing—and pretty much out of contact with most of his friends and colleagues. I was of course saddened by this turn of events, but hoped that *The Ancient Track* could find a home somewhere. Jason Williams of Night Shade Books, which had begun a few years earlier by publishing a curious book on the *Necronomicon* (*The Necronomicon Files* [1991] by Daniel Harms and John Wisdom Gonce III), came to my rescue. He was happy to publish the book and, using Marc's page design, issued the book in 2001.

The book came close to being a comprehensive edition of Lovecraft's poetic output, even including scraps of poetry found in letters. In the interim, some new scraps (and two whole poems—mostly poems from amateur journals of whose existence I knew but which I had not been able to locate) have emerged, but overall I think *The Ancient Track* did a good job in presenting the corpus of Lovecraft's poetry in a sensible arrangement. I did not organise the poems chronologically, as I felt a thematic arrangement was a better way to go. This meant that the category of "Occasional Poems" was a bit unwieldy, but at least I had gathered Lovecraft's weird poetry (which I had already culled for the Necronomicon Press edition of *The Fantastic Poetry*) in one compact section, along with his satiric poetry (the only other aspect of his verse that has genuine merit) and other branches of his work, including a fairly large section of (rather tedious) poetry relating to amateur

8. New York (1995–2001)

affairs. A selection of the best of Lovecraft's poetry—something Derleth attempted but failed to accomplish with *Collected Poems* (1963)—would still be a useful volume.

Along the way, I continued my investigation of other writers of weird fiction. I assembled a volume for Tartarus Press (Henry Ferris's *A Night with Mephistopheles* [1997]) and one for Ash-Tree Press (a volume of Arthur Quiller-Couch's collected weird fiction, entitled *The Horror on the Stair* [2000]). The Ferris book came about in an odd way. I was investigating the authorship of a story called "A Night in the Bell Inn," which had been attributed to J. Sheridan Le Fanu. According to the *Wellesley Index to Victorian Periodicals*, the story was actually written by Ferris (1801?–1853?), a very little-known Irish writer on "strange lore." It turns out, however, that Ferris wrote a sheaf of other works, both tales and essays, for the *Dublin University Magazine* between 1841 and 1851, enough to make a book. Ray Russell of Tartarus readily accepted it. It later turned out that some of Ferris's essays were actually translations from the German.

The Quiller-Couch volume was indirectly a result of my Lovecraft work, since in compiling Lovecraft's library I had found that he owned three of Quiller-Couch's collections of stories, each of which contained a modicum of ghostly fiction. But much more of this sort of work lay scattered throughout Quiller-Couch's writings, and it was not a matter of great difficulty to gather it all.

I was also happy to work with Chaosium on some projects. Ever since it issued Robert M. Price's *The Hastur Cycle* (1993)—which, I'm sorry to say, I excoriated in an unduly harsh review in *Lovecraft Studies*—Chaosium had been intent on publishing fiction that either influenced Lovecraft or was influenced by Lovecraft. I first proposed a volume of Lord Dunsany's early tales, specifically his tales set in the imaginary realm of Pegāna. This came to be as *The Complete Pegāna* (1998), which merely reprinted *The Gods of Pegāna* (1905) plus three stories from *Tales of Three Hemispheres* (1919). But I then assembled a much more ambitious book—nothing less than the complete weird short fiction of Robert W. Chambers. The result was an immense volume, *The Yellow Sign and Others* (2000), which contained all his weird fiction taken from all his short story collections, ranging from *The King in Yellow* (1895) to *Police!!!* (1915), and including the complete *In Search of the Unknown* (1904). The one thing I did not include was the late novel *The Slayer of Souls* (1920), not only because of its length but because it is a pretty dreadful piece of work. (Lovecraft himself found it wanting, and

I've always imagined a reprint of the book featuring a blurb that would run like this: "What a disappointment!"—H. P. Lovecraft.) The book in any event was a hefty 600 pages. And yet, Centipede Press is now envisioning a new edition of the book with the addition of *The Slayer of Souls!*

A final project is of some interest. Through my work on Bierce, I had become interested in the little-known writer W. C. Morrow, who had published one of the most pungently titled short story collections in all literature—*The Ape, the Idiot and Other People* (1897). At the New York Public Library I was able to pore through many bound volumes of the *Argonaut* and other San Francisco papers, with the result that I had amassed quite a lot of short fiction by Morrow well beyond the one story collection he published. This included a curious psychological detective story, *A Strange Adventure* (1880), along with much other interesting matter. (I also read Morrow's stirring mainstream novel *Blood Money* [1882].) Only a relatively small fraction of this material was weird in the strictest sense, but some of the crime/suspense stories were quite meritorious. I worked with Stefan Dziemianowicz to publish a selection of this work as *The Monster Maker and Other Stories* (2000) with Midnight House, one of several imprints managed by John Pelan, then residing in Seattle.

What is of specific interest about my work on Morrow is that it led to the resurrection of my fiction-writing career. I had been struck with the story "The Removal Company" (1891)—not because it was a particularly good story (it was a kind of mix between a crime story and a sentimental love story), but because I felt that Morrow had failed to realise the full potential of the basic scenario. In fairly short order I devised a plot that I felt *would* realise the potential of the story; but I would do much more than merely spin out the tale to novel length, which I felt it deserved. I would transform the tale into a kind of hard-boiled crime story, set in the 1930s, with a tough-guy detective along the lines of Sam Spade or Philip Marlowe. I named my detective Joe Scintilla (I have no idea whether that name even exists as a surname in any language), and in about three weeks I produced *The Removal Company*, a novel of just over 50,000 words. I simply couldn't carry on the narrative beyond that length—and didn't want to. I felt I had done what I had set out to do, and that any further wordage would be merely padding. I can't recall if any publishers actually looked at the manuscript—I think one did, but didn't bite on it. So the book lay fallow for a time.

As the new millennium approached (on January 1, 2001—*not* 2000, as I tried to tell everyone who would listen), other projects came to fruition. I

8. New York (1995–2001)

had long wished to write a full-scale critical study of Ramsey Campbell, who I felt had by this time produced a sufficient body of work that such a study would be justified. I had been disappointed with Gary William Crawford's brief and sketchy Starmont Reader's Guide to Campbell (1988), which I felt had wrongly proposed that Campbell had merely reworked old-time Gothic themes; anyway, that work was very much out of date, failing to take note of such vibrant novels as *Midnight Sun* (1990) and *The Long Lost* (1993). So I wrote to Twayne Publishers—and, lo and behold, received a contract.

I wrote the study according to their specifications sometime in the late 1990s—and duly submitted the book. What was my surprise when it was rejected! The editor claimed that I had engaged in too much plot synopsis and not enough analysis. There was some justification to that claim, although I felt that the plot synopses were essential to any proper study of the works in question; but what was really going on, I believe, was that Twayne had decided that a Ramsey Campbell volume simply would not sell very well, as he was still not widely known to the mainstream literary—and academic—community. So I turned down Twayne's offer for a major rewrite, thinking I could land the volume elsewhere. My decision ended up being providential, for Twayne itself collapsed in the early 2000s, so that my book would have been orphaned if it had appeared under that imprint.

I believe it was Ramsey himself who suggested that I approach Liverpool University Press. Ramsey certainly qualified as a "local author" whom Liverpool might wish to promote; moreover, the publisher had a strong line of science fiction books, and my study might fit more or less within that line. So I signed a contract with Liverpool and did rewrite the book to some degree, tightening up the prose and cutting down some of the plot description. The book appeared in 2001 as *Ramsey Campbell and Modern Horror Fiction*, with a gorgeous cover (previously published) by J. K. Potter, who seems to have had an uncanny ability to interpret Campbell's hallucinatory prose in art. Campbell himself added a fine autobiographical piece, "My Roots Exhumed," as a sort of foreword to the book.

Liverpool signed me up to do another project—nothing less than a substantially abridged version of my Lovecraft biography. Recall that *H. P. Lovecraft: A Life* was already abridged from the manuscript version (from 508,000 words to 350,000 words); now Liverpool proposed a volume that would be no more than 150,000 words! How on earth was I to whittle down even the 350,000-word version to less than half that length? Well, I simply ended up cutting out a lot of plot synopses of the stories, which readers could be expected to know. That was the easy part. Over successive waves of revision, I pruned and clipped and filed and cut and chopped. The whole process took weeks, and I quite frankly (and perhaps a little egotistically) felt as if I were cutting out parts of myself. But the job got done somehow, and the result was *A Dreamer and a Visionary: H. P. Lovecraft in His Time,* also published in 2001. I suppose it is a fair version of a compact Lovecraft biography; unfortunately, it appeared only in England, with little distribution in the U.S.

Another book that emerged in 2001 was *The Modern Weird Tale.* This came out from McFarland, whose line of books on various aspects of popular culture—especially horror film—led me to think it might be interested in such a book. It was—but McFarland objected to the book's length, with the result that I ended up having to cut out whole chapters (on Les Daniels, Dennis Etchison, and David J. Schow) along with the introductory notes to some other sections. In other words, I ended up having to make pretty much the same cuts that I would have had to have made when Southern Illinois University Press was considering the volume back in 1992! Some reviewers noted the fact that the book was about a decade out of date, as I made no effort to update the book in the nine years it had sat unpublished. Well, at least it had come out, and it sold reasonably well. McFarland issued the book only in paperback (at an outrageous list price of $34.95) and kept it in print for a good many years; a Kindle edition is still in print. Amusingly enough, at about the same time as the McFarland edition appeared, the book was translated into German (as *Moderne Horrorautoren*) in two volumes by Festa Verlag, with the restoration of the chapters I had had to drop!

One final project at this time concerned my favourite contemporary weird writer, Ramsey Campbell. I can't recall whether it was he or I who suggested a volume of his collected essays on weird fiction; I may have been inspired by the fact that he had written so many outstanding pieces for *Necrofile,* which I felt should be preserved in more permanent form. Ramsey had also written a number of essays on other writers, ranging from Clive Barker to Stephen King to James Herbert, as well as introductions to books by Donald R. Burleson, Dennis Etchison, and many others. Finally, he had written interesting forewords or afterwords to new editions of his own books, notably the Scream/Press edition of *The Face That Must Die* (1983), where he had talked of his sad upbringing after his parents had become estranged. So I assembled all this material, and Ramsey gave it the title *Ramsey Campbell, Probably.* It appeared in 2002 from PS Publishing, a British small press that was on the verge of becoming Ramsey's default publisher. I believe the book came out pretty well. It is perhaps the only book I have edited that does not contain a single word of writing from me.

By the late 1990s I had begun to sense that we needed more venues for the publication of Lovecraft scholarship as well as some of Lovecraft's lesser works. Much as I was encouraged by the continual growth of Lovecraft's reputation and popularity, both here and abroad, I realised that in the short term the dissemination of such material would still have to occur by way of small presses. I was immensely grateful to Marc for having issued *H. P. Lovecraft: A Life*, and he kept the paperback edition in print for at least a decade (there were paperback printings in 1996, 1997, and 2004, each of about 2000 copies). But with Necronomicon Press flagging as a venue for specialised material, I sensed the need to find someone else to take over the load.

I had no idea, when Derrick Hussey began attending New Kalem Club meetings in the mid-1990s, that he would be the saviour I was looking for. Derrick had been working for Routledge, a leading academic firm, but was dissatisfied with his progress within the company and had recently resigned. He seemed to be somewhat at loose ends, so in an almost jocular fashion I said at one Kalem meeting, "Why don't you become a publisher yourself?"

Derrick was intrigued at the possibility. By this time, of course, the increasing sophistication of desktop publishing and the advent of print-on-demand outlets made the task of preparing attractive books far easier. One still needed a certain initial outlay of capital, but that didn't seem to be a problem for Derrick; and when I flatly told him that I could keep him supplied with an unlimited array of viable books, either of my own or by my colleagues, he decided to take the plunge.

Sometime earlier I had dug out my old annotated edition of "Supernatural Horror in Literature," prepared all the way back in 1981, and typed it into my computer. I had updated the bibliography on several occasions, wishing to include up-to-date citations to the authors and works Lovecraft had discussed in his essay. I had sent the file of the book to David E. Schultz, who purely as a lark had set it up as a book, just as a kind of practice effort in book design. Derrick seized on this item and brought it out as *The Annotated Supernatural Horror in Literature* in 2000 under the imprint of Hippocampus Press. On my recommendation, Derrick chose as the cover art the splendid line drawing by Vrest Orton on the cover of the *Recluse* (1927), where the original version of "Supernatural Horror in Literature" had appeared. The cover design was prepared by Barbara Briggs Silbert (Scott Briggs's mother), who is a professional graphic designer.

Derrick had come upon the rather odd name for his press by way of a letter by Lovecraft to Frank Belknap Long: "be a nice little amethystine hippocampus, write your Old Grandpa, and prepare to visit Providentia's sequester'd shades when the sun is warm and genial." I suppose the name is as evocative as any that could have been chosen, although it does not evoke specifically Lovecraftian echoes in most people's minds—but perhaps that is for the best, since the press has expanded well beyond the realm of Lovecraftiana.

I believe this initial publication did reasonably well for Derrick, and so we moved on to our next project—nothing less than the corrected text of "The Shadow out of Time," based on my consultation of the autograph manuscript back in 1994. David and I had annotated the text as extensively as we had "The Shadow over Innsmouth" for the Necronomicon Press edition, and we asked John Stanley to write a brief statement about the discovery of the manuscript. I was pleased that, after seven years, the text of this important Lovecraft story was finally available to the public. What's more, Hippocampus Press was off and running, and I would devote a substantial bulk of my attention to it over the next decade and more.

I was continuing to work on projects well outside the realm of supernatural fiction. One of the most interesting was a book inspired by my study of Lovecraft's racism. Various books I had read on the subject led me to understand that there was an immense amount of appalling racist material, written by well-known figures of their day and published in prestigious venues, that had been all but forgotten—justifiably so, because it presents both its authors and the culture in which they functioned in a poor light. I felt that present-day Americans needed to confront this material so that they could understand the long and cruel history of racism from the very beginning of European occupation of this continent.

The result was *Documents of American Prejudice,* issued by Basic Books in 1999. My former Chelsea House friend Richard Fumosa was now working at Basic Books, and he directed me to the editorial staff, where my book was accepted. I included all manner of writings on African Americans, Latinos, Asians, Jews, and other areas, including a long concluding section on anti-immigrant screeds. Needless to say, I included some works that Lovecraft had read—the most piquantly titled of which was Lothrop Stoddard's *The Rising Tide of Color against White World-Supremacy* (1920), a best-selling volume of its day. There were also pieces by Thomas Jefferson, Oliver Wendell Holmes, Ralph Waldo Emerson, Madison Grant, Theodore Roosevelt,

8. New York (1995–2001)

Andrew Jackson, William Gilmore Simms, Abraham Lincoln, Thomas Nelson Page, Thomas Dixon, Jr. (an extract from his racist novel *The Clansman*), Mark Twain, Ambrose Bierce, Jack London (*The Yellow Peril*), Walt Whitman, Henry James, Calvin Coolidge, Madison Grant (*The Passing of the Great Race*, which Lovecraft probably read), and many others—107 pieces in all. I wrote headnotes to each piece and introductions to each of the twelve sections of the book, along with a general introduction.

I believe this was a fine and necessary compilation, but the publisher chose not to promote the book to any significant degree. It received almost no reviews, although a brief notice did appear many months after publication in the *New Yorker* (and this, I believe, was because Mindi had given a copy to a colleague who worked at that magazine). So sales were not exactly robust. But I had gotten the book out. I recall reading one notice (possibly a reader's comment) that the book was covertly meant to promote racism by broadcasting these ugly views, but I very much doubt that any sane person could plausibly arrive at such a view. I decided to omit Lovecraft, although obviously there would have been a wealth of material to choose from, because he had had no influence on the public discussions of race during his lifetime.

While *Documents of American Prejudice* had taken many months to compile, another project came together far more quickly. In the course of my research on W. C. Morrow and Edward Lucas White, I had stumbled on some Civil War stories they had written that had never been reprinted. I wondered if I could assemble an entire volume of lesser-known stories of the type—and in a matter of two weeks had come up with a book! It was actually quite simple to consult other anthologies of Civil War writings, and then comb some standard authors (Henry James, Louisa May Alcott, Kate Chopin, Sarah Orne Jewett, Thomas Nelson Page—and, of course, Ambrose Bierce) to find stories that, if not actually unreprinted, were at least not very well known. I pitched the volume to a publisher that specialised in such books, Rutledge Hill Press in Nashville. The book was quickly accepted and appeared in 2000. I had titled the book *Lost Stories of the Civil War*, but the publisher used the strange title *Civil War Memories*, which made the book sound as if it contained true accounts of the war by those who had served in it. I complained, but to no purpose.

The amusing thing is that this project has proved to be among my most successful books. It was reprinted by two other publishers (Gramercy Books in 2003 and Barnes & Noble in 2009) and sold well in each of its incarnations. Not bad for two weeks' work! And as a matter of fact, I think the book has some fine tales. One of the W. C. Morrow stories, "The Bloodhounds" (1879), is a grim account of an escaped slave hunted down by hounds. I even found a little-known story by Stephen Crane ("Three Miraculous Soldiers"), and one of Bierce's tales that fuse a Civil War setting with psychological terror ("Three and One Are One").

A more serious project—and another one that, although I did not know it at the time, would lead to several more projects of the same sort—was *Atheism: A Reader*. My work on Lovecraft's atheism (as discussed in *H. P. Lovecraft: The Decline of the West*) and on ancient philosophy had been leading me in this direction for years. I had noticed that Prometheus Books, a leading publisher of atheist/freethought books, had published two large anthologies of atheism compiled by Gordon Stein in the 1980s; but I felt that these volumes were missing some significant authors and works that were vital in portraying the history of atheism in the West. Accordingly, I set about assembling a volume of my own. I knew I had to include something by Lovecraft, as I wished to give his incisive remarks on the subject a wider audience; I chose his pungent letter to Maurice W. Moe (May 15, 1918). Beyond that, I chose a section of Lucretius' *De Rerum Natura* arguing against the immortality of the soul; works by my chief philosophical influences, Bertrand Russell and A. J. Ayer; an essay by Leslie Stephen (a leading nineteenth-century British philosopher and critic, and the father of Virginia Woolf), whose work I had come upon while at Chelsea House; and many other interesting pieces by Percy Bysshe Shelley, Emma Goldman, H. L. Mencken, John Stuart Mill, George Eliot, Anatole France, Charles Darwin, Robert G. Ingersoll, Clarence Darrow, Carl Sagan, Friedrich Nietzsche, Elizabeth Cady Stanton, and others. The book was accepted by Prometheus and published in 2000. It received quite good reviews (although some reviewers criticised my harsh introduction, where I basically branded religious believers as brainless asses)—and, more significantly, has sold exceptionally well for Prometheus. It remains in print to this day.

*

It was at the end of the period covered in this chapter that I underwent the most intense and torturous experience of my entire personal life.

My relationship with Mindi had reached a certain plateau. For five years we had been content to meet each other on weekends, go to the occasional

8. New York (1995–2001)

opera or other performance, take in a movie nearly every week, and so on. The strange thing was that, not only did the issue of cohabitation never come up (or, rather, it was already settled: the prospect of cohabitation was simply deemed unworkable, for the reasons I've outlined), but the subject of marriage never came up once in those five years. My mother, who had not yet given up hope that I would spawn offspring, would probably not have approved of marriage to a woman so far beyond her childbearing years—not that that would have made any difference to me.

Things took a rather bizarre turn in 2001. Leslie—with whom I had remained sporadically in touch since I had re-established contact in 1991—had said she wished to pay me a visit. Actually, all she said was that she wished to visit New York City—would I be around for a day or two to be her tour guide? Because she had just been laid off from her job as a Latin teacher, she was choosing a cheap vacation spot—not that New York itself was cheap, but she had a friend who lived on the Upper East Side who had offered to put her up, so that a hotel bill could be avoided. And I was almost the only other person in the New York area whom she knew.

Leslie's life since our fleeting engagement had been a bit mixed. She had gained her library science degree from the University of Washington, but had never secured a position in a library. Instead, she had utilised her Latin skills to teach at the high school level, most recently at the Villa Academy, a Catholic school in Seattle. This job had essentially been terminated because of financial difficulties at the school, so Leslie was wanting to take a little break before plunging back into the job market.

I had of course told Mindi of my previous involvement with Leslie, and as the time for her trip approached Mindi became quite nervous. I tried to reassure her that whatever feelings I had had for Leslie had long ago dissipated. This was especially the case because, around 1995, Leslie had actually married someone else. It struck me as odd, however, that in our communications she rarely if ever mentioned her husband (one Jeff Godden). Maybe she was just trying to spare my feelings: she had waited some months before even telling me of her marriage, fearful that I would be angry or hurt; in fact, I reacted to the news with bland resignation, sensing that whatever dim hopes I had had in that direction had been essentially negated. Then, in 2000, Leslie quietly announced that she had divorced Jeff. Again I reacted calmly to the news, not thinking that it really altered our relations in any significant way. So I looked forward to seeing her merely as an old friend whom I had known for nearly two decades.

The plan was to meet her on the steps of the New York Public Library around noon on a Thursday. I was there a bit ahead of schedule, so I was waiting at the top of the long stairway leading up to the library entrance. Presently Leslie appeared—and my heart seemed to do a back flip. She looked radiantly beautiful, and of course all my memories of our prior involvement flooded over me.

We had lunch somewhere, then simply walked about. I can't even remember where we went, but I remember ending up at some spot overlooking the Hudson River, where I told her that I felt I had changed quite a bit since she had known me back in 1989: I was less intolerant and dogmatic, more able to understand other people's points of view, and in general far less agitated than I had been in what I considered to be my protracted youth, which had extended into my early thirties.

We parted, with plans to meet the next day at a spot near where she was staying so that we could take a bus to the Cathedral of St. John the Divine, which she had never seen. I duly met her; as we sat next to each other on the bus, she took my hand and said, "Are you feeling what I'm feeling?" I admitted that I was. There was, in short, no question that I was still in love with her—in a way that I would never be with Mindi.

When we got to the cathedral, Leslie impulsively sought to kiss me in some secluded corner. I was pretty discombobulated by this turn of events—on top of which, my lips were somewhat chapped, so that I wasn't sure I was really ready for that kiss! But we kissed anyway. After eighteen years, I had somehow won her heart! I had no idea how it had happened, but it had happened nonetheless.

We later sat in Bryant Park wondering what to do. For of course there was Mindi to consider. She had done nothing to bring this fate upon herself; Leslie's assertion that Mindi might be prepared to recognise Leslie's "prior claim" upon me was too preposterous for words. We couldn't just spring this upon her—and yet, we were set to meet her for dinner in a few hours!

The situation was unresolved by the time we came to Mitali West, one of my favourite Indian restaurants, on Seventh Avenue South. Leslie and I got there first, and Mindi duly arrived, sitting next to me as she felt was her due. That dinner was an excruciating affair: somehow Leslie and I managed to conceal our true feelings while Mindi chatted with us without a care in the world. Leslie took a cab back to her friend's apartment, and Mindi and I strolled back to my co-op.

On Sunday, while Mindi was in the shower, I managed to make a surreptitious call to Leslie. All I could say was that we would work the situation out somehow. As Leslie returned to Seattle, we began planning. She of course wished me to break it off with Mindi at once, but my residual shyness and my understandable unwillingness to cause anyone emotional heartache prevented me. Initially Leslie and I hatched a plan whereby she would come to New York and I would see her during the week while still maintaining my weekend rendezvous with Mindi; but Leslie later put the kibosh on that ridiculous idea. For her own self-respect, and for our future happiness, she stressed that I had to tell Mindi sooner rather than later.

Well, I did—shortly after a trip we took to Philadelphia. She could sense that I was seriously disturbed, but I put her off and said I would explain later. I did so in the most cowardly manner imaginable: I wrote her an email about the whole situation. I knew I couldn't dodge her entirely, but I felt that this was the best way I could explain my side of the situation without interruption. Well, that was only the beginning. Mindi later called me, heartbroken and outraged, and we spoke for hours. It was an agonising conversation, but she had no choice but to admit that she had been kicked out of my life.

The task of separation was not a simple one. She had many belongings at my co-op, and she demanded that I vacate for some hours while she came over to clear out her stuff. The task was accomplished, although she neglected to leave behind the spare set of keys I had given her; she eventually mailed them back to me.

So now I was in the clear, even though I had felt as if I had gone through the ringer in the process. No doubt what Mindi had suffered was much worse: she had to face the humiliating prospect that the man she had loved for more than five years had discarded her like an old shoe for someone he loved better. I'm sure I could have handled the matter better, but my general inexperience in situations of this sort had probably made me come off as brutish and cruel.

But there was Leslie's next visit to consider. She was now planning to stay for a full month in New York; later I would stay for a comparable time in Seattle. The first order of business we had to settle was whether we would live in one place or the other. Since I was now a full-time freelance writer who was (more or less) self-supporting, I could theoretically work anywhere. But perhaps Leslie wished to live in New York for a while—and my place would make a nice haven for her.

We were well aware that we had not actually spent a great deal of time in each other's company in all the years we had known each other. The summer of 1989 loomed large as an example of what trouble we might face: the week in June we had spent together had been wonderful, but the six-week period later that summer where we had lived together in a "normal" working situation was very different. But we also realised that circumstances had changed dramatically for both of us. I was no longer having to report to an office and could set my own hours; I was also living in an apartment far different from my dreadful flat in Jersey City. Moreover, we both felt that we had matured somewhat since 1989: Leslie had been married once, and I had had several close relationships with various women, although none of them really amounted to a "living" situation.

The month Leslie spent in my co-op was a wonderful experience. I no longer remember the exact details of what we did, but we visited some standard tourist sites and met some of my friends in the area. At one point we rented a car and drove around New England. Again, my memory as to details is vague, but I'm sure we spent a few days in Providence as well as in the Boston area.

We had convinced ourselves that we were well matched, but I was by no means certain that Leslie would be happy in New York—and I had come to sense that I myself might need a change. I had lived in the area for seventeen years, and I was no longer the young man I was. New York takes a great deal of energy: even the simplest tasks require going out into crowded streets or congested subways, and the city is filled with hostile and dangerous people at every turn. Also, I had grown tired of living in apartments—as I had for the past twenty-five years, if one counts the dorm rooms and other places I had occupied in college—and yearned to live in an actual house with a yard and a neighbourhood.

So I looked forward to visiting Leslie in Seattle. The one benefit of her marriage to Jeff Godden was that in the divorce settlement she had obtained full title to the house they had occupied—a nice but smallish two-bedroom place in the coveted Wedgwood district of the city. The only issue was whether I could work successfully in the Pacific Northwest. At the time, I still felt I needed a large university library to conduct my research. I didn't doubt that the University of Washington library was adequate for the purpose, but there were other factors to consider as well.

My trip to Seattle was also highly successful. I was glad to meet her family again (although her father had died in 1996, only two years after my father had passed away). Her older sister, Eleanor (called Elie), professed bluntly not to have remembered me from my earlier visits of more than a decade before, to which I coolly remarked, "I suppose I'm not very memorable." But Leslie's mother was gracious and welcoming, as she always was.

The trip occurred during a month-long span from mid-August to mid-September, and toward the end of it we were convinced that we were meant for each other. I myself was so determined not to let Leslie slip through my fingers again that I pleaded with her to have a quick marriage ceremony before I was scheduled to leave on September 9. She agreed, and we duly filled out the paperwork and were married on September 1, 2001. The idea of a church wedding was of course out of the question in light of my atheism, and anyway there was no time for such a thing. We hired a rather New Age-ish pastor at a dime-store chapel who hastily conducted the ceremony. My best man was Kirk Sigurdson, a young devotee of weird fiction who had written a fine thesis on Lovecraft (which I published in part in *Lovecraft Studies*) and was in Seattle to attend an annual music festival, Bumbershoot. He was stunned when, as he sat down with us at a pub a few days before the event, we said, "If you're not doing anything on Saturday, why don't you be best man at our wedding?" Only three other people—all friends of Leslie's—were in attendance. Afterward, we came back to her house and had pizza and ice cream.

So it was done: I was married to Leslie after pursuing her (rather sporadically) for eighteen years! And we had resolved to live in Seattle. I of course had to return to New York to begin the tedious task of wrapping up my affairs and getting ready to move, so I left Seattle on September 9.

9. Seattle I (2001–05)

> "I see the world peopled with dupes and knaves."—Robespierre

I scarcely need inform readers what occurred two days after I returned. In fact, I slept through the events of 9/11, as I was still so jetlagged that I did not awaken until about 10:30 on that fateful Tuesday morning. My copy of the *New York Times* was waiting for me on schedule on my doorstep, but of course it only told of the events of the previous day. I never turn on the television or the radio in the mornings, so I knew nothing of the events until Scott Briggs called me up around noon, babbling incoherently about how he had been told to go home from his midtown office. When it became obvious to Scott that I didn't know what had occurred (I had, to be sure, heard sirens here and there—but in New York City one always hears sirens, so I thought this was nothing special), he told me, "You'd better turn on the TV—something very strange has happened." Well, I did—and then called Leslie at once. She herself was only just waking up in Seattle.

I was living about two or three miles north of the World Trade Center, but that was far enough for me to have little sense of the cataclysmic nature of the event. Scott later came to my apartment, and we strolled outside. Other people were wandering around in a daze, and when I saw the sudden absence of the twin towers in the lower skyline, I felt a sense of outrage—not because my country had been attacked, but because the city I felt had become my home and the focus of my literary and personal life had suffered this grotesque mutilation. It was as if someone had extracted a tooth violently and without anaesthetic. I of course had been to the World Trade Center many times—I once took my mother to the observation deck there, as I felt that one could get a far more interesting view of the general area than from the Empire State Building's observation deck. And one line of the PATH trains dropped people off there, and I had ridden that line more times than I can remember. But since the events of 9/11 I have never ventured down there—and don't think I will.

The immediate effect of 9/11 was to speed up my departure from New York. In spite of the fact that I was now a married man, I had planned a leisurely move to Seattle, perhaps by November or December. But Leslie urged me to come sooner. I agreed with the plan—not because I feared another terrorist attack, but because I saw little reason for delay, and I wished to be settled in my new house sooner rather than later. I could of course not take anything like all my possessions—which now amounted to at least 5000 books, along with my collection of LPs and my ever-increasing files of papers, documents, etc.—with me; they would have to be brought over by professional movers. But I needed some essential items with me, and I shipped them to Leslie's house while starting the process of discarding certain items (such as back issues of the *New York Review of Books*) that I had saved simply because I was too indolent to throw them away.

So on October 12, 2001, I left New York for good, at least as a resident. I of course knew that I would have to come back at least once; but, as I settled into Leslie's house at 3158 NE 81st Street, I felt that I had left New York behind and was on the verge of becoming a Seattleite—whether temporarily or permanently, I was not clear. In fact, this move began a period in which I moved six times in eleven years—not good for stability or for keeping track of things!

My first order of business was to get my effects in order. The movers I hired packed my belongings themselves after I had left, and in a week or so they arrived on our doorstep. There were a grand total of 173 large boxes, of which 101 consisted of books. These were stacked in our garage, filling the space from floor to ceiling. It took weeks for me to unpack all the material and arrange it in our small house. My workspace was in the partially finished basement, a large area where I could house my entire library collection along with a desk for my computer and other equipment. The arrangement was adequate, but no more; at times I felt a bit like a mushroom working entirely with artificial light, even during the sunny days of Seattle's dry season.

One adjustment I was entirely happy to make was to get acquainted with Leslie's two cats, Pinkley and Chessie. Pinkley was an old gray shorthaired cat who was at least seventeen years old. I had first met him in 1989, when Leslie actually had to move out of her apartment temporarily because it had suffered some water damage; we took Pinkley to her mother's house, where we stayed for the duration of my visit then. He was diabetic, so we needed to make sure he was available for his twice-daily insulin injections. Accordingly, we set up a system whereby he could go out into the front or back yard on a harness, with a long cord attached to a clothesline that allowed him to roam nearly the entire yard, but that permitted him to be "reeled in" if necessary. (He did, however, on one occasion escape from his harness, and after some anxious searching I found him cowering in fear in a neighbour's yard.)

Chessie, on the other hand, was young—maybe only a year old at this time. Leslie had gotten her as a kind of emotional ballast in the event that Pinkley (whom she had had for nearly his entire life) died. She was a regal but energetic short-hair who was a bit on the skittish side, but who in the end welcomed me into her heart, as I did her. But Pinkley was the cat I bonded with more readily. Late at night, when I would lie at full length on the sofa in the living room, he would jump up and lie on my chest, staring into my face. No doubt he wanted some of my body heat, but I felt gratified at his attention.

I was thrilled to be in the presence of cats for the first time since I had left Muncie to go to college. I had always felt that, because I had lived alone and in apartments up to this time, it would be irresponsible of me to own a cat. I hated the idea of leaving a cat cooped up in a small apartment, all alone (assuming I was either in college or working at an office), unable to have its freedom in the great outdoors. And I didn't know what I would do with such a creature during my frequent absences on vacations or research trips. But the moment I came into daily contact with Leslie's cats, I knew that I would never again live without one—and more than one, if I could manage it.

Leslie had by this time secured a position as the receptionist/office manager of the Classics Department at the University of Washington—a position that her mother had held years before. This was fortuitous for more than one reason, for she urgently needed a hysterectomy, and now we could rely on the university's excellent health plan. I believe she had the operation in late October: I stayed at the hospital all morning while the operation was in progress, and I was the first to see her as she groggily emerged into consciousness after the anaesthetic wore off. Her recovery was understandably slow, but by early December she was back at work.

It was, however, becoming quickly obvious to us that we needed to find a larger house. My belongings had filled Leslie's house to the brim, and there was very little space to move about. So, early in 2002, we began looking for another place to live. I did not relish the thought of moving again, although a local move would presumably be easier than a move across the continent. It was also determined that I should sell my New York co-op: by this time it had become clear that we would never occupy it, and we would need the revenue from it to purchase a new house. Our local real estate agent, Jeff Perkins, found a competent agent in New York, and my co-op was put on sale on the Ides of March, when an open house was held. It got three offers that very day; I shall not go into details, but let's just say that I ended up selling the place for more than two and a half times what I paid for it. The events of 9/11 had not in any way dampened the compelling desire of many to live in Manhattan! And my apartment was quite a bit larger than most, and in a central location. So the sale went through.

Jeff took us house-hunting for weeks, perhaps months, until we finally found a place we liked: a four-bedroom house at 5525 16th Avenue NE, in the University District. This place—built in 1905, which for Seattle is very old indeed—was within walking distance of the university, on a shady and placid street. It was a magnificent house with an immense living/dining area, kitchen, and a kind of "extra room" on the first floor, and four bedrooms—one on each corner of the house—on the second floor. I of course earmarked the bedroom overlooking the street (a sort of "corner office") for my main study. The only drawback was that the yard was quite small: the front yard was adequate, but there was no back yard at all, because the lot had been subdivided and a small house (currently serving as an apartment building with three units) had been built directly behind ours. One could almost touch it from our back door. But we weren't exactly diligent gardeners, and the front yard allowed ample room for whatever plants we wished to grow.

But the property—a corner lot, one side facing 16th Avenue, the other facing 56th Street—was not fenced, and we noticed that passersby had a tendency to cut across the yard when going from one street to the other. Therefore, we had a fence built soon after we moved in. The company we hired used plain, unpainted lumber, and so there was the need to paint it. That task devolved upon me, even though I had never done any such thing before. I first put on primer for the fence—which stretched a total of 134 feet—and then two coats of white paint. The whole process took weeks, but I was immensely proud of the finished product. I do not generally consider myself handy around the house, but I think I did this job more than adequately. (I may note that, in attempting some work in our previous house, I skirted disaster. In trying to pull out some vegetation that had grown in the gutter, I tumbled off a ladder and fell hard on my right shoulder. The whole experience was, from a sensory perspective, very bizarre: I felt as if I were suspended in the air for a moment, only to crash hard on the ground. Leslie wanted to take me to the hospital, but after painfully moving the affected shoulder, I concluded it was not broken. I recovered slowly but satisfactorily over the next several weeks.)

It was only a few weeks after we had moved into the house that Pinkley quite suddenly came down with an illness. It turned out to be a tumour in his kidneys, and less than a month after his diagnosis he was dead. He had, indeed, lived to the ripe old age of eighteen and a half—but he was the first cat I had known whose death I had personally witnessed. (He would not be the last.) Even though I had lived with him for only about a year, I wept in grief over that little ball of fur.

Two days after Pinkley's death, we strolled over to an animal shelter and adopted a cat that the shelter had named Jack o' Hearts. This cat, already ten years old, had been owned by a young man who had died in a motorcycle accident. His mother had absurdly wanted the cat to be euthanised, but the shelter adamantly refused to do that. But the cat remained in the shelter for *nearly a year* because, being diabetic, it was regarded as too much of a bother for potential owners. We came to the cat's rescue, since we were already used to dealing with a diabetic cat. The shelter told us that they had held a bottle of champagne in reserve for the time when the cat would be adopted.

We promptly renamed the cat Sneakers, because he had four white paws. Otherwise, he was a rather fat and quite curmudgeonly tabby with whom I had my difficulties at the start, although we eventually got along splendidly. In one unfortunate incident, Sneakers lashed out at me while I was holding him and scratched my face just above my left eye, causing me to drop him. He fell awkwardly, and we thought he had broken his leg; but eventually it turned out that he had only sprained it. He recovered well enough, although he walked with something of a limp thereafter. But he eventually settled down and became a good and lovable cat.

Another curious thing that happened in the winter and spring of 2002 was that I became a choral singer again. I had not done anything of the kind since high school; I still remembered how I had failed to pass the audition for the Brown University Chorus. But Leslie had been involved in a local community choir for years (this was, indeed, one of the reasons why she hadn't wished to move to New York back in 1989), one of many in the Seattle area. This one was led by an African American man named Lynn Hall—a very pious gent who concluded each rehearsal with a brief prayer to Jesus. Leslie was worried that this might offend my atheism, but it didn't (and doesn't) bother me in the slightest. Lynn is not a government official, and it doesn't take much effort to sit quietly while the prayer is being uttered. Anyway, the prospect of singing great works of music—mostly sacred, admittedly, but it is a brute fact that some of the greatest choral music in Western civilisation is sacred—was too much to pass up. The choir—the Northwest Chorale, of which I am still a member—performs twice a year, in winter and in spring; every odd-numbered year it performs Handel's *Messiah* for its winter (Christmas) concert, with other works (sometimes a medley of short works, sometimes one long work) performed during the other times. Rehearsals are every Monday for about two to two and a half hours.

During the decade or more in which I've been in this chorus, I've performed such incredible works as Bach's *B Minor Mass*, Mendelssohn's *Elijah*, Verdi's *Requiem*, Mozart's *Requiem*, Britten's *Ceremony of Carols*, and many other works. I have performed Handel's *Messiah* so many times that I know it by memory. Lynn Hall is an outstanding musician who knows everything there is to know about choral music; and he has the gifts to elicit the best out of his fundamentally amateur group of singers (there are no auditions). Our choir generally numbers about sixty members, but in the *Messiah* years we have had as many as eighty.

It took me a full year to get my voice back into decent shape. I still hoped to be able to sing tenor, as I had done in high school; but as my speaking voice had now become rather low, I wondered if I could still manage. I could—barely. I at times have to resort to "head voice" (i.e., falsetto) for the higher notes; but when I am in good practice I can sing the A above middle C (generally the highest note required of tenors in most choral works) without falsetto. I have a pretty wide range and can sing bass at times—indeed, I *did* sing bass when our choir performed William Byrd's haunting *Mass in F minor*. I can go as low as the D nearly two octaves below middle C, which even most basses cannot manage.

One hilarious thing that occurred as a result of my joining the Northwest Chorale was—hold on to your hats, folks—my joining a church choir! Can you imagine the absurdity of such a thing? It came about because a bass in the chorale, Ed Bossert, who was a member of the choir at Queen Anne Lutheran Church, begged me to join the church choir because it had *no tenors at all*, meaning that it could only sing three-part music (soprano/alto/bass). I was pretty dubious about venturing into a church every Sunday, but Leslie joined me for a while for solidarity. We had to go to the church (quite a distance from our house) on Thursday for a rehearsal (usually only about an hour), and of course had to show up for the service on Sun-

9. Seattle I (2001–05)

day. The choir overall was quite small, totalling ten to fifteen people; but the music we sang was surprisingly interesting. For the "performance" I had to put on a white muslin robe that stretched to my feet. I felt like a perfect idiot doing so, but figured I could stomach it once a week. The pastor was a rather engaging fellow who delivered interesting sermons full of wit and humour, although he tended to get serious and emotional toward the end. What he was saying was of course windy nonsense, but he was a good performer.

My friends were so incredulous that I, a fire-eating atheist, had joined a church choir that some of them refused to believe it. When Linda Aro and Chris Pfaff came to visit us in Seattle, they attended a service—and, I believe, videotaped at least a part of my "performance." I suppose they must still have the incriminating footage, although I've never seen it. I kept up attendance for about two years—long after Leslie herself, pleading fatigue, had dropped out. This meant that, because I still wasn't driving a car, some other member of the choir had to undertake the tedium of driving all the way to my house on Thursday evenings and Sunday mornings, pick me up, take me to the church, and then take me home afterwards. This woman (an alto, as I recall) must have been truly devoted to endure this for well over a year!

But at last I dropped out. I felt increasingly irked at having to sit through the sermon, and, although I found the music we sang fairly engaging (we actually received a thunderous round of applause—something generally not allowed in a church service—when we performed a setting of the magnificent Anglican hymn "Jerusalem," with trumpet and flute accompaniment), I eventually decided that I preferred to watch football on Sunday mornings in the fall rather than go to a church service.

*

It is uncanny that during this period I ended up doing major work on all four of Lovecraft's "modern masters"—Arthur Machen, Algernon Blackwood, Lord Dunsany, and M. R. James.

First up was Machen. Around 2000 I had received an offer from Chaosium to prepare a three-volume set of Machen's collected weird fiction. I jumped at the task, for I had been doing random Machen research for many years. Using Wesley D. Sweetser and Adrian Goldstone's 1965 bibliography, I had hunted up many of Machen's fugitive writings in British magazines while I was at Princeton: the library had a vast array of such periodicals, and in off moments I had made copies of the Machen items. I had continued this work at the New York Public Library. Machen's newspaper contributions—especially in such a paper as the *London Evening News*—were harder to locate, as these articles were generally available only in England; nonetheless, I had amassed an extensive array of Machen's uncollected work.

I planned to print the stories in absolute chronological order, based on the date of composition. In *The Weird Tale* I had included an appendix supplying dates of writing of nearly every story of Machen's, based on evidence found in his autobiographies and elsewhere. For the first volume, *The Three Impostors and Other Stories* (2001), I was able to resurrect my planned reprint of *The Three Impostors,* which Dover had initially accepted but then rejected. I had been lucky enough to secure a copy of the first edition, locating it at the Strand Bookstore for all of $5.00. (On another occasion, when one of the last bookstores along lower Fourth Avenue, which even in Lovecraft's day had been a haven for used books, was closing, I had snatched the first edition of *The Secret Glory* for $6.00, latching onto it a few seconds before Steve Mariconda saw it. But this is not a weird novel.) The second volume, *The White People and Other Stories* (2004), contained not only the magnificent prose-poems in *Ornaments in Jade* (1924—the works themselves had been written in 1897), but the first known reprint of "The Coming of the Terror," an abridged version of *The Terror* that had appeared in the *Century Magazine.* Machen himself had testified that the abridgement had been done with exceptional skill, and I myself thought this version was superior to the full-length short novel. Strangely enough, I did not have *The Terror* itself in any edition except *Tales of Horror and the Supernatural* (1948). So I contacted Sam Gafford, who had extravagantly purchased the magnificent nine-volume Caerleon Edition of Machen (1923), and he sent me a photocopy of the short novel. This was for the third volume, *The Terror and Other Stories* (2006), which also included some of the stories in the late collections *The Cosy Room* and *The Children of the Pool* (2006). I did not include the late weird novel *The Green Round* (1933), as it was a pretty sorry piece of work; but I did include an unreprinted novelette, "The Dover Road" (1936).

Overall, I think this edition came out quite well, and my introductions to the three volumes expanded upon—and in some regards revised my opinions on—my chapter on Machen in *The Weird Tale*. That chapter had provoked some Machenians, like Roger Dobson, who thought it unduly harsh. I came to agree with this verdict and lessened the severity of some of my judgments on Machen's lesser work.

9. Seattle I (2001–05)

For Algernon Blackwood I did nothing more than assemble a substantial volume, *Ancient Sorceries and Other Weird Stories* (2002), for Penguin Classics—but, I think, that was enough. I had lobbied hard that Blackwood deserved to be in this series, and Michael Millman agreed with me. The problem with Blackwood is that his best work mainly consists of lengthy novellas, so I was not able to include a great many stories in the book. No volume of this sort could exclude "The Willows" and "The Wendigo"; but I also included "The Man Whom the Trees Loved" and "Sand," both from *Pan's Garden* (1912). The latter has one of the most evocative lines in all weird fiction: "The desert stood on end." I had also found great merit in *Incredible Adventures* (1914), a collection of five long tales that I declared in *The Weird Tale* to be one of the premier weird collections of all time. (Ted Klein ended up disagreeing with me on this point. After reading my praise of the book, he had re-read his copy and found he didn't care for it—so he generously gave me his copy of the first U.S. edition!) But I ended up not including any stories from it in the Penguin book, because I felt that the tales hung together so well that it would be a crime to present just one or two of them torn from their context. I think this was a mistake, and I probably should have included "A Descent into Egypt," which I am half inclined to think is superior even to "The Willows." But "Sand" had never been reprinted up to that time, so I thought it was a choicer item.

For Dunsany the case is very different. For years I had been pressing Millman to issue a Dunsany volume, but he had resisted; he himself didn't like Dunsany very much and questioned whether such a volume would sell. But finally I managed to get the nod from him for such a book, and I assembled *In the Land of Time and Other Fantasy Tales*, which appeared in 2004. I had long been irked by Lovecraft's and others' refusal to consider the entirety of Dunsany's writing, which to my mind was brilliant from beginning to end; and so, while I of course selected many classic tales that Dunsany had written in his early period (from *The Gods of Pegāna* [1905] to *Tales of Three Hemispheres* [1919]), I also made a point of including a number of late tales, including some Jorkens stories that Lovecraft had contemptuously dismissed as "tripe." I was more or less vindicated: not only did the book sell reasonably well, but it received a glowing review from Ursula K. Le Guin (whom I had not yet forgiven for using de Camp's biography to write an attack on Lovecraft in the *Times Literary Supplement* back in 1976) that appeared in the *Los Angeles Times Book Review*. But Le Guin, like Lovecraft, expressed a marked preference for the early tales!

But this was only the tip of the iceberg of my Dunsany work at this time. Not long after my critical study had come out in 1995, I had heard from the Honourable Edward Plunkett, the grandson of the writer and the son of the current (19th) Lord Dunsany, Randal Plunkett. He was married to a vibrant Brazilian woman, Maria Alice, who was even more enthusiastic about Lord Dunsany than his grandson was. The fact was that Randal, out of a sense of envy at being overshadowed by his illustrious father, had stood in the way of many projects that could have helped resurrect Dunsany's reputation. But his grandson, and especially Maria Alice, were intent on changing that.

They contacted me in 1996 and asked me to meet them for lunch at a swank hotel in New York, the Sherry Netherlands, where they were staying. I ambled over there; but I didn't realise that the hotel restaurant had a dress code, so I had to borrow a jacket and put on a tie clumsily over the polo shirt I was wearing. The lunch went very well, and I was pleased to learn that copies of both my bibliography and my critical study were being sold at Dunsany Castle in County Meath!

I kept up steady contact with the Plunketts. At long last, Randal Plunkett, the 19th Lord Dunsany, died in early 1999. Soon thereafter, a man named Joe Doyle became the archivist at Dunsany Castle, and he began poring through the masses of manuscripts reposing there, many of which had probably not been looked at in decades. He made some fascinating discoveries, notably the unearthing of a sixth book of Jorkens stories that Dunsany had assembled just before his death. The book did not have a title, but it contained not only the few uncollected Jorkens tales that I had found (several of them published in *Ellery Queen's Mystery Magazine*) but a number of unpublished stories. Doyle sent me this text, and I arranged with Night Shade to publish it under the title *The Last Book of Jorkens*. This book was dated 2002, but actually appeared in March 2003. But by this time Night Shade had commissioned me to prepare a complete edition of the Jorkens stories, and this came out in three volumes in 2004–05 as *The Collected Jorkens*. I wrote detailed introductions to each volume, expounding on the stories in a more extensive manner than I had done in my critical study.

Joe Doyle had also made another thrilling discovery: a complete short novel that Dunsany had written around 1956, titled *The Pleasures of a Futuroscope*. When he sent me the typed manuscript, I read it in one sitting, lounging on the sofa in the living room and staying up long after Leslie had gone to bed. It was a fascinating read. The work was a kind of science fiction tale, in which a man devises a "futuroscope" that allows him to peer into the future; he discovers that the world had (presumably through a nuclear holocaust) reverted to primitivism, but—in consonance with Dunsany's long-held belief in the superiority of the natural world over the artificialities of urban civilisation—human beings were happier in that condition. Derrick Hussey of Hippocampus Press was thrilled to publish the book in 2003. We tried to get a major publisher to issue the book in paperback, but found no takers.

The most surprising turn of events, perhaps, was my work on M. R. James. My chapter on James in *The Weird Tale* had been by far the shortest and also by far the least enthusiastic. I had found James's ghost stories quite uninspiring and had said so bluntly. My chapter had first appeared in one of Bob Price's spinoff magazines, *Spectral Tales* (June 1988) and, like my Machen chapter, had excited the wrath of devoted Jamesians, including Rosemary Pardoe. They had written vehement letters of protest that were published in the second issue; but since I myself was the "typesetter" for those two issues, I was conveniently able to add a brief rebuttal to their comments.

Millman had for years been after me either to edit an M. R. James edition myself or to find some other capable hand to do so. He wished such a book not because he had any great admiration for James, but because he wished to present competition to the World's Classics edition of James's *Casting the Runs and Other Ghost Stories* (1987), assembled by Michael Cox. Millman regarded this series, published by Oxford University Press, as Penguin Classics' chief rival, and he wanted to make sure that he had a counterweight to the James book.

After years of pleading from Millman (and also after my attempts to find someone else to edit the book proved futile), I agreed to edit the book myself. We quickly decided that we could issue James's complete ghost stories in two moderately sized volumes, and so I set about editing *Count Magnus and Other Ghost Stories*. I now sat down and re-read the two standard biographies of James (by Richard William Pfaff and Michael Cox), along with all manner of other articles about him; and I ended up revising my opinions somewhat. I was still not especially enthusiastic about James's stories, but I found James himself a more interesting figure than I had before, at least in terms of his place in English intellectual and cultural history. In *Count Magnus* (2005), I included the first two of James's four ghost-story collections, along with some nonfiction matter in an appendix; in *The Haunted Dolls' House and Other Ghost Stories* (2006) I included the contents of James's two remaining ghost-story collections along with all manner of miscellany, including the long essay "Some Remarks on Ghost Stories." I was of course not able to include James's children's fantasy *The Five Jars* (1922), a book that I have still not read to this day. But overall I think these books came out reasonably well. I annotated the stories quite carefully—and was smugly proud of myself for discovering that James had made an error in translating a Greek word in one of his stories! (My work on these editions led directly to my collaborating with Rosemary Pardoe to assemble a pretty good volume of criticism about James, *Warnings to the Curious* [Hippocampus Press, 2007], containing both original and reprinted items.)

So now I had prepared editions of Lovecraft, Dunsany, Blackwood, and James for Penguin Classics. I was hoping Machen would follow someday, but that proved to be quite a struggle. I may mention that the Penguin Classics edition of Ambrose Bierce—the very project I had first approached Penguin about in 1998—came out in 2000 as *Tales of Soldiers and Civilians and Other Stories,* edited by Tom Quirk. But I am forced to say that this is one of the most incompetently edited Penguin Classics editions ever issued. Its annotations are paltry, and Quirk does not even provide information on the first magazine or newspaper publication of the stories in question—information he could easily have found in my bibliography of 1999.

But I myself, in tandem with David E. Schultz, was continuing my own work on Bierce. We had already issued four volumes of Bierce's writings with academic publishers; but we were far from done. I myself wished to make available at least some of the masses of unpublished letters that I had accumulated, and David and I persuaded Ohio State University Press to let us edit a volume of selected letters. This emerged in 2003 as *A Much Misunderstood Man: The Selected Letters of Ambrose Bierce.* It is a slender volume that contains only about a quarter of Bierce's collected surviving correspondence, but at least it includes some letters that Bertha Clark Pope had inexplicably excluded from her *Letters of Ambrose Bierce* (1922), including some tart letters Bierce wrote over the years to his employer, William Randolph Hearst. Of course we included Bierce's letter to George Sterling where he praises Clark Ashton Smith's "Ode to the Abyss," and many other letters to Sterling. And we included his final letter, written to Blanche Partington from Chihuahua, Mexico, on December 26, 1913, which includes a postscript that reads: "As to me, I leave here tomorrow for an unknown destination." After that—silence!

But I was convinced that we needed an entirely new and annotated edition of Bierce's fiction, arranged in strict chronological order (by date of publication, as no information existed on the actual dates of writing of Bierce's stories) and with authoritative texts. Ernest Jerome Hopkins's pathetic compilation of Bierce's *Complete Short Stories* simply had to be superseded. The University of Tennessee Press, which had published two of our previous Bierce books, happily went along with the idea. The result was a three-volume edition, *The Short Fiction of Ambrose Bierce: A Comprehensive Edition* (2006).

For this immense task, we enlisted the assistance of Lawrence I. Berkove, an elderly professor at the University of Michigan at Dearborn who was probably the leading authority on Bierce at the time. Berkove was set to the task of writing the general introduction, the introductions to the various sections of the book, and introductory notes (which actually were included at the end of the story) to each of the more than two hundred stories the book contained. David and I did the actual annotations to the stories (which Berkove supervised), and I was in charge of establishing the texts.

In the absence of any significant number of manuscripts, we had to resort to printed sources, notably Bierce's own meticulously prepared *Collected Works*. But we did locate the proof copies of the relevant volumes of the *Collected Works*, located at the Huntington Library, and secured microfilm copies of these documents. They showed how carefully Bierce revised not only the contents of his two major story collections but also the texts from previous versions. There were many, many uncollected stories—nearly eighty of them, many of them early tales from English magazines (some had appeared in *Cobwebs from an Empty Skull*, but most were unreprinted). In some cases we were in doubt as to what really counted as a "short story" as opposed to a sketch or a squib or whatever; but eventually we set up a fairly coherent set of criteria to decide this question.

I believe this edition came out quite well, but it received almost no notices in either the academic or the general literary community. I imagine a fair number of the larger university libraries bought the edition, but aside from that it appears to have made not the slightest difference to Bierce's reputation. And yet, I am happy to have done the job. The result was not nearly as revolutionary as my preparation of the corrected texts of Lovecraft's stories, but students and scholars now finally have a reasonably authoritative edition of Bierce's fiction to work with.

I was becoming more and more involved in the study of weird fiction in general. After the publication of *The Weird Tale* and *The Modern Weird Tale*, I persuaded Derrick Hussey to issue a volume of my scattered writings (many taken from introductions I had written) on various horror authors, from W. C. Morrow to Poppy Z. Brite. The book appeared in 2004 as *The Evolution of the Weird Tale*. Perhaps the best thing about it is the cover art—taken from one of Wallace Smith's striking illustrations to Ben Hecht's *Fantazius Mallare* (1922). I do think I have done good work on analysing the work of such writers as F. Marion Crawford, Edward Lucas White, and L. P. Hartley; and I had a section on Lovecraft and his disciples, such as Frank Belknap Long, Robert Bloch, and Fritz Leiber. Among contemporary writers I included the three chapters (on Daniels, Etchison, and Schow) that I had had to omit from *The Modern Weird Tale,* along with an essay on Rod Serling that had appeared (as had several of the other essays in the book) in *Studies in Weird Fiction*. I also included my essay on L. P. Davies, a relatively little-known Anglo-Welsh writer of mystery/horror/science fiction novels whom I had been reading since high school. (I had actually written a crude essay on Davies as part of my old *Mystery and Horror Writers of the Twentieth Century* project and had sent it to Davies's agent, who professed to be pleased with it and said he would pass it on to the author.)

But a much larger project loomed in the offing. Greenwood Press proposed that I edit a multi-volume reference work—nothing less than an encyclopaedia of weird writers and works from the dawn of time to the present day. I blanched at the immensity of the undertaking and insisted that Stefan Dziemianowicz, who not only knew a lot more about many aspects of weird fiction than I did but also had much wider contacts among critics and scholars, be my co-editor. Even so, the work on this project—*Supernatural Literature of the World: An Encyclopedia,* which appeared in three volumes in 2005—took the better part of two years.

Stefan and I first had to plan out the list of entries. We naturally wished to include as many significant writers—and many lesser writers—as we could, but I insisted that the length of the entry on each writer be determined by our judgment as to his or her importance in the field. I felt that only four writers—Edgar Allan Poe, Algernon Blackwood, H. P. Lovecraft, and Ramsey Campbell—deserved the longest entries (stipulated as 3000 words); Machen and Dunsany received less, the latter only because his predominant work was in fantasy, not the supernatural as such. Bestselling writers like King, Straub, Barker, and Rice also received less wordage than the "big four."

I exercised supreme restraint in *not* writing the Lovecraft entry; I figured I'd had my say on Lovecraft many times over, so I entrusted this article—

along with eleven different short articles on individual works by Lovecraft—to Steve Mariconda. I did write the articles on Bierce, Campbell, Dunsany, Shirley Jackson, and Machen—but these were just the tip of the iceberg. In the end I ended up writing dozens of articles, long and short. I was happy to dredge up the remnants of my classical knowledge to write entries on horror literature in Greek and Latin. I also felt that I was qualified to write the articles on Criticism, Supernatural Poetry, Humor/Satire, and the lengthy article on "American Literature [Supernatural in]."

But because, over the course of the project, a certain number of writers whom we had tapped to write articles either failed to turn the articles in or had other difficulties, I ended up writing entries on all manner of authors and works I would otherwise have not written. I see that I wrote an entry on one Jeffrey Sackett. Who on earth is he? Apparently he wrote some horror novels in the 1980s and 1990s, in the wake of the horror boom. Did I even read any of his books? I suppose I must have. I also wrote the article on Stefan Grabinski, although why I wasn't able to get Miroslaw Lipinski to write the piece, I cannot now remember. I also wrote entries on Don Burleson and Stefan Dziemianowicz, while I got Steve Mariconda to write an entry on yours truly. His entry reads largely like an annotated bibliography, but it is still a capable piece of work.

Our contract with Greenwood Press stipulated that we revise the book for subsequent editions (including online editions) if the publisher requested us to do so; but mercifully, it has so far not done so. I do believe the work came out quite well—it is certainly the most comprehensive reference work on the subject ever published. It won the International Horror Guild Award and was nominated for the World Fantasy Award.

In terms of my work on Lovecraft, David E. Schultz and I were focused on publishing Lovecraft's letters. Night Shade had done fairly well with *The Ancient Track,* and so we persuaded Jason Williams to let us undertake an ongoing series of books collecting Lovecraft's letters. We started with the joint correspondence of Lovecraft and Donald Wandrei. The John Hay Library had acquired Lovecraft's letters to Wandrei—and, of course, it already had Wandrei's letters to Lovecraft, as these had come to the library when R. H. Barlow had donated Lovecraft's papers in the years following Lovecraft's death. Wandrei's spidery handwriting was a challenge to read, but somehow I managed the job. The book appeared as *Mysteries of Time and Spirit: The Letters of H. P. Lovecraft and Donald Wandrei* (2002). This was the first time that both sides of a correspondence with Lovecraft had been published.

I felt that Lovecraft's letters to his aunts—especially the letters he had written to Lillian Clark during his New York stay (1924–26)—were an untapped gold mine, providing vital insights into Lovecraft's state of mind during this difficult period. The problem was that, even if we focused just on those two years, the amount of material was immense. So we took a different tack, printing extracts of many letters in which Lovecraft talks of first visiting New York in 1922, proceeding to the 1924–26 period and continuing on to late letters to Annie E. P. Gamwell where he visited New York in the 1930s during Christmas. The result was *Letters from New York* (2005). I didn't like the idea of presenting extracts, but in this case I saw little alternative.

But right around this time, Night Shade shifted its focus to publish more commercially viable books, and the Lovecraft letters project was cancelled. This didn't bother David and me very much, because we felt that these books didn't quite have the scholarly authoritativeness that we wished. In any case, we were now directing our editing of the letters to a different publisher—Hippocampus Press. In short order David and I edited and annotated the *Letters to Alfred Galpin* (2003) and *Letters to Rheinhart Kleiner* (2005), including a fair amount of writing by these individuals in an appendix.

At this time, however, I felt the need to tackle the last body of work by Lovecraft that had not appeared in a complete or definitive edition—his essays. As early as my undergraduate years at Brown, I had made fairly detailed outlines of a grandiose project called *The Collected Works of H. P. Lovecraft,* which would contain three volumes of original fiction, two volumes of revisions and collaborations, six volumes of essays, and two volumes of poetry. In the event, the fiction and revisions had fit into four volumes and the poetry into one. Would six volumes be needed for the essays? I managed to get them into five, even though the result—*Collected Essays* (2004–06)—was a set of books that differed widely in their page counts.

We published two volumes per year for the first two years: Volumes 1 (Amateur Journalism) and 2 (Literary Criticism) came out in 2004, Volumes 3 (Science) and 4 (Travel) were dated 2005 but actually came out in February 2006, and Volume 5 (Philosophy; Autobiography and Miscellany) was dated 2006 but appeared in January 2007. I think this was a satisfactory arrangement of a very diverse body of material. I had obtained the texts—a fair number of them unpublished, and many of them unreprinted since their original appearances in amateur journals, newspapers, and other venues—long ago; but the actual task of arranging, editing, and annotating them took a bit of effort. It might not have been the wisest tactic, from a sales perspective, to have begun with Lovecraft's writings on amateur journalism; but this was meant to be an archival edition, and we figured that readers would buy the whole set regardless of what was in it. We started with a hardcover edition, but it appeared later in paperback as well as on a CD-ROM that David expertly designed.

I compiled a final volume of stories for Penguin Classics, *The Dreams in the Witch House and Other Weird Stories* (2004). I was disappointed that my suggestion (actually Steve Mariconda's) that a striking painting of a house with a single light inside, by Charles Burchfield (an American artist whom Lovecraft admitted to liking), was deemed insufficiently spooky by the Penguin staff; they ended up using the now-hackneyed *Nightmare* by Fuseli, which Penguin had already used long before for its edition of *Three Gothic Novels* (1968), which I owned. But now we had nearly the totality of Lovecraft's fiction available in annotated editions from Penguin Classics.

I am quite confident that these editions led to the ultimate canonisation of Lovecraft—the volume of *Tales* issued by the Library of America. This project was entrusted to the editorship of Peter Straub, because the publisher wished an author with a wide general reputation as editor. That was fine with me, and I was also happy to provide, free of charge, my corrected texts. Straub's annotations largely cribbed my own, although they were far fewer in number: the Library of America editions are very austere in the amount of notes they include. The book was widely praised in reviews, ranging from the *New York Times Book Review* (Daniel Handler) to the *Wall Street Journal* (John J. Miller) to the *Times Literary Supplement* (Michael Saler). Michael Dirda, who had become increasingly interested in genre literature in general and weird fiction in particular, wrote a splendid review in the *Weekly Standard*. But the review by one Stephen Schwartz in the conservative *New Criterion* berated the Library of America for publishing this pulp hack in its distinguished series. And yet, this hostile review was an outlier in the general chorus of approbation. The book also sold the fastest of any Library of America book published up to that time: about 25,000 copies were sold in a few months!

About this time another volume came out: *At the Mountains of Madness: The Definitive Edition* (Modern Library, 2005). Now who, pray, could have prepared the "definitive edition" of this difficult text? Even I did not claim that my text of the novel was "definitive," because by the very nature of things it is impossible to fashion such a text, given the peculiarities of its publishing history. The book would also contain "Supernatural Horror in

Literature" to flesh out the slim volume. When I heard about this impending project, I politely dropped an email to the Modern Library, declaring that my contract with Arkham House stipulated that I be acknowledged as the editor of any texts from my editions that are reprinted or translated. I never heard back from the publisher, but sure enough the book does say on the copyright page, "These versions of *At the Mountains of Madness* and *Supernatural Horror in Literature* were edited and prepared by S. T. Joshi." There was also an introduction by China Miéville.

Otherwise, a fair amount of my time was devoted to establishing Hippocampus Press as a viable small press in the field of weird fiction. From a fairly early stage, Derrick Hussey and I determined that we would not restrict ourselves to publications relating to Lovecraft, even if these remained our core focus; we had to expand our potential audience by publishing works in the entire realm of weird fiction. To some degree even these publications might be related to Lovecraft—if, for example, they were works that had influenced him or had been influenced by him.

Derrick agreed to publish my transcript of Smith's *Black Diamonds* (2002), along with a selection of Smith's best fantastic poetry that David and I had assembled, *The Last Oblivion* (2002). David and I, with the assistance of Douglas A. Anderson, also put together a fairly complete edition of R. H. Barlow's fiction and poetry, *Eyes of the God* (2002). We also began a campaign of reprinting works that Lovecraft either had in his library or had expressed enthusiasm for, under the series "Lovecraft's Library." The first such volume was Herbert Gorman's *The Place Called Dagon* (2003), which I had always found to be a striking weird novel, even though the supernatural ultimately does not come into play. We have published many more titles since then. I myself revised my 1980 listing of *Lovecraft's Library*, fleshing out many of the entries (e.g., with tables of contents of anthologies or short story collections); the new edition appeared in 2002. Derrick charitably published a slim collection of my essays on Lovecraft, *Primal Sources* (2003).

One compilation—Samuel Loveman's *Out of the Immortal Night* (2004)—is of some interest. The volume is largely a product of my New York years. I had been fascinated by Loveman's poetry ever since I purchased *The Hermaphrodite and Other Poems* (1936) from the rare book room at the Strand Bookstore for $15. I had wept over parts of the title poem, which evoked the spirit of classical antiquity about as well as any twentieth-century poem did, and so I began a campaign of tracking down as much of his work as I could find. I knew that Loveman had published extensively in

9. Seattle I (2001–05)

the amateur press, and I made sure to make copies of any poems of his that came to light while I was looking through any amateur journals. But at one point I decided a more systematic effort was needed, so I sat down at the New York Public Library (mercifully, the amateur journalism collection had been brought back to the main library from the annex) and went through each of the 181 batches of journals in the collection. Sure enough, I turned up a fair amount of Loveman poetry. I also knew that Lovecraft, after he learned that Loveman was so careless of the preservation of his work that he did not even write down some of his poetry, had transcribed some poems by making Loveman recite them from memory.

But there was more. By this time I had secured letters between Loveman and other important colleagues, such as Lovecraft, Bierce, Sterling, and Smith. Using these and other documents, I fashioned a fairly extensive (although still spotty) account of Loveman's long life (1887–1976). This information was included in the lengthy introduction I wrote.

I have no idea how well this volume has sold; strictly speaking, Loveman is not a "weird" poet, and interest in him will inevitably stem (at the moment) from his association with Lovecraft, Smith, and others. But the publication of this volume was a matter of personal satisfaction to me. It also bolstered Hippocampus Press's line of poetry volumes, which was also augmented by a small selection of Sterling's weird poetry that I assembled, *The Thirst of Satan* (2003). Derrick has informed me that that book has sold quite poorly, and I suspect some of the other poetry volumes have also. What an indictment of our culture that great poetry is no longer marketable!

Continuing the promotion of Clark Ashton Smith, Hippocampus published *The Shadow of the Unattained: The Letters of George Sterling and Clark Ashton Smith* (2005). David and I wrestled a bit as to who would get top billing on the book; the nod finally went to him, even though I believe I transcribed all the letters. Carol Smith had sold Sterling's letters to Smith to the New York Public Library, and the library had also obtained Smith's letters to Sterling. But some dimwit at the library had separated the enclosures (usually poetry manuscripts) from the letters themselves, forcing us to make educated guesses as to which enclosures went with which letters. We also included Smith's several poems about Sterling (especially the poignant elegy he wrote after Sterling committed suicide in 1926) as well as Smith's articles on Sterling. (I may mention that I am in effect an editor of the *Selected Letters of Clark Ashton Smith*, which came out from Arkham House in 2003. After I became *persona non grata* at Arkham House, I was told that this project would only proceed if I were not listed as editor. I shrugged my shoulders and let David E. Schultz and Scott Connors take editorial credit, even though I had assembled a manuscript for the book myself. I also compiled the index.)

I did one final compilation for Dover, the anthology *Great Tales of Terror* (2002). I included a fair number of quite scarce items, including a story by William Waldorf Astor, "The Ghosts of Austerlitz" (I had found that Astor had written a fair number of weird tales, but I was unable to persuade a publisher to issue a collection of them); Robert Hichens's "The Return of the Soul" (I had previously assembled a volume of Hichens's tales, *The Return of the Soul and Other Stories* [2001], for Midnight House, but plans to issue two more volumes of his weird tales floundered); James Hopper's "The Night School" (I had somehow stumbled upon this story, written by a colleague of George Sterling); Bierce's first weird tale, "The Discomfited Demon"; and rare or uncollected stories by Barry Pain, E. Nesbit, Thomas Burke, and Gertrude Atherton (I would later assemble collections of weird tales by all these authors); and so on. A pretty sound volume—and we made sure not to use "Weird Tales" in the title!

*

Non-weird projects also progressed. My research on H. L. Mencken had already progressed to the point that I could contemplate assembling volumes of his uncollected work. First on the agenda was *H. L. Mencken on American Literature*, which consisted largely of his reviews from the *Smart Set* (1908–23) and *American Mercury* (1924–33) of such writers as Theodore Dreiser, F. Scott Fitzgerald, Sherwood Anderson, James Branch Cabell, Sinclair Lewis, and many others. I also included some hilarious take-down reviews of hack writers ranging from O. Henry to Thomas Dixon, Jr. (the racist author of *The Clansman*). The book was published in 2002 by Ohio University Press and got a lengthy and flattering review in the *Atlantic Monthly*. Around the same time I published *H. L. Mencken on Religion* (Prometheus Books, 2002), which reprinted for the first time Mencken's complete writings on the Scopes trial of 1925, the first week of which (in sweltering Dayton, Tennessee) he had attended in person. (He left before Clarence Darrow, in a stunning manoeuvre, put the plaintiff's attorney, the religion-besotted William Jennings Bryan, on the stand, destroying his credibility and forcing the Christian fundamentalist movement to go underground for half a century—would that it had remained there!)

A few years later I came out with *H. L. Mencken's America* (Ohio University Press, 2004), the core of which was based on a series of articles, "The American," that Mencken had written in the *Smart Set* in 1913–14 and that had never been reprinted before. I fleshed this out with other articles on American religion, politics, literature, and culture. As an epilogue I printed Mencken's "Testament" (1927), also previously unreprinted. It features the three doctrines that Mencken claimed guided his life:

1. That it is better to tell the truth than to lie.
2. That it is better to be free than to be a slave.
3. That it is better to have knowledge than to be ignorant.

The world would certainly be a better place if more people observed these rules.

But by this time I was ready to undertake more ambitious projects of my own. By 2002 I had produced a full-length treatise called *God's Defenders: What They Believe and Why They Are Wrong*. Prometheus Books, bolstered by the good sales of my *Atheism: A Reader* and the Mencken collection, published this book in 2003. It had started in an odd way. I had casually read William James's treatise *Varieties of Religious Experience* (1902) and was appalled at discovering that, far from being a neutral psychological study of the subject, it was a blatantly tendentious tract designed to bolster belief in Christian doctrine. I was floored that other scholars had not come to the same conclusion; perhaps scholars of James himself had a vested interest in promoting the obvious lie of the book's objectivity. I wrote a screed against James (drawing upon Bertrand Russell's criticism of James's overall philosophy of pragmatism) in a white-hot blaze of anger. Then I figured I could similarly eviscerate other pious gents who had written Christian apologetics of various kinds. I found many juicy targets: G. K. Chesterton's fallacious use of clever tricks of language to justify religious dogma; T. S. Eliot's ever-increasing religiosity, laced with anti-Semitism; the multiple buffooneries of Jerry Falwell (whose book *Listen, America!* [1980] is a hilarious venture into unwitting self-parody); and so on and so forth. I couldn't help skewering William F. Buckley (whose silly book *God and Man at Yale* [1951] I lampooned in the very title of my chapter on him, "God and the Yale Man"). And I used books by other writers to focus on issues relating to the intersection of religion and politics, religion and morals, and so on.

Prometheus Books liked my book but had some reservations at the start.

First, they wanted me to write a chapter on C. S. Lewis, who had somehow developed a saintly reputation as a leading Christian apologist. I felt I didn't have much to say on him beyond what John Beversluis, in the slashing treatise *C. S. Lewis and the Search for Rational Religion* (1985), had already said; but I wrote a pungent chapter in any case. But Prometheus also expressed some trepidation at my blunt title (or, rather, subtitle) and wanted me to come up with something a bit less offensive to religious sensibilities. I patiently explained to the editor, Stephen L. Mitchell, that being offensive to religious sensibilities was a fairly central part of the book's function; indeed, I felt that I had developed a whole new subgenre of literature, which might be called *satirical criticism*. I had unconsciously worked in this subgenre (which, I will acknowledge, I really derived from my work on Bierce and Mencken) with my "hanging-judge" reviews in *Necrofile* and elsewhere, but here I was taking it to a new level. So I stuck to my guns and demanded that my subtitle remain; and Prometheus finally caved on the matter. I dedicated the book to Bob Price, who was also becoming more and more forthright in the expression of his own atheism.

The book did ruffle some feathers among the pious and elsewhere. The religion editor at *Publishers Weekly* (whoever he or she may have been) wrote an outraged review in which he or she shed bitter tears at my labelling most or all religious believers as dupes and morons. Well, I stand guilty of the charge. I naturally got some better reviews in the atheist/freethought press.

A few years later I used the same basic methodology on another book, but this time directed toward politics. I had by this time become increasingly liberal in my political outlook—indeed, I theoretically adopted Lovecraft's moderate (i.e., non-Marxist) socialism, although I had also adopted the anti-democratic tendencies exhibited in the work of Bierce, Mencken, and Lovecraft himself (the idea of limiting the suffrage is one whose time, I suspect, may now have come). The end result was *The Angry Right: Why Conservatives keep Getting It Wrong* (Prometheus Books, 2006). Here I lambasted such darlings of the right as Russell Kirk, William F. Buckley, Jr. (again), William Kristol, the ineffable Phyllis Schlafly, Rush Limbaugh and his brother David (who had written a whiny and fallacy-laced treatise, *Persecution: How Liberals Are Waging War on Christianity* [2003]), and the odoriferous trilogy of Ann Coulter, Michael Savage, and Sean Hannity. Again, Prometheus Books happily published the book. They had wanted me to write a chapter on Bill O'Reilly, but at that time O'Reilly's actual books did not contain a sufficient amount of right-wing lunacy for me to skewer him adequately, so I begged off. I dedicated this book to my mother-in-law, Elizabeth Boba, a gracious old woman who looks like Queen Elizabeth. This book does not seem to have made a great many waves in political circles, but I enjoyed writing it in any event.

I had now written or compiled books on what I believed to be the two of the three great evils afflicting humanity—religion and far-right politics. The third curse—misogyny—I treated in my anthology *In Her Place: A Documentary History of Prejudice against Women* (Prometheus Books, 2006). The book was obviously structured along the lines of my *Documents of American Prejudice* (1999), and indeed I had initially titled the book *Documents of American Misogyny;* but the publisher (amusingly, to my mind) felt that the word misogyny would be a mystery to most Americans, so they came up with the title themselves. Here again, as with my racism book, I was flabbergasted by the sheer *extent* of the material I came upon—by illustrious authors, and published in respectable venues. We have screeds by such figures as Charles W. Eliot (president of Harvard), Sigmund Freud (the essay "Female Sexuality"), Sir William Blackstone (vindicating the inferior status of women as enshrined in British common law), and on and on and on. This too makes for extremely depressing reading—especially if one reflects that, in some regards, not a great deal of progress has been made on this issue. Indeed, that point is emphasised by the fact that I reprinted some material of quite recent vintage, such as Steven Goldberg's *The Inevitability of Patriarchy* (1973) and George Gilder's *Men and Marriage* (1986).

But, like my racism book, this volume didn't seem to make much of an impression, if the relative paucity of reviews is considered. But I was happy to have compiled it. Prometheus had hinted that it might reprint my *Documents of American Prejudice* if the misogyny book did well; but the fact that it made no such offer suggests that the book did not in fact sell very well.

*

Leslie and I didn't do a great deal of travelling during this period, but we did take a few trips of some interest. I believe we went twice to the Bay Area, at least once on Penguin's dime; that is, Penguin scheduled a little book tour to promote the second Lovecraft volume, *The Thing on the Doorstep and Other Weird Stories* (2001), and I recall going to several of the more prominent weird and science fiction bookshops in San Francisco and Berkeley and drawing adequate crowds in each venue. I took the occasion to promote *The Ancient Track* as well. We had pleasant dinners with Alan Gullette and his wife, Julie Hodge, and I believe I met Dick Lupoff as well as several other notables in the area.

On a second book tour that I took on my own, I was ferried to bookstores from San Francisco all the way down to San Diego. In the latter venue, it turned out that the hotel where Penguin had lodged me was very far from the bookstore I would be speaking at, necessitating a long taxi ride. After my spiel at the bookstore, I asked if there was anyone who could give me a ride back to my hotel so that I wouldn't have to take another taxi. Two friendly Lovecraftians volunteered to do so. We swung by the city's international district and picked up some toothsome Japanese victuals and some sake, and one of the gents invited his wife to come and join us. We sat in my hotel room, munching snacks and talking away about all matters Lovecraftian, far into the night.

In the spring of 2003 Leslie and I attended the International Conference on the Fantastic in the Arts (ICFA) in Fort Lauderdale, sponsored by the International Association for the Fantastic in the Arts (IAFA), as I was set to receive the IAFA's Distinguished Scholarship Award for that year. We were happy to have an all-expenses-paid trip to a warm climate during a part of the year when Seattle is cold and rainy. I had initially been rather dubious about attending the ICFA, since I feared it would simply be a gathering of pompous-ass academics who would spout impenetrable jargon (of the sort they habitually wrote in ponderous articles) on the various panel discussions; but to my relief the handful of panels I attended and participated in were fairly lively affairs. My own address as Distinguished Critic, entitled "Establishing the Canon of Weird Fiction," appears to have ruffled a few feathers—not so much for my nose-thumbing of Stephen King and Clive Barker as for my temerity at engaging in such an elitist and anti-democratic business as attempting to establish a canon of weird writing at all. Evidently, in the opinion of some of the members, actually passing an evaluative judgments on the merits (or lack of them) of a literary work or an author was somehow beyond the bounds of a critic's function—in spite of the fact that, as I took pains to point out, the very word *criticism* is derived from a Greek verb meaning "to judge" or "to distinguish." The speech was supposed to have been published in the *Journal of the Fantastic in the Arts*, but after more than a year passed without the piece appearing, I threw it into the last issue of *Studies in Weird Fiction* (Spring 2005). The IAFA did, however, give me a little plaque and an honorarium.

9. Seattle I (2001–05)

Another trip was complicated by some cat matters. In early 2004 we had welcomed a third cat to our household, to join Chessie and Sneakers. This was a cat we named Taffy because of his lovely orange colouring. He was one of many cats who roam the University of Washington campus; these cats—some mere strays, some actual feral cats—are looked after (insofar as it is possible to do so) by two ladies who call themselves Campus Cats. Leslie had frequently noted Taffy's presence, along with that of another cat (clearly feral), as she saw them outside the window of her office at the Classics Department. After she had expressed to Campus Cats an interest in adopting Taffy, they set a trap for him and caught him easily; this led them to believe he had been a domesticated cat who had been abandoned, rather than a feral cat. (Taffy's companion could not be caught.)

We were happy to have him, but for the first few weeks Taffy was so terrified that he did little but remain in his cage (or work his way *behind* some of my bookshelves on the wall) in my "corner office." He would eat the food I placed near his cage, but would otherwise not venture out at all. We had kept him confined in my office until he became habituated to the house; but one day I had left the door open, and Taffy took occasion to stroll out. He went all the way down to the basement, and as I followed him and tried to capture him, he suddenly turned wild (well, it didn't help that I tried to seize him by his tail) and ended up scratching or biting me on my right hand, right around the knuckle of my middle finger. In the end we collared Taffy, and my wound didn't seem terribly serious: it bled quite a bit, but otherwise it didn't seem too bad.

There wasn't much to be done about it, because the very next day I was set to go to Washington, D.C., to participate in a panel discussion on Mencken at the Smithsonian. So I boarded the flight and took off. But the wound continued to hurt; and what is more, my hand began swelling up to almost twice its size. The morning before the 2 P.M. panel, I took a hasty trip to a clinic in Alexandria, Virginia, to have the wound looked at. The doctor gave me some antibiotics and said that if the swelling did not go down, I should go to an emergency room at once. Well, the swelling did not go down—and even though I managed to get through the panel adequately enough, my hand by this time was hurting so much that I had to hold it upright if I were to avoid excruciating pain. I had planned to stay a few extra days in D.C. doing research at the Library of Congress; but the situation clearly required that I go home immediately. So I changed my flight, notified Leslie, and left the next day.

When she picked me up at the airport, we immediately went to the emergency room at the University of Washington Medical Center. The doctors quickly diagnosed that I had developed an abscess, and they did what they could to clean up the wound. All this took several hours, and I was worried that I would at last be required to spend my first ever night in a hospital; but by 8 P.M. the doctors said there was nothing more they could do for me, and we went home.

It took some weeks for the injury to heal, but it did heal. For years, however, the middle knuckle of my right hand was noticeably larger than the other knuckles, because of the amount of scar tissue underneath it. And as for Taffy—well, he eventually got over his fear of his new environment, and we became the best of friends. He was a peculiar cat in that he *did not meow*. He purred quite loudly, but never meowed: he would at times open his mouth as if to meow, but no sound came out. We later learned that cats in the wild do not in fact communicate with one another by meows; this is how domesticated cats communicate with humans. Even if Taffy had been with a human family as a kitten, he had been so long on his own (he was probably about four years old at this time) that he had forgotten how to speak.

Nonetheless, he proved to be a wonderful cat. He had the most *honest* face of any cat I have ever seen. As he was a very mild-mannered cat, he got along well enough with Chessie and even the cantankerous Sneakers. But one incident with the latter proved most amusing. Not long after he arrived, Taffy became fixated with the fringe at the bottom of our sofa in the living room, playing with it constantly and becoming more and more agitated as he did so. One day, Sneakers was snoozing on an ottoman near the couch and was annoyed at Taffy's rambunctiousness. He gazed up at me with a look that could only have said, "What does a cat have to do to get some sleep around here?" And so he calmly extended a paw and bopped Taffy on the head, causing the latter to bolt out of the room. "Ah!" Sneakers must have said to himself. "Now I can sleep."

A final trip we took in the summer of 2004 is of some interest. Leslie had some cousins—three young men whom she had met so often that they came to seem like brothers—now living in Payson, Illinois, in the western part of the state, near Quincy and the Mississippi River. They and their father (Leslie's uncle by marriage) had a fine old house and property of many acres outside of town, and we went there for a visit. But this visit was not merely to look up these relatives; we were now contemplating moving away from Seattle.

9. Seattle I (2001–05)

Leslie professed at this time that she was no longer happy in Seattle and yearned to live somewhere else. She had lived in Seattle her whole life, with the exception of two years in Portland (attending Lewis and Clark College before she finished her undergraduate degree at the University of Washington), and felt the need for a change. But where to go? Theoretically we could go just about anywhere, for as a freelance writer I could function anywhere there was a reasonably good library, and Leslie could presumably find any number of jobs—as a librarian, a Latin teacher, or something else—just about anywhere in the country.

The idea of being near to her beloved cousins was appealing, so our trip combined interaction with the cousins and her uncle with some exploration of houses in Quincy. We were shown around by a realtor known to Leslie's uncle, and we also made sure to examine Quincy University, which—even though it was a Catholic liberal arts college—seemed to be adequate for my research purposes. We in fact ended up liking one house so much that we tentatively made an offer on it. It was a house of new construction a bit outside the city, but with ample space for our belongings and an expansive yard.

But then we developed cold feet. We went on to visit my mother in Muncie after leaving Quincy, and we then decided that we had acted in some haste. So we pulled out of the deal on the house; it cost us nothing to do so, but Leslie's uncle was not pleased—not so much because he regretted not having his niece nearby on a permanent basis, but because he felt we had treated his friend, the realtor, a bit shabbily. I will not deny the charge, but it probably would have been a mistake to move there.

But that didn't stop us from contemplating the same course. By the summer of 2005 we had indeed uprooted ourselves from Seattle—and ended up in a little town called Moravia, in the Finger Lakes area of upstate New York, about twenty miles northeast of Ithaca and the prestigious Cornell University.

10. Moravia (2005–08)

> ". . . really our one and only recourse is to give up thinking altogether, if we are not to feel too cruelly the tragic absurdity of living."—Anatole France, *The Garden of Epicurus*

How did we decide upon such a locale to live in? I wouldn't say it was entirely an accident, although I do believe that at some point we looked at a map of the United States and pondered, "Where would be a good place to live?" New York City was out of the question: even if we could afford to buy property there (and we couldn't), we were both determined not to return to that seething mass of humanity, for all the friends that I had there. Providence, R.I., was considered, but real estate was getting expensive there also. Ithaca presented itself as a viable location chiefly because property was affordable, the library of Cornell University was more than adequate to my research needs, and we were within relatively easy driving distance of many other places—Providence, Boston, New York, Philadelphia, Baltimore, and so on.

We must have made an exploratory trip out there in the spring to check on real estate. We did canvass Ithaca itself, in the company of a real estate agent, but didn't find anything to our liking. Then we expanded our territory, and the agent took us to a house at 31 Congress Street in Moravia. This place had been a former boarding house that had been allowed to fall into a state of near-ruin; but a local man, now retired, had taken up the hobby of restoring old houses (I believe the house dated to the late nineteenth century) just for the fun of it. He had done a splendid job of restoration, and we fell in love with the place almost at once. The lot was also ample—perhaps three-fourths of an acre. And so we bought it.

The task of packing up our belongings and moving was not simple. Of course, we hired professional movers to handle the heavy stuff (furniture, my 5000+ books and 1000 LPs, and mountains of files and papers); but we had to decide exactly how to move ourselves and our three cats. We momentarily considered flying, taking on all three cats as carry-on baggage. But we quickly discounted the idea: it was not clear that any airline would allow us to take all three cats on as carry-on, and anyway we had to get Leslie's car over to our new house. And so we felt our only option was to drive across the country. I wanted to make sure that Leslie was up to the task, since she would have to do all the driving. She was, however, an experienced and skilled driver, and she expressed confidence that she could manage.

And she did. We did have some difficulties with the cats, of course. Each of them was in his or her own carrier in the back seat; but on the first day of the trip they cried and howled pitiably. Chessie, the most high-strung of the cats, had actually been given some "kitty Valium," but it had the opposite effect, making her more agitated than before. We discovered that the secret of keeping them relatively calm and quiet was to drape a dark sheet over their carriers. What was bothering them was the rapid motion they saw out the window as we drove along; cats' eyes are extremely sensitive to motion, and they were freaking out at so much visual stimulation. The dark sheet prevented the sensory overload, and they became relatively quiet. One afternoon we did find that Sneakers was having a sort of seizure from lack of insulin; but we quickly solved that problem by forcing a bit of corn syrup down his throat.

We took five or six days to drive across the country, beating the movers by a day or two. The setting up of the household was an enjoyable task. It was a fairly spacious house with three large bedrooms, one of which I commandeered for my study. By this time I had accumulated so many files and papers that I needed as many as eight four-drawer file cabinets to house them all. The movers managed to lug these incredibly heavy cabinets up the back stairs and into position where I wanted them. The master bedroom was of course filled with my king-size four-poster bed, although the heavy dresser that went along with it was left on the main floor in the dining room as a kind of sideboard.

Moravia is a very small town. Its total population is about 1200 people, and it seems much smaller than that. It consists largely of a single main street (called, logically enough, Main Street) with streets branching off of it. Congress Street is one of these, toward the south side of the town. But, aside from Ithaca, it is close to other, larger cities by good state or county roads. Moravia itself has, essentially, one of everything: one grocery store (there is also a convenience store that has some groceries, but we never shopped there), one drug store, one post office, one medical clinic, one Chinese restaurant, one veterinarian (very important for us—we got to know her well), and so on. It does have several banks, and we opened an account at one of these.

Naturally, we expected to go to Ithaca and other locales often for its restaurants, theatres, and other amenities—and indeed we did so. I regularly travelled to Cornell for research, since the main library was open to anyone. I quickly settled into a pattern of work, while Leslie took some time off to figure out exactly what she wished to do—if anything—as far as unemployment was concerned. By happenstance, however, the librarian at the town's one public library (quite a venerable institution, with one part of the building dating to the 1880s) quit or retired not long after we arrived; Leslie applied for the vacant position and was quickly hired. She held that position for nearly the entire time we lived in Moravia. The library was small but choice, and Leslie did good work in bringing it up to date and making it more user-friendly. She had her difficulties with the library's rather stodgy board of trustees, and occasionally she expressed frustration at their ignorant vetoing of important reforms she wished to institute; but overall she felt herself a useful member of the community.

There was, of course, the matter of our choral singing. Leslie herself had become a somewhat sporadic participant in the Northwest Chorale, but we both wished to keep up our singing if we could find a viable group. Ithaca seemed to offer one, and we joined; but, although we sang for one season, we found the group unsatisfactory. It was very large (well over a hundred members), but the real problem was that we both felt the director was a very arrogant and high-handed individual, and so we dropped out after the end of the term. We doubted that a small town like Moravia even had a community choir, but we noticed an ad in the local paper for a group called the Horizon Chorus. We decided to try it. It was quite a small group (about twenty-five members), and the music it performed was pretty elementary; but we found it adequate to our needs and remained in it for nearly our entire stay in the town. I alternated between singing tenor and bass; I often sang the latter because the other basses, aside from being few in number, were somewhat unskilled and needed a sound musician to lead them.

A number of issues regarding cats came up during our Moravia stay. In the fall of 2005, Leslie noticed a stray cat who seemed to be hanging around the Methodist church two doors down from us. Once she even saw the cat standing disconsolately in the rain—the poor creature didn't even have enough sense to take cover! (Water is very bad for cats' fur.) We managed to lure the cat into our enclosed back porch with a plate of food, and then we took it to the vet to see what its condition was. We somehow thought the cat was a female—but the vet informed us that it was an unneutered male, probably about a year old. We had him neutered at once. Otherwise, he seemed to be in reasonably good health, although a bit undernourished.

At the start he was not particularly good-looking: his face had a kind of ratlike expression, and he was long and big-boned. But, after getting hefty doses of Fancy Feast (he would eat an entire can at a time), he gained three pounds in four months and became a strapping grey cat with a fine white bib under his chin. We named him Henry—as his generally regal bearing reminded us of Henry VIII. He was decidedly an alpha cat, and he quickly gained supremacy over the old and decrepit Sneakers and the gentle Taffy. Chessie didn't care for him very much, but she had enough moxie to be able to keep him at bay.

Then, sometime in 2006, we were wandering around a pet store in Ithaca and came upon a number of cats who were being offered for adoption by the Humane Society of Schuyler County. Leslie immediately fell in love with a doe-eyed two-year-old tabby, and we adopted her. It turned out, however, that the cat—whom we named Phoebe, because she struck us as a bit *feeble*—had, unbeknownst to her previous owners, broken her back right leg, and it had healed badly, so that she walked with a limp. Only a few months after we got her, she came back from a stroll outdoors, dragging that same back leg. It was broken again. The vet informed us that repairing it would be difficult and tedious, requiring her to be immobilised for weeks. The best alternative, she suggested, was to amputate the leg. We reluctantly followed her advice. In fact, it was the best thing that could have happened to little Phoebe. She has adjusted to the loss of her appendage splendidly and can still outrun any of us if she puts her mind to it. Even after all these years, she still exhibits the classic behaviour of a "scaredy-cat": she must have received some serious trauma in her youth. But she is a wonderful cat, and everyone loves her.

Finally, in the fall of 2007, our vet notified us that a stray cat that tended to hang out in a nearby horse farm had given birth to a litter of four kittens. Being unable to say no to more cats, we first took one of the two females, then quickly took the other female also, as we wished to have them grow up together. They were both calicos—and were the most adorable creatures on earth! We named them Mollie and Lily. Most of our other cats—we now had six—took to the kittens well enough; Phoebe even groomed them, as if she were their mother. Chessie, however, was very standoffish, and the gruff Henry did not conceal his distaste at being jumped upon by these energetic balls of fur. As for Taffy: he was so gentlemanly that he would politely stand aside while the aggressive Lily shoved him out of the way to eat his food! We had to stand over him and ward Lily (and others) off so that Taffy could actually get some food in his mouth. It was all perfectly delightful.

But tragedy was in the offing as well. It was probably in 2006 that Sneakers came down with a serious ailment. It turned out that one of his kidneys had developed a tumour. Our vet said our options were to operate and remove the kidney, hoping that he could function with only one, or to euthanise him. Well, there was really no choice, so I told the vet to proceed with the operation. It seemed to go well: Sneakers emerged from the anaesthetic and even ate a bit of food. But that night he died: his old and decrepit body could simply not take the trauma it had undergone. But at least I had given him a chance at life. So he was the second cat I had to bury.

One thing I realised I had to do was to learn how to drive. The county we were in had very few services—and in fact no public transportation of any kind (aside from a bus that drove from the centre of Moravia to the local prison!). I could not impose on Leslie to drive me repeatedly to Ithaca and Cornell University, then pick me up again after my research was over. So in 2006 I took a driving course and, after flubbing the exam once, got my licence the second time around. This was one day after my forty-eighth birthday—June 23—and exactly thirty years after I had previously secured my Indiana licence.

My mother had decided to reward me for securing the licence by purchasing a car for me—a 2006 Chevrolet Malibu. The only drawback was that I would have to come to Muncie to pick it up. But that problem was providentially solved by the fact that Burris was holding a reunion in mid-July—my thirtieth, of course. So I figured that both Leslie and I would attend the event, then drive the car back the 900 or so miles to Moravia.

But things didn't go quite according to plan. I headed out first, and Leslie was to come the next day. But that day, there was such heavy rain in Syracuse that many flights were cancelled, and in the end Leslie gave up and didn't come out at all. So this left me with the prospect of making the long drive all by myself, after having my licence for only three weeks and with relatively little experience at highway driving. But nothing ventured, nothing gained! I figured I could always stop overnight somewhere along the way if I got too tired. So I headed out, making sure to call both Leslie and my mother every two hours to let them know I was still alive and uninjured. I managed well enough—and decided to make the whole trip in one day. I had left at about 8:30 A.M. and pulled into our driveway in Moravia around 9:30 P.M. No accidents! Once in a while another car honked at me as I did something not quite kosher, but otherwise I seemed to manage well enough. I do not profess to be the greatest driver in the world, but to this day I have not had an accident with another car.

*

Not long after we settled into our house in June 2005, we decided to make our first foray into my old residence—New York City. The visit was triggered by the fact that my off-and-on colleague Charles (or Danny) Lovecraft was coming all the way from Australia, along with his charming wife, Margaret. I had been in touch with Charles since the early 1980s, when he was using the quaint pseudonym C[harles] D[exter] Whateley. At that time he sent me some poetry that I thought was quite good, and I managed to place it in some fan magazines of the period. We had dropped out of touch for a while, but then Charles wrote again and resumed communication. His devotion to Lovecraft and weird fiction was so great that he had legally changed his name to Charles Alveric Lovecraft (Alveric being derived from a central character in Dunsany's *The King of Elfland's Daughter*).

Leslie and I met Charles and Margaret at our usual rendezvous, O'Reilly's Pub, along with Derrick Hussey, Ben Indick, Stefan Dziemianowicz, Peter Cannon, and others. The next day we took them around the Lovecraft sites in Brooklyn—and made sure to warn them not to venture into Red Hook, as they had naively expressed the intention of doing. Charles has gone on to found P'rea Press, a small press devoted to the dissemination of weird poetry.

With my new car, I ended up making many research trips during my three years in Moravia—chiefly to Providence, New York, Baltimore, and Washington, D.C. Many of these trips were devoted to my ongoing study of H. L. Mencken—or, more specifically, my quest to obtain the totality of Mencken's published writings and transcribe them on my computer. I got to know the Enoch Pratt Free Library (the main branch of the Baltimore Public Library system) very well, since it owned Mencken's papers and manuscripts, including his scrapbooks of his newspaper work. The curator of the collection, Vince Fitzpatrick, was exceedingly helpful in my work. I also spent a lot of time at the library of the University of Maryland at College Park. I went to this library chiefly because it was on the Washington Metro system, hence easily reachable from the nation's capital. It also had a full run of both the *Baltimore Sun* and the *Baltimore Evening Sun*, with convenient microfilm machines so that I could print out the thousands of articles Mencken published there. I would mail sheafs of copies back to myself from a nearby post office. I also became thoroughly versed in using the Library of Congress—and was especially delighted to discover that an underground passageway allows one to go to all three of the libraries (the main [Jefferson] branch as well as the Madison and Adams branches) without having to venture outdoors and go through the tedious security checks all over again. There are even restaurants and coffee shops down in that basement level, so that one could spend the entire day there without stepping outside at all. I frequently did so.

I did not publish any Mencken books at this time, but I was constantly gathering and transcribing material that would lead to one or two future projects, to say nothing of the seemingly Sisyphean task of actually completing the transcription of Mencken's complete published writings. I did assemble an edition called *H. L. Mencken on British Literature;* but, in spite of the fact that it contained highly stimulating reviews of Joseph Conrad, H. G. Wells (not his science fiction, but his novels of social realism), Arnold Bennett, D. H. Lawrence (whom Mencken despised), and others, I could not find a publisher for the book. I believe I reprinted Mencken's evisceration of Arthur Machen (in the course of which Mencken reveals that he did not even understand the plots of some of Machen's weird tales) and his generally favourable reviews of Lord Dunsany, whom he knew slightly and published extensively in the *Smart Set.*

Otherwise, what I did was, as was now becoming customary, to work on (a) Lovecraft-related projects, (b) projects relating to weird fiction, and (c) projects of other sorts, chiefly on atheism.

On the Lovecraft front, the ongoing publication of letters was front and centre. I had always believed that one of the richest batches of correspondence was the letters written to R. H. Barlow. It was no accident that Lovecraft named Barlow his literary executor: he seemed to establish a rapport with the young man (twenty-eight years his junior) in a way that he never did with August Derleth or even Donald Wandrei. After all, he had spent several months in the summers of 1934 and 1935 in Barlow's company. The annotation of the letters was not an easy task, but David E. Schultz and I managed it after many months. As for publication, we turned to a new venue. We had somehow gotten in touch with Sean Donnelly, who was a devotee of amateur journalism (he published a volume on the legendary amateur writer, editor, and publisher W. Paul Cook with Hippocampus Press in 2007). Sean was an editor at the University of Tampa Press; and given the fact that Barlow was a Floridian, we wondered whether the press might be interested in the book. It was. I think it was Sean who came up with the title *O Fortunate Floridian: H. P. Lovecraft's Letters to R. H. Barlow*. This came out in 2007, both in a signed-limited slipcased edition and in a trade hardcover edition. It was a beautiful job of book production, and we were duly proud of it.

But this was only the beginning. I had long envisioned the seemingly insane idea of publishing the entirety of Lovecraft's surviving correspondence. In an essay on the letters that I had written around 1990, I had conjectured that Lovecraft's correspondence, if by some miracle it had survived intact, might fill 500 volumes! Mercifully, only a fraction of his letters survived, but by my estimate it would still fill at least 25 volumes of about 180,000 words each. I set about preparing a tentative outline of how such an edition would be configured. We would publish both sides of a correspondence in those instances where the other side survived and was of particular interest—specifically, letters by Donald Wandrei (already published), Clark Ashton Smith, and Robert E. Howard; we had other batches of incoming correspondence available (letters by Ernest A. Edkins, E. Hoffmann Price, C. L. Moore, and a few others), but were doubtful of the merits of publishing these letters. In the case of Edkins, we have virtually no letters to him; in the case of Price, his correspondence dwarfs Lovecraft's at least threefold in total wordage, and it tends to ramble on and on to little purpose; Moore's letters proved to be intensely interesting, and we have published them in a recent edition.

But the book we chose as the initial instalment of our "Collected Letters" project was the letters to August Derleth—among the first letters we had transcribed. David had also done plenty of annotation on these letters already, in spite of the fact that he despised Derleth as a writer and especially as Lovecraft's editor, publisher, and interpreter even more than I did. So we began assembling the edition. At a late stage we decided to include Derleth's relatively few surviving letters (about 40, as compared to more than 400 on Lovecraft's side): as David mentioned to me, these letters actually show Derleth to be cocky, immature, and otherwise rather repulsive, and that justified publishing them! We received permission from the Derleth Estate to do so.

This would be a Hippocampus Press job, since Derrick had agreed to publish the "Collected Letters"—both in a print edition and in an eventual electronic edition—even if the process took several decades (in fact, we may wrap up the project by around 2020). The edition came out in 2008 as *Essential Solitude: The Letters of H. P. Lovecraft and August Derleth*. David did yeoman's work on the edition and deserved the top billing he received. He had spent a great deal of time ascertaining the exact (or at least the approximate) dates of many undated Lovecraft letters, based on other correspondence and other sources; and he had unearthed many of the works by Derleth discussed in the letters, by consulting the August Derleth Papers at the Wisconsin Historical Society. The edition was limited to 250 copies, but some years later Hippocampus issued a paperback edition.

This set the stage for an even more ambitious project—the joint letters of Lovecraft and Robert E. Howard. Rusty Burke, a leading Howard authority, had long ago sent me these letters; indeed, I had (minimally) assisted in the publication of Howard's *Selected Letters*, which had come out in two volumes in 1989 and 1991 from Necronomicon Press. These books were Marc's customary stapled booklets, and the type was almost illegibly small because of the amount of text that needed to be included. But an edition of the joint correspondence was a tempting prospect. The surviving wordage by Howard actually exceeded that of Lovecraft, but that may partially be due to the fact that not every one of Lovecraft's letters survived; indeed, the 32-page letter that Lovecraft said he sent to Howard in May 1936 is not extant.

Strictly speaking, *none* of Lovecraft's letters are extant, if by that one means the original autograph manuscripts. It appears that these documents, in the possession of Howard's father, Dr. I. M. Howard, were inadvertently destroyed in the 1940s. But luckily, Dr. Howard had sent the letters to Arkham House to be transcribed, and the Arkham House typist (on Derleth's instructions, no doubt) had typed the letters mostly intact, although with some abridgments here and there. So the Arkham House Transcripts were our only source for Lovecraft's side of the correspondence. Howard's side (consisting uniformly of typed letters) survived reasonably intact, as Lovecraft himself had sent them back to Dr. Howard after his son's death.

The two-volume edition came out as *A Means to Freedom: The Letters of*

H. P. Lovecraft and Robert E. Howard, with David E. Schultz and Rusty Burke as my co-editors. This edition was limited to 345 hardcover copies. Derrick had quite a time dealing with the entity that controlled Howard's estate, a company called Paradox Entertainment. Indeed, once the hardcover edition sold out, it took us several years to negotiate for a paperback edition, but finally one was issued (1000 copies) in 2011.

Around this time Stefan Dziemianowicz, who was working for Barnes & Noble Publishing, proposed a one-volume omnibus of Lovecraft's entire corpus of original fiction. I leaped at the chance to prepare such an edition, since I could now finally fulfil my dream of presenting Lovecraft's stories in absolute chronological order, so far as could be ascertained (in fact, there is only one story, "Sweet Ermengarde," where we do not have a reasonably precise date of writing). And given the fact that David E. Schultz had electronic (Word) files of the stories, the job of assembling the volume would seem to be fairly straightforward. I wrote brief (about 100 words) headnotes to each story, along with a general introduction. "Supernatural Horror in Literature" was also included.

But the original printing of *H. P. Lovecraft: The Complete Fiction* (2008) was a boondoggle. This was because, even though Stefan had sworn up and down that he would assign in-house proofreaders to check the text against the Arkham House editions, this job was clearly not done; and I myself, faced with the task of looking over about 1100 pages of printed text, did no more than eyeball the proofs and catch some obvious errors. In the end, I (or maybe David and I) take responsibility for the errors. We ourselves were so busy that we had assigned to random colleagues the task of typing this or that Lovecraft story into a Word file, and we had never done a thorough proofread of these transcriptions. They contained many errors. Indeed, Michael Millman had pointed out that on the first page of "Dagon," the transcript I supplied read "navel" when it should have read "naval"! The Penguin staff had proofread these texts fairly carefully; I am not entirely sure that the Library of America staff did so, for I heard reports of people complaining about the typos in that edition.

In any case, Stefan and I knew that something had to be done. The Swedish Lovecraftian Martin Andersson came to our rescue. He performed a laborious comparison of the Barnes & Noble text with the Arkham House editions—and ended up preparing a *22-page list* of corrections! These corrections were duly made in a new printing, so that I can now rest easy and recommend this volume (still available at a bargain price) to anyone wishing

10. Moravia (2005–08)

a one-volume edition of the complete Lovecraft fiction.

Martin actually came to visit me in Moravia at one point, and we had a most entertaining time. He of course also spent plenty of time with the New York Lovecraft gang. I suspect he also went up to Providence: how could a Lovecraftian from Europe come all the way across the Atlantic and not go to that all-important locus of the Lovecraftian universe?

But we had other plans for Hippocampus beyond the publication of Lovecraft letters. First, I wished to re-establish some kind of venue for the publication of Lovecraft scholarship. After 1999, *Lovecraft Studies* had become highly irregular; a double issue (nos. 42/43) had come out in the fall of 2001 from Hippocampus Press. A perfect-bound issue (no. 44) had come out from Necronomicon Press in 2004, and the final issue (no. 45) had appeared in Spring 2005. After that—silence. I persuaded Derrick to start a new journal, which I titled the *Lovecraft Annual*. I had wished to continue using the name *Lovecraft Studies,* but Marc properly claimed ownership of that title and refused to allow us to use it. Well and good; I was in any event unprepared to edit a journal that appeared more than once a year, and so the idea of an annual magazine (more like a book than a magazine) seemed viable. The first issue came out in 2007, and we have come out regularly in the late summer of every year (as close to August 20, Lovecraft's birthday, as possible) from then till now.

We used the *Lovecraft Annual* as a venue to publish small (and sometimes not so small) batches of Lovecraft letters that David and I were editing. This also helped fill up space when we were a bit short of actual critical articles. But I believe the level of scholarship in the magazine is quite as high as in *Lovecraft Studies,* if not a tad higher. In particular, I was very happy to publish T. R. Livesey's groundbreaking 85-page article on Lovecraft's interest in astronomy (in issue no. 2), J.-M. Rajala's 90-page article on "lost" stories by Lovecraft (in issue no. 5), and much else of interest. Ken Faig wrote a number of biographical pieces that required an heroic amount of research, and Robert H. Waugh continued sending me his trenchant analytical articles on a wide variety of subjects. By this time I myself was writing relatively little in the way of critical articles on Lovecraft, and my contributions were largely restricted to reviews—some of them, admittedly, quite pungent.

Derrick also volunteered to publish a review journal for the weird fiction field. This idea had actually been suggested by Jack Haringa, who had come up to me at a convention and suggested that we team up on such a journal. For a title, I resurrected a name we had come up with when we were bruiting about the title for *Necrofile,* and the first issue of *Dead Reckonings* appeared in the spring of 2007. I had mellowed a bit since the days when Ellen Datlow had called me the "*nastiest* reviewer in the field," and some of my reviews (especially of new books by Ramsey Campbell and Caitlín R. Kiernan) were actually positive. But every now and then the need to expel venom came over me, as when I excoriated Kenneth Hite's superficial *Tour de Lovecraft* in issue no. 5 (Spring 2009). I continued co-editing this twice-yearly journal until issue no. 10 (Fall 2011), when I begged off because of too many other commitments.

Hippocampus had no plans to revive *Studies in Weird Fiction,* which had also limped to a humiliating close: there was a long gap between no. 23 (Summer 1998) and no. 24 (Winter 1999); no. 25 came out from Hippocampus Press, dated Summer 2001; then Necronomicon Press resumed the journal, but the next issue was also numbered 25 (dated Summer 2003); and the final issue (no. 27) was dated Spring 2005. Sean Donnelly and others at the University of Tampa Press then approached me about editing a journal that would contain both fiction and criticism, and so *Studies in the Fantastic* was born. But it lasted for only two issues (Summer 2008 and Winter 2008/Spring 2009) under my editorship, because I chafed at having to have the material I accepted approved by an editorial board consisting of people whom I did not believe to be sufficiently attuned to weird fiction or criticism. So we called it quits after these two issues. Tampa has now revived the journal under its own editorship, and it seems to be doing well.

I suppose it is a mistake to say that I was no longer interested in writing Lovecraft criticism. I now embarked on one project that did exactly that— *The Rise and Fall of the Cthulhu Mythos.* This book was born of my increasing interest in Lovecraft-inspired work by contemporary weird writers, although in all honesty I began it with a severe prejudice against such material. I think that prejudice was justified in the case of such hacks as August Derleth and Brian Lumley; but as I began reading other work that I had either read in haste or put off reading altogether, I found that some of this material—especially some very recent work—was in fact fairly creditable.

I began the book with several chapters specifically focusing on how Lovecraft himself had gradually and unsystematically devised his Mythos over the course of his entire career. In the course of this new look at Lovecraft's tales I myself came to revise my previous understanding of the exact particulars of some Lovecraft stories. And when I wrote chapters focusing on the Lovecraftian work of his colleagues and contemporaries (Clark Ashton Smith, Robert E. Howard, Frank Belknap Long, Robert Bloch, and others), I again found some of this work not at all bad—and, more vitally, not as slavishly dependent on Lovecraft as I had initially assumed.

I actually went to the trouble of re-reading Derleth's Mythos writings— not only such abominations as *The Mask of Cthulhu* and *The Trail of Cthulhu* but his noxious "posthumous collaborations." I swear that I tried to approach even this material with an unprejudiced eye, but for the life of me I couldn't see more than a smidgeon of merit in all this mass of rubbish. And when I actually sat down to read Brian Lumley's novels and tales, I found them even worse than I had dimly suspected. Other atrocities, such as Basil Copper's *The Great White Space* (1974), also stank to high heaven.

But when I came to works like William Browning Spencer's *Résumé with Monsters* (1995) and Donald Tyson's *Alhazred: Author of the* Necronomicon (2006), I was taken aback. The Tyson novel in particular—a full 600 pages in length, and a splendid historical/supernatural tale set in eighth-century Damascus—was a revelation. I of course knew that some meritorious Mythos writing existed—the later work of Ramsey Campbell, tales by Karl Edward Wagner ("Sticks"), T. E. D. Klein ("Black Man with a Horn"), Thomas Ligotti ("The Last Feast of Harlequin"), and others—but I found merit in other unexpected sources, such as the first two *Shadows over Innsmouth* anthologies edited by Stephen Jones, as well as the tales of C. Hall Thompson, published in *Weird Tales* in the 1940s. And I was also taken with the work of my friend W. H. Pugmire, whose tales long and short featured a perfumed prose-poetry and a true understanding of the essence of the Lovecraftian vision that Lovecraft himself would have appreciated.

Rise and Fall was published in early 2008 by David Wynn's Mythos Books. Wynn had emerged some years earlier as a bookseller who featured an extensive catalogue of Mythos-related items for sale. Then he decided to get into publishing, and he had issued a number of fine books (by Stanley C. Sargent, Michael Cisco, and others) of Lovecraftian fiction. He accepted my book readily and did a good job in bringing it out—although the first edition lacked an index, which I hastily added for a reprint.

A project of much broader scope was my eighth book for Penguin Classics, *American Supernatural Tales*. I had actually devised the table of contents to pitch to the Library of America, as I was in sporadic touch with the editorial director, Geoffrey O'Brien. He had declined on the project (later it turned out that Peter Straub was chosen to edit a somewhat similar project, the two-volume *American Fantastic Tales* [2009]), so I pitched it to Penguin.

Michael Millman accepted the proposal—and, because it would require me to secure reprint permission for those works that were still under copyright, I was given a substantially higher fee than for my previous Penguin editions. I of course knew what stories from the nineteenth and mid-twentieth centuries (from Washington Irving to Ray Bradbury) I wished to include; but the difficulty was in choosing recent work. What stories (and authors) really qualified as "classics"? I knew I had to include Stephen King, much as I disliked the great majority of his work; but I managed to choose a kind of weird/science-fiction hybrid, "Night Surf" (from *Night Shift,* 1978), that I thought was passable. Peter Straub's relatively small number of short stories were generally too long to include, so he had to be excluded. I was thrilled to use Ted Klein's immortal "The Events at Poroth Farm"—and Ted even sent me a slightly revised version of the story. As for other contemporaries, I believe it was Stefan Dziemianowicz who convinced me that both Dennis Etchison and Caitlín R. Kiernan were sufficiently "classic" to include; and I agreed with him.

However, the book as I compiled it did exceed Penguin's space limitations, so I was compelled to omit some earlier tales—notably some ghost stories by Edith Wharton and Mary E. Wilkins Freeman. But I preserved Robert W. Chambers, who was close to the chopping-block. Overall, I think the book is a pretty fine compilation.

I had proposed a *British Supernatural Tales,* but the new editor of Penguin Classics, Elda Rotor, declined on the project, claiming that the London office was doing something similar. In fact, the book that that office produced—*The Penguin Book of Ghost Stories* (2010), edited by one Michael Newton—is nothing like what I was proposing. In the first place, it was not restricted to British writers (American writers Fitz-James O'Brien, Ambrose Bierce, Lafcadio Hearn, Mary Austin, and others were included), and the scope was very narrow—essentially late nineteenth and early twentieth centuries. I had wished to compile a volume that stretched from the Gothic novels of the late eighteenth century up to Ramsey Campbell (and, grudgingly, Clive Barker). But it was not to be. I have a feeling that *American Supernatural Tales* did not sell as robustly as Penguin had wished, so that there was little appetite in giving me another assignment of that sort.

But I had other fish to fry. By this time, David E. Schultz had done incredible work in assembling nearly the totality of Clark Ashton Smith's published and unpublished poetry: through repeated trips to the John Hay Library, he had pored over Smith's manuscripts (which I had catalogued) and come up with a mountain of material that never made it into Smith's various poetry collections. So we proposed to Derrick that he publish our edition of Smith's *Complete Poetry and Translations*. We planned the edition in three volumes—the first two to consist of his original poetry, the third to consist of his translations. Curiously enough, that third volume was farther along than the rest: because David did not know French (like many Americans, he is proudly monolingual), he had assigned to me the task of preparing transcripts of Smith's translations of Baudelaire, Verlaine, Hugo, and other French writers—and also his translations from Spanish writers. (My own grasp of Spanish was poor, but I could struggle through it by drawing upon my knowledge of French and Latin.) Smith had translated nearly the totality of Baudelaire's *Les Fleurs du mal*, but most of these were fairly literal prose translations: his plan was to make verse translations at a later date, but he only did so with a relatively small number of poems.

So we set about preparing Volume 3 for publication first, and it came out in 2007. David felt obliged to place my name before his as editor—but this had the unfortunate effect of suggesting that I was the dominant editor of the entire series, as my name remained first on even the first two volumes (which appeared in 2008), even though David had done about 90% of the work on them. I felt mortified that he seemed to have been robbed of the credit that was due him. In any event, the preparation of Volume 3 was ticklish in that we wished to present the French and Spanish texts on the versos, facing Smith's English versions. We had difficulty ascertaining which edition of Baudelaire he owned, since his numbering didn't seem to match any that we found. But we somehow overcame that problem. As for the original poetry: we decided on a conjectural chronological arrangement, disregarding any date of publication. In most cases we could either definitively assign a date of composition to a given poem or make a reasonably good conjecture. In an appendix we put Smith's juvenile poems and other miscellaneous items (including some obscene limericks).

I myself was proud of the result, because I had long maintained (and still do) that Smith was substantially superior as a poet than as a fiction writer. So I was particularly glad to get this important body of work into print in a reasonably comprehensive edition. A later paperback edition included some poems that had come to light after the first edition appeared.

Greenwood Press, apparently pleased with how the encyclopaedia of supernatural literature had turned out, now commissioned me to prepare a book called *Icons of Horror and the Supernatural*. The idea was not to discuss specific authors, but to choose broad themes—the ghost, the haunted house, and so on—and to have contributors write lengthy (about 15,000 words) essays on them, discussing literature, film, and other media on the topic in question. I got colleagues old and new—Don Burleson, Brian Stableford, Darrell Schweitzer, Steve Mariconda, Mike Ashley, and others—to contribute. I myself wrote a long piece on "The Cthulhu Mythos"—which was in fact the preliminary version of *The Rise and Fall of the Cthulhu Mythos*. The two-volume set came out in 2007.

*

I was also doing plenty of work on non-weird topics. I had long been interested in Clarence Darrow, chiefly because of his central role in the Scopes trial of 1925. I began investigating his life and work, and found that he had actually written far more than most people realised. Some collections of his writings had been published, but I felt there was plenty of room for a book that contained his little-known writings. I put together a book called *Closing Arguments: Clarence Darrow on Religion, Law, and Society*. It was published by Ohio University Press in 2005. Naturally, I focused on Darrow's writings on religion, including a fiery piece, "The Lord's Day Alliance" (1928), which even H. L. Mencken had found too inflammatory to publish in the *American Mercury*. Darrow had also engaged in a number of public debates on religious and other issues, and many of these debates were later transcribed and published as little booklets. These were some of the hardest items in his corpus to find, but I managed to locate a number of them and include them in the book. Darrow was also a vigorous proponent of woman suffrage and a strong opponent of capital punishment. I don't know that the volume had great sales or much of an impact, but I'm glad to have done it.

I don't know how I developed an interest in a Gore Vidal bibliography, but I set to work on such a project in 2006. The Cornell University library was as impressive as advertised, and I spent many hours tracking down material both by and about Vidal on its shelves. I also wrote to Phillips Exeter Academy, where Vidal had gone to school; he had published some material in the school paper, the *Phillips Exeter Review*. But the bulk of the bibliography was a listing—the first ever—of criticism about him, including a small number of monographs, collections of essays, magazine articles, and many, many reviews of his various books. These reviews were so extensive that I decided to present capsule summaries of them—something that is rarely done in bibliographies. *Gore Vidal: A Comprehensive Bibliography* came out from Scarecrow Press (the same firm that had published my Dunsany bibliography in 1993) in 2007. It therefore beat into print another bibliography that I knew was in the works. This came out as *Gore Vidal: A Bibliography* (2009) by Steven Abbot. But this book featured painstaking descriptions only of Vidal's own works (chiefly his book publications) and had next to nothing about secondary sources. I sent a copy of my book to Vidal (who by this time had had to leave his villa in Italy and settle in Los Angeles), and he sent me a nice note of acknowledgement.

Prometheus Books now commissioned me to assemble an *Agnostic Reader*. I had not been greatly interested in agnosticism, which I felt was a somewhat pusillanimous stance by those who couldn't bring themselves to "come out" as full-fledged atheists. But once I began examining the literature on the subject—including several trenchant articles by Thomas Henry Huxley, who coined the term—I came to a slightly different view. I still don't think this book—which appeared in 2007—is quite as lively as *Atheism: A Reader*, but it still has good work by Clarence Darrow ("Why I Am an Agnostic"), Bertrand Russell, Robert G. Ingersoll, Albert Einstein, Isaac Asimov, Arthur Schopenhauer, Leslie Stephen, H. L. Mencken, and others.

Greenwood Press came back at me with a proposal to do a one-volume *Icons of Unbelief*. I was happy to oblige. This book would perforce focus on individual atheists, agnostics, secularists, and freethinkers: no doubt it was meant to take an advantage of the emergence of the "New Atheists" (Richard Dawkins, Sam Harris, Daniel C. Dennett, and Christopher Hitchens), whose bestselling books were making atheism popular for perhaps the first time in Western history. (The cover of the book has a photograph of Dawkins.) Once again I appealed to old colleagues, notably Don Burleson, Richard Bleiler, and Robert M. Price; but I was now in touch with an array of other scholars in the field, notably Tom Flynn (who had edited *The New Encyclopedia of Unbelief* [Prometheus Books, 2007], to which I had contributed four entries), Edd Doerr (president of Americans for Religious Liberty), and others. But in other instances I had to do some homework to figure out who would be the best person to write on, say, Nietzsche or Sigmund Freud or Carl Sagan. I believe I assembled a fine crew of scholars; I myself wrote four entries (H. L. Mencken, John Stuart Mill, Leslie Stephen, and Gore Vidal). Price wrote the article on H. P. Lovecraft. These articles were nowhere near 15,000 words—more like 5000 words. The book appeared in 2008. I do not know of a single review of it (we had reached the point where publishers no longer sent reviews to the authors, as they used to do, or even notified authors of any reviews that appeared online), but I suppose the book was purchased by the larger academic and public libraries.

*

I have already mentioned the various research trips I took during this time. Naturally, these trips were generally taken alone, as there wasn't much Leslie could do (aside from sightseeing) while I was holed up in a library all day. But we did make frequent trips to Providence—not only for research, but because Linda Aro had proposed me to become a member of the Board of Trustees of the Friends of the Library of Brown University. This sounds like a prestigious position, but in fact the Friends of the Library is a small group that seeks to raise money for the library, put on interesting lectures, and in other ways promote the various Brown libraries to whoever might be interested. I was happy to come to the twice-yearly meetings (spring and fall), and Leslie, as a librarian, also joined in unofficially. Those board members who showed up in person were treated to a fancy luncheon at the Brown Faculty Club, after which there would be a business session. I rarely contributed very much, but hoped I could persuade whatever wealthy friends I had to donate to the library, perhaps specifically earmarking the Lovecraft Collection. (Derrick Hussey did exactly that, although I had nothing to do with his decision.)

One meeting at Brown was particularly interesting. In March 2007 there was to be a conference on pulp writing, and I was invited to deliver a speech (maybe the keynote address). I was happy to oblige, discussing Lovecraft's tortuous relations with *Weird Tales* and other pulps. After the lecture, Bob Harrall came up to me, and we talked a bit. But I noticed that a tall man with a shock of white hair was tentatively approaching Leslie, who was standing off to the side as I hobnobbed with various attendees. She dragged him by main force over to me, saying that this person wished me to read some of the weird tales he had written.

This was how I first met Jonathan Thomas.

I was by this time frequently bombarded (usually via email) with novices who hoped to gain a few crumbs of praise for their crude and ungrammatical stories. Every now and then a meritorious work would come in, but not often. However, I knew how difficult it was to establish a foothold in this field (or any field), so I was happy to do what I could to help these apprentices out. Jonathan Thomas didn't exactly strike me as an apprentice, at least in the chronological sense: he was clearly older than I was (I only learned years later that he was born in 1954). He seemed quite literally to be shaking in his boots as Leslie forced him to introduce himself (maybe he'd read some of my killer reviews!); she managed to convince him that in person I was not quite the ogre I may at times have appeared in print. He mumbled a few words and shoved a manila envelope containing three stories into my hand. I'm not sure that he informed me at that first meeting that he had already published a slim book, *Stories from the Big Black House* (1992), with a tiny press in Providence; at any rate, he sent me a copy later.

At some point after I came home from the conference, I sat down to read the three stories. The first one, "Eben's Portrait," started off with deceptive placidity—but then the unexpected climax nearly made me jump out of my seat. Good God! this guy could write! I can't even remember what the other two stories were, but I'm sure they were almost as good. I immediately got in touch with him, expressing the hope that he could assemble an entire book of stories for Hippocampus. I did read his 1992 collection, but felt that only a few of the stories in it might profitably be resurrected, if revised; but Jonathan had in the interim written a fair number of other tales, and fairly soon we put our heads together and got a volume together. It came out in 2008 as *Midnight Call and Other Stories*. Its dedication acknowledges, among others, "Leslie, for the gracious benefit of the doubt." Jonathan has gone on to write five more collections to date, plus a novel. In my judgment he is, with Caitlín R. Kiernan, the leading weird writer of his generation (setting aside the older Ramsey Campbell as in a class by himself).

Only a year later, I came in touch with another highly promising writer, Michael Aronovitz. He sent me some stories that I felt had a great deal of promise—and more than promise. I suggested some revisions, and he came back with a collection of five stories (one of them a 40,000-word novella) called *Five Deadly Pleasures*. I made the obvious point that maybe he should write two more . . . and he did, and we published the book as *Seven Deadly Pleasures* in 2009. Michael has also gone on to write prolifically, and well. Although he works splendidly in the short story, he also is skilled at the novel, where his powers of character portrayal can come into their own. *Alice Walks* (2013) and *Phantom Effect* (2016)—both of which I read in manuscript and copyedited for the publisher—are to my mind two of the outstanding weird novels of the new millennium.

In 2007 I was happy to make the three- or four-hour drive to Saratoga

Springs to attend the World Fantasy Convention there. Aside from spending many pleasant moments with Ramsey Campbell, I was also pleased to make the acquaintance of Joseph S. Pulver, Sr. My relationship with Joe had not gotten off on the right foot, since I had harshly reviewed his Lovecraftian novel *Nightmare's Disciple* (1999) in *Weird Tales* (Summer 2001); so I was fearful that he might be less than cordial to me. And even though he claimed (absurdly, I thought) that my review had caused him to give up writing for several years, he now was writing material of a very different sort. Inspired by the cryptic references and overall atmosphere of Robert W. Chambers's *The King in Yellow*, Joe had taken to writing pungent and impressionistic vignettes that melded allusions to Chambers with his own noir idiom. He later read one such piece, "Carl Lee and Cassilda," aloud, and I was extremely taken with it. I encouraged him to assemble a volume of his short pieces for Hippocampus, and was happy to write a foreword to it: *Blood Will Have Its Season* (2009). Joe also took a number of us to a nearby cemetery where Chambers himself was buried. It was a touching site, and I was glad to have seen it.

But the call of Lovecraft was never very far from my mind. I was painfully aware that my bibliography, dating to 1981, was now ludicrously out of date—especially as far as secondary sources were concerned. To be sure, that book, along with *H. P. Lovecraft: Four Decades of Criticism, Lovecraft Studies,* and other publications, had been largely responsible for both the outpouring of Lovecraft scholarship and the gradual elevation of Lovecraft's reputation over the past two or three decades. Leigh Blackmore and I had prepared a hefty supplement to the bibliography in 1985, but even that was quite outdated. So I set about preparing an entirely new version—getting rid of the elaborate descriptions of books that Kent State University Press had insisted upon, and deciding to divide up the main chapter on criticism (in books and periodicals) into various categories, so that this extensive body of material could be more conveniently used by readers. The result was *H. P. Lovecraft: A Comprehensive Bibliography*, published by University of Tampa Press in 2009. I doubt if it will be the last incarnation of the work. John H. Stanley, although he has largely retired, is still seeking out foreign editions of Lovecraft, and he sends me regular updates. Lovecraft has now been known to have appeared in Russian, Chinese, Turkish, and many other languages previously unknown. (But the supposed Bengali edition of *The Case of Charles Dexter Ward* [1976], cited in the Indian National Bibliography, has not turned up!)

10. Moravia (2005–08)

Speaking of Lovecraft, it was in 2007 that Leslie and I accompanied Steve Mariconda in an exploration of central Massachusetts—specifically, the Quabbin reservoir area where Lovecraft set "The Colour out of Space." Steve had consulted detailed maps of the area and felt he could find some specific locales that had inspired the story. The region proved to be a bit frightening—very remote and sparsely populated. What few individuals there were seemed to be of the survivalist type with whom one did not wish to fraternise too closely. We were attempting to find a cemetery of the Gardner family that Steve had seen indicated on a map, and we were forced to ask directions from the occupants of what looked to be a well-fortified compound in the area. The fellow directed us to some place that sounded like "scary road"—but proved to be Skerry Road. There we had to leave our cars and proceed on foot—and sure enough a cemetery hove into sight!

Now we thought it would be far beyond the bounds of coincidence to find any names actually used in Lovecraft's story—but lo and behold! Leslie alerted us to the existence of a headstone that clearly read "Nabby Gardner"! Yog-Sothoth Neblod Zin! I had scoffed at the very idea that such a name could exist on a gravestone: Nabby is merely a nickname for Abigail, and surely no one would have the nickname imprinted on their place of eternal rest. But there it was! It was a thrilling moment, even though it was not absolutely clear that Lovecraft had ever been to the site. We never got to Athol (home of W. Paul Cook, whom Lovecraft visited frequently), but we did skirt the edge of the reservoir itself and stopped off at a building that housed an interesting museum that displayed both texts and photographs detailing the history of the reservoir's construction.

*

I myself was enjoying being back in the eastern part of the United States, as I'd spent so many pleasant years of my life in Rhode Island and the New York/New Jersey area. I was grateful to have access to the major cities of the East Coast without actually having to live in one of them; I myself had become quite comfortable in the small town of Moravia, even though it itself offered little in terms of amenities. There was always Ithaca, of course, and I went there often also.

But Leslie was not happy. We had made some friends in town and elsewhere, but she seemed to feel the absence of her longtime friends and family in Seattle keenly. Even though it had been her decision to leave her hometown, she now realised that she missed it more than she had expected. As early as 2007 we were contemplating a return there; and finally, in the summer of 2008, our minds were made up. Our decision was aided by the fact that Leslie, finding the board of the public library intolerable, had abruptly resigned.

So we packed up all our belongings, put our house for sale, and headed back to Seattle in late September of 2008. This was exactly the time when the American and world economies were tanking as a result of the housing bust, and we listened to the radio with increasing alarm at what appeared to be one of the cataclysmic events of our time. But we had more immediate concerns: this time we were driving in two separate cars, each with three cats in cages in the back seat (Chessie, Henry, Taffy, Phoebe, Mollie, Lily). Somehow we managed; Leslie had affixed a shiny piece of paper or foil to the back of my car, as I tended to drive faster than she did and she wanted to make sure to keep me in her sights. We took a full six days to get across country, staying two nights in a hotel in Montana before making the final portion of the trip to her mother's house in Seattle. The cats were not particularly happy, but they managed reasonably well. We pulled in to her mother's driveway in the View Ridge district at the very end of September. How she would deal with the sudden entry of two humans and six cats into her modest house was one of the many issues we would face in the coming months and years.

Linda Aro, Chris Pfaff, Leslie, and S. T. in New York, April 2003

Sunni K Brock and Jerad Walters in Lakewood, Col., 2014

S. T. and Lady Dunsany at Dunsany Castle, 2013

S. T., Mary, Sunni K Brock, Jason V Brock, and William F. Nolan at our wedding, 2014

S. T. playing the violin, 2014

Greg Lowney, W. H. Pugmire, and S. T., 2017

Above: S. T. and Mary in Santorini, 2017; *Right:* S. T., Jonathan Thomas, and Derrick Hussey in Seattle, 2016

11. Seattle II (2008–12)

> "'Why was I condemned to live in a democracy where every fool's vote is equal to a sensible man's?'"—John Wyndham, *Out of the Deeps*

The first order of business, once we had reached Elizabeth Boba's house, was to get the cats settled. This proved to be a surprisingly easy affair, as they all adjusted well to their new environment. We managed to arrange it so that there was a little gap in the French doors so that they could venture into the back yard: our cats were all used to going outdoors and would have gone stir-crazy if they had been confined to the house. On her own initiative, Elizabeth bestowed upon Mollie the new name of Mimi. She noticed that the cat had a cute little black spot on one side of her head, making her look as if she were wearing a black beret—hence the name Mimi, evocative of Puccini's *La Bohème*. I privately felt it a bit high-handed of Elizabeth to rename one of our cats; but as she was making the substantial sacrifice of opening up her house to our eight-member family, I figured she was entitled. Anyway, the name fit the cat better than Mollie, so it stuck.

This living arrangement was, of course, temporary, as we had not had a chance to come out to Seattle ahead of our move to look for a house of our own. And while we all got along pretty well, Leslie and I did feel a bit like teenagers in the house, even though I had just turned fifty and Leslie would do so in about two months. No later than the beginning of 2009 we began house-hunting. The economic crash hadn't yet affected Seattle housing prices, and we had considerable difficulty finding a house that suited us. Finally we resolved on a house that we thought was just passable—one at 12545 19th Avenue NE, quite a bit north of the university and rather close to the boundary of the separate community of Shoreline. The neighbourhood wasn't the greatest (our street had no paved sidewalk), but it was the best we could find. By this time it was already spring, and we were eager to get a place of our own.

So we moved in. But almost at once two disastrous events occurred. First, Leslie lost the job she had taken at the University of Washington Medical Center. The second event was even more painful—nothing less than the tragic death of little Lily when she got hit by a car. I saw this happen while I was watching her from the living room; and although I rushed to get a carrier so that we could take her to a vet, Leslie announced that she was no more. Lily had lived only a year and three months. The fact that we had five other cats made little difference, and I shed bitter tears at the loss.

It took Leslie about five months to find another job, but finally she got one at the University of Washington's Bothell campus. Then, in the spring of 2010, another catastrophe occurred. Taffy was diagnosed with a severe cancer on his jaw, about which nothing could be done. Leslie wished to euthanise him at once, but I felt that he was not in any actual pain, although the cancer had somewhat disfigured his face. He carried on for several weeks, but then one day it became obvious to us that he had gone blind. This was too much to endure, so we had him put to sleep. Now we were down to four cats; but almost at once, a friend of ours who lived on Bainbridge Island donated a stray cat that had wandered into their yard (they would have kept it, but their son was allergic). We named this cat Georgie. So now we had five.

Our return to Seattle allowed us to renew our acquaintance with friends and colleagues in the area. Of course there was Wilum Pugmire, who was gratifyingly thrilled to see us return. During our years at the house in the University district (2002–05), he had frequently stopped by on his way to a Mormon temple nearby. Now he introduced us to his friends, Greg Lowney and Maryanne Snyder, a married couple who lived in the rather remote eastern suburb of Redmond. We met them often and always enjoyed their company.

Then there was Philip Haldeman. I had met him as far back as 2002, when he came up to me during a mass book signing (which included Octavia Butler) at the University of Washington bookstore. At that time he had given me the manuscript of a horror novel, *Shadow Coast*. I read it and found it full of promise, but felt some revisions were needed. In the course of time he made the revisions, and Hippocampus Press published the book in 2007. It sold very well indeed—more than 1000 copies over a period of two or three years—and also garnered some nice reviews. But Philip became dissatisfied with the way Derrick Hussey was marketing the book and (unwisely to my mind) initiated legal action to wrest the rights of the book back to himself. This process ate up a good deal of the revenue Philip had gained

11. Seattle II (2008–12)

from the book. In the course of time he republished the book under his own imprint, English Hill Press. Philip and I subsequently had disputes of our own, so we had a parting of the ways.

It was at this time that I became a truly regular attendee of the H. P. Lovecraft Film Festival in Portland, Oregon. The festival had begun in 1995 under the direction of Andrew Migliore, and at some point (presumably in my initial stay in Seattle, 2001–05) I had been chosen to receive the Howie Award (a splendid statue of the standing Lovecraft designed by the talented Bryan Moore, who is also a filmmaker) in conjunction with Stuart Gordon. I confess that the initial films put on at the festival were quite bad, but with the passing of years they became substantially better. Moore's 44-minute *Cool Air* was a splendid production, and a number of other independent films were highly creditable.

I think it was at the 2007 festival that I first met Jason V Brock and his smart, versatile, and beautiful wife Sunni, who lived in Vancouver, Washington, just across the Columbia River from Portland. Because Sunni was doing freelance consulting work for Microsoft and other tech companies, the couple came up to Seattle frequently, and we were happy to meet them. Sometimes they brought with them the venerable William F. Nolan, who was then about eighty years old but in good shape—thanks largely to Jason and Sunni, who spent a considerable amount of time and effort looking after him. They were all vegetarians—a stance I wholeheartedly respect, while admitting to a moral failure in my own inability to follow it. If someone could ever come up with a genuinely tasty vegetarian substitute for bacon, then maybe I'll convert! Until then, I will remain a regretful carnivore (or, more precisely, omnivore).

It was at the film festival in 2002, I think, that I was interviewed by Shawn R. Owens for a documentary on Lovecraft, *The Eldritch Influence* (2003). This was a worthy effort, but it was surpassed by Frank H. Woodward's *Fear of the Unknown* (2008), where I appear extensively, along with Ramsey Campbell, Guillermo del Toro, Peter Straub, and Neil Gaiman. Around this time Jason and Sunni interviewed me for a documentary they were working on about Charles Beaumont. I didn't know a great deal about Beaumont, but I provided some background on the weird fiction scene in the post-Lovecraft years, so I appear briefly in the film (*Charles Beaumont: The Short Life of Twilight Zone's Magic Man* [2010]). I appear even more briefly in their documentary about Forrest J Ackerman, *The AckerMonster Chronicles!* (2012).

But while all this was going on, something less pleasant was happening: the disintegration of my marriage. It is not to my purpose in this memoir to go into intimate details of my private life, but let me say frankly that the marriage's failure was largely my fault. It may seem remarkable that my relations with Leslie fell apart after only nine years, after I had spent the previous eighteen in a (very sporadic) effort to win her heart; but in point of fact, we had spent very little of those eighteen years in each other's actual company, and the act of living together revealed major differences in our whole approach to life that eventually became insurmountable. I was bursting with energy, whereas Leslie tended for various reasons to be a bit sluggish; I was usually bubbling with optimism, whereas Leslie was inclined toward melancholy. There were plenty of other issues involved, but the end result was that she left me in August 2010. The marriage had really been failing for years, but I was caught in a kind of inertia whereby I did not wish to face the uncertainties of living alone, even though I myself wasn't particularly happy. But Leslie forced the issue. Our parting was tolerably amicable, and we were able to divide our assets without rancour. I got the house—and the hefty mortgage that came with it. We also divided the cats: I got the upstate New York cats (Henry, Mimi, and Phoebe), while Leslie took Chessie and Georgie.

Almost immediately upon her departure, I began hunting for another partner. Putting up a profile on match.com, I went out with one woman after the other over the next few months—a total of about fifteen, I believe. I did have one brief fling with a woman who lived in Everett (where she ran a daycare center out of her house)—I even spent a weekend with her in Cannon Beach in Oregon. But this woman had a *dog*, and I can't imagine what I was thinking in trying to link up with her. But she calmly dismissed me in a few weeks, for which I ultimately breathed a sigh of relief. Thereafter I determined to focus on women who either had no pets or who were definitely "cat people."

This is how I met one Mary Krawczak Wilson. She was a widow whose husband, a man who had worked in the tech industry, had died of a brain tumour only a few months before; but her profile on match.com featured several pictures of cats, both living and deceased. Wonderful! For a while we merely corresponded by email, and also spoke for hours on the phone. I wished to meet her, but sensed that she was a bit uncomfortable with a face-to-face encounter until she knew me better. I understood her concerns and waited for her to decide when we would meet. At last, in early December, we had a nice dinner at a nearby Mexican restaurant. We talked for three hours while a small band played in the background. Within a few weeks we were a couple. By early 2012 I had moved into her house in the Ravenna district, and in 2014 we married.

Mary herself had chosen exactly the opposite path toward meeting a suitable mate from the one I chose. For all that Seattle has some of the most well-educated citizens in the nation, she encountered a distressing number of people on the dating site whose chief virtues appeared to be that they were rugged outdoorsmen who "enjoyed huntin' and fishin'" and suchlike activities. The end result was that she *refused to meet anyone on the site except myself*. Well, that was most flattering! And, as it happened, she batted 1.000. She has repeatedly stated that it was my simple ability to write a complete sentence when exchanging emails that made her inclined to give me a chance—that and, of course, my own love of cats. The fact that I had three at home must have been appealing.

Not long after I had first met Mary, in January 2011, I flew down to Phoenix to attend MythosCon. This was a convention set up by Adam Niswander, an author of several Mythos novels who funded the convention almost entirely out of his own pocket. He also expended considerable sums trying to drum up interest for the event at the World Fantasy Convention and other venues. I believe it was at the World Fantasy Convention in San Jose in the fall of 2009 that Adam hosted a party for his convention that included immense amounts of hard liquor (which he had brought in a van from Phoenix, where he resided) along with *104 boxes of pizza*. He figured that nearly every one of the attendees would wish to pay a visit to the room and would consume at least one slice of pizza; hence the need for 832 slices. Needless to say, many of those boxes remained unconsumed. I helped the cause by quietly picking up the airfare for Ramsey Campbell (who was deemed the chief special guest) and his wife.

The convention itself was even better than advertised. It was by far the best convention focused specifically on Lovecraft ever held, surpassing any of the NecronomiCons of the 1990s. A great many of my colleagues were there—Steve Mariconda, Ken Faig, Bob Price, Will Murray, Jason & Sunni Brock, and many others. Don and Mollie Burleson couldn't make it, and David E. Schultz boycotted because he so loathed the "Cthulhu Mythos" (i.e., stories written by authors other than Lovecraft) that he could not bring himself to participate in even the scholarly aspects of the programme (of which there were many). I was also glad to meet again Donovan K. Loucks and his wife Pam. I had met them in the late 1990s in New York; and although Donovan is a fundamentalist Christian, our mutual passion for Lovecraft outweighed our religious (and political) disagreements. I was also delighted to meet again Martin Andersson from Sweden, and to meet for the first time Juha-Matti Rajala, a brilliant young Lovecraftian from Finland. These two, among others, may well carry on the tradition of Lovecraft scholarship after my passing!

*

In terms of work, my career took a surprising turn in 2008, when I assembled the first *Black Wings* anthology of Lovecraftian tales. My emergence as an editor of original anthologies (as opposed to anthologies of criticism or anthologies of reprinted weird fiction) came about through the confluence of various disparate events. First and foremost, of course, there was my writing of *The Rise and Fall of the Cthulhu Mythos,* during the course of which—to my own surprise, since I had intended that volume not to praise but to bury the Mythos—I found that creditable Mythos work was being done by a multitude of writers today. Then there was my work on *American Supernatural Tales,* which had put me in touch with such leading writers as Caitlín R. Kiernan, David J. Schow, and others. I believe some writers had also sent me Mythos tales for my examination, and so the idea came to me to assemble a volume of all-original tales. I felt I could do at least as well as August Derleth or E. P. Berglund or any of the others who had put together similar volumes in the past.

But one of my central reasons for compiling the volume was to help Arkham House get back on track. It had not published a book since 2006; and although I was not welcome with Peter Ruber after writing my eviscerating review of *Arkham's Masters of Horror,* I had actually re-established contact with April Derleth, who did not hold it against me that I still regarded her father's effect on Lovecraft's work and reputation as more harmful than helpful. I thought that this book—which I perhaps immodestly regarded as a *Tales of the Cthulhu Mythos* for a new generation—might help Arkham House regain its footing as a leading small press in the field.

And so I began actively contacting those authors whom I felt could do a good job at the kind of indirect, non-slavish Mythos writing that I was looking for. In the end, I believe the volume came out splendidly, especially in its three longest stories—Laird Barron's "The Broadsword," Jonathan Thomas's "Tempting Providence," and W. H. Pugmire's "Inhabitants of

Wraithwood." (I had made the mistake of reading Wilum's story during one of my travels, when I was exhausted and unable to concentrate; and I had wounded him by telling him I didn't care for the story. Sometime later, I reread the story—and recognised it as the masterwork that it was.) Caitlín contributed a splendid story ("Pickman's Other Model (1929)"), and other writers such as William Browning Spencer, Norman Partridge, Michael Shea, Nicholas Royle, Michael Cisco, Donald Tyson, and many others contributed superb items.

But when I submitted the book to Arkham House, April sat on it for many months without making a decision. To be sure, the book would have required a not insignificant initial expenditure, to pay contributors and myself; but I still thought it would have made an excellent addition to the Arkham House line. But finally my patience was exhausted and I reluctantly pulled the book from her consideration. Where to go next? I cannot recall how I had chosen Pete Crowther of PS Publishing; to be sure, I had assembled *Ramsey Campbell, Probably* for him back in 2002, but I had had little contact with him since then. When I queried him by email, all I did was to give him a brief précis of the volume and a list of the table of contents. He accepted the book instantly—without reading it.

Naturally I was thrilled, and PS Publishing did an outstanding job of issuing the book—both in a trade hardcover and a signed/limited traycase edition. Pete had also twisted Ramsey Campbell's arm into writing a half-parodic story ("The Correspondence of Cameron Thaddeus Nash"), and also got Michael Marshall Smith to send in a story ("Substitutions")—a story that I thought was pretty good but not particularly Lovecraftian.

The book, appearing in 2010, was received quite well by readers and reviewers, so I set about assembling a follow-up volume. *Black Wings II* came out from PS in 2012 and contained outstanding stories by John Shirley, Caitlín R. Kiernan, Jonathan Thomas, Richard Gavin, Melanie Tem, Steve Rasnic Tem, Nicholas Royle, Jason V Brock, the veteran (and erstwhile EOD member) Chet Williamson, and others; but I think the best story in the book was John Langan's novelette "Bloom." Jason Eckhardt wrote a poignant story called "And the Sea Gave Up the Dead." This book too was well received, and Pete Crowther gave me blanket permission to assemble as many more *Black Wings* books as I wished at intervals of twelve to eighteen months.

One amusing series of publications related to my own work—both fiction and criticism. Robert Reginald, having subsumed his Borgo Press imprint within John Gregory Betancourt's Wildside Press line, gave certain authors blanket permission to assemble whatever books they wished, and he would guarantee their publication. I was one of these authors. I could not resist throwing my detective novel *The Removal Company* at him, and he was happy to publish it in 2009. I had wished it to be published under the pseudonym J. K. Maxwell—a name I had devised as early as 1975 or thereabouts, but had never actually used for a published work of fiction. What was my annoyance when I discovered that there were already in print several books by J. K. Maxwell (whether this was someone's real name or a pseudonym, I never bothered to ascertain), at least one of which was a mystery story! So I hastily had Reginald issue a new edition with my real name affixed as author. So those who have the paperback edition (with a splendid cover chosen by Betancourt) with the J. K. Maxwell pseudonym have a rarity indeed! I myself sent out the book for review in various venues, and Peter Cannon (who had been working at *Publishers Weekly* for years) managed to get a review of it in that prestigious venue. It was quite a favourable review, and I was tickled at having taken this baby step toward becoming a bona fide detective writer.

Around this time I wrote another short detective novel called *Conspiracy of Silence*. Betancourt wished to publish a series of books similar to the Ace Doubles of the 1950s, whereby two works would be included in a single volume, the second one printed at the end of the volume and upside-down, so that the reader would flip the book over to read it. I told Betancourt that I wasn't certain I had another work that I could pair with this one, but I decided to rework my 1979 short novel *Tragedy at Sarsfield Manor*—but in doing so I ended up with a work of only about 27,000 words. But Betancourt didn't seem bothered by the disparity in size between the two works (*Conspiracy* was just over 50,000 words), and he issued them as a double in 2010. This book didn't get a very good review in *Publishers Weekly*, even though I feel that *Conspiracy* at least is somewhat superior overall to *Removal*.

I only published one further work with Borgo Press—*Junk Fiction: America's Obsession with Bestsellers* (2009). This book was meant to be what *God's Defenders* and *The Angry Right* was for literature: an example of "satirical criticism," in which I would ridicule such bestselling writers as Danielle Steel, Dan Brown, Jackie Collins, James Patterson, Dean Koontz, and others; but the execution of the book wasn't quite up to its conception. I made the mistake of having too much plot summary of the books I chose to skewer, without a sufficient amount of analysis (satirical or otherwise). The only good that came out of the project was that I discovered that Sue Grafton was a surprisingly able hard-boiled detective writer—and the more unusual because she herself was female and had created a vivid female detective, Kinsey Millhone. Otherwise, *Junk Fiction* was pretty much of a flop and has made virtually no impression, even among my most devoted fans.

Mencken work continued apace. I decided to assemble a new bibliography of Mencken based on all the work I had done in gathering up his fugitive writing. Richard J. Schrader had already prepared a meticulous bibliography (University of Pittsburgh Press, 1998), but this focused almost exclusively on Mencken's book publications. Aside from that, scholars had to rely on Betty Adler's old and inadequate compilation from 1961. So I set about the task, listing Mencken's 92 books, 15 edited books, 1074 magazine articles, 2346 signed newspaper articles (and hundreds—or perhaps thousands—of unsigned editorials that I had discovered he had written), and much else besides. The book came out as *H. L. Mencken: An Annotated Bibliography* (Scarecrow Press, 2009). I did not have room to include Mencken criticism, which would really require another whole volume.

This bibliography was the first that I know of to include the *exact wordcounts of every single item listed in the book*. Yes, folks: by this time I had completed my transcription into Word files of every single published work by H. L. Mencken—a total of 12 million words. The process had taken nearly a decade, and by the time I was done I did not know what to do every morning—during which I usually spent two hours transcribing Mencken texts. What I am to do with this immense body of work remains a mystery. I will at some point have to get into negotiations with the Mencken Estate to issue some kind of electronic edition, for of course no publisher could ever issue print books of all this material.

One book project that did emerge was called *Mencken on Mencken: New Autobiographical Writings* (Louisiana State University Press, 2010). Mencken had written three substantial autobiographies late in life—the so-called "Days" books (*Happy Days, Newspaper Days, Heathen Days*); but he had written a series of further autobiographical articles in the *New Yorker* and elsewhere that he may or may not have meant to assemble into a fourth volume. I did assemble these and other articles, and I think the result was pretty interesting. The book was politely reviewed here and there and sold adequately.

I assembled three other Mencken books—a slim volume of his *Collected Poems* (2009), which Derrick charitably published; a volume of his collected plays, *The Collected Drama of H. L. Mencken* (Scarecrow Press, 2012), and a selection of his short stories, *Bluebeard's Goat and Other Stories* (Dufour Editions, 2012). It does not appear as if these volumes made the slightest impact, but I find them entertaining nonetheless. Mencken's play *Heliogabalus* (1920; co-written by George Jean Nathan) is riotously funny.

On the atheism front I published only one book during this period: *The Unbelievers: The Evolution of Modern Atheism* (Prometheus Books, 2011). This was based on those four articles I had written for *Icons of Unbelief.* I went ahead and wrote other articles on such figures as Thomas Henry Huxley, Mark Twain (using the introduction I had written for my compilation of Twain's writings on religion, *What Is Man? and Other Irreverent Essays* [Prometheus, 2009]), Madalyn Murray O'Hair, and three of the "New Atheists," Richard Dawkins, Sam Harris, and Christopher Hitchens. (I did not write about Daniel C. Dennett, as his work is heavily based on science and I felt ill-equipped to discuss his work.) I think this was a pretty good book; but Prometheus had now developed a policy of publishing nearly all books in trade paperback format, meaning that sales would have to be particularly robust for an author to gain a substantial amount of royalties. Sales of my book were not especially robust, but it continues to sell little by little.

*

Once again I was involved in preparing editions of various writers of weird fiction. Some of these volumes can be dispensed with quickly. I rather liked my compilation of Edna W. Underwood's weird tales, published as *Dear Dead Women* (Tartarus Press, 2010). I had found her one volume of stories, *A Book of Dear Dead Women* (1911), but this was not quite large enough to be worth reprinting on its own; but then I stumbled upon an unreprinted novella she had published in *Asia*, "An Orchid of Asia" (1920); and adding this made a respectable volume. In the introduction I told what little there was to know about Underwood's life, drawing upon a small monograph written by Carol Wood Craine.

I was happy to assemble a volume of W. H. Pugmire's stories, *The Tangled Muse*, for Jerad Walters's Centipede Press. I believe this was my first book for Centipede, but it would certainly not be the last. The book first came out in late 2010; but because of a snafu with the artist, the entire edition had to be scrapped and a new edition published in early 2011. Among many other fine stories, it included "Inhabitants of Wraithwood" from *Black Wings I*.

11. Seattle II (2008–12)

My next book for Centipede was a volume of Maurice Level's *contes cruels*. Level (1875–1926) had gained celebrity by writing many plays for Paris's Grand Guignol theatre, but I focused on his short stories and novels—at least those that had been translated into English. My French had by this time become so rusty that I did not have the confidence (nor, indeed, the time) to translate any new works. However, his *Tales of Mystery and Horror* (1920) contained an abundance of stories. When I lived in New York I had managed to secure a photocopy of Level's rare novel *In the Grip of Fear* (1911), and there was also a novel translated as *Those Who Return* (1923). I also found some other stories—including some highly interesting stories about World War I—in various magazines or anthologies. The result was a pretty fat volume. Jerad's initial printing (100 copies!) was so small that he printed 300 more a few years later.

Jerad then agreed to publish my edition of Donald Wandrei's two novels, *Dead Titans, Waken!* (the early—and to my mind superior—version of what was published as *The Web of Easter Island*) and the unpublished mainstream novel *Invisible Sun*. Brown University had purchased the manuscripts of these novels when they were sold by the Wandrei Estate, and I had secured a microfilm of them. I had prepared an edition that was to be published by Fedogan & Bremer, the default publisher for material by Donald and Howard Wandrei; indeed, the publisher had even generated proofs of the book—although I never received them! But Fedogan suffered financial and other difficulties at the time (the late 1990s), and my edition went begging. Jerad's edition, published in 2011, is a superb job of book production, as all his publications are. I have high regard for *Invisible Sun:* apart from some crudities because of Wandrei's relative inexperience at novel-length mainstream fiction, the novel (highly autobiographical in many sections) is a powerful piece of work. (It is, however, amusing to note that one chapter is a stream-of-consciousness description of a woman masturbating.)

I also produced two books that achieved considerably greater visibility in the general literary world. First was the Library of America edition of Ambrose Bierce, published in 2011. I had been discussing with Geoffrey O'Brien the makeup of the book for many years, and we finally agreed that it should contain *The Devil's Dictionary,* the contents of his two major story collections (*In the Midst of Life* and *Can Such Things Be?*) as finalised in his *Collected Works,* and—at my insistence—the "Bits of Autobiography" essays. As I've mentioned, the Library of America prefers very austere annotation; and since I'd already annotated these works before, it wasn't difficult for me to prepare the edition. I had vaguely suggested a second Lovecraft volume (to contain additional stories and also a selection of essays, poetry, and letters), but so far O'Brien hasn't bitten on that project, and perhaps never will.

The other book was, at long last, the Penguin Classics edition of Arthur Machen. The new Penguin editor, Elda Rotor, had resisted such a book because she didn't think Machen would sell adequately; but between the two of us, we persuaded Guillermo del Toro to write a foreword to the book. I had been in touch with del Toro on a highly sporadic basis for years—he had wanted me to be a consultant on his film version of *At the Mountains of Madness*—and he was happy to write a piece on one of his favourite weird writers. I don't know if his foreword has actually made the book—*The White People and Other Weird Stories* (2011)—sell well, but at least the book was out. Now I had edited the key works of all four "modern masters," as well as Lovecraft himself!

*

Lovecraft-related projects were almost too numerous to count during this period. I was approached by the University of Tampa Press to prepare an annotated edition of *The Case of Charles Dexter Ward*, even though I had already annotated the text in my second Penguin edition. But I had written even more annotations than what appeared in that edition, so I was happy to do the job. And I received some splendid photographs of Providence sites relating to the story from Donovan Loucks, who had undertaken an immense project to present photographs or other images of every single landmark that Lovecraft had visited or mentioned in stories, essays, letters, and poetry. His photographs added a great deal to the book. I later learned that the Rhode Island School of Design had assigned the book to all incoming freshman at least two years running!

A person named Alex Smith approached me about preparing an edition of Lovecraft's atheistic writings, and I was happy to oblige. The book—*Against Religion*—came out under the curious imprint of Sporting Gentleman and was generally available only on lulu.com. It contained some essays but mostly extracts from letters. Smith somehow managed to persuade Christopher Hitchens to write a foreword. The first edition was very poorly designed, and I complained bitterly that Smith (or whatever underling he had assigned the task) seemed to know very little about book design. A later edition rectified these errors.

David E. Schultz and I published only one volume of letters during this period, but it was a fat one: the *Letters to James F. Morton* (2011). Regrettably, we had to rely almost exclusively on the Arkham House Transcripts for the texts of the letters. I had long heard rumours that someone in the amateur journalism field possessed the original documents, but they have not come to light. Even so, the book was more than 500 pages, and Morton was a supremely important correspondent, eliciting many fascinating discussions on philosophy, politics, and other subjects. So I was glad to get the book out.

Perhaps the most momentous project was the full version of my biography, which I now titled *I Am Providence: The Life and Times of H. P. Lovecraft*. Derrick charitably brought this out under the Hippocampus Press imprint in 2010 in two volumes (hardcover, paperback, and ebook), and it seems to have sold adequately. I did not do a great deal of revision, but a certain amount of new information had come to light since the publication of *H. P. Lovecraft: A Life* in 1996, so I was happy to update the book. Otherwise, David E. Schultz probably had more difficulty designing the book than I had in preparing it for publication.

I now developed a relationship with Larry Roberts, the somewhat reclusive publisher of several imprints, including Bloodletting Press and Arcane Wisdom. Under the latter imprint I published a two-volume set of *The Annotated Revisions and Collaborations of H. P. Lovecraft* (2011–12), in which I prepared reasonably definitive editions of the texts of the revisions (most of which, of course, had already appeared in corrected editions in *The Horror in the Museum and Other Revisions* [1989]) and annotated the stories. Nothing of great note came out during the annotation process, although I believe Ken Faig had discovered that the poetry extracts in "Poetry and the Gods" (1920) were actually from a published poem of the period (I had conjectured that these extracts were the work of Lovecraft's collaborator, Anna Helen Crofts). I also printed the original versions of various revisions, including William Lumley's hilariously illiterate first draft of "The Diary of Alonzo Typer."

Then Roberts agreed to publish a two-volume project called *H. P. Lovecraft's Favorite Horror Stories*. This is a project that had originated decades earlier. Marc Michaud and I had, around 1980, actually prepared a full manuscript of such a book, but we found no takers for it. Now I resurrected the idea, although in the interim several other books claiming to print Lovecraft's favourite horror stories had appeared. I felt that all these books had various deficiencies, so I was happy that Roberts gave me the go-ahead for the project. I had already written headnotes for each story, in which I discussed how the stories had influenced Lovecraft's own work.

Another project that had a long gestation period was *A Weird Writer in Our Midst: Early Criticism of H. P. Lovecraft* (Hippocampus Press, 2010). This was one of several projects (including a *Best of Lovecraft Studies*) that I had prepared in the early 1980s for Necronomicon Press, but which for one reason or another never achieved print. *Weird Writer* expanded considerably upon the earlier project, as I included a number of significant reviews that Lovecraft's posthumous publications (mostly from Arkham House) had received in mainstream magazines and newspapers. I also reprinted the letters about Lovecraft from the *Weird Tales* letter column (first printed in *H. P. Lovecraft in "The Eyrie"* [1979]) and also the letters in *Astounding Stories* about the two Lovecraft stories published in 1936. I think this book is highly useful—and I may draw upon it if I ever write my history of Lovecraft studies (and the history of Lovecraft's recognition) that I have long contemplated.

In 2011 the fiction bug hit me again, and I wrote a weird novel with Lovecraft as the central character. I called it *The Assaults of Chaos*. I had read any number of books that feature Lovecraft as a character; indeed, I had written a tongue-in-cheek review of Richard A. Lupoff's *Lovecraft's Book* (1985), in which I claimed that the work was a nonfiction treatise that unearthed a secret chapter in Lovecraft's life. In fact, I didn't care for the book very much; and when Dick later sent me the full version, titled (curiously) *Marblehead*, I wrote him a long letter outlining the numerous factual errors and some other issues in the text. But Dick was probably weary of the book, and he made no revisions when this version was published in 2007. Peter Cannon had written a fine novel, *The Lovecraft Chronicles* (2004), although it was not supernatural as such but a kind of alternate-history narrative in which Lovecraft finds literary fame and ventures to England.

I wished my book to be both historically accurate and also supernatural—and perhaps the mixture doesn't work so well. I also put on stage such other revered writers as Ambrose Bierce (who, in this scenario, had not died in 1914), Arthur Machen, Lord Dunsany, Algernon Blackwood, M. R. James, and William Hope Hodgson. Of course, in my book Lovecraft also ventures to England (in the company of Bierce) to meet these gents. The supernatural element emerges by way of a battle between these titans of weird fiction and Nyarlathotep.

In an afterword I explained that the book was a pastiche in the literal sense of the term: I drew upon the original Italian word *pasticcio*, meaning a medley (but it can also mean "a botch" or "a potboiler"—perhaps a more accurate description of my novel!). By this I meant that I drew heavily upon my scholarship and used the various authors' own words at key points in the text. Nearly every single utterance by Lovecraft, Machen, Bierce, etc., was taken from their actual writings—essays, stories, letters, or whatever. I was particularly proud of one scene where the authors had gathered in M. R. James's office at Cambridge to discuss the nature and practice of weird fiction.

The novel received some charitable reviews, but others apparently disliked it violently. This may have been because I included a romance element: I had (inspired in this regard by Ken Faig, who had suggested such a thing in a story in his fine collection *Tales of the Lovecraft Collectors*) put on stage an Irish girl in Providence with whom Lovecraft was carrying on at the time (the novel is set in 1914, just before the outbreak of World War I), and who goes with him to England. Some readers were mortified that I depicted Lovecraft and the Irish girl having their first sexual encounter; but others told me that I had handled this scene, and the romance in general, with a certain tenderness. But I don't plan on writing Harlequin romances anytime soon!

*

The major project on which I was working during this entire period was, of course, *Unutterable Horror: A History of Supernatural Fiction*. I had long contemplated writing a comprehensive history of weird fiction, since I felt that there still wasn't anything that truly served this purpose. David Punter had written a one-volume history, *The Literature of Terror* (1980), later expanded into two modest volumes (1996); but Punter's judgments—especially his relatively low opinion of Lovecraft and Ramsey Campbell—left much to be desired. Of course, I learned a great deal about the history of the field through my compilation of the Greenwood Press encyclopaedia of supernatural literature.

I had begun the work as early as 2007, and of course proceeded in a roughly chronological manner. Like Lovecraft when he undertook "Supernatural Horror in Literature," I felt the need to re-read a great many works I had read in the past, since my memory of them was quite weak. In volume one (proceeding up to the end of the nineteenth century), I made my first serious attempt to grasp the nature and parameters of Gothic fiction (the novels and tales of the late eighteenth and early nineteenth century); and I believe I came up with a division of these novels into six types, which works rather well. I did enjoy re-reading Lewis's *The Monk* and Maturin's *Melmoth the Wanderer*, but concluded that Shelley's *Frankenstein* is the only truly great work produced during this period. Ann Radcliffe I found unspeakably tiresome.

I also grappled for the first time with Poe, after a thorough re-reading of his tales. I had long avoided dealing with Poe (aside from his influence on Lovecraft) because I felt that nothing new could really be said about this author. And although I myself don't think I said anything terribly innovative, I think I produced a sound account of Poe's historical importance and of some of the key elements in his work. My 18,000-word chapter was published in a Centipede Press book, *The Man That Was Used Up* (2009).

The greatest revelation in this volume, although from a negative perspective, was my drastically *lower* evaluation of J. Sheridan Le Fanu after a thorough re-reading of his tales and the novel *Uncle Silas*. I came to the conclusion that Lovecraft was quite right in dismissing Le Fanu as a mediocrity (even after reading "Green Tea," Le Fanu's one great contribution to weird fiction, Lovecraft had decided that "I'd hardly put him in the Poe-Blackwood-Machen class"). I dutifully read much of the criticism on Le Fanu, but found that it rarely addressed Le Fanu's actual *competence* as a weird writer.

I found significant flaws in two celebrated later works, Stevenson's *Dr. Jekyll and Mr. Hyde* and Oscar Wilde's *The Picture of Dorian Gray*. And the later Victorian ghost story writers (Rhoda Broughton, Mrs. J. H. Riddell, Amelia B. Edwards, etc. etc.) were all yawn-inducing. And upon re-reading Henry James's *The Turn of the Screw* I came to the conclusion that those many critics (beginning with Edmund Wilson and carrying on through Tzvetan Todorov) who maintain that it is impossible to tell whether this is a supernatural or a psychological horror tale are all wet: the novel is undeniably supernatural, and James intended it to be perceived as such. (An academic critic, Peter G. Beidler, had come to the same conclusion in a book published in 1989, but I had not read his work before I came up with my theory.)

I believe I finished the first volume around 2009. Pete Crowther of PS Publishing had already agreed to publish the book, and although I wanted the fruits of my labours to be disseminated at once, I later determined that the book would have greater impact if the two volumes came out simultaneously. So I told him to hold off as I began work on volume two. This volume started off with long essays on the four "titans" (Machen, Dunsany, Blackwood, M. R. James). I of course had to have a long chapter on Lovecraft and his immediate disciples. For this book I thoroughly re-read (or, in some cases, read for the first time) the work of Walter de la Mare, Oliver Onions, Ray Bradbury, Charles Beaumont, Richard Matheson, and many others. I do not know that I made any great discoveries here—except, perhaps, the work of David Case, with which I had been entirely unfamiliar. Naturally I drew extensively upon both *The Weird Tale* and *The Modern Weird Tale* for this volume. I ended up running out of space to write about contemporary writers beyond Caitlín R. Kiernan, Laird Barron, Jonathan Thomas, and a few others.

The two-volume edition came out in 2012 and did make something of an impact. Naturally, Jim Rockhill, a Le Fanu enthusiast, didn't care for my low opinion of that author, and also didn't agree with my low estimation of Russell Kirk, whose ghost stories had left me thoroughly underwhelmed. But I think the book is a reasonably comprehensive history of the field, although no doubt I omitted numerous authors and works that might have deserved inclusion. I now intend to add an informal third volume, covering contemporary writers, titled *21st-Century Horror*.

*

I do not intend to go into the details of my relationship with Mary. Let us just say that it was a breath of fresh air to meet someone who, aside from her youthful and attractive appearance, had such an even-tempered and mild-mannered bearing. Mary has been endlessly tolerant of my numerous idiosyncrasies. I admit that on a day-to-day basis I can be somewhat high-maintenance, but Mary easily takes all my gruffness and OCD tendencies in stride.

By early 2011 we were already seeing each other on a daily basis. This was made the easier by the fact that we only lived seven minutes away from each other by car. Mostly I was spending evenings at Mary's house, getting to know her and her lively and friendly Maine coon cat, Paolo. We also began taking trips here and there—something we both found highly enjoyable. Mary took me for the first time to Mt. Rainier. In all the years I had lived in Seattle I had never once visited this imposing site—a fragment of cosmic immensity that would have brought raptures from Lovecraft. We of course did not do any serious hiking up the mountain (that is something only professionals should do), but we did take walks along some of the lower foothills. And we made two separate visits to the Olympic Peninsula. On one trip I was compelled to light a fire in the fireplace after the power went out for a few hours in our cabin. I am not exactly an outdoorsman, but I managed the task after some struggling with the damp wood. We also visited the Hoh Rainforest—a remarkable and rather eerie sight.

Mary was also a good sport and accompanied me to my niece Anne Gieseker's graduation from Clark University (Worcester, Massachusetts) in the spring of 2011. The ceremony itself was tedious, but it was nice to see my two sisters (Nalini had herself graduated from Clark many years before) and other relatives.

As time went on, it became increasingly absurd to maintain two separate houses and two separate (and expensive) mortgages. Indeed, I was reaching the stage where I would be unable to afford paying the mortgage on my house. But I did not feel I could simply demand (or even ask) Mary to let me move into her house, although it was the obvious move to make; I had to wait for her to make the offer. And she did, sometime in late 2011 or early 2012. We did have a brief discussion about which house to live in, mine or hers; but there was really no question that it should be hers. My house may have been somewhat larger as far as square footage was concerned, but it was not in as nice a neighbourhood as Mary's house; and moreover, I had made very little acquaintance with any of my neighbours—aside from one woman who lived in a house behind me and complained that my cat Henry was beating up her aged (but large and aggressive) orange cat, Jack. In fact, Jack had become quite a pest, sauntering into my yard and actually entering my house through the cat door in the basement, moseying on up to the main floor and eating my cats' dry food (always left out for them) whenever he liked. During my trip to MythosCon in Phoenix, I had Mary look after my cats; and she found Jack calmly sitting on a cat tower in the living room, as if he owned the place. Aside from all this, my own house had a lot of bad memories—not only from my breakup with Leslie, but from the deaths of two cats. So I was glad to see the back of it.

I moved my two female cats, Phoebe and Mimi, into Mary's house first, in late February 2012; Henry and I followed a week later. My cats got along fairly well with Paolo, although he seemed to recognise Henry as a superior alpha cat to himself and became something of a sidekick to him. Meanwhile, there was the matter of my possessions. Of course, my mediocre furniture was largely discarded or sold; but there was the issue of my enormous collection of books, LPs, papers, and other paraphernalia. We decided to have a shed built in the back yard for the sole purpose of housing a good many of my books, especially those of lesser value or importance (e.g., my collection of detective stories; my classical volumes, which I could not bear to give up even though I no longer had any great facility in reading Greek or Latin; and my collection of general literature). The shed had built-in bookshelves to house the books. My horror collection of course went in the house, largely on built-in bookshelves in the basement. The basement (which had a bedroom and a full bathroom along with a large open space) became my man cave, and it suited me splendidly. I should mention that Jason and Sunni Brock helped me prodigiously with the move—much appreciated!

My house, of course, had to be put on the market. In early 2012 Seattle was just recovering from the Great Recession, and housing prices were climbing, although they were still lower than what they had been in 2008. It took several months for my house to sell, and I did have to take a bit of a loss. But that was not of any great importance: the critical issue was that I no longer had to pay the mortgage. I had done good work in that house (*Unutterable Horror* had largely been written there), but I was not sad to leave it.

12. Seattle III (2012–18)

> "I am truly not sanguinary except when confronted by an imbecile."—Wyndham Lewis to Ezra Pound

One of the many benefits resulting from cohabitation was that Mary forced me to go to a doctor to get a physical. Given that I had never broken a bone or needed to spend a night in a hospital, I had felt there was no need for me to get regular checkups. Well, my first checkup established that I had high blood pressure—and may have had it for years if not decades. I had long been plagued with mild headaches, and no doubt high blood pressure was the cause. So I was put on some medications that made a significant difference in my general well-being.

My work progressed seamlessly as I settled into Mary's house. One project I found particularly amusing was the editing of the *American Rationalist*. This magazine, now appearing six times a year, was the oldest continuously running freethought journal in the United States, having begun in 1953. The current editor, however, was running the paper in a highly idiosyncratic manner—and in the process losing subscribers in great numbers. The Center for Inquiry, which now published the paper, approached me in 2011 about taking over the editorship. I initially blanched at the thought, since I was already editing several other magazines; and I also wondered if I truly had the connexions in the atheist/freethought community to solicit contributions. But Robert M. Price, who had recommended me, promised to be a regular contributor, as did Don Burleson. So I tentatively accepted the position. The first issue under my editorship was the July/August 2011 issue.

Within a relatively short interval I became accustomed to the rhythm of editing a new issue of the journal every two months. I had insisted that I be allowed to write a regular column in each issue (always on the last page), called "The Stupidity Watch." My focus would principally be on instances of stupidity as exhibited in the realm of religion; but fairly soon the realm of politics—mostly Republican politics, which of late has provided an inexhaustible fund of buffoonery—came under my purview. I gradually began writing book reviews as well, and found great entertainment in skewering various books of Christian apologetics and other ventures into absurdity. Tom Flynn of the Center for Inquiry told me a few years later that the circulation of the *American Rationalist* had increased from less than 1000 to about 1500—so I must be doing something right! By early 2017 I had written enough material for the paper to assemble a small book's worth of material, which I published under the title *The Stupidity Watch*. This was a self-published volume, issued under an imprint I had devised, Sarnath Press.

In some early issues I instituted an informal series of articles by various individuals telling of their "deconversion" from the religious beliefs in which they had been brainwashed as children. Thus, I got interesting articles from Jason Brock (who had been raised as a Southern Baptist), Sunni Brock (who had been raised, incredibly, as a Jehovah's Witness), and others. Mary herself wrote an article on how she had fallen away from Catholicism, as did William F. Nolan. Ray Garton told about his deconversion from Seventh-Day Adventism. My neighbour, Jim Dempsey, is a firebrand who is even farther to the left than I am, and he has written some pungent articles and reviews on the political scene.

The only other atheism project at this time was *The Original Atheists* (Prometheus Books, 2014). I had always been fascinated with the French Enlightenment, which had featured some of the pioneering atheists and freethinkers of Western history—Voltaire, Diderot, and many others. I had even contemplated a full translation of Paul Thiry d'Holbach's *Système de la nature* (1777), an immense and comprehensive treatise on atheism. Prometheus wasn't interested in this project, but it did bite on *The Original Atheists*. I of course included work by German, British, and American writers of the period, including Jefferson and Madison.

But the great majority of my work during this period focused on Lovecraft or other weird writers. Let me discuss the latter first.

I was doing a great deal of work for Centipede Press. Jerad Walters had in fact talked me into editing an annual magazine, the *Weird Fiction Review,* whose first issue came out in 2010. This magazine would feature about 30,000 words of fiction and the same amount of nonfiction. I had initially hoped to obtain a fair number of scholarly articles from various contributors, but had some difficulty doing so. So Jerad helped the process along by securing contributions of all different sorts (interviews, articles on films, television, comics, and other media) that substantially bolstered the contents, both in bulk and in quality. I was particularly pleased to get Dennis Etchison's interview with Clive Barker and Dave Roberts's interview with Ted Klein. These interviews appeared in issue 6 (2015), which had an amusing cover based on the Beatles' *Sgt. Pepper* album, with the faces of leading horror writers from the past and the present displayed. Among the articles, the Canadian critic James Goho wrote a series of papers on Caitlín R. Kiernan's work that I thought were brilliant, and that Goho hopes to assemble into a full-scale monograph on her work. The production values of this journal are exceptionally high, with a great many full-colour illustrations. I don't believe there is any journal in the field quite like it.

Jerad also wished me to compile volumes for a new series called the Centipede Press Library of Weird Fiction. These would be very large volumes presenting exhaustive (or at least extensive) editions of the weird work of classic authors. We began with four volumes—containing the work of Poe, Lovecraft, Blackwood, and Hodgson—published in 2014. These books were substantially less expensive than Centipede's usual hardcover editions, costing a mere $60.00. Jerad promised to keep these books in print, but so far he has not done so. Volumes on Bierce, Machen, and Stoker came out in 2017 and 2018.

I did other books for Centipede Press. There was a collection of Sax Rohmer's best weird tales (*Brood of the Witch-Queen* [2013]). I had gone through Rohmer's various story collections when I was living in New York, earmarking the better weird tales for eventual reprinting; and the opportunity finally arose. With John Pelan I edited a large omnibus of Carl Jacobi's writings for the Masters of the Weird Tales series (2014). In a sense, this project dates to the very dawn of my interest in weird fiction, for the very first book I ordered from Arkham House was Jacobi's *Portraits in Moonlight*, around 1974. In all honesty, Jacobi is not a particularly stellar horror writer—and the book was made the poorer by Pelan's insistence that we include a lot of his corny and contrived "weird menace" tales. But I suppose the book will be useful to collectors. Also for the Masters of the Weird Tale series, I edited large volumes of the work of Fred Chappell (2014) and David Case (2015). I worked with both authors on these books.

Another author I worked with was Dennis Etchison, for a Masters of the Weird Tale book of his stories (*It Only Comes Out at Night and Other Stories*, 2015). I actually prepared Word files of at least sixty stories by Etchison from his various collections and sent them to him, in the event that he wished to do some revisions. But in the end he chose only thirty-eight stories for the book. To add insult to injury, I was not credited as editor—but I did indeed edit the book, and it appears in my bibliography as such. I had spent some entertaining time with Etchison and his wife at the World Fantasy Convention in San Diego (2011).

Jerad continued to solicit other projects from me. I assembled a large volume of John Metcalfe's collected short fiction—both weird and otherwise (not yet published as of this writing). Other reprints of Metcalfe's work had chosen only the weird specimens in his early collections, *The Smoking Leg* (1925) and *Judas and Other Stories* (1931). But I thought the other tales were worth including. On top of that, I had discovered that Metcalfe had assembled a third collection, *The Feasting Dead and Other Stories,* in the early 1950s and submitted it to Arkham House. But Derleth had published only the title novella (a mediocre vampire tale). The full manuscript resided in the Harry Ransom Center at the University of Texas, and I secured a copy of it and transcribed it.

I had assembled a slim volume of D. H. Lawrence's weird tales years earlier, and Christopher Roden of Ash-Tree Press had expressed interest in it; but Ash-Tree Press's difficulties had doomed the book to limbo until Jerad came to my rescue and brought it out in 2018. Jerad also had me assemble an immense Robert W. Chambers omnibus—including virtually the complete contents of my *Yellow Sign* edition (2000), but this time with the addition of *The Slayer of Souls*. This mammoth book also appeared in 2018.

And Jerad wanted to do an edition of the collected weird tales of Robert Aickman, which I assembled in two volumes; it also was published in 2018. In all honesty, my opinion of Aickman actually declined as I re-read his weird fiction: I now feel that only a very small number of his stories truly succeed, with the others suffering from various flaws large and small. But it is always useful to have them in one place. Years before, I had secured the typescript of Aickman's last work of fiction, a mainstream novel called *Go Back at Once.* This was at Bowling Green State University, which had purchased Aickman's papers. I spent years casually transcribing the work, then went to Bowling Green in 2012 to check some hard-to-read passages in the text. But Aickman's agents and estate did not think the work would do him credit and have refused to sanction its publication. I can well understand their reluctance: it is a very curious account of two young women who head to Italy to participate in a small revolution, and quite frankly it lacks focus and dramatic tensity. The volume did appear in print from Tartarus Press in 2020, although I was not consulted on this edition.

I have also assembled large omnibuses of the work of J. Sheridan Le Fanu,

E. F. Benson (two volumes), and W. C. Morrow (in collaboration with Stefan Dziemianowicz) for Centipede, but these have yet to appear.

Perhaps the most notable book I did for Centipede Press was *A Mountain Walked: Great Tales of the Cthulhu Mythos* (2014). This was an anthology that I had compiled, in rudimentary form, for David Wynn's Mythos Books as early as 2008, when it was titled *Spawn of the Green Abyss* (after the C. Hall Thompson story). But Mythos Books became moribund before it could get around to issuing the book. Jerad decided to publish it, although he didn't care for the pulpish title I had chosen; so we went with the celebrated comment about Cthulhu in "The Call of Cthulhu" ("A mountain walked or stumbled"). The result was, in my opinion, one of the most spectacularly beautiful books ever designed—a gorgeous signed/limited slipcased edition with numerous evocative illustrations. Jerad added some stories as well as illustrated versions of "Pickman's Model" and "The Lurking Fear" (neither of them Mythos stories, in my estimation), and I omitted these when Dark Regions Press issued the book in paperback in 2016.

*

Naturally, I was doing a great deal of work for Hippocampus Press as well. One of the most ambitious projects I undertook was an entirely new historical anthology of weird poetry. I had long been dissatisfied with Derleth's *Dark of the Moon* (1947), admirable in many ways as that anthology was. (I have heard rumours that it was actually Donald Wandrei—far more knowledgeable about weird poetry than Derleth was—who was responsible for many of the selections.) At a minimum, its omission of George Sterling was appalling. I sought the collaboration of Steve Mariconda, whose knowledge of poetry in general (he is a great devotee of Hart Crane and Wallace Stevens, two poets I can take or leave) and weird poetry in particular is much greater than mine. And so we set about compiling *Dreams of Fear: Poetry of Terror and the Supernatural,* which Hippocampus published in 2013. I have to say I am rather proud of this book. I dredged up my classical learning to find poems (or portions of poems) by Homer, Euripides, Catullus, and Horace. I myself had previously translated the Euripides (a section from *Medea*) and Catullus (Poem 63—the "Attis" poem) selections, but we decided to go with more authoritative published translations. Steve did good work selecting some European writers (Emile Verhaeren, Georg Heym) with whom I was not very familiar. One ticklish issue concerned which contemporary poets to include, and I think we made a good selection by printing the work of Richard L. Tierney, Stanley McNail, G. Sutton Breiding, W. H. Pugmire, and others, all the way down to the youngest contributor, Ann K. Schwader, who is probably the preeminent weird poet today.

This set the stage for a project that David E. Schultz and I had been casually working on for years—nothing less than the collected poetry of George Sterling. I have mentioned that we had begun our work on Sterling as far back as 1995. Now, once Derrick made the incredibly charitable gesture of offering to publish the edition in hardcover, we set about our work. We had accumulated a fair amount of poetry, but knew that many unpublished poems remained in various institutions. The major Sterling repository was at the Bancroft Library (which, in fact, owned the literary rights to Sterling's work—the rights were bestowed upon it by Sterling's heirs), so at some point I spent a week or more with my laptop transcribing dozens, perhaps hundreds, of unpublished poems there.

The three-volume edition of Sterling's *Complete Poetry* emerged in 2013, in a beautiful slipcased edition. We were fortunate to get a foreword from Kevin Starr, a leading authority on California literature and history. As expected, it sold quite poorly, and Derrick was forced to offer it at a steep discount sometime after publication. But I was happy that I had done the work. Sterling's poetic dramas in particular (notably *Lilith* and *Rosamund*) are some of his most scintillating works, and they occupied pride of place in the edition.

Another poetry project was the establishment of a twice-yearly journal of weird poetry, which we titled *Spectral Realms*. The first issue was dated Summer 2014, and it and subsequent issues have, I believe, featured outstanding weird poetry from a wide variety of contributors. Certainly, it has proved popular with the poets themselves, chiefly because its high production values make each issue a thing of beauty to behold. But actual sales were poor, and after issue 6 (Winter 2016) Derrick was on the verge of pulling the plug on the venture; but I persuaded him to keep it going by eliminating some of the more costly design elements so that it could be offered at a lower price, thereby perhaps inducing more people to buy it. It is still not clear how much longer the journal will survive, but I hope to keep it going in some fashion or other.

Another project of some importance was an anthology of essays on William Hope Hodgson, *William Hope Hodgson: Voices from the Borderland,* published in 2014. I collaborated on this book with Sam Gafford and Massimo

Berruti. It fit into a line of similar critical anthologies Hippocampus had already published, including those on M. R. James (my own *Warnings to the Curious*) and J. Sheridan Le Fanu. The Hodgson book was of some importance because it allowed for the publication of the bibliography of Hodgson that Sam and I, in conjunction with Mike Ashley, had been working on for years. This meant that I had now published bibliographies of Lovecraft, Dunsany, Bierce, Campbell, Vidal, and Mencken. (I had also been working on a revision of the Sweetser-Goldstone bibliography of Arthur Machen and a new bibliography of Clark Ashton Smith; the latter was published in 2019. I also prepared, with assistance from Alan Gullette, a comprehensive bibliography of George Sterling, but it proved impracticable to include it in the edition of Sterling's poetry, so it remains an orphan.)

I was also continuing to do work for Larry Roberts's Arcane Wisdom imprint. First on the agenda at this time was an edition of Edward Lucas White's collected weird tales, published as *The Stuff of Dreams* (2013). This project was also many years old: as early as the mid-1980s, some English publisher had solicited such a project, but never carried through on it. So the book languished until Larry gave the go-ahead.

Not long afterward, I obtained a document that everyone thought was lost: the original version of Fritz Leiber's novella "Adept's Gambit," written in 1936. In fact, this may not have been absolutely the *first* version; but it was an earlier version than what had been published in *Night's Black Agents* (1947), and closer to the version that Lovecraft had read, as recorded in his immense letter of December 19, 1936, where he discusses the work in detail. Lovecraftians had always been puzzled at Lovecraft's mention in his letter that Leiber had dropped references to his myth-cycle in the story, for of course all such references were removed in the published version. Sure enough, this version has the passing exclamation "By Cthulhu!" and other random and insignificant citations. At any rate, I solicited permission from Leiber's agents to publish the text, wrote an introduction and some learned notes, and added Lovecraft's letter as an appendix. This book—*Adept's Gambit: The Original Version*—appeared in 2014.

A highly interesting book that appeared in 2014 was *Letters to Arkham: The Letters of Ramsey Campbell and August Derleth, 1961–1971*. Peter Ruber had long ago given me copies of Campbell's letters to Derleth, and now Ramsey provided the other side of the correspondence. It took me quite a while to edit the texts, aside from the mere transcription. The two authors had discussed a great many books, films, and other material that required annotation of various kinds. The book provided a fascinating window into the weird fiction scene in the decade covered by the letters. The book won the British Fantasy Award.

In 2014 Joe Morey—who had founded Dark Regions Press and then turned it over to his son, Chris—asked me to compile several volumes for a series he wished to call Classic Weird Fiction, to be published under his new imprint, Dark Renaissance Books. These books would be on a somewhat smaller scale than the Centipede Press Library of Weird Fiction, but I hoped to be able to include pretty much the complete weird writings of the authors in question.

Joe asked me to prepare six volumes at the start. I began with Mary E. Wilkins Freeman. I had done enough research on Freeman by this time to realise that previous volumes of her weird work—especially the Arkham House *Collected Ghost Stories* (1974)—were quite incomplete, so I set about rectifying the deficiency. I titled my volume *Lost Ghosts*, and also included Freeman's non-supernatural play about the Salem witch trials, *Giles Corey, Yeoman*, which Lovecraft had enjoyed.

Then I turned to E. Nesbit, who had published two volumes of horror tales early in her career, *Grim Tales* (1893) and *Fear* (1910). What startled me about Nesbit was not so much her weird tales (which are interesting but not revolutionary) as the turbulent life she led, which at one point involved her decision to run away with H. G. Wells (both were married at the time, and in the end their romance was nipped in the bud).

Then I directed my attention to two American short story writers in whom I had long been interested, Irvin S. Cobb and Gouverneur Morris. The former's celebrated tale "Fishhead" had been much appreciated by Lovecraft, while the latter's "Back There in the Grass" was a splendidly creepy tale; both had been in Alfred Hitchcock anthologies that I had read as a teenager. While in New York I had gone systematically through their various short story collections and found a small modicum of weird work (some of it psychological suspense) in each author; neither was enough to publish as a volume on its own, but the two together worked well.

Théophile Gautier was an author whose weird work I had long wished to collect. It extended well beyond Lafcadio Hearn's famous translation of *One of Cleopatra's Nights and Other Fantastic Romances* (1882), and included the novellas "Avatar" (which Lovecraft owned in a translation by Edgar Saltus), "Spirite," and some other works.

The fifth book was another old favourite—Thomas Burke, whose *Night-*

Pieces (1935) I had read in the Muncie Public Library as a teenager. (I never ended up getting a physical copy of this book but had to settle for a photocopy.) Burke wrote a great deal of other work (he was best known for *Limehouse Nights* [1921], a splendid series of tales about the Chinese immigrants in London), and I canvassed his entire corpus of work for weird specimens.

Then I came to W. W. Jacobs. In all honesty, I was not particularly taken with this author, although a re-reading of "The Monkey's Paw" for *Unutterable Horror* still gave me a jolt. But this is just the tip of the iceberg of his weird writings, and I canvassed his various collections to find more. Indeed, I found what I believe to be his very first weird tale, published in a magazine in 1889 and never reprinted. I also included some dramatic versions of his stories that he had done, and the famous dramatic version of *The Monkey's Paw* by another author.

In late 2015 Joe Morey wished me to do two more volumes. I chose Robert W. Chambers, even though I had already prepared that enormous omnibus of his weird work for Centipede. In addition, Morey wished me to do an edition of Mary Shelley. Beyond *Frankenstein*, there are some shorter weird tales that could be included. (Her post-apocalyptic novel *The Last Man* was too long to include; in any case, it really should be regarded as a proto-science-fiction tale.) I learned that most modern editions of *Frankenstein* radically alter Shelley's (very archaic and idiosyncratic) punctuation, so I painstakingly restored her usages, following a recent scholarly edition.

Just at this time, however, health difficulties forced Joe to suspend his press. I wondered if anyone would pick up these eight books and was on the verge of publishing them myself; but then Derrick Hussey came to my rescue and said he would issue them, one or two at a time. The first two appeared in early 2018 under the series title Classics of Gothic Horror.

Around this time a new editor at Dover, Drew Ford, asked me to assemble some books. Dover reprinted my Edward Lucas White collection (*The Stuff of Dreams*) and partially reprinted my Maurice Level edition (leaving out the novels and calling the edition *Thirty Hours with a Corpse*), but Ford also commissioned me to do a new historical anthology of weird writings by women, which I titled *The Cold Embrace* (2016). This contained material from Mary Shelley up to the early twentieth century (in other words, material that was all in the public domain). Ford had planned to assign me to do two further volumes of weird stories by women, bringing the series right up to the present day; but he left the company at this time, and the project was dropped.

One reprint project was of considerably greater importance. My tenth book for Penguin Classics was nothing less than a volume of Clark Ashton Smith's fantastic writings, both poetry and prose. As with the Machen book, it took some time to persuade the Penguin editors to undertake such a volume; but my edition of Smith's collected poetry, and a concurrent edition of Smith's *Collected Fantasies,* edited by Scott Connors and Ron Hilger, seems to have persuaded Penguin that Smith was on the verge of becoming canonical.

I wished to include a heavy dose of Smith's poetry, since I felt this was self-evidently the most aesthetically meritorious of his output; but Penguin insisted that poetry fill only 20% of the book—because, of course, "poetry doesn't sell." Given that restriction, I decided to exclude the 600-line *Hashish-Eater;* but after I submitted the book, Penguin surprised me by insisting that *The Hashish-Eater* be included, since it was by all accounts one of Smith's more recognisable works. Penguin did not insist that I remove any other poems to make room for it. I did a thorough re-reading of Smith's stories, finding a bit more merit in them than I had previously thought; and I believe I came up with a pretty good selection that spanned the range of Smith's imagined worlds (Zothique, Hyperborea, Averoigne, and so on). The book was titled *The Dark Eidolon and Other Fantasies* and came out in 2014. It was well received in the weird community, but I have no idea how well it has sold.

A more scholarly enterprise at this time was my role as editor of a series, Studies in Supernatural Literature, for Scarecrow Press (now subsumed by Rowman & Littlefield). I commissioned a number of scholars to assemble either anthologies of essays or original monographs. Among the former was Robert H. Waugh's *Lovecraft and Influence* (2013), Gary William Crawford's *Ramsey Campbell: Critical Essays on the Master of Modern Horror* (2013), and *The Unique Legacy of* Weird Tales (2015), edited by Justin Everett and Jeffrey L. Shanks; among the latter were books by William F. Touponce, Jason V Brock, and James Goho. I assembled a volume of *Critical Essays on Lord Dunsany* (2013), which included both an extensive selection of reprinted criticism and some original pieces. Darrell Schweitzer and I revised our Dunsany bibliography for a kind of twentieth anniversary edition (2013). But the series sold poorly (not surprisingly, as the books were very expensive hardcover editions), and the series was terminated in late 2015.

After completing *Unutterable Horror,* I felt so overdosed on horror fiction that I actually indulged in "pleasure" reading of a sort, returning to my first love, detective stories. But soon this desultory reading led to a more concrete project, albeit one that I worked on at a very leisurely pace: *Varieties of Crime Fiction*. It was a project I had conceived long before, the idea being to focus on given writers of mystery or suspense fiction who might represent various phases of the broad field of crime fiction. It took several years for me to finish the project, but I finally did so in early 2017. My coverage ranged from the classic detective stories of the 1920s and 1930s (during which I was once again regaled by John Dickson Carr, while also examining Margery Allingham and Philip MacDonald), the hard-boiled writers (Hammett, Chandler, Ross Macdonald), writers of psychological mysteries (Margaret Millar, Patricia Highsmith, and my old friend L. P. Davies), and some recent writers (P. D. James, Ruth Rendell, Sue Grafton). I came away with a very low impression of the sainted James, who struck me as a pseudo-literary poseur whose work was in fact thin and insubstantial. Publication prospects for my book are still uncertain as of this writing.

Derrick charitably published another volume of my miscellaneous essays on weird fiction, this one titled *Varieties of the Weird Tale* (2017). Much of this book was made up of my various introductions to books on Bierce, M. R. James, Dunsany, and others that I had edited, but I nonetheless think the compilation hangs together reasonably well. I might have one or more books of this sort left in me before I call it a day.

*

I carried through on my promise to Pete Crowther to edit more *Black Wings* volumes. Four more appeared, in 2014, 2015, 2016, and 2017. Moreover, I entered into negotiations with Steve Saffel of Titan Books to issue paperback editions of the series. I had met Saffel many years before, in the 1990s, when he was an editor at Del Rey (a division of Ballantine) and in charge of the Lovecraft programme there. Our various discussions at that time were somewhat inconclusive, and I could not persuade Saffel to start using my corrected texts in any new editions of Lovecraft (although in 2007 Del Rey reprinted my edition of *The Horror in the Museum and Other Revisions* without my knowledge or authorisation). In any event, Saffel now picked up the *Black Wings* series—but made the egregious decision to retitle it *Black Wings of Cthulhu!* He maintained that the word Cthulhu was a kind of magic talisman that would make any book featuring it in the title fly off the shelves. I was not entirely convinced by this argument, but the series did begin appearing in paperback in 2012.

I'm not sure I have anything of consequence to say about the last four volumes of the series. In *Black Wings IV* I was thrilled to publish an original novelette by Fred Chappell, "Artifact," along with a fine story by Ann K. Schwader. I was so taken with Schwader's Mythos tales that I urged Derrick to publish a volume of them, *Dark Equinox and Other Tales of Lovecraftian Horror* (2015), with Hippocampus. *Black Wings IV* also included the first story by Stephen Woodworth, who has contributed a number of splendid stories to various anthologies of mine. The volume also introduced the pattern of concluding the book with poetry—either a single long poem or, as in this case, a series of sonnets (Charles Lovecraft's splendid cycle "Fear Lurks Atop Temple Mount," a poetic reinterpretation of "The Lurking Fear"). *Black Wings V* introduced Nicole Cushing to the series. I later wrote a foreword to her story collection *The Mirrors* (Cycatrix Press, 2015). Jason Eckhardt contributed a splendid story about the ghost of Lovecraft, "The Walker in the Night," set during the hurricane that hit Providence in 1938. It also had a story by David Hambling. Hambling was a British journalist who had written a number of superb Mythos stories, and I persuaded Pete Crowther to issue a volume of them, *The Dulwich Horror and Others* (2015).

After compiling *Black Wings VI*, I decided the series deserved a break. A number of my "regular" authors had stated that they were pretty much tapped out of ideas for Lovecraftian fiction, so I felt that a little respite would do everyone some good. Meanwhile, I was busy with other projects. Saffel signed me up to do a two-volume series called *The Madness of Cthulhu* (Titan, 2014–15). The project would theoretically include stories playing riffs off of *At the Mountains of Madness*. One of the key selling points was that I would get Guillermo del Toro to write a foreword; but although he had promised to do so, he failed to come through—and failed even to write a blurb for the first volume. And yet, the books came out quite well. Either Saffel or I or my agent, Cherry Weiner (who had taken me on as a client on Adam Niswander's recommendation) managed to get some prominent and otherwise unusual contributors to the two volumes, including Harry Turtledove, Heather Graham, Robert Silverberg (a reprint), Kevin J. Anderson, Alan Dean Foster, William F. Nolan, and Greg Bear (in collaboration with his son, Erik). But I do not believe these two volumes have sold quite as robustly as Titan would have liked.

Another project that did a bit better was *Searchers After Horror* (Fedogan & Bremer, 2014). This was my first attempt at a *non*-Lovecraftian anthology, although a few Lovecraftian stories crept in by happenstance. I was already getting tired of being typecast as just as a "Lovecraft scholar" or a "Lovecraftian anthologist," so I sought to break out of the mould. Even though the title uses a phrase from "The Picture in the House" ("Searchers after horror haunt strange, far places"), I deliberately wished to include general weird stories; if there was any "theme" to the book, it was that of topographical horror. I was lucky to get a splendid new story by Ramsey Campbell, along with other fine stories by Michael Aronovitz, Gary Fry, Brian Stableford, and many others. Dwayne Olson had passed on to me an unpublished story by Hannes Bok, "Miranda's Tree"; it was not the most scintillating story in the world, but I believed it deserved to be published, so I included it. The book was nominated for some awards but did not win any, but I believe it has sold fairly respectably.

There were, of course, many Lovecraftian publications. I decided the time was right for the publication of my collected essays on Lovecraft, and Derrick was happy to oblige. *Lovecraft and a World in Transition* came out in 2014, filling nearly 650 pages. Of course, it did not include every scrap of non-book-length material I had ever written about Lovecraft; at a minimum, my many introductions to various Lovecraft editions were not included (although I decided to reprint my introductions to the different sections of *Miscellaneous Writings* as a single essay). The real reason for the book's compilation was that I had largely given up the writing of critical essays on Lovecraft. I had, indeed, not written any significant ones for years, since I felt I had had my say on Lovecraft and needed to step aside and let others have their say. I had, as I have mentioned, contributed almost nothing to the *Lovecraft Annual* except for random reviews. The book concluded with my keynote address at the 2013 NecronomiCon (for which see below), which I transcribed from an audio recording.

I also felt it was time to revise my *Rise and Fall of the Cthulhu Mythos*. Even the first version should probably have been titled *The Rise, Fall, and Rise of the Cthulhu Mythos*, since Mythos writing even in the early years of the twenty-first century had shown a marked improvement over the mechanical pastiches of Derleth and his ilk. So the book appeared under this title in 2015. I was happy to include extensive sections on Caitlín R. Kiernan, Jonathan Thomas (whose *The Color over Occam* [2012] is, to my mind, perhaps the best Mythos novel ever written by someone other than Lovecraft), Donald Tyson, and numerous others who had come to the fore over the past decade. There were by this time a bewildering number of Mythos anthologies, and I could not be troubled to cover every single one of them.

As for Lovecraft letters, David E. Schultz and I proceeded with volumes of the letters to Elizabeth Toldridge (also including the letters to Anne Tillery Renshaw); Robert Bloch (also including letters to Kenneth Sterling, Donald A. Wollheim, Willis Conover, and others); J. Vernon Shea (also including letters to Carl F. Strauch and Lee White); F. Lee Baldwin (also including letters to Duane W. Rimel and Nils Frome); and C. L. Moore (also including letters to Fritz Leiber, Henry Kuttner, and others). The letters to Wollheim had surfaced thanks to Paul La Farge, who was acquainted with Betsy Wollheim. The Moore volume included mostly letters *by* Moore (more than 60,000 words of them), as the letters to her were in a fragmentary condition.

This set the stage for the massive joint correspondence of Lovecraft and Clark Ashton Smith. This enormous (800 pages) hardcover volume was the result of decades of work—mostly by David; I actually got involved only toward the end of the process. It required the assembly of hundreds of disparate documents, since the Lovecraft letters had been sold individually by Smith's literary executor at the time, Roy A. Squires (whom I had met at conventions on a number of occasions, the last time at the World Fantasy Convention in Baltimore in 1980). Squires had, however, kept a (more or less) complete set of photocopies of the letters before selling them; around 2007 I and others had arranged with Squires's successor, Terence McVicker, to purchase these photocopies along with the final remaining original letters and donate them to the John Hay Library. The library eventually allowed us access to these photocopies, and David spent years transcribing and annotating them. The volume, entitled *Dawnward Spire, Lonely Hill,* seemed to receive universal accolades, and I think it deserved it.

I am obliged to mention the momentous publication of *Collected Fiction: A Variorum Edition,* which appeared in three volumes in 2015. (A fourth volume, containing the revisions and collaborations, came out in 2017.) In a sense, this project brought my whole Lovecraftian work to a grand conclusion. The idea of a variorum edition—an edition, in other words, that prints the textual variants found in all relevant appearances of a given work, from manuscript to book—was a pipe dream from the dawn of my work on Lovecraft's texts in 1976–77. I had kept track of textual variants as I consulted stories in amateur journals, in *Weird Tales* and other pulp magazines, and in key Arkham House editions.

I felt that it was now time to publish these notes—especially since certain individuals had felt that I had on my own initiative revised the texts of

12. Seattle III (2012–18)

Lovecraft's stories without authorisation. (One individual had claimed that I had done so in the case of his ghostwritten tale "Under the Pyramids"; but this fellow had not realised that I had meticulously followed the *first* appearance in *Weird Tales*, rather than a later appearance, where numerous alterations had occurred.) I had, of course, made tiny revisions in Lovecraft's stories, but chiefly only when no manuscript existed: in such cases, the alteration of the American spellings used in the first appearance (and, indeed, most subsequent appearances) to the British spellings that Lovecraft preferred was an uncontroversial editorial decision.

So the preparation of the edition began. In the course of it, Derrick Hussey did a monumental amount of work in going over my textual notes: he found a substantial number of textual variants I had missed and made numerous other suggestions for revision. At one point I was contemplating giving him a co-editorship; but the fact that I had been working on these texts for decades, while Derrick only contributed (even if vitally and essentially) toward the end dissuaded me. Still, he saved me from an enormous number of errors, and I remain eternally in his debt for it.

We received three splendid pieces of cover art—subdued but nonetheless evocative—by Fergal Fitzpatrick. I am not entirely sure that the edition made a great impact on the Lovecraftian community: I suspect that many of them did not fully realise the significance of a variorum edition. Nonetheless, I was happy to have prepared it. Sometime later, Lovecraft's typescript of the humorous squib "Old Bugs" surfaced, revealing a fair number of minor textual alterations that August Derleth had made when publishing the text in *The Shuttered Room and Other Pieces* (1959). We were able to make revisions in this story for the paperback edition that appeared in 2017.

*

This entire period was, in part, one of contention and dispute on various fronts. After a time, I felt that the Lovecraftian and general weird fiction community had descended to the petty infighting and backbiting that had characterised the "fan" movement of the 1970s, and I was not happy with this development. I do not believe that in most instances I have instigated any of these disputes; rather, they have erupted after I felt the need to defend myself (or Lovecraft) from unwarranted attacks. It has caused a great deal of bad blood, hurt feelings, and severed relationships, and that cannot be good for the field as a whole.

One feud centred around the publication of John D. Haefele's *A Look*

Behind the Derleth Mythos (dated 2012, but apparently only available in the spring of 2013). I had been casually acquainted with Haefele, who was then a member of the EOD living in Wisconsin. Although his book began with flattery ("This author admires and respects the work of S. T. Joshi and David E. Schultz, whether as a team or individually, especially in the field of Lovecraft Studies"), it proved to be a regressive attempt to re-enshrine August Derleth's flawed interpretation of the Cthulhu Mythos (as an echo of the Christian mythos, as a battle between good and evil, and so on) after it had already been annihilated by Richard L. Tierney, Dirk W. Mosig, and others. But because I was—and had been for decades—the chief spokesman of this "anti-Derlethian" approach, Haefele directed his guns on me. His book lacked an index, but if it had one, it would probably have shown that I was cited more frequently than Lovecraft himself.

Haefele was, however, an amateur as a literary critic. He had not received any formal training in the discipline, and his interpretations were invariably tendentious and implausible. He was also motivated by an inexplicable fondness for Derleth's own writing, which then translated into a frenzied defence of everything Derleth had ever said about Lovecraft (even when these statements were contradictory or plainly erroneous), and even a defence of Derleth's sorry Mythos writings, including his wretched "posthumous collaborations."

And so I lowered the boom on him, in a lengthy review (running to nearly 7000 words) that I posted online. Haefele whined to me that I had roughed him up unjustly, and he soon dropped out of the EOD; but I felt a fairly strong response was needed, because what Haefele was really trying to do was to overturn the central pillars of Lovecraft scholarship as they had been unequivocally and irrefutably established over the past half-century—and that was something I could not tolerate. Later I learned that Haefele had self-published a revised version of his book (2014)—which was *200 pages longer than the original*. I am not enough of a masochist to have read this version; I daresay most of those 200 extra pages are devoted to further abuse of me. Mercifully, no one pays any attention to John Haefele, so the effect of his screed is pretty close to nil.

Then there was the case of Roger Luckhurst. This fellow is a professor at Birkbeck College, University of London, and he took it into his head to edit an annotated volume of Lovecraft stories, entitled *The Classic Horror Stories* (2013). Somehow he got the prestigious Oxford University Press to issue it in its World's Classics edition. (Perhaps Oxford envies the Penguin Classics line just as Penguin seems to envy the World's Classics line.) The only problem is that Luckhurst, who had no knowledge of Lovecraft and apparently no knowledge of text editing, produced a fantastically botched job.

In order to avoid using my corrected texts (which would have required an acknowledgement to me, since they are my intellectual property), Luckhurst claimed that he based his texts upon the original appearances of Lovecraft's stories in pulp magazines, even though he surely knows these texts are significantly flawed. In fact, Luckhurst hasn't even followed his own stated principles; what he has actually done is to use the uncorrected Arkham House texts.

This is only the first and greatest of the malfeasances in Luckhurst's edition. His annotations are both parsimonious and largely cribbed from my own. Wherever he departs from cribbing me, he makes errors. His introduction is lacklustre, and his bibliography is a disgrace. So what else could I do but write a scathing review of this misbegotten tome? This review appeared both online and in *Lovecraft Annual* (2013). So far as I know, the eminent scholar made no attempt to reply to my criticisms. As I write these lines (spring of 2017), the hardcover edition has already been withdrawn, and a paperback edition issued on January 1, 2017, isn't exactly flying off the shelves (it is ranked #522,902 on Amazon).

At this point, the disputes compounded themselves, as I unwittingly blundered into a mare's nest of cliques and sub-cliques within the horror field. First of all, I wrote a less than rapturous review of Laird Barron's third short story collection, *The Beautiful Thing That Awaits Us All* (2013), published online on a site called *Former People*. (Don't ask me what that is meant to signify.) I had admired Barron's earlier collections as well as his novel, *The Croning* (2012), for which I had in fact supplied a blurb for the publisher; in fact, I had met Barron a few times while he was living in the Pacific Northwest (he has now moved to upstate New York) and was grateful to receive a copy of *Beautiful Thing* from him at the NecronomiCon convention of 2013.

But evidently I had committed some kind of *lèse-majesté* by daring to maintain that everything Barron wrote wasn't golden. I received predictable abuse from various Barronistas on social media—which, mercifully, I do not participate in myself, even though I receive regular reports from those who do. I then compounded my error by being not quite as enthusiastic as I apparently should have been over a book entitled *Ana Kai Tangata* by one Scott Nicolay. This book had appeared from Fedogan & Bremer in 2014, about the time of my own *Searchers After Horror*. I had never heard of Nicolay, but the book contained over-the-top encomiums from the aforementioned Laird Barron as well as John Pelan. Well, in all honesty no one—not Thomas Ligotti, nor even H. P. Lovecraft himself—could have lived up to the flamboyant praise these uncritical critics bestowed upon the unknown author of a first book. I did not read the entire book, but I did read about half of it (five of the eight stories); and in a blog I bestowed both some praise and some criticisms on Nicolay, feeling (rightly, so far as I can tell) that he was a beginning author who would benefit from constructive advice on how to improve his work.

But it seems that Nicolay had come to feel (perhaps based on those floral bouquets from Barron and Pelan) that he had already attained the pinnacle of literary greatness; moreover, he had somehow garnered a tiny but fanatically devoted following who looked upon the slightest derogation of his talents as something to be furiously combatted and rebutted. But the manner in which my comments were "rebutted" was merely by insult and billingsgate. I shall not dignify those who most viciously abused me—let them dwell in ignominious anonymity. What is more, when Jason V Brock attempted a fairly mild-mannered defence of me (which really was nothing more than a defence of my right to speak my mind), he too was caught up in the abuse: he was simultaneously deemed both my "lapdog" and my "Svengali"—quite a neat trick! Nicolay himself, in an email to me, spoke of Jason as a "sociopath"—a comment I have now come to suspect might be an instance of Freudian projection.

None of this would be worth recording if it did not lead to a slightly (but only slightly) more significant kerfuffle—the blatantly manufactured dispute over the appropriateness of the bust of Lovecraft (designed by Gahan Wilson) that served as the World Fantasy Award. This controversy was apparently initiated by one Daniel José Older, a young New York writer (I use the term loosely) who seemed so startled by the revelation of Lovecraft's racism that he began lobbying for the bust to be discarded or changed. Others, such as China Miéville, joined in this ridiculous movement. Now Lovecraft's racism has been known for many decades, and so I was reminded of the old joke of the Christian and the Jew:

A Christian meets a Jew and beats him up. When the Jew says, "Why did you do that?" the Christian says in a rage, "Because the Jews killed Christ!" When the Jew says, "But wasn't that a long time ago?" the Christian replies, "Maybe—but I just heard about it!"

12. Seattle III (2012–18)

At first, I laughed at the whole business, because it seemed so preposterous. It quickly became clear to me that Older himself simply didn't like Lovecraft and was looking for a way to knock him down a few notches. He made the incredible statement that Lovecraft was a "terrible wordsmith"—this from a person whose own prose verges upon neo-hipster illiteracy. But the unfortunate part about the whole business is that those people, like Barron, Nicolay, and others, whom I had already offended by my candour now took up the anti-Lovecraft cause, chiefly as a way of gaining vengeance on me, as I was Lovecraft's chief scholar and champion.

I then decided to have some fun with the issue. Older had proposed that the Lovecraft statue be replaced with one of Octavia Butler. It was transparently obvious to everyone but him and his cabal that this choice was made merely because Butler was an African American woman; she had next to no contributions in the field of weird fiction or even fantasy fiction. But arguing logically on this matter wouldn't accomplish much, because Older and their ilk aren't very logical. So I wrote a spoof in which I proposed a new figure for the bust—*myself!*

Yes, folks, there ought to be a likeness of *me* on the World Fantasy Award statue. After all, I am also a person of colour (even though I have the crippling drawbacks of being male and heterosexual); and a close comparison of my work against Butler's shows pretty clearly that I have contributed a great deal more to the weird field than she has (this, indeed, is a plain fact). My lampoon wasn't received terribly well by the other side, which had now been joined by one Laura Miller, a journalist who had written silly and uninformed pieces on Lovecraft and Lord Dunsany for the *New Yorker* and elsewhere. She referred to my various blogs on the subject as "egregious," whereupon I lowered the boom on her in a pair of withering blog posts.

But Older and others kept up the pressure, to the point where the World Fantasy Convention took an informal vote among those attending the 2014 convention in Arlington, Virginia, about whether to keep the statue or replace it. I attended that convention (the last World Fantasy Convention I have attended and ever will attend) and of course voted to keep the statue. Evidently a slight majority agreed with me. Nevertheless, the rather opaque World Fantasy Committee (led by David G. Hartwell, with whom I had had various sporadic contacts over the years) decided to scrap the statue. I understood that Ellen Datlow was instrumental in making this decision.

A more craven instance of caving in to political correctness would be difficult to find. In the first place, the award is designed merely to reward excellence in the weird field, and secondarily to acknowledge (what everyone aside from Older and his cohorts will readily acknowledge) Lovecraft's centrality in the history of weird fiction and the intrinsic excellence of his literary work. It says nothing about Lovecraft as a person—just as the John W. Campbell Award in the science fiction field says nothing about the fact that Campbell himself was a racist. Moreover, Lovecraft's racism is far more nuanced than most people realise—chiefly because the average person (and that includes many weird writers) has little or no knowledge of history. If we were suddenly to be prohibited from recognising the merits of every historical individual who had some character flaw, we would not recognise very many people from the past—or, indeed, from the present.

So I felt honour-bound to return my two World Fantasy Awards to Hartwell, with an open letter to him that I posted online. I received support from a number of individuals, ranging from Stephen Jones to Ramsey Campbell to Caitlín R. Kiernan, although they could not bring themselves to follow my lead and return their awards. That was their choice, and I did not fault them for it. But I felt I had no other recourse. To my surprise, my act was discussed in an article in the *Guardian* (London), which also included portions of my letter.

It is unfortunate that the anti-Lovecraft gang—many of whom have benefited from the very fact that Lovecraft has helped to make weird fiction popular—were so ungrateful and short-sighted on this matter. But that is, I suppose, how some people are. I like to think I have had the last laugh. This silly event has had not the slightest effect on Lovecraft's popularity or his high standing as a literary figure. And conversely, the next several World Fantasy Conventions were quite poorly attended, proving that the committee's decision was not met with great favour.

As a pendant to this whole business, I can discuss the widely diverging response to the appearance of Leslie Klinger's *New Annotated Lovecraft* (W. W. Norton, 2014). This immense book also borrowed a fair number of my notes to the Penguin editions, although Klinger did his research well and came up with some interesting findings of his own. But the prominence of the book, issued by a major publisher, led to correspondingly wide coverage in the press. Many reviews—ranging from John Gray in the *New Republic* to Michael Dirda in the *Times Literary Supplement*—were highly complimentary and gave Lovecraft a great deal of favourable coverage.

But one was quite otherwise. One Charles Baxter, who proved to be a professor at the University of Minnesota, was chosen for mysterious reasons—since he clearly knows nothing about Lovecraft or, indeed, about weird fiction as a whole—to write a lengthy review-essay in the *New York Review of Books*. This review was such an appalling attack on Lovecraft that both Klinger and I were floored by it. He urged me to write a response that might be published in the letter column. I initially resisted, but the more I thought about the matter the more I felt that some kind of response was needed. Less than twenty years after Joyce Carol Oates had written a penetrating and insightful analysis of Lovecraft in this same venue (while reviewing *H. P. Lovecraft: A Life*), we were now once again backsliding to the era when Lovecraft was considered a pulp hack—and, now, a racist and (Baxter's new and unsupported claim) a misogynist to boot.

Well, I ended up writing a 4200-word rebuttal that I sent to the *New York Review of Books*. I later received a response from Robert Silvers, the lead editor, saying that my response was obviously too long to publish as such (even though the journal had in fact published many lengthy responses of exactly this sort); Silvers went on to say that my response would have to be limited to 400 words if it were to be published in the letters column. I did not think that 400 words would really accomplish the purpose, but I went about preparing such a version, meanwhile posting my full response on my website. The 400-word letter was indeed published in a subsequent issue; but it quickly became clear that Baxter's halting reply was based on my *full* rebuttal, as it addressed points that I did not make in the 400-word piece! I wrote to Silvers, saying that his readers might be puzzled at this discrepancy, but he did not trouble to reply.

I doubt that Baxter's attack has had much effect on Lovecraft's reputation either, so it is probably best left to find merciful oblivion.

*

Now that I had settled into Mary's house, my personal life attained a stability and calm that it had not had in quite some time. At a minimum, I felt that this sixth move since 2001 would be my last for some time, since our house was adequate to our purposes and we both liked the neighbourhood we were in. We actually *knew* our neighbours—a refreshing change from my previous house! Aside from Jim Dempsey across the street, his wife, Janice Klain, proved to be an engaging friend. I even persuaded her to join the Northwest Chorale, where—in spite of her habitual diffidence—she eventually rose up to the august level of president of the chorale's board, working closely with Lynn Hall on finding venues for our performances and in general trying to make our chorale operate in a more efficient and professional manner.

On our trips, we customarily drew upon the services of another choir member, Mila Webb, who was a professional catsitter. She did an excellent job, eliciting a particular fondness from the curmudgeonly Henry. It also turned out that Mila was a devotee of fantasy and was an excellent poet. This came in handy for *Spectral Realms,* where she has appeared frequently. Much to my delight, Mary herself contributed some powerful weird and cosmic poems. She had written poetry earlier in life, but now her poetry took a dark, brooding turn inspired by her reading of Lovecraft and other weird writers.

Our travels were largely governed, in the earlier years covered by this chapter, by my professional obligations. We went to Vancouver, British Columbia, twice, once to attend the Modern Language Association convention held there. A professor from Wisconsin, Alison Sperling, had invited me to speak on a panel discussion on weird fiction. It proved to be rather less stuffy and pompous than I had been expecting. On both Vancouver trips we made sure to look up the exemplary poet Wade German, and we had lively discussions with him on the nature and craft of weird poetry.

We attended the World Horror Convention in New Orleans in June 2013—the first WHC I had attended since 1993, when it was in Stamford, Connecticut. I was thrilled to see both Ramsey Campbell and Caitlín R. Kiernan there. We also spent a lot of time with Jason and Sunni Brock and Bill Nolan. But the weather was frightfully hot and humid, and I was also disappointed with some of the cuisine we sampled. This was my first time in New Orleans since, I believe, 1988, when I went to the Modern Language Association meeting on behalf of Chelsea House.

Then there was, of course, the first NecronomiCon as organised by Niels Hobbs and others. They made it clear that they were not at all connected with the earlier NecronomiCons held in the 1990s. This one, in August of 2013, was held at the Biltmore Hotel in Providence and was overall a splendid affair. I was on an unprecedented *twelve* panel discussions—four a day over the three days of the convention—and since these panels ran to an hour and a quarter, I was pretty wiped out after a full day of blabbing. Indeed, Jason Brock claimed to have overheard one attendee say in exasperation, "Man, I'm getting tired of listening to that Joshi guy!" Me too, my dear chap.

I also gave the keynote address on the Thursday prior to the convention, held at the First Baptist Church (where I had graduated from Brown thirty-three years earlier), giving a potted history of Lovecraft's recognition. As soon as that was over, we had to head over to the Athenaeum for a ceremony unveiling the superb bust of Lovecraft designed by Bryan Moore. (I was amused when I later saw Woody Allen's film *Irrational Man*, which takes place in a fictitious Rhode Island university. The bust is prominently visible in one scene that purportedly takes place in the university's library.) Of course, it was wonderful to see all my colleagues, old and new, ranging from Steve Mariconda to Joe Pulver. Wilum Pugmire had made the long trip from Seattle also. It was astounding to learn that the convention attracted as many as 1200 attendees, and it received wide coverage in the local press.

Later that year, Mary and I ventured over to Brighton, England, to attend the World Fantasy Convention. This was my first time in England since 1988. The convention itself was rather dull, but we made sure to visit some of the historic sites in town. After the convention we spent a few days in London, where I was interviewed by Digby Rumsey for a documentary on Lord Dunsany, oddly titled *Shooting for the Butler*. It appeared in 2014, but I was disappointed that he had only interviewed me, Joe Doyle, and one or two others. Nonetheless, it was a fine piece of work. Then we went over to Dublin for two days. I made sure to look up the site where Handel's *Messiah* had first been performed in 1742. There was a plaque on the inconspicuous-looking building commemorating the event.

The reason why we were in Ireland was because we had received an invitation from Maria Alice, Dowager Lady Dunsany, to visit Dunsany Castle, about an hour's drive northwest of Dublin. We were picked up by a driver and taken deep into the Irish countryside where the castle—built in the late twelfth century—lay. Only a relatively small portion of the castle is now in use, and incredibly Lady Dunsany lives in it pretty much on her own, with no regular servants. Some people come in from the nearby village of Dunsany to lend a hand now and then. She received us cordially, and we had a wonderful time. We spent only one night in the castle, but it was thrilling to come to the place where Dunsany had written so many of his great works of fantasy. (Of course, he had also lived at Dunstall Priory in Shoreham, Kent, but this residence was no longer in the family.) There is also a ruined chapel on the grounds; the writer is not buried there but in Shoreham.

Then we went back to London to participate in a conference on the weird held at Birkbeck College. (Mercifully, Roger Luckhurst, whose edition of Lovecraft I had excoriated, was not in attendance!) I gave the keynote address, on the revolutionary work of Poe and Lovecraft—more or less a duplicate of the lecture I gave to the Edgar Allan Poe Society in Baltimore in October 2012, where I also participated in a charming ceremony at Poe's gravesite. I was also on a panel discussion or two. Otherwise, the conference was a bit on the stuffy and academic side, and I didn't find many of the other presentations of any great interest.

The visit to Dunsany set the stage for a much more ambitious visit that I made without Mary in the summer of 2014. The purpose of this visit was nothing less than to catalogue the totality of Dunsany's literary manuscripts. For this task I enlisted the assistance of Martin Andersson, who had already visited the castle on a number of occasions and in fact may now know more about Dunsany than I do. We planned to stay for two weeks, hoping that would be enough time to do the work.

The trip did not get off on the right foot, as my suitcase did not make it on the flight to Dublin. It took about five days for it to reach me at the castle, during which time I had to borrow clothes (including underwear) from Randal Plunkett, Maria Alice's son and the current Lord Dunsany (the 21st). But Martin and I got to work without delay. I had instructed Maria Alice to get a certain type of box to hold the manuscripts, along with plenty of file folders to fill the boxes. We worked like lunatics, from 8:30 A.M. to about 11:30 P.M. I do not believe Martin and I set foot outside of the castle for the first eight days we were there. Of course we were provided with meals—indeed, Maria Alice supplied us with such an immense quantity of food that I could scarcely consume it all. For a time I felt as if I had entered into Robert Aickman's "The Hospice," which takes place at a roadside inn where the elderly guests were eating "as if their lives depended on it."

It quickly became clear to me that the task of cataloguing the literary manuscripts—novels, tales, poetry, essays, plays—would be quite enough for us to do. I had initially hoped that I might tackle the mounds of correspondence (mostly to Dunsany, of course, although the letters he wrote to his wife, Lady Beatrice, from his far-flung travels were also in evidence); but I soon realised there was no hope of that. So I tackled the plays, essays, and poetry, and Martin took on the stories. The novels were fairly easy to document, since most of them were in large scrapbooks, usually in several volumes (Dunsany's handwriting was quite large, so he couldn't get many words on a page). I found a number of unpublished plays among the material and made copies of them for later transcription. At one point we sensed that there must be more manuscripts than what we had at hand; and Maria

12. Seattle III (2012–18)

Alice, Martin, and I conducted a systematic exploration of the castle to see if we could find them. Sure enough, a trunk that Maria Alice thought she had examined proved to have—under a layer of books—many more manuscripts!

We quite literally finished the work a few minutes before we had to leave for the airport and back to our respective homes. But the job was done, and we had clear electronic records of every work by Dunsany that existed at the castle. I felt immense satisfaction at having completed the task, for now that cache of manuscripts might serve as the basis of new projects. Indeed, I had earlier conceived the idea of a *Collected Plays* of Dunsany, and I transcribed the new plays and threw them into the book. Some time before, Joe Doyle had passed on some manuscripts of unpublished plays he had discovered. One of them was a three-act play called *The Strange Lover* that proved to be a version of the Frankenstein story told from the monster's point of view. I'm hoping that the project—which may come to nearly 1000 pages—may find print soon.

Another project on which Martin and I were working was a volume of Dunsany's uncollected stories. This project dated back years, when Darrell Schweitzer realised that there was a great deal of uncollected material beyond what he had gathered in *The Ghosts of the Heaviside Layer and Other Fantasms* (1980). I had initially wished to include stories from a wide chronological range, as well as some splendid essays, and perhaps even some plays; but as the project progressed, I decided to drop the essays and plays, and I also focused on the later stories, since Lady Dunsany had given exclusive permission to a tiny publisher, Pegana Press, to issue limited editions of some of the early uncollected tales. Joe Doyle sent me a list of some stories that Dunsany had wished to gather into a collection around 1956; I knew of some of these stories, but others were unfamiliar. Later Doyle found the manuscripts of a good many of these, and eventually Martin found other unpublished stories that were worth including. Securing permission from Dunsany's agents took a very long time, but the volume finally appeared as *The Ghost in the Corner and Other Stories* (Hippocampus Press, 2017).

I got back home from Ireland only five days before another momentous event—my marriage to Mary on July 27, 2014. I had quaintly proposed marriage to her on the previous Valentine's Day, and now we prepared for a modest-sized wedding—chiefly for our respective families and any friends who might be able to come. In the end, as many as fifteen of Mary's relatives showed up, along with my mother, my two sisters, my two nieces, and my nephew. Linda Aro and Chris Pfaff came over from New York, as did

Lois Gresh from Rochester, New York. Of course, Jason and Sunni were there, along with Wilum and Greg Lowney. In reality, our life really didn't change much with the event, but it felt good to be married.

The NecronomiCon convention of 2015 was of some interest. I was only on six or seven panels this time. The attendance was even larger than at the previous convention—about 1800, I was told. Bob Price made a bizarre keynote address in which he tried to affirm that Lovecraft would have been in consonance with right-wingers in his hostility to Muslims, but aside from gaffes of that sort the convention was entertaining enough.

From a personal perspective, the chief event at this NecronomiCon was a brief ceremony at the John D. Rockefeller Library of Brown to announce the S. T. Joshi Endowed Research Fellowship. This had been set up by Derrick Hussey and was intended to promote scholarship on Lovecraft and related writers by providing a stipend to scholars who might come to Brown and make use of the research materials at the John Hay Library. I confess that I felt somewhat posthumous when this fellowship was set up, but I took it in good stride.

Mary and I had fallen into the habit of going on cruises one year and road trips the next. Our first cruise was an ambitious one to the Baltic, in the summer of 2013. After flying to Copenhagen, where the cruise originated, we were taken to Stockholm, Helsinki, St. Petersburg (two days), Talinn (Estonia), and Berlin (by train). In nearly every stop, I was able to rendezvous with some Lovecraftian colleague who showed us around the city: Martin Andersson in Stockholm, Juha-Matti Rajala in Helsinki, Joe Pulver and his wife in Berlin (also Mateusz Kopacs, the Polish translator of my biography, who brought several friends with him from Warsaw), and Henrik Harksen in Copenhagen. It was a spectacular trip, although we were rushed through the Hermitage museum in St. Petersburg during a swelteringly hot day by a tour guide who literally ran from one room to the other.

The next year, we did not in fact take a proper honeymoon, but we decided to take a road trip to Denver to look up Jerad Walters and others in the area. Jason and Sunni drove separately from Vancouver. Naturally, we stopped at various places along the way—chiefly Yellowstone National Park, where we spent several days. In Denver, we not only looked up Jerad, his wife, and his young son, but also Mary's niece, Emily Kurmis, who was teaching in the area. And we had a wonderful dinner with Melanie and Steve Rasnic Tem. It was, of course, our last visit with Melanie before she died the next February.

In 2015 we took our belated honeymoon—a river cruise down the Danube. We flew into Munich, then took a train to the charming historic town of Passau, on the Danube. We attended a concert in a church there—which has the largest cathedral organ in Europe. Then the cruise began, and we stopped at Vienna, Salzburg, Bratislava, and Budapest. It was criminal to restrict the Vienna visit to only one day, and I had no chance to go to the Vienna Central Cemetery and pay my respects to Beethoven; but we did hear a nice orchestra concert that evening. At Salzburg we made sure to see many of the Mozart-related sites. Budapest was a remarkable city, and we spent two days there before flying home.

Some travels during 2015 and 2016 were for a very different purpose. In the fall of 2015 my mother had to have emergency gall bladder surgery. After spending a full thirteen days in the hospital, she spent several additional weeks in a skilled care facility in Muncie. Ragini, Nalini, and I then decided that my mother could no longer feasibly live on her own in her house: while her mind remained incredibly keen, her mobility was severely restricted and she was in constant danger of injuring herself. So we arranged to place her in an assisted living facility in the northern part of Muncie; we also realised that we would have to deal with the accumulation of possessions that my mother had accumulated over a lifetime. We may have been perhaps a bit hasty in this undertaking, discarding some items that perhaps had some value; but the end result was that, over five separate visits over the next year and a half, I helped to clear out the house that my mother had lived in for more than forty-five years and get it ready for sale. We of course did preserve some materials of real or sentimental value, including my mother's remarkable collection of family photographs, filling up many scrapbooks and extending back to our life in India. No doubt the transition to a smallish apartment in the assisted living facility was difficult for my mother; but she keeps herself busy with numerous projects relating to mathematics and other subjects, and the physical therapy she is receiving at the facility has somewhat improved her physical condition.

On one of those trips, in the summer of 2016, I combined a checkup on my mother with my attendance of my high school's fortieth reunion. But this one was not nearly as entertaining as the thirtieth reunion, especially given that only five other classmates were present. Where's your school spirit, people? Some of them might have balked at the high price of the actual reunion dinner, and in fact I met other classmates privately during that weekend. But I'm hoping the fiftieth reunion in 2026 will be better attended.

In September 2016 we took a road trip to the Southwest. We flew into Phoenix, then drove to the quaint city of Sedona, then on to the Grand Canyon. The cosmic splendour of this site is not to be believed. Our first day there was a bit overcast, and the canyon itself was smothered in an eldritch fog or mist; the next day the weather cleared up a bit. Some of the trails take you very close to the edge of the canyon, and my fear of heights caused me several moments of acute terror.

During this period we got into the habit of spending the Christmas holidays either at Nalini's house in Carmel Valley or Ragini's house in Los Angeles, usually the former. The gatherings usually include Nalini's daughter Anjeli and Ragini's daughter Anne (Joshi) Gieseker. On one trip to Los Angeles, however, I was delighted to meet K. A. (Kyle) Opperman and his girlfriend, Ashley Dioses, two young poets who lived in the area. Kyle published a strong book of poetry, *The Crimson Tome,* with Hippocampus Press in 2015, with deserved encomiums by Donald Sidney-Fryer and W. C. Farmer. His poetry is perhaps a bit derivative of Poe, Lovecraft, and Clark Ashton Smith, but it is technically polished and highly evocative. Ashley later submitted a splendid poetry collection, *Diary of a Sorceress,* that appeared from Hippocampus in 2017.

After one trip to Carmel Valley (in 2013), however, we came home to a sad event. When we arrived back home, we found our cat Paolo absent. We notified our catsitter, Mila Webb, and she told us that she had not seen Paolo for the entire preceding day. Well, Paolo never came back. About two months earlier a cancer had been detected in one of his back legs, and the leg had to be amputated; unlike Phoebe, whose amputation had occurred when she was quite young, Paolo never truly adjusted to the loss of the appendage. We suspected that he had been killed by a raccoon or some such thing. For weeks I roamed the neighbourhood in the hope that I might find him, lost, disoriented, or even kidnapped by some nefarious individual, but he never turned up. We mourned him deeply and cherished even more our three remaining cats—all of them, curiously enough, the cats I had obtained during my Moravia years. I keep lobbying Mary for more felines (especially kittens), but so far she has cruelly denied me.

*

The summer of 2016 was memorable for a number of reasons. I have already mentioned our trip to the Grand Canyon. Upon our return, I became

12. Seattle III (2012–18)

enthralled by the remarkable ascendancy of the Chicago Cubs. The previous year they had reached the league championship series but had come up short; now they were dominating professional baseball as few other teams had. Could they actually achieve their first World Series championship since 1908? It seemed too good to be true, but on November 1 they achieved that goal. I could barely endure to watch that seventh game of the series, tuning in only toward the end when they pulled out a victory from the jaws of defeat.

Somewhat the reverse happened exactly a week later, when the nation was stunned by the triumph of Donald J. Trump over Hillary Clinton in the presidential election of 2016. I suddenly began to question what kind of country I was living in. Did I really wish to acknowledge that the United States was so full of racists, religious bigots, gun nuts, and other such canaille? It was cold comfort that Clinton won the popular vote by a considerable margin; and it may be true (as I suspected from the start) that Trump's "victory" was more than a little Pyrrhic; if nothing else, he and his administration of liars, sycophants, and incompetents have energised the left as it has not been for many years.

I myself have become increasingly radicalised, lambasting the hypocrisy, duplicity, and corruption of right-wingers (including the religious right) in my "Stupidity Watch" columns for the *American Rationalist.* (Alas, for reasons in no way connected with my editorship, the Center for Inquiry pulled the plug on the journal in the summer of 2017.) But the election had more personal effects, and I felt compelled to break with certain colleagues with whom I could no longer endure to associate because of their political views. One of these was Scott Connors. I long knew that he was a fervent and almost irrational hoplophile, but I subsequently learned that he had spent much of the presidential campaign in unleashing attack after attack on Clinton. (Whether any of it came from the "fake news" generated from Russian sources, I have no idea.) So Scott contributed his mite to Clinton's defeat; indeed, the brainwashing of many millions by Fox News (which Scott watches religiously) was the ultimate factor in Trump's "victory," for its decades-long campaign of demonising the Clintons had its effect on many voters who should have known better. As for Scott, I had already been appalled by his attitude on guns. Some time before, he had paid me a visit, and in a late-night discussion (in which Jason Brock also participated), we had become quite heated on the subject. Some of Scott's views were so astonishingly wrong-headed that I felt obliged to discuss them in a "Stupidity Watch" column some time later, although I did not mention his name.

But, unlike other liberals who seemed to have been stunned by the election results, I myself quickly resumed literary activity; indeed, I have rarely been so prolific as I have been in the past year or so. One surprising development was that I returned to fiction writing. I began writing what I felt would be a novella (I did not think I could extend it to a full-scale novel, and I was right) that I ultimately titled *Something from Below*. This was a non-Lovecraftian horror tale set in the coal-mining country of Pennsylvania (an area, I confess, of which I have no first-hand knowledge). I worked on it in fits and starts, but eventually finished it in the summer of 2017, at a length of more than 37,000 words. I was pretty pleased with this—and more pleased when Pete Crowther of PS Publishing quickly accepted it. He promised to get it out in the fall of 2018, but it took him another year to get it into print.

I also assembled another original—and non-Lovecraftian—anthology entitled *Apostles of the Weird*. The point of this anthology was a kind of tacit rebuke of the increasingly artificial "theme" anthologies that have so dominated weird fiction in the past few decades. I deliberately set out to demonstrate the wide scope of the weird by including tales ranging from pure supernaturalism to imaginary-world fantasy to post-apocalyptic science fiction to psychological terror. In this anthology I included not only many of my "regular" contributors but also such authors as Michael Washburn (a talented and diverse writer from Brooklyn, who has also visited me a few times in Seattle) and George Edwards Murray, a protégé of Nancy Holder. PS will publish this volume in the fall of 2018.

I also took advantage of Amazon's self-publishing programme (print books through CreateSpace; ebooks through Kindle Publishing) to issue some titles that I did not feel it worth while to burden Derrick Hussey or other real publishers. One of these was *Driven to Madness with Fright* (2016), a volume of my collected reviews subsequent to those included in *Classics and Contemporaries*. This book featured a splendid cover by Allen Koszowski: he had generously passed on a dozen or more of his illustrations for my use, and I was happy to place it on the cover. I collected some of my more interesting and controversial blog posts under the title *Lovecraft and Weird Fiction* (2017), which also had a fine cover illustration by Koszowski.

My prime work during this period, however, was editing Lovecraft letters. David E. Schultz and I actually could see the light at the end of the tunnel of this immense project, and we picked up the pace in getting books ready for publication by Hippocampus Press. In 2016 we issued *Letters to J. Vernon Shea, Carl F. Strauch, and Lee McBride White* and *Letters to F. Lee*

12. Seattle III (2012–18)

Baldwin, Duane W. Rimel, and Nils Frome; in 2017 we came out with *Letters to C. L. Moore and Others* and, as mentioned earlier, *Dawnward Spire, Lonely Hill: The Letters of H. P. Lovecraft and Clark Ashton Smith. Letters to Maurice W. Moe and Others* appeared in 2018.

But by this time, and perhaps exacerbated by the election, the weird fiction field had become riven by cliques, feuds, and hostilities of various sorts. I have already mentioned that people like Scott Nicolay and, to a lesser extent, Laird Barron had come to regard me as their enemies; and now they were, for various reasons, joined by a motley crew of other writers, editors, and publishers. Much of this hostility—insofar as it was directed at me—was ignited by the unfortunate events surrounding the third NecronomiCon convention, held in Providence in August of 2017.

The 2015 convention had already had its awkward moments, and after it was over I engaged in a rather heated discussion with the organiser, Niels Hobbs, about how to avoid such missteps at the next event. Hobbs did not seem eager to take my advice; indeed, as I continued discussions with him I became concerned that he himself actually sided with those whom I took to calling the "Lovecraft-haters"—people like Daniel José Older, Laura Miller, and others who seized upon Lovecraft's racism in an attempt to drag him down and, in essence, throw him out of the literary arena. (It is curious that these ardent devotees of social righteousness do not exhibit similar outrage at the racist, anti-Semitic, and misogynist sentiments of much more influential writers of the period, such as T. S. Eliot, Ezra Pound, Jack London, Roald Dahl, and many others one could name.) Hobbs had arranged a panel on Lovecraft's racism at the 2015 convention that was nothing but one long rant at Lovecraft's views without the slightest attempt to contextualise them or understand their origins and motivations. Indeed, I was stunned to learn that Hobbs had actually extended an invitation to Older to that event. Imagine! One might as well have invited the Grand Wizard of the Ku Klux Klan to an N.A.A.C.P. conference.

So I felt obliged to take a tough line with Hobbs for the 2017 convention, noting that there were a handful of individuals—including Nicolay, Nick Mamatas (who had written a fatuous *roman à clef* about the 2015 convention, entitled *I Am Providence,* which contains caricatures of Robert M. Price, Jason Brock, and myself, among others), and certain others who had both shown themselves to be implacably hostile to Lovecraft and generally worthless as authors or critics of weird fiction—whose presence at the 2017 event would necessitate my own absence from that same event. Hobbs had, to my mind, already made the error of inviting Ellen Datlow—who I knew for a fact was instrumental in having the Lovecraft bust removed as the emblem of the World Fantasy Award—as a special guest, but I felt that the banishment of certain others might at least salvage the convention to some extent.

I thought I had received Hobbs's agreement to my conditions, but apparently he thought differently. At the last moment he invited Nicolay to host some sort of event—neglecting, of course, to inform me of his decision. I only found out about it when someone directed me to the NecronomiCon website, where the event was displayed. I immediately wrote to Hobbs and said that I felt obliged to withdraw from the convention altogether unless he removed Nicolay; he refused, and I forthwith announced my boycotting of the convention.

This resulted in an uproar in which a fair number of people lost their heads. Hobbs himself, a few days before the convention was to begin, actually posted a lying and deceitful statement condemning me (without naming me) for establishing a "blacklist," even though he had (at least to my understanding) initially agreed to it, promising me in fairly explicit terms that those people I had named would not be involved in any capacity in the formal programming of the convention. Others chided me for my decision, claiming that Hobbs could do what he wished. Evidently I was not granted the same freedom of action.

It was too late to change my travel plans, so Mary and I went to Providence in any case, spending a few days in Boston beforehand. In the Boston area I ventured for the first time to such Lovecraftian locales as Rafe's Chasm in Magnolia (where Lovecraft took Sonia in 1922) and revisited Mt. Auburn Cemetery for the first time in nearly forty years. In Providence we mostly spent time with Jonathan Thomas, who took us around to various sites—ranging from Lovecraft's ancestral domain of Foster, in western Rhode Island, to Quinsnicket Park (one of Lovecraft's favourite haunts), to Neutaconkanut Hill, where Lovecraft had wandered a few months before his death—that I myself had never seen before. We also explored the grounds of Butler Hospital and also Swan Point Cemetery, where we at last found the gravesite of Lillian D. Clark (Lovecraft's elder aunt), which I had never seen before. We made an expedition to Foster, in western Rhode Island, but aside from finding the house where Lovecraft's mother was born, we had trouble locating other relevant sites. I did stop by very briefly at the convention, talking with Derrick Hussey, Jeffrey Thomas, and a few others. (Later, one Scott R. Jones maintained that I was "skulking" around the convention and, furthermore, that I was an ingrate for taking money from the convention for my travel and hotel expenses but refusing to fulfil my obligations on the program. In fact, I was not offered a penny by the NecronomiCon to cover my expenses.)

The furore continued in the weeks and months following the convention, becoming especially furious when I singled out Ellen Datlow as the prime mover (as in fact she was) in the whole World Fantasy Award kerfuffle. Neither she nor her many devotees took kindly to my remarks, but they could only rebut me with lies: Datlow herself claimed that there had been a "unanimous" vote among the World Fantasy Committee to retire the Lovecraft bust, when I knew (after discussing the matter with a member of the committee) that in fact there had been no vote at all, and that the removal of the bust was a fait accompli. But as a result of my pointing all this out, still more people—among them Paul Tremblay, Brian Keene, and the publisher Ross E. Lockhart—began raining imprecations down on my head on social media.

All this amused me no end, and I began resorting to the practice of deliberately baiting these earnest individuals by various comments of my own on my blog and elsewhere. There was, in truth, not very much sport in it, since it was so easy to rile these touchy individuals, who would fly off the handle at the least provocation. I myself used my "satirical criticism" to twit some of these folks. By this time I had plunged into my quasi-sequel to *Unutterable Horror,* entitled *21st-Century Horror,* in which I would cover writers of weird fiction who had come to prominence in this new century. I wrote—and posted on my blog—critical essays on Laird Barron, Brian Keene, Joe Hill, Nick Mamatas, Jeff VanderMeer, and others that were perhaps a trifle less than charitable, even though I genuinely felt that the deficiencies of their work required a frank evaluation that took no regard of the authors' popularity; but of course, the authors themselves, as well as their lickspittles and sycophants, all expressed fury and outrage at my remarks. It provided me some transient amusement to witness their discomfiture.

However, when I came to seek a publisher for this book, I understandably had some difficulty, as the controversy surrounding some of the chapters I had posted online made the book essentially radioactive. Well, that didn't bother me in the slightest, and I issued the book myself under my Sarnath Press imprint in 2018. I doubt that it has sold many copies, but it is out there for anyone to read.

*

There were, of course, pleasanter things afoot in 2017. Chief among them was my choir's performance of Handel's *Israel in Egypt,* an oratorio (nearly all of which consists of choruses, many of them double choruses of some difficulty) that I had wished to sing ever since I heard it in the late 1970s. Because of the expense of putting on such a major production, I anonymously contributed about $7,000 to the venture. I wouldn't say that our two performances, on May 13 and 20, were flawless; but they were good enough. And because both of them had been recorded, we later produced a 2-CD package (which I paid for, also anonymously) that is more than creditable.

The big trip of the year was an extended trip overseas (July 7–24), much of which involved a cruise on a Holland America ship that took us to Italy, Albania, and Greece. The voyage started with (ugh!) a red-eye flight from Seattle to Venice, where the cruise would begin. We arrived in Venice a day or two early, on the afternoon of July 8, and immediately had a splendid meal near our hotel. It sounds like an absurd truism, but the Italians sure know how to make pasta!

On Sunday, July 9, was our major exploration day in Venice. We of course took in the Piazza San Marco. When we arrived, a service was in progress at the basilica; but we were allowed to go upstairs to the museum of the basilica, which afforded us a fine view of the church's interior as well as a bird's-eye view of the square itself. Fabulous! Then we trudged all the way to the majestic domed Basilica di Santa Maria della Salute—but because it was a Sunday, the church was closed from noon till three P.M.! So we satisfied ourselves with gazing at the exterior. We returned to our hotel and took a dip in the pool—rather small, and in effect a kind of oversized hot tub. We had another splendid meal that evening. We did some minimal exploring the following day before heading to the place where the cruise ship was docked.

Of course, the advantage of a cruise is that nearly all your meals are provided for, you don't have to pack and unpack your clothes, and you do not have to worry too much about transportation from one place to another, as this is generally provided (for a fee, of course) by the cruise ship. The cruise left port on July 10 and spent the entirety of July 11 at sea, landing at the Albanian beach resort of Sarandë on July 12. This was a moderately interesting place, but really it was meant as a replacement for the cruise's initial plan of going to Istanbul—a plan that political events in that increasingly authoritarian country have rendered hazardous to Americans (and others).

On July 13 we ventured to one of the Greek islands in the Ionian Sea, Kefalonia, where we were taken around the town of Argostoli and also to

Melissani Lake and the Drogararti caves—my first true experience of caves. This was a fairly spooky place, and the acoustics in the cave are such that actual concerts are occasionally held. Our tour guide urged me (the only halfway decent singer in our group) to belt something out, and I obliged with a few bars from a tenor solo from Handel's *Messiah*.

At last the cruise reached mainland Greece, where we saw the ruins of ancient Mycenae (one of the oldest civilisations on earth, dating to at least the second millennium B.C.E.) and Olympia, where the first Olympic games were held in 776 B.C.E. The chief distinction here was the superb Hermes of Praxitiles, housed in the archaeological museum in Olympia, one of the towering masterworks of world art. Then we ventured to Athens itself, where of course we saw the Acropolis with its majestic Parthenon and other sites. I would have liked to have gone to the archaeological museum there (one of the greatest in the world), but we didn't have time.

We also took in the ancient remains of Corinth, which once rivalled Athens for supremacy. Indeed, we had an awkward moment in the museum in Corinth, when Mary had me pose for a comical photograph standing behind a headless statue, as if it were my head on the statue. A female guard noticed our shenanigans and brusquely demanded that Mary delete the photograph from her phone. I calmly walked away from the encounter, pretending I didn't know this rude American woman who was being so disrespectful of classical antiquity.

We then went to two Greek islands, Mykonos and Santorini. Both of these islands feature distinctive architecture—nearly all the buildings are painted white, with the occasional blue roof or dome. The vistas that can be obtained from various lookout points are beyond description, with extraordinary views of the blue Aegean. Then we made the long trip through the Straits of Messina to Naples. We did not explore that city itself, but did take a tour of ancient Pompeii, where we saw a few examples of human bodies covered in lava (although it appears that these are not genuine but copies or casts made of chalk). The whole site was remarkable—not least of which was the *lupanar* (whorehouse), where pictures of various sex acts on the wall were designed for the purpose of allowing the patrons to select which exact position was desired.

The cruise ship left us off in Rome on July 22, and we spent that day touring the Vatican Museum (Sistine Chapel and all), having another great Italian meal, and then spending the next day on a largely pedestrian tour of the major sites—Colosseum, Forum, Pantheon, Trevi Fountain, and St. Peter's. We only went into the square of St. Peter's, as the line for actually getting into the church was immense. That evening, incredibly, we had dinner with my sister Nalini and her daughter Anjeli, along with some of Nalini's co-workers. She just happened to be in Rome for business at the time, and it was wonderful to get together with her and Anjeli so far from home. We enjoyed our momentary fantasy of being jetsetters ("Yes, let's meet in Rome this summer").

The entire trip was sensational, but the weather was so cripplingly hot and humid that we both felt the need to take shelter in the afternoon with long naps on the ship or in a hotel. The virtues of the siesta became very obvious to us! If we go to the Mediterranean again, we will have to go at some other time of year—not only because of the weather, but because of the mobs of tourists at every turn. As it was, I developed a heavy tan that makes me even more of a person of colour than before!

Mary and I ventured to Minnesota twice, around Labor Day and also in November, to attend weddings of a niece and nephew, in the course of which I was able to become better acquainted with her side of the family. And my sisters and I, along with Mary, returned to Muncie in early October for a slightly early celebration of my mother's ninetieth birthday (officially on October 17).

We have also tried to keep in touch with the local gang of weird fiction devotees (and other friends) with festivities of various kinds. In what could be considered a West Coast affiliate of the New Kalem Club, we periodically round up such luminaries as Wilum Pugmire, Greg Lowney, Dave (D. L.) Myers, Mila Webb (and her husband, Sean Chitwood), our neighbours Jim Dempsey and Janice Klain, and others for a meal at an excellent Thai restaurant near our house. Afterward, we come back to our house for general discussion, sometimes livened by poetry readings—for it happens that a number of these individuals (Wilum, Mila, Dave, and of course Mary herself) are all weird poets of some accomplishment, who all appear frequently in *Spectral Realms*. We also have cookouts on Memorial Day and Labour Day, where we host not only the persons mentioned above but also Jason and Sunni Brock, who manage to whip up toothsome vegetarian items along with the largely carnivorous fare that we provide.

A nice and comfortable life! Neither of us are extravagant, and we both work pretty hard (Mary has fallen into the occupation of being a ghostwriter, working with some interesting individuals in writing "as told to" books about their lives and travails), but make sure to enjoy ourselves by dining out occasionally, going to the theatre (Seattle Repertory Theatre is one of the best in the country) and the symphony, getting together with friends, taking trips long and short, and otherwise making sure that we avoid anything approaching an "all work and no play" scenario. That said, I can confirm that I am definitely not finished with my work.

13. Seattle (2018–2022)

> "Oh! my dear Sir, don't you find that nine parts in ten of the world are of no use but to make you wish yourself with that tenth part?"—Horace Walpole to John Chute, 20 August 1743

The hardcover edition of this book appeared in June 2018, and my publisher, Derrick Hussey, kindly arranged a lavish publication party in New York for the occasion. It was held on my sixtieth birthday, June 22, at O'Reilly's pub, our favourite hangout—and I was immensely pleased and flattered that Peter Straub, Donald Sidney-Fryer, and a host of other friends and colleagues attended the event. It was even enlivened by the reading of several poems about me written by Leigh Blackmore, Adam Bolivar, and others.

Mary and I spent more than a week in the general area. We flew into Syracuse on the 16th and spent several days exploring my old stomping-grounds in the Ithaca area. Of course we visited my old house in Moravia, which had been transformed by the new owners into something far more elaborate and appealing than Leslie and I had had the chance to do during our three years there. In New York City we visited the always lovely Brooklyn Botanical Gardens and also (a first for me) the Tenement Museum in the Lower East Side.

But upon my return to Seattle on the 24th, it was of course back to work. As previously mentioned, Hippocampus Press had taken over the series I had initially compiled for Joe Morey of Dark Renaissance Books, Classics of Gothic Horror, and the first two books came out in early summer 2018. These covered the work of E. Nesbit and Mary E. Wilkins Freeman. Several other volumes soon appeared: Thomas Burke (2018), W. W. Jacobs (2018), Mary Shelley (2018), Théophile Gautier (2018), May Sinclair (2020), Irvin S. Cobb and Gouverneur Morris in one volume (2020), and Sir Walter Scott (2021). The last was a very old interest of mine, and I had made tentative plans for it as early as my college days. I had somehow stumbled upon a brief tale by Scott, "Phantasmagoria" (*Blackwood's Edinburgh Magazine*, May 1818), which had almost never been reprinted. I was also impressed by Scott's critical essays and reviews on Gothic fiction, including biographies of several of the leading weird writers of the period as collected in Scott's *Lives of the Novelists* (1825). And, of course, there was Scott's weird poetry, some of which was collected in the early volume *Apology for Tales of Terror* (1799). As a result, my volume contains a miscellany of fiction, poetry, and criticism that I think is quite distinctive.

I continued work for Centipede Press, assembling large volumes for the Masters of the Weird Tale and Library of Weird Fiction series. My two-volume edition of Robert Aickman's tales for the former series appeared in a somewhat abridged edition for the latter. A volume of Bram Stoker's best weird work appeared in 2019, and a fairly comprehensive edition of Ambrose Bierce's weird tales was issued in 2021.

Jerad Walters, the publisher of Centipede Press, talked me into assembling a volume of Frank Belknap Long's best weird stories for the Library of Weird Fiction. Jerad had already published an immense volume of Long's fiction for the Masters of the Weird Tale series in 2010. In all honesty, I was quite dubious about the merits of Long's work overall; but as I investigated his stories and novels, early and late, I found quite a bit more to praise than to deprecate. I believe my selection (published in 2022) represents Long to best advantage. I chose to include one of his later novels, *Journey into Darkness* (1967), an able horror/science fiction hybrid, in the volume. I had also recommended to Jerad two other novels, *The Horror Expert* (1961; in spite of its title, it is in fact a hard-boiled crime/detection novel) and *The Night of the Wolf* (1972; a capable werewolf tale), and he has promised to issue these two books separately, each with an introduction by me.

My volume on Machen for the Library of Weird Fiction (2017) reignited my interest in assembling his complete fiction. I came to believe that I had the totality of his fiction among the extensive collection of Machen texts (print copies, photocopies, etc.) that I had accumulated over the years, so I felt I was in a good position to compile such a volume. Much of this material had of course appeared from Tartarus Press, which specialised in issuing Machen's writings; but those editions were very expensive and rarely made it over here from the United Kingdom. So I undertook the edition—which would include his novels (*The Hill of Dreams, The Secret Glory*, etc.) along with his short fiction, weird or otherwise. It came out in three paperback volumes from Hippocampus Press in 2019. I recall receiving some criticism that I had omitted a few early items; but it is very difficult to determine whether some of the work Machen wrote during this period really constitutes fiction, as opposed to sketches or vignettes or other matter.

In the summer of 2018 I was encouraged by Marc A. Michaud's plans to revive Necronomicon Press after a long hiatus. To help this venture along, David E. Schultz and I compiled *Ave atque Vale: Reminiscences of H. P. Lovecraft,* which appeared in late 2018. Peter Cannon had, of course, prepared an exemplary volume of this sort in *Lovecraft Remembered* (Arkham House, 1998), but we felt that a different arrangement and a somewhat different selection of material—such as the original version of Sonia H. Davis's memoir rather than the edited version that Peter had used—would make for a better book. In any case, Peter's volume was long out of print, and although we had made some tentative queries with Arkham House to reprint that book with Hippocampus Press, those overtures came to nothing.

I believe the book turned out well, and I went on to compile a book that both Marc and I had long wanted: *The H. P. Lovecraft Cat Book,* as well as volumes of Lovecraft's *Selected Essays* and *To a Dreamer: Best Poems of H. P. Lovecraft.* All these volumes came out in 2019. Alas, Marc suffered a further deterioration in his health, and the press has once again gone moribund.

In regard to my own fiction, I issued *The Recurring Doom: Tales of Mystery and Horror* with Sarnath Press (2019). It contained my two detective novels and a detective novella, along with a sheaf of my weird short fiction. Two years later I couldn't help issuing *Back from the Dead: Early Fiction and Poetry,* consisting mostly of the tales and poems I had published in the *Forum* during my high school years. No doubt this was an indulgence—but I am not forcing anyone to buy this book, and I also did not burden a legitimate publisher with the onerous task of issuing it.

I also used Sarnath Press to begin a project of staggering scope and extent: nothing less than the collected essays and journalism of H. L. Mencken. I had of course completed the transcription of Mencken's entire literary output (including all his books) years before, and I had already mined this body of work—some 12,000,000 words—for my numerous editions of Mencken's rare and uncollected writings. The last such volume had appeared in 2017, and I now resolved to issue the totality of the work that had appeared in magazines and newspapers. The project began in October 2018 with the first of eight volumes of his writings in the *Smart Set* (1908–23), which contain the majority of his brilliant book reviews of

English and American writers of the period. I then began issuing the journalism that had appeared in the Baltimore newspapers, from 1899 onward. By the end of 2022 I had published forty-six volumes. At this point I hit the limit of what was in the public domain, so from now on I shall be able to publish only a single volume containing the material for a given year, as soon as that material goes into the public domain.

In late 2020 I brought out the first of my editions of the complete essays of Leslie Stephen (1832–1904), the brilliant English literary, cultural, and philosophical critic whose work I have always admired. The first three volumes covered his essays on religion and philosophy, which I regard as among his most perspicacious writing. He was an agnostic whose searing criticisms of the religious theory and practice of his time are bracing. In my edition I made the fateful decision to annotate the texts—and this proved so time-consuming that I was obliged to suspend the project after I published the eighth volume in mid-2021. I hope to resume the edition (which may extend to more than fifteen volumes) at some future date.

In 2022 I began issuing the collected essays and journalism of Ambrose Bierce. David E. Schultz and I had gathered and transcribed this material decades ago, and it had come to something like five million words. But how to get it into print was a quandary. David had initially pitched it to Derrick Hussey of Hippocampus Press; and although Derrick charitably agreed to publish it, or at least a limited sampling of it, I convinced my colleagues that this was simply not a viable Hippocampus Press project, so David and I began bringing it out under the Sarnath Press imprint in the summer of 1922. It could easily extend to fifty volumes or more; and of course there is no worry about the copyright status of this work, as it is all in the public domain. All these Sarnath Press books benefited immensely from the expert and attractive typesetting and design by David E. Schultz, whose free work in this capacity is something akin to saintly benevolence.

What Hippocampus Press did issue in 2021 was a three-volume edition of Bierce's collected fiction. This was, in essence, a reconstitution of the collected edition that Schultz, Lawrence I. Berkove, and I had assembled for the University of Tennessee Press in 2006; but I felt that a thematic or topical arrangement would be more appealing to readers than the strict chronological arrangement of the Tennessee edition. I had in fact pitched such an edition to Tennessee, but the press did not follow up on the idea. I do think that this is the most accessible edition of Bierce's entire fiction that is currently available. We of course jettisoned our critical commentary as being something that Hippocampus Press readers would probably not find of any great interest.

But in the realm of H. P. Lovecraft and his work, Schultz and I took a very different approach. We continued issuing heavily annotated editions of Lovecraft's letters, bringing out ten hefty volumes from 2018 to 2022. Perhaps the most impressive—or, at any rate, the most informative in terms of the biographical and other information on Lovecraft that it provided—was a two-volume edition of Lovecraft's *Letters to Family and Family Friends* (2020). We had contemplated issuing the book in hardcover, because of the importance of the material: it contained the more than 400,000 words that Lovecraft wrote to his aunts, Lillian D. Clark and Annie E. P. Gamwell, at least 250,000 of which were written during his tormented years in New York (1924–26). A hardcover edition, however, proved unfeasible, so we went ahead with two large paperback volumes. I had largely been responsible for transcribing these letters back in the 1990s, so I was deemed the top editor of this book. In other editions Schultz was appropriately given top billing, as he did the majority of the editorial work. We ended up reissuing (with further revisions) our earlier editions of the letters to Rheinhart Kleiner, Alfred Galpin, and Donald Wandrei.

We had all manner of difficulties, however, reissuing volume 4 of my variorum edition of Lovecraft—the revisions and collaborations, which had initially appeared in 2017. In this volume we were forced to omit the four stories that Lovecraft had revised for C. M. Eddy, Jr., because Eddy's grandson, Jim Dyer, claimed to own the copyright on these stories. His claim was questionable, but Derrick did not think it prudent to publish the stories without his authorisation and then be subject to litigation. The Eddy stories went into the public domain on January 1, 2021; but although I prepared the variorum texts of these stories later that year, various factors caused the book to be delayed month after month. A new paperback edition finally did appear at the very end of 2022, but the hardcover edition has not yet been published.

On the editorial front, my editorship of *Weird Fiction Review* came to an end with the ninth annual issue (2018), as Jerad Walters and I mutually decided that it would be best if a new editor with a fresh vision were installed. Jerad enlisted a succession of guest editors for the next few issues before taking over the editorship himself. But I had gotten into the habit of publishing both original fiction and good criticism of weird fiction, so I persuaded Derrick Hussey to let me edit a new magazine for him. We had some difficulty coming up with a title, but finally we resolved on *Penumbra*. This would also be an annual, and the first issue appeared in 2020. The breakdown was, approximately 30,000 words of fiction (in some issues I included as much as 40,000 words), for which authors would be paid 3 cents a word, and about 70,000 words of essays and criticism (unpaid). I also included a sheaf of poetry. I was gratified that such writers as Mark Samuels, Michael Aronovitz, Darrell Schweitzer, and Stephen Woodworth sent me original short fiction (but the prize here was Ramsey Campbell's "Lost for Words," in the 2021 issue). Among essays, I published fine work on Thomas Ligotti, Simon Strantzas, Lord Dunsany, Edith Wharton, John Collier, Caitlín R. Kiernan, Greg Bear, Clark Ashton Smith, Bram Stoker, William Hope Hodgson, and others, as well as thematic essays on important motifs in weird fiction.

Another important editorial project was the issuance of an unpublished novel by Michael Shea, *Mr. Cannyharme*. When Shea's widow, Linda, sent me the typescript of this work some years after his death in 2014, I was struck with its brilliance. It is nothing less than a vast expansion of the core idea of Lovecraft's "The Hound" (!), vividly set in 1960s San Francisco and carefully etching the array of distinctive characters who figure in the book. Incredibly, it had been written in 1981, well before the majority of Shea's other fiction. At the last minute Linda found a partially expanded version of the text, so I had to do some hasty re-editing to include the new or revised portions into my edition. Hippocampus Press issued it in 2021.

*

The year 2019 did not get off to a good start. Sometime in February Wilum Pugmire took ill, apparently with pneumonia. He had been subject to this ailment from time to time, but in this instance he seemed unable to shake it. He remained in the hospital a full month, and Mary and I visited him a number of times. Eventually a doctor notified us of the dismal prognosis: either Wilum would have to remain hooked up to a machine that would facilitate his breathing or he would die if he were taken off his respirator. Wilum chose the latter.

I have never seen a man face death with such calmness, even indifference. Wilum frankly told me that his fervent Mormon faith—by which he was convinced that he would, upon his demise, meet not only his own relatives who had passed on, but such figures whom he revered as H. P. Lovecraft,

Oscar Wilde, and Shakespeare—sustained him during this time. As an atheist I could not accept such a view, and he knew it; but I did nothing to rob him of the comfort his faith provided. Wilum left the hospital in late March, wishing to die at home. Mary, Greg Lowney, several of Wilum's relations (including his sister, Holly White), and I were present on March 25, when Holly disconnected the respirator by which he was kept alive. We thought he might expire on the spot, but somehow he managed to carry on, although his breathing was extremely laboured and he was barely conscious of his surroundings. After a time we held his hand and bid him adieu for the last time, and he died early on the morning of the 26th.

Prior to his death, Wilum had expressed his desire that I be his literary executor and that I take possession of his immense library. Even though these points were not incorporated in his will (indeed, I am not certain he had a will), Holly was happy to adhere to them. The literary executorship was formally validated following a meeting with her lawyer. I agreed to turn over all funds accruing from the sale of Wilum's work, keeping nothing for myself.

The matter of the library was much more significant. As Holly's two sons moved into the family home, Mary, Greg, and I undertook the onerous task of moving his thousands of books out of the house and placing them in our own homes. It was decided to segregate the books by category: I took the books pertaining to genre fiction (weird, horror, science fiction, fantasy, mystery, etc.), general literature (including a large number of books about poetry), books pertaining to Oscar Wilde, and some other batches of books; Greg took the books pertaining to Henry James, William Shakespeare, Judaism, and Mormonism.

Since I myself owned many of the books that I obtained, and in any case did not have the space to house them (they filled up my shed and garage to repletion), I decided to sell them. Greg had set up a database of Wilum's library on a website, LibraryThing. Mary input hundreds if not thousands of titles, and I later did the same. I then undertook the laborious procedure of determining a fair price for these books; some were inexpensive paperbacks, others were highly valuable limited editions. Greg then generated a list of titles, with the prices affixed to them, and created a website (an offshoot of the sesqua.net website he had previously established for Wilum's writings), By late summer we were ready to offer the books for sale.

The response was staggering, and in short order I found that I was generating thousands of dollars' worth of sales. The amount was so immense that I consulted with Derrick and others to see if this money could be put to use in acquiring what had become something of the "white whale" of Lovecraft scholarship—the 500 pages of Lovecraft's letters to Frank Belknap Long, which the bookseller L. W. Currey had been offering for sale since at least 2007. Currey's asking price was $150,000 (not at all unreasonable, all things considered), but he was prepared to sell the letters at $120,000 if they were purchased as a single lot. Our idea was to purchase the letters and donate them to the John Hay Library of Brown University, where they rightly belonged.

Derrick arranged to supply nearly half of the total amount through his Aeroflex Foundation. The sale of Wilum's books over two years generated more than $30,000, and I devoted this entire sum to the purchase of the letters. Sean Branney and Andrew Leman of the H. P. Lovecraft Historical Society set up a crowdfunding campaign that supplied most of the remaining amount. By the spring of 2021 the money was in hand. A last-minute snafu almost dynamited the effort, but we managed to get it back on track; Currey was paid, and the letters arrived at the John Hay Library in May. In reasonably short order, the librarians there prepared scans of the letters and provided them to David E. Schultz, who began transcribing them at once. The letters are astonishingly illuminating—far more so than the extensive extracts prepared by August Derleth (or, rather, his secretary) in the Arkham House transcripts. With a substantial number of Long's letters to Lovecraft surviving, the entire volume—*Letters with Frank Belknap Long,* due out in late 2023—will be one of the most revealing volumes in the entire Lovecraft Letters series, and will be a fitting capstone to that twenty-three-volume set.

My work as Wilum's literary executor was relatively light, although I received several requests from foreign publishers—in Spain, Germany, Italy, and elsewhere—to translate his work. I myself arranged for the publication with Hippocampus Press of a selection of Wilum's best work, *An Imp of Aether;* it appeared in August 2019. Wilum read proofs on, but did not live to see the appearance of, his second Centipede Press book, *An Ecstasy of Fear,* which appeared in July 2019.

*

The year 2019 proved to be unprecedented for the amount of travel that I (mostly, but not always, accompanied by Mary) undertook. In late April I was asked to go to Auburn, California, for a public showing of a fine documentary on Clark Ashton Smith, *Clark Ashton Smith: The Emperor of Dreams* (2018), prepared by Darin Coelho Spring. I appear occasionally in the film, and I spoke at a Q&A session following the showing of it, along with Darin and several others who are featured in it.

In May I went to France, as I had been invited to one of the two major conventions in that country devoted to imaginative fiction that are held every year. This was called Les Imaginales, and it took place in Épinal, a town near the border with Germany. The occasion of my visit was the publication of the French translation of *I Am Providence* by the publisher ActuSF, which funded my trip. This enormous undertaking (1400 pages in print) required ten different translators, supervised by Christophe Thill, a leading French authority on weird fiction. Mary and I made the long trip to Paris, where we spent two days before the convention. I was kept busy conducting interviews on radio and also with some newspapers, as well as appearing in a few bookstores. In one of these I met Patrice Louinet, a leading Robert E. Howard scholar who had written a Ph.D. dissertation on Howard for the Sorbonne.

It was not all work, however, as Mary and I had some wonderful meals at various cafés and restaurants in Paris as well as taking a tour of the Catacombs—something I had always wanted to see. We tried to get into the Louvre, but after waiting in line for well over an hour we were informed that the museum staff had gone on strike. We made our way to the Musée d'Orsay (which specialises in Impressionist art) and were overwhelmed by the paintings, sculptures, and other work there, including Rodin's *Gates of Hell* and many other spectacular items by Van Gogh, Gauguin, and others.

Moving on to Épinal by train, we found that the event was held in a succession of tents or pavilions near the river. I was assigned my own translator, Morgane Saysana, who, whenever I appeared on a panel discussion or any other public event, translated my English words into French almost as soon as they were out of my mouth. Christophe Thill and several of the translators of my book were there, and we spent much time with them. Upon our return to Paris after the convention, we met Gilles Menegaldo, a prominent authority on Lovecraft, who filmed an interview of me for a proposed documentary. Also present was Martine Chifflot, who has written a charming play about Lovecraft and his wife, *Lovecraft, mon amour*, which I believe has been staged. She has now arranged for its translation into English as *Lovecraft, My Love* (2022).

The French translation of my biography, titled *Je suis Providence*, has sold remarkably well in spite of its size. It was published in two trade paperback volumes and later later appeared in two mass-market paperback volumes as well as a one-volume hardcover that cost 100 euros. It won at least one award in France. My biography has also appeared in German (*H. P. Lovecraft: Leben und Werk* [2017–20; 3 vols.]), Italian (*Io sono Providence* [2019–21; 3 vols.]), Spanish (*Yo soy Providence* [2022]), and Russian (the first volume of which appeared in 2022).

In June and July Mary and I spent nearly three weeks in Australia. This trip was arranged by David Bottrill, who set up speaking engagements for me in Canberra, Melbourne, Sydney, and Hobart (Tasmania). It was an incredible journey, although I regret to say that Bottrill overestimated my drawing power, and few of the public events in which I appeared were well attended. I wish I could give him his money back!

Mary and I decided to break up the long trip in each direction with an overnight stay in Hawaii, since I had never been there. We didn't do much there except have a meal or two and stroll along Waikiki Beach. On June 20 we flew to Sydney and immediately caught another plane to Canberra, the nation's capital. David set up a nice dinner for us and some others at a Malaysian restaurant. One of those in attendance was Ellen Greenham, a professor at Murdoch University in Perth, all the way across the continent on the far western coast. She had written a perspicacious dissertation focusing on Lovecraft and his influence upon the science fiction writers Robert A. Heinlein, Philip K. Dick, and Frank Herbert. I later assisted her in preparing this dissertation as a book, and then recommended it to Hippocampus Press, which issued it in 2022 as *After Engulfment*.

The event in Canberra featured one Larry Sitsky, who had composed a piece some years earlier called the *Necronomicon Suite*. This piece for clarinet and piano was performed live at the event; it was a somewhat puzzling modern piece that didn't make much sense to me or most of the others in the audience. Afterward, Sitsky, Greenham, Leigh Blackmore (who had come up from Sydney for the event), and I held a Q&A session.

I later spoke in Melbourne in the company of Perry Grayson, the devotee of Frank Belknap Long (and a rock musician), and in Hobart, accompanied by Steve Dillon, a prominent Australian weird writer. In each of these cities I conducted a radio interview. The Sydney event featured Leigh Blackmore, Danny Lovecraft (who filled in for another speaker who never showed up), and myself.

Because Bottrill had arranged for these events to occur every other day

13. Seattle (2018–2022)

(the intervening day devoted to travel), Mary and I had abundant opportunities for sightseeing. So we managed to take in the Australian National Gallery (Canberra), Centennial Park (Sydney), and much else. But this was only the beginning of our exploration. With incredible generosity, Danny Lovecraft and his wife Margaret offered to put us up in their home in Sydney for a full week after the lecture tour was over, and they were tireless in taking us all around the area to take in the abundance of sites there. Of course we ventured to the spectacular Sydney Opera House, one of the world's great landmarks. But even more impressive—or, at least, compelling for me—were the numerous opportunities we had to investigate the distinctive flora and fauna of the continent, in such locales as the Featherdale Wildlife Zoo and the Australian Reptile Park. We saw kangaroos, koala bears, and, yes, Tasmanian devils. A trip to the Norman Lindsay Museum Gallery was stimulating.

We did some specifically Lovecraftian exploration, taking in the vast Hyde Park and the "Hyde Park Museum" (now the Australian Museum) mentioned in "The Call of Cthulhu." At Macquarrie University Danny and I looked up copies of the *Sydney Bulletin*, which proved to be quite different from Lovecraft's description of it in the story, meaning that it would have been unlikely to have featured a news item of the sort that Lovecraft purportedly quotes in the text.

One evening we ventured to the suburb of Wollongong to look up Leigh Blackmore (who was celebrating his sixtieth birthday) and his companions, the poet Margi Curtis and her husband Graham. Another time we attended an event where we met Kyla Lee Ward, one of the finest weird poets of our time.

In September Mary and I took a trip to the Midwest—first to look up her many friends and relatives in the Twin Cities, and then to take a trip to Chicago, where we thoroughly canvassed the Art Institute and the Field Museum. But for me the highlight of the trip was a visit to Wrigley Field to watch the Chicago Cubs play (in an odd coincidence) the Seattle Mariners. The Cubs won, 5–1, and the experience of being in that venerable stadium was one I had longed for since I was a boy.

This is by no means a complete account of my travels in 2019; in fact, Mary determined that I ended up taking a grand total of twenty-two different airplane flights that year! I shall relate some of the other trips later in this chapter, but I may mention here a curious by-product of all these travels: the unexpected revival of my work as a composer.

The idea of resuming the composition of classical music had been gradually filtering into my consciousness as a product of my ongoing participation in the Northwest Chorale; this time, naturally, I would take a stab at choral music, something I had never attempted during my youthful ventures as a composer. I had come to believe that I had developed a sufficient understanding of choral music to do the job adequately; and I also felt I had things to say as a choral composer that extended beyond mere mechanical imitation of my beloved Baroque composers. I had, indeed, been significantly affected by the powerful choral pieces of such modern composers as Stephen Paulus, Morten Lauridsen, and others whose work I had sung in the Northwest Chorale; so I decided to give it a go.

I had long found Lovecraft's three-stanza poem "Sunset" to be an ideal work to set to music, and I undertook the task in late 2017, but after a few bars I got stalled and set it aside. Then, in February 2018, I was inspired to take it up again and managed to finish it. It was quite a short piece (probably no more than three or four minutes in length), but I later showed it to Lynn Hall, our choir director, and he scheduled it for our Spring 2019 concert.

Working on the piece during our rehearsals was a curious experience. Every so often Lynn would halt the practice and ask me pointed questions as to whether I really wanted certain passages to be as I had written them; in some cases I accepted his suggested emendations, in others I stuck to my guns. Everyone in the choir appeared to enjoy the piece, and the performance of it went quite well. Greg Lowney kindly filmed the performance and then posted it on YouTube.

This set the stage for future work, although I did not then have any idea of how extensive that work would be. All those plane trips in 2019 provided the ideal opportunity to whip out my composition book and get to work. By this time I no longer needed the crutch of my electronic keyboard to set down the notes. Indeed, I recall one man seated next to me asking in amazement, "Can you really hear those notes in your head?" I calmly replied, "Yes," and got back to work.

Over the next several years I ended up composing a total of fourteen pieces, all for *a cappella* (unaccompanied) four-part choir. The best of them, "Continuity," I dedicated to the memory of W. H. Pugmire; another, "Little Sam Perkins" (based on Lovecraft's poem to a deceased kitten), I dedicated to Henry the cat, who had perished in June 2019. In the end, I set poems by Lovecraft, Clark Ashton Smith, George Sterling, Edgar Allan Poe, Lord

13. Seattle (2018–2022)

Dunsany, Ernest Dowson, and one Mary K. Wilson to music. Derrick charitably published the scores of these pieces as *Songs from Lovecraft and Others* (2022). My music notation software was able to generate sound files (it could not articulate the words but it did play the notes in a computerised imitation of the human voice), which listeners could access on the Hippocampus Press website.

*

It is difficult to discuss this period of American and world history without talking about the pandemic and its multifarious ramifications.

I first heard of the pandemic in late December 2019 or early January 2020. One of the first significant outbreaks was at a nursing home in nearby Kirkland; but this facility had been notoriously badly run for years, and so I did not think much of it. In early February, our choir had to face the decision whether to continue or to suspend operations. I initially scoffed at the disease, thinking we could tough it out. Could it really be much worse than the flu? Well, obviously it was, and our choir took an enforced holiday for the better part of two years.

Otherwise, my own life did not change significantly during this whole period. To be sure, Mary and I gave up going to restaurants and movies (but we were very occasional moviegoers in any event—by which I mean seeing movies in theatres), and our meetings of the local gang also came to an abrupt end. We did get abundant takeout meals from local restaurants as a way of helping them stay in business. I dutifully wore a mask when in public and practised social distancing when necessary. I was bemused—nay, appalled—at the politicisation of these safety measures by conservatives, the only result of which was to ensure that many of those same conservatives would be sickened or even perish because of their mulish insistence on "freedom."

Incredibly, Mary and I both managed to avoid infection during the whole of the pandemic. In mid-September into early October 2020, I developed a mild fever, a hacking cough, and some chest congestion—which seemed unmistakably to be the symptoms of COVID-19. But later testing confirmed that neither I nor Mary (who came down with similar symptoms at the time) had in fact contracted the disease. This, indeed, was the only sickness of any kind that I suffered for a full two years, until August 2022, when I got a mild cold after a trip to New England.

As the presidential election of 2020 approached, I was understandably concerned, in spite of the fact that Joe Biden maintained a small but consistent lead over Donald Trump right up to election day. I was prepared for the strong possibility that no victor would be declared for days, and rolled my eyes as Trump proclaimed victory in a bombastic speech on the day after the election. But the counting of mail-in and other ballots in various states continued. Optimistic as I was, given the probability of a Biden victory, I did suffer a few sleepless nights—until on the Saturday after election day the verdict came in: Biden had won!

I naively thought that was the end of the matter. As the official tabulation of electoral votes in the various states occurred on December 14, I felt more and more confident that we would see the back of Mr. Trump.

Then January 6 happened.

Since I was 3000 miles away from Washington, D.C., I paid only minimal attention to the events in the nation's capital on that day. At one point my mother called up frantically, stating that the Capitol had been invaded. I shamefully pooh-poohed her concerns, saying it was nothing to be worried about. It was clearly very much otherwise, but neither I nor anyone else at the time was aware of the true scope of the event. I did not stay up to see the final count of electoral votes in the Capitol, after the turmoil had been suppressed.

As I continued to learn of the events leading up to January 6, and what had occurred on that day itself, I was more and more appalled at how close this country had come to a coup. My mother, now ninety-three, expressed grim relief that she was in an assisted living facility, since as a woman of colour she no longer felt safe on the streets of Muncie. I made a pretence of dismissing similar fears of my own in liberal Seattle—but then became aware of various white supremacist groups right here in this state, and began to think twice about taking my customary late-afternoon constitutional around the neighbourhood.

More to the point, I gained an even more ferocious loathing of Republicans than before—not just the seemingly endless array of incredibly vile, corrupt politicians, but the rank-and-file voters who supported them in spite of their ignorance, dogmatism, deceit, and in some cases treasonous speech and activity. Chief among them was, of course, Trump himself. Back in 2018 I had written an article for *Free Inquiry* (the freethought magazine that had signed me up as an occasional columnist upon the demise of the *American Rationalist* in 2017) entitled "The Party of Traitors." It appeared

13. Seattle (2018–2022)

in *Free Inquiry* for April/May 2018, but the instances of Republican "treason" I pointed out in that piece were trivial compared to what was going on now.

As a result, I gained rich satisfaction at the ever-increasing display of G.O.P. contemptibility, from Trump on down, in the media (especially the *New York Times,* which I continued to read daily) and, especially, in the January 6 congressional commission. I yearned to see Trump indicted for the multifarious crimes he had clearly committed—and am still waiting. But I am confident it will happen. I did not actually see any of the televised January 6 hearings of 2022, but did read about them extensively after the fact.

I became somewhat obsessed with day-to-day politics, to the detriment of my state of mind. I had latched on to the liberal website Daily Kos—initially just to be amused at its pungent exposés of Republican folly and duplicity. But for the sake of my own sanity I ceased looking at this site altogether as the midterm elections of 2022 approached. I was not entirely surprised at the strong showing Democrats made: for months I had been privately stating that the Democrats would actually gain seats in the Senate, based on the demographics of the states where senate races were being held and the hideously bad candidates the G.O.P. had nominated. In the end, Democrats gained only one seat—but one is better than none. I also predicted (not, indeed, a very bold prediction) that the Supreme Court's overturning of *Roe v. Wade* that summer would create a furious backlash that would help the Democrats, and so it did.

On February 24, 2022, a new source of anger and torment occurred—Russia's invasion of Ukraine. I was stunned by this event, as I found it hard to believe that Vladimir Putin would make such a horrendous blunder. And yet, as the initial days of the war seemed to signal a quick Russian victory, I feared the worst for the whole of Europe and the world. But then the Ukrainians, with incredible courage and resilience, battled back, and the world presently became aware of the comical Potemkin army that Putin had fielded. Kyiv did not fall; Mariupol did, but at great cost to the Russian army. Sudden and not entirely surprising counter-attacks by the Ukrainians that resulted in the regaining of significant territory bolstered my faith that Russia might actually be definitively defeated in this unprovoked war. The strong prospect of that blessed event sustains me even as the war drags on into 2023.

I did my best to carry on with my work during this turbulent and distracting time—and, in fact, I accomplished a great deal. I undertook the writing of a full-scale treatise for the first time in years: *The Recognition of*

H. P. Lovecraft. For several years I had meant to write such a work—a detailed history of Lovecraft's rise in fame and critical recognition from his own day to the present, with a survey of the criticism and scholarship on Lovecraft over the past eighty years. The book came out from Hippocampus Press in late 2021, and I was reasonably happy with the result. Some of the reviews were not entirely favourable, as a certain umbrage was taken at my less than charitable assessments of recent Lovecraft scholarship, but I stand by what I said and may perhaps add successive chapters to the book in the years to come, as I am doing for this work.

I also felt the need to revise my study of Ramsey Campbell, which had come out in 2001 and was now woefully out of date, as Campbell had continued producing book after brilliant book over the past two decades. I had reviewed a number of these titles in various venues, so I stitched these reviews together and wrote new matter; the result was *Ramsey Campbell: Master of Weird Fiction*. PS Publishing agreed to publish the work and brought it out in 2022.

The year 2020 saw the publication of (at long last) a new and comprehensive bibliography of Clark Ashton Smith. I was deemed the lead compiler, with David E. Schultz and Scott Connors as my co-authors. I am not sure I deserve the honour, since Schultz was almost entirely responsible for the extensive listing of publications of Smith's poems (taken largely from our edition of 2007–08) and Connors largely assembled the bibliographical information on Smith's books and the publications of his short fiction in magazines and anthologies. I suppose I compiled most of the material on Smith criticism. Of course, the bibliography could not have been compiled without the pioneering research of Donald Sidney-Fryer, whose own bibliography—*Emperor of Dreams* (1978)—laid the groundwork for all subsequent work in this realm. Sidney-Fryer, however, did not follow orthodox bibliographical method in his compilation, so I felt that at a minimum our work would be somewhat more rigorous in that regard, to say nothing of taking account of more recent publications by and about Smith.

As we realised that we were coming to the end of our programme of publishing Lovecraft's letters, David E. Schultz and I turned our attention to publishing those of Smith. Of course, these survive in far smaller numbers than Lovecraft's immense correspondence. We had already published the Smith–Sterling letters in 2005, and now we prepared the Smith correspondence with August Derleth and with Samuel Loveman; these volumes appeared in 2020 and 2021, respectively. Two more volumes of this sort are forthcoming, and that will all but complete the publication of Smith's extant letters.

I used Sarnath Press to issue books that I could not trouble other publishers with. Four more volumes of my miscellaneous criticism of weird fiction—*The Advance of the Weird Tale* (2020), *The Progression of the Weird Tale* (2021), *The Parameters of the Weird Tale* (2022), and *Miscellaneous Writings* (2022)—appeared, along with *Bits of Autobiography and Interviews* (2020). I had been interviewed a surprising number of times over the decades, going all the way back to the 1980s, and I decided to gather up the more interesting of these, along with some autobiographical essays I had written over the years.

Along the same lines I issued three volumes of my *Journals*. I had been keeping these journals from as early as 1974 (my junior year of high school, when my English teacher, Robert C. Rose, asked his students to write journal entries that he would read and evaluate) up to 1987. The later journals were written in blank books that I purchased, each of them about 240 pages in length. There was an immense amount of material here (more than 300,000 words), and it was all in my nearly illegible handwritten scribbling. So you can imagine that it took quite a while to transcribe. Amusingly enough, not long after writing the journals of 1974–76 I typed up the entries on my old Smith-Corona typewriter—and had even *annotated* them! So of course I printed these pompous and self-important notes along with the text, as an exhibition of my utter narcissism and self-obsession during this period. I wrote a small number of new annotations for the later parts of the journal. I will admit that I expurgated a few passages here and there—not so much to protect my own privacy (I wrote very little that I did not wish anyone to read) but that of some close friends or family members. I daresay the three volumes have sold in the tens of copies, but what of it? Once again, I am forcing no one to buy or read these books.

Not quite so self-indulgent was a volume of my *Classical Papers* that I issued in 2021. These were nothing more than a collection of the papers on classical literature, history, and philosophy that I wrote during my undergraduate and graduate years at Brown and Princeton, and in all honesty I think some of them—notably my honours thesis on "Juvenal and Ancient Philosophy" and my master's thesis, "Lucretius Satiricus"—are rather good and even stand up to the orthodox scholarship on these authors or topics.

I also published my short detective novel *Honeymoon in Jail* (2022) through Sarnath Press. I had begun this work as early as 2015 but only finished it in early 2019. Initially I had conceived it as another novel featuring my tough-guy private eye, Joe Scintilla; but I later sensed that it might be amusing to have Lovecraft and his wife Sonia as the detectives. I set it in the spring of 1928, when Lovecraft in fact went to Brooklyn to spend six weeks with Sonia to help her set up a new hat shop; I then involved other members of the Kalem Club, notably James F. Morton, whose wedding to Pearl K. Merritt I moved from its actual date (1934) to this period. I confess that I liked the way it came out, even though it was barely 50,000 words in length—a very short novel indeed!

I first offered it to Sam Gafford, whose Ulthar Press was doing good work in publishing books relating to William Hope Hodgson. Sam had also been forced to publish his magnificent novel *Whitechapel* (2017) through his press. I had read this entire work—a brilliant tale of Jack the Ripper (a subject on which Gafford was an authority), with the young Arthur Machen as a detective and also a suspect in the murders (!)—in manuscript and done the copyediting on it. Its length (250,000 words) and Sam's relative lack of standing as a novelist made it impossible for him to find a publisher for the book.

Sam accepted my novel readily, but had trouble finding the wherewithal to issue it. In June 2019 he had made an arrangement with Necronomicon Press to publish it under a joint imprint. But then Sam died suddenly in September 2019; he was only fifty-six years old. This grievous circumstance, and the inability of Marc Michaud to continue the revival of his press, compelled me to issue my novel with Sarnath Press in 2022.

In February 2021 I undertook a major project—nothing less than a comprehensive history of atheism. I initially conceived it as a world history of atheism, but as I began the research I realised that I did not have the means to conduct a worldwide survey, so I focused only on atheism in the West. This work—to which I eventually affixed the title *The Downfall of God*—may be one of the two or three texts I am remembered for. Certainly, it embodies some of the most profound and all-encompassing research I have ever conducted.

I began it at this time because the easing of the pandemic allowed me to access the University of Washington Library for the first time in more than a year. Even so, for much of 2021 I had to request books online, then come to one of the entrances of the library, where the books would be brought to me in a paper bag. Later I could actually go into the library and fish for books myself.

13. Seattle (2018–2022)

For the earlier chapters of the book—especially those on atheism, freethought, and secularism in Greek and Roman civilisation—I drew heavily on my classical studies of some forty years before. I had kept most of my classical texts and books of classical scholarship, and these were immensely useful in certain phases of my work, although of course I consulted more recent scholarship as well. I was quite surprised at the rapidity with which I wrote the first volume of the book. It was completed (at just under 200,000 words) in September 2022—in spite of the fact that I had to do considerable library research on the mediaeval and Renaissance periods, about which I knew relatively little. I was quite happy with the way it turned out, and I expect to finish the second volume by the end of 2024. Of course, a book of this size and scope is going to be difficult to market to a publisher, either academic or commercial; but I believe I will succeed in finding an appropriate publisher for this work.

A very different type of work in which I somehow became engaged was my appearance in a variety of media projects relating to Lovecraft and weird fiction. I have, of course, been featured on numerous podcasts over the years, and these seem to have augmented my reputation to some degree; I have also appeared in documentaries on Lovecraft, Bierce, and other writers on whom I can claim some expertise. In the spring of 2018 I heard from Qais Pasha, a young filmmaker in Canada of Pakistani origin. He had conceived the plan of making a documentary on Lovecraft's involvement with Quebec. I was happy to help him, and in May I flew to Quebec to examine a number of locales that Lovecraft had visited on his three trips to Quebec (1930, 1932, 1933). To my surprise, I found a plaque in French commemorating a house where Lovecraft had stayed during one of those visits. This plaque was set up in 2001.

As Qais continued to work on his project, he secured additional funding from the Canadian government, and so we envisioned a much more expanded documentary—not an orthodox summary of his life, but one that focused on the places where he had lived and written about in his fiction and other writings. In August 2019 I spent more than a week with Qais and his crew canvassing sites in New York City, central Massachusetts (the Quabbin Reservoir area), Boston, Salem, Marblehead, and of course Providence. Along the way I met Curtis M. Lawson, whose *Black Heart Boys' Choir* (2019) is a splendid evocation of terror in music. Lawson has gone on to write several other fine works and is emerging as a leading weird writer of the younger generation.

COVID understandably delayed Qais's work, but in due course of time he finished the documentary, bestowing upon it the somewhat esoteric title *Exegesis: Lovecraft*. I saw several drafts of it and made extensive comments on how it could be improved or reshaped. A version of it was shown as part of the streaming programme of the H. P. Lovecraft Film Festival in October 2021, and I believe the response was fairly positive. Qais had, of course, filmed interviews with numerous other commentators on Lovecraft, including Jonathan Thomas, Molly Tanzer, Donovan K. Loucks, and Steven J. Mariconda. The result may perhaps be somewhat heavy in its emphasis on Lovecraft's racism; but one of the arcs of the film, as Qais conceived it, is how persons of colour such as he and myself have wrestled with this issue while maintaining a general devotion to and admiration for Lovecraft. The film was shown again in Mexico City in August 2022, and the reaction was enthusiastic.

The travel-filled year of 2019 saw me heading to Providence in July for a brief meeting with a Japanese TV crew shooting a documentary on Lovecraft as part of a programme called *Dark Side Mystery*. I am not clear whether the Lovecraft segment actually aired, but I suppose it must have. In April 2022 I was summoned to Providence again, this time by a French film crew headed by Alexis Metzinger, who was shooting four segments of a proposed TV show, one of which was to be about Lovecraft (the others would be about the Brothers Grimm, William Morris, and Robert E. Howard); the overall title would be something like "The Roots of Modern Fantasy." The moderator or narrator of the programme was John Howe, the Canadian concept artist for the *Lord of the Rings* movies. We had great fun walking around the usual Providence sites as I rattled on about Lovecraft's life and work. I believe the episode will be broadcast sometime in 2023.

All this work was entirely separate from a very different kind of media project I became involved in—nothing less than a biopic focusing on Lovecraft. Such things have become quite popular of late, and I have seen fine biopics of such diverse figures as Thomas Wolfe, A. A. Milne, and J. R. R. Tolkien. And who can forget the poignant biopic about Robert E. Howard, *The Whole Wide World* (1997)? I was contacted in the summer of 2017 by Ryan Grulich—a filmmaker who lived near me and who had prepared some short films for Disney—for an interview about Lovecraft. He came to my house and we did the interview, which was posted online. At some point we hatched the idea of the biopic. I felt that the relationship between Lovecraft and Sonia should be at the heart of the film, since this

13. Seattle (2018–2022)

was the only way that a major female character could appear. Ryan enlisted the aid of a colleague (who shall remain nameless here) who would be tasked with writing the screenplay. This person, apparently, did not know a great deal about Lovecraft but promised to spend a month on research and then write the screenplay.

The result was a perfect disaster. Aside from the fact that the fellow's research was woefully inadequate, parts of the screenplay were virtually unintelligible even from the standpoint of English usage. I pleaded with Ryan to let me write my own screenplay (which I had already plotted out in my mind), in spite of the fact that I had no experience at such a thing. In February 2019 I banged it out in eight days—it came to more than 100 pages, meaning that it would be close to two hours long (one page of a screenplay generally translates to one minute of screen time). Ryan seemed to like the result, but felt some modifications were needed. I later added several scenes (including one where Lovecraft is in Charleston and has an amusing encounter with little black boys who help him mail his postcards). The climactic scene, which I had envisioned from the start, would be a dramatic series of back-and-forth images showing, on the one hand, Lovecraft on his deathbed at Jane Brown Memorial Hospital, and on the other hand Sonia going out into a field and burning Lovecraft's letters. (This latter event apparently occurred a year or two before Lovecraft's death—but in filmmaking that doesn't matter.)

Of course, the major sticking-point was money. A film of this sort, requiring the re-creation of 1920s New York (the film would largely focus on Lovecraft's marriage to Sonia and their time in that metropolis from 1924 to 1926) would be an expensive matter; and, of course, there would be the issue of securing an actor who could pass for Lovecraft. (Getting an actress to play Sonia would probably be an easier business.) That is where the situation lies at the moment, but I still have some hope that the film can eventually be made. Meanwhile, Ryan and I are now working on a smaller-scale project—a selection from Lovecraft's letters discussing his life and work, which I will read on camera; there will be appropriate images in the background, including reproductions of some of the handwritten letters at the John Hay Library. We hope to finish this project by early 2023.

I continued to do work on all manner of fronts. For Centipede Press I was happy to prepare comprehensive editions of the weird work of M. R. James and Guy de Maupassant. In the latter case, I discovered in the course of my research a website that revealed the appalling fact that certain older editions of Maupassant had included tales not by him, and several of these had been embalmed in editions of Maupassant's tales of supernatural and psychological horror. I made sure to excise them from my own edition. These two books add to the pile of titles that are forthcoming from Centipede, which include editions of John Metcalfe, E. F. Benson, J. Sheridan Le Fanu, Lord Dunsany, W. C. Morrow, and Robert W. Chambers. For Hippocampus I (in conjunction with David E. Schultz) have assembled a heavily annotated volume of the joint correspondence of Ambrose Bierce and George Sterling and a volume of Sterling's collected essays; for Weird House I have prepared editions of the work of such pulp writers as Robert Barbour Johnson, Everil Worrell, and Anthony M. Rud, with a volume of John Martin Leahy's tales in the planning stages.

A final, immense project that will appear in early 2023 is *The Horror Fiction Index*. This is nothing less than a listing of the tables of contents of all single-author horror collections from 1808 (the first such volume to appear, M. G. Lewis's *Romantic Tales*) to 2010. The title reflects that the work is meant to be a companion to Mike Ashley's *Supernatural Index* (1995), an authoritative index of horror anthologies. I list nearly 3300 books, which contain nearly 30,000 short stories. While much of this information is available online, I believe there is some virtue in having it all listed in a single volume, which will be available in both print and ebook editions from Sarnath Press.

But it is not all work and no play here. The easing of pandemic restrictions in our state allowed us to resume our Memorial Day and Labor Day cookouts for the local weird fiction gang—a group that has now been augmented by Ovidio Cartagena (one of the most talented weird artists I have encountered, and who also has keen and provocative opinions on art, politics, and other areas) and David Ray, a devoted collector of Lovecraftiana and weird fiction who lends a genial presence to our gatherings.

I have of course reached the stage of life when the deaths of colleagues and family members is a not entirely unexpected occurrence. Most consequentially, William F. Nolan died on July 15, 2021. He had gone into the hospital for pneumonia, contracted COVID while receiving treatment, and died of COVID and other complications. It was true that he was ninety-three years old, but it would seem that his death might have been avoided. His physical condition had been in decline for years, but his mind was sharp up to the end and I always enjoyed his genial chatter about colleagues old and new (especially, of course, Ray Bradbury, Charles

Beaumont, Richard Matheson, and other members of the Group) and his charmingly eccentric views on everything from John Dillinger to the building of the pyramids.

I also mourned the passing of Peter Straub and Greg Bear within a few months of each other in late 2022. I had been to Greg's house in Lynwood (a northern suburb of Seattle) a few times, in the company of Jason and Sunni Brock. Then, on January 1, 2023, my mother died at the age of ninety-five. Anytime a parent dies, the result is at the very least a certain sense of disorientation. She was a flawed individual—but who isn't? But I cannot fail to acknowledge that her role in my life—at least in terms of her inculcation of a love of classical music and the financial and other support she lent to me over the decades, especially at a time when my freelance writing was not terribly remunerative—was immensely beneficial.

And I must make note of the passing of my beloved cats Henry (2019) and Phoebe (2021). Both lived to relatively advanced ages (fifteen and seventeen, respectively), and I hope they had a good life with me and Mary. This leaves us with only Mimi, now a grand dame of fifteen but still very kittenish in her way. May the years weigh lightly on her!

I myself have many more things I wish to accomplish, many more places I wish to see, and many more ways in which I wish to better myself. Let me hope that I am allowed some further years to do so.

Epilogue

"To every man comes, sooner or later, the great renunciation."—Bertrand Russell

I am not sure I have any grand reflections about the course of my life. And yet, if I were at all inclined toward religiosity—which, mercifully, I am not—I might be inclined to speculate whether some cosmic hand were ensuring that my life proceeded in exactly the direction I wished it to go. Since the age of fourteen, I had wanted to become a full-time writer. My discovery of Lovecraft facilitated that goal: because Lovecraft was then (in the early 1970s) quite unrecognised as a literary figure but (as I and others were convinced) was ripe for elevation to canonical status, even a tyro like myself could make contributions to scholarship at an early age. The six years I spent at Brown, and in Providence, led me to soak up far more knowledge about Lovecraft than I could have done in any other locale, and my preparation of corrected texts of Lovecraft's work was instrumental both to Lovecraft's rising reputation and my own.

My two years at Princeton were largely unhappy ones, but they simultaneously made me realise that the academic arena was not where I belonged and allowed me to become acclimated to the pace of life in New York, so that I could be comfortable working there. My employment at Chelsea House permitted me to broaden my general understanding of literature well beyond the realm of weird fiction, and it also gave me the copyediting and other skills that I would use to good effect later. My early collaboration with Marc A. Michaud of Necronomicon Press was tremendously fruitful, and it led inexorably to my even more fruitful working relationship with Derrick Hussey of Hippocampus Press. My work on Lovecraft led to the dissemination of his (and my) work through Penguin Classics and other prestigious venues. And my expanding work on weird fiction—led by my interest in understanding the bases for Lovecraft's own appreciation of Poe, Machen, Dunsany, and others—allowed me to become a leading authority on many other writers, from Ambrose Bierce to Ramsey Campbell. The collapse of Chelsea House in 1995 forced me to become a full-time freelance writer—and while it took some years for me to become even partially self-supporting, in the course of time I attained that long-sought goal. Today, I am doing exactly what I have always wished to do as a writer, editor, and scholar.

In my personal life, equally fortuitous results have occurred. My decision to visit England in 1983 led to my acquaintance with Leslie Boba, whom I eventually married eighteen years later. Our marriage dissolved, but it had the good effect of prying me away from the East Coast and landing me in the tranquil haven of Seattle, where I met the woman with whom I hope to spend the rest of my life.

I do not say that everything in my life has worked out providentially. As I approach my sixty-fifth birthday, I do find the frenetic energy that carried me on in my twenties, thirties, and even forties flagging a bit. I am a bit tired. Perhaps I have already achieved more than most, but I remain driven to do more. Whether I retain the mental and physical energy to do so remains an open question.

I have, incredibly, prepared reasonably comprehensive editions of many of the greatest writers of weird fiction and a fair number of the lesser ones. By the time I am done, there may remain relatively few weird writers whose work I have not assembled—aside, perhaps, from certain authors who are still under copyright (e.g., Walter de la Mare) and whose estates may not be amenable to negotiation. I have also written chapters or critical articles on many of these authors (including introductions to the aforementioned editions), including *The Weird Tale, The Modern Weird Tale, The Evolution of the Weird Tale, Varieties of the Weird Tale,* and other items.

If I am remembered for anything by future generations, I suspect it will be for (a) my corrected texts of Lovecraft, (b) my biography of Lovecraft (in its full version, *I Am Providence*), (c) my editions of other weird writers (especially Ambrose Bierce and Lord Dunsany), (d) *Unutterable Horror,* and (e) my history of atheism. All these projects could theoretically be superseded by later scholarship, but for the foreseeable future I think they will stand as respectable accomplishments.

As I age, I take heart that I have achieved long-lasting relationships—in some cases lasting decades, and dating to my earliest ventures in the Lovecraft fan community of the 1970s—with such individuals as David E. Schultz, Scott Briggs, Steve Mariconda, Bob Price, Ken Faig, Don Burleson, and others. More recent friends and colleagues from whom I have benefited are Derrick Hussey, Jason and Sunni Brock, Greg Lowney, and Wilum Pugmire. And yet, I have reached the stage where I no longer find it productive to engage in disputes with colleagues or acquaintances, old or new. In recent years I have severed relationships with a number of individuals, since—in spite of what my public or online persona may seem to be—I do not enjoy disputes, especially if they descend to bitterness or vitriol. I find it easier simply to have nothing to do with the parties in question.

The question that might occur to anyone reading this memoir is: Do I have anything left to accomplish? The question is not meant to sound arrogant, in spite of the fact that, if all the books I have already published and also the ones that are waiting to be published were to be enumerated, the number would already surpass 400. Derrick had charitably published my comprehensive bibliography, *200 Books by S. T. Joshi* (2014); a *300 Books* appeared in 2020, and, incredibly, a *400 Books* is likely to appear in late 2023. What else do I wish to do that I haven't already done?

I have long contemplated several grandiose projects of varying sorts, among which are these, among them biographies of Ambrose Bierce, George Sterling, and Lord Dunsany. But I am not sure I have the energy to pursue any of these projects. Specifically in the weird field, I would like to do yet more to promote the work of Lord Dunsany, but I am not sure how I can do so. I toy with the idea of persuading Neil Gaiman to write the screenplay for *The King of Elfland's Daughter,* to be directed by Guillermo del Toro; but that is probably a pipe-dream. Making Dunsany's work more accessible to contemporary readers would be a worthy goal; I have already transcribed several Dunsany novels for proposed ebook editions, but so far this effort has not come to fruition. There is certainly more work to be done on Arthur Machen, Algernon Blackwood, and even M. R. James, but I am not sure I am the person to do it. Someone should write a biography of Ramsey Campbell (one was in the works some years ago, but the author later dropped the project), but again, I do not feel I am the right person for the job. I would like to continue reading and editing weird fiction, whether through Centipede Press, Hippocampus Press, or other publishers.

In terms of Lovecraft, I do not believe I have anything more to say. David E. Schultz and I are close to completing the publication of all surviving Lovecraft letters, and that is about all I care to do. I have had my say in terms of the charting of his life and the analysis of his work, and I am happy to leave it to others to carry on the task of studying this most distinctive literary figure through other approaches. Lovecraft has enriched my life immensely and has led, directly or indirectly, to most of the other intellectual and aesthetic interests I have pursued. My life and career would have been inconceivably different had I not come from India to the United States and become fascinated with him at an early age. In that sense, my life is largely a pendant to Lovecraft's own. I hope I have done some service in elucidating his writing and promoting him as a writer of merit. If that is the case, then that seems to me sufficient justification for my own existence.

Index

Abbey Road (Beatles) 43
Abbot, Steven 257
"Account of Charleston, An" (Lovecraft) 172
Ackerman, Forrest J 265
Acolytes of Cthulhu (Price) 52
Adams, Fred C. 67
Adelaide Concerto 57
"Adept's Gambit" (Leiber) 289
Adler, Betty 271
Advance of the Weird Tale, The (Joshi) 337
Aeroflex Foundation 328
Aeschylus 110
Aesop 189
After Engulfment (Greenham) 330
Against Religion (Lovecraft) 274
Agnostic Reader, The (Joshi) 257
Aickman, Robert 163, 286, 306, 322
Alas, Babylon! (Frank) 47
Albright, Andy 44
Alexander, Ed 44, 68–69, 71, 99
Alfred Hitchcock's Ghostly Gallery (Hitchcock) 41
Alfred Hitchcock's Mystery Magazine 54
Alhazred: Author of the Necronomicon (Tyson) 253
Alice in Wonderland (Carroll) 21
Aliotta, Jerry 158
All Quiet on the Western Front (Remarque) 47
Allen, Woody 305
Allingham, Margery 41, 293
"Allurements of the Abyss" (Prawer) 111

Ambrose Bierce: An Annotated Bibliography of Primary Sources (Joshi–Schultz) 188, 224
American Fantastic Tales (Straub) 253
American Literature 154, 162
"American Pie" (McLean) 72
American Rationalist 283–84, 311, 312, 334
American Supernatural Tales (Joshi) 253–54, 268
Amsterdam, Netherlands 131
Ana Kai Tangata (Nicolay) 299–300
Ancient Sorceries and Other Weird Stories (Blackwood) 221
Ancient Track, The (Lovecraft) 198–99, 227, 236
Anderson, Douglas A. 230
Anderson, James A. 183
Andersson, Martin 250–51, 268, 306–7, 308
André, Maurice 57
Angry Right, The (Joshi) 234–35, 270
Annotated H. P. Lovecraft, The (Lovecraft) 195, 196
Annotated Revisions and Collaborations of H. P. Lovecraft, The (Lovecraft) 275
Annotated Supernatural Horror in Literature, The (Lovecraft) 203
Ape, the Idiot, and Other People, The (Morrow) 200
Apology for Tales of Terror (Scott) 322
Apostles of the Weird (Joshi) 312
Arabian Nights Murder, The (Carr) 153
Arcane Wisdom (publisher) 275, 289

Arkham House 41, 42, 55, 66, 73, 74, 88–89, 90, 99, 113, 125, 126–27, 138, 162, 171–72, 175, 194–95, 196–97, 198, 230, 231–32, 249, 250, 268–69, 276, 285, 286, 290, 296, 299
Arkham House Companion (Jaffery) 194
Arkham House Transcripts 148–49, 155, 249, 275
Arkham Sampler 67, 194
Arkham's Masters of Horror (Ruber) 194–95, 268
Arnoldo Mondadori (publisher) 158
Aro, Linda 120, 121, 137, 192, 219, 258, 307
Aronovitz, Michael 259
Around the World in Eighty Days (Verne) 49
Ash-Tree Press 286
Ashley, Mike 149, 153–54, 289, 342
Asimov, Isaac 47, 104
Assaults of Chaos, The (Joshi) 276–77
Association, The 21
Astor, William Waldorf 232
Astounding Stories 89, 90, 174–75
Astro-Adventures 145
At the House of Sebastian (Joshi) 51
At the Mountains of Madness (Lovecraft) 42, 53, 89, 90, 92, 96, 174, 195, 197, 274, 294
At the Mountains of Madness: The Definitive Edition (Lovecraft) 229–30
At the Mountains of Madness and Other Novels (Lovecraft) 42, 52, 90, 92, 126
Atheism: A Reader (Joshi) 206, 257
Atlantic Monthly 54
Auburn, Cal. 328–29
Australia 330–31
Autobiographical Memoir (Long) 142
"Autobiography in Lovecraft" (Joshi) 106, 107
Ave atque Vale: Reminiscences of H. P. Lovecraft (Joshi–Schultz) 323
Ayer, A. J. 206

Bach, J. S. 38, 56, 68, 109, 120, 218
Bach, Richard 60
Back from the Dead (Joshi) 323
"Back There in the Grass" (Morris) 290
Bacon, Delia 137
Ball State University 29, 32, 33, 37, 39, 44, 45, 58, 60, 68, 72, 74, 176
Ball State University Forum 63
Ballantine Books 126, 162, 196, 293
Baltimore, Md. 117–18, 246–47
Baltimore Sun/Evening Sun 247
Bancroft Library (University of California) 186, 288
Banks, Ernie 35
Baring-Gould, S. 195
Barker, Clive 140, 163, 236, 254, 285
Barlow, R. H. 96, 99, 113, 159, 170, 174, 175, 181, 186, 193, 227, 230, 247–48
Barnes & Noble Publishing 250
Barron, Laird 268, 299–300, 301, 313, 315
Barron, Neil 116, 165, 183
Bartlett, Matt 63
Basic Books 204–5
Bass, Ben 147
Batman 28
Baudelaire, Charles 255
Baxter, Charles 302–3
"Beast in the Cave, The" (Lovecraft) 52
Beatles, The 20–21, 43–44, 63, 82, 285
Beaumont, Charles 265
Bear, Greg 343
Beautiful Thing That Awaits Us All, The (Barron) 299
Beckert, Glenn 35
Beckwith, Henry L. P. 91
Beethoven, Ludwig van 39, 52, 57, 309
Beidler, Peter G. 278
Bender, Barry 129
Benson, E. F. 287
Béraud, Henri 101

Index 351

Bergier, Jacques 91
Berglund, Edward P. 62, 268
Berkove, Lawrence I. 225
Berruti, Massimo 288–89
Best Ghost Stories (Stoker) 193
Best of Forum, The 61
Betancourt, John Gregory 269, 270
Beversluis, John 234
Beyond the Wall of Sleep (Lovecraft) 66
Bierce, Ambrose 52, 59, 153, 154, 186–91, 195, 200, 206, 224–25, 232, 234, 273–74, 276–77, 285, 324–25, 342
Biden, Joe 334
Bilmes, Joshua 196
Birds, The (film) 40
Birkbeck College (University of London) 305–6
Bishop, Zealia 106
"Bits of Autobiography" (Bierce) 188, 273
Bits of Autobiography and Interviews (Joshi) 337
Black Diamonds, The (Smith) 115–16
Black Heart Boys' Choir (Lawson) 339
Black Wings series (Joshi) 268–69, 272, 293–94
"Blackbird" (Beatles) 20
Blackmore, Leigh 260, 321, 330, 331
Blackstone, Sir William 235
Blackwood, Algernon 59, 146, 147, 153, 193, 221, 226, 276, 285
Blatty, William Peter 140, 163
Bleiler, E. F. 193
Bleiler, Richard 257
Bloch, Robert 83, 296
Blood Money (Morrow) 200
Blood Will Have Its Season (Pulver) 260
Bloom, Harold 135–36, 137, 185
Bluebeard's Ghost and Other Stories (Mencken) 272
Blumberg, Diana 130
Boba, Elizabeth 235, 262, 263
Boba, Leslie G. 129–30, 138–39, 151–52, 154, 169, 191, 207–11, 213–19, 235–39, 241–46, 258–59, 261–62, 263, 266, 280, 346
Boerem, R. 105
Boerwinkle, Tom 20
Bok, Hannes 125, 295
Bolivar, Adam 321
Bombay Finance (Joshi) 11
Book of Knowledge, The 25
Book Review Digest 167
Books at Brown 160
Borgo Press 164, 269–70
Boskone 102–3
Bossert, Ed 218
Boston (band) 151
Boston, Mass. 102–3, 121, 144, 210, 314
Bottrill, David 330–31
Bowers, Fredson 90
Bowling Green State University 286
Bowling Green State University Popular Press 153
Bowman, Erin 71
Bowman, Lisa 44, 71
Bradbury, Ray 47, 55
Bradofsky, Hyman 96
Branam, Cathy 56
Brandenburg Concerti (Bach) 68, 120
Branney, Sean 328
Brashear, Iris 43, 49
Breiding, G. Sutton 288
Brennan, Joseph Payne 47–48, 118
Bride of Re-Animator (film) 159
Briggs, Scott 125, 137, 146, 159, 203, 213
British Fantasy Award 290
Britten, Benjamin 218
Brock, Jason V 62, 265, 281, 284, 292, 300, 304, 308, 311, 313, 318, 343
Brock, Sunni K 265, 281, 284, 304, 308, 318, 343
Brontës, the 60
Brood of the Witch-Queen (Rohmer) 285
Brown Daily Herald 91
Brown Film Society 121

Brown Student Chamber Players 118
Brown University 73, 75–76, 78, 79–80, 81–85, 86, 87, 88, 91, 93, 95, 102, 106, 109–11, 113, 118–19, 121–23, 128, 132, 157–60, 217, 273, 305, 345
Browne, Karyn 137
Bryan, William Jennings 232
Buckley, William F., Jr. 32, 233
Buhle, Paul 105, 146
Bullen, John Ravenor 107
Burchfield, Charles 229
Burgess, Thornton 26
Burke, Rusty 249, 250
Burke, Thomas 290–91, 321
Burleson, Donald R. 103–4, 107, 108, 111, 114, 116, 117, 123, 124, 143, 157, 161, 162, 174, 227, 257, 283
Burleson, Mollie L. 114, 146
Burning Court, The (Carr) 41
Burr (Vidal) 61
Burris Laboratory School 37, 38–39, 40, 44, 47–49, 52, 55–58, 61–64, 67–72, 82, 90, 245, 309
Butkus, Dick 20, 34, 48
Butler, Octavia 301
Butler University 29, 30
Butterworth, George 120
Byrd, William 218
Byrds, The 21

Cabell, James Branch 185
Caesar, C. Julius 122
Caligari's Children (Prawer) 111
"Call of Cthulhu, The" (Lovecraft) 287, 331
Call of Cthulhu and Other Weird Stories, The (Lovecraft) 195–96
Cambridge, England 129
Campbell, Jenny 169, 267
Campbell, John W., Jr. 302
Campbell, Ramsey 55, 140, 163, 165–66, 169, 201, 202–3, 226, 252, 254, 259, 260, 267, 269, 277, 289–90, 295, 304, 326, 336, 347

Cannon, Peter 75, 105, 107, 116, 117, 124, 137, 140, 141, 142, 146, 157, 158, 174, 183, 196, 246, 270, 276, 323
Captain Kangaroo 22
Carr, Erik 44
Carr, John Dickson 41, 47, 51, 54, 153, 293
Cartagena, Ovidio 342
Carter, Lin 125–26, 193
Case, David 279, 285
"Case for Classicism, The" (Lovecraft) 84
Case of Charles Dexter Ward, The (Lovecraft) 53, 197, 260, 274
Case of the Constant Suicides, The (Carr) 54
Casting the Runes and Other Ghost Stories (James) 223
Catman and Bobbin 28
Caton, Marcia 25, 36
Catullus, C. Valerius 110, 287
Centipede Press 200, 272–73, 278, 284–87, 290, 291, 322, 341–42
Cerasini, Marc A. 125
Ceremonies, The (Klein) 140
Chalker, Jack L. 66, 76–77, 86, 117
Chambers, Robert W. 199–200, 254, 260, 286, 291
Chandler, Raymond 55, 293
Chanler, Josephine 17
Chaosium 199–200, 219
Chapman, Walker 180
Chappell, Fred 285, 294
Chariots of Fire (film) 121
Charleston, S.C. 181
Chelsea House Publishers 132–33, 135–38, 139, 146, 150, 157, 172–73, 183–86, 206, 304, 345, 346
Chessie (cat) 214, 215, 237, 238, 242, 244, 245
Chesterton, G. K. 233
Chicago, Ill. 17–18, 20, 70, 138, 331
Chicago Bears 20, 34, 138
Chicago Blackhawks 20
Chicago Bulls 20

Chicago Cubs 20, 35, 311, 331
Chicago White Sox 20
Chifflot, Martine 329
Chitwood, Sean 318
Christianity 17, 41, 114, 129, 232–34, 283–84, 300
Christie, Agatha 41, 43, 47, 51, 53–54
Christmas Concerto (Corelli) 119
Chronicles of Narnia (Lewis) 41
Chuidian, Sonny 44
Cicero, M. Tullius 122
Civil War Memories (Joshi) 205–6
Clark, Lillian D. 148, 149, 228, 314, 325
Clark Ashton Smith: The Emperor of Dreams (documentary) 329
Clark University 280
Classic Horror Stories, The (Luckhurst) 298–99
Classical Papers (Joshi) 337
Classics and Contemporaries (Joshi) 165
Classics of Gothic Horror 321–22
Clinton, Hillary 311
Closing Arguments (Darrow) 256
Cobb, Irvin S. 290, 321
Cobwebs from an Empty Skull (Bierce) 189, 225
Cohen, Philip 135, 150, 185
"Coffin, The" (Joshi–Marhoefer) 51
Cold Embrace, The (Joshi) 291
Collected Drama of H. L. Mencken, The (Mencken) 271
Collected Essays (Lovecraft) 228–29
Collected Fables of Ambrose Bierce, The (Bierce) 189
Collected Fantasies (Smith) 292
Collected Fiction: A Variorum Edition (Lovecraft) 296–97
Collected Ghost Stories (James) 147
Collected Jorkens, The (Dunsany) 222
Collected Plays (Dunsany) 307
Collected Poems (Lovecraft) 52, 53, 199
Collected Poems (Mencken) 271
Collected Poems (Wandrei) 141
Collected Works (Bierce) 188, 189, 225

Collins, Tom 97–98, 108
Color over Occam, The (Thomas) 295
"Colour out of Space, The" (Lovecraft) 53, 195, 196, 261
"Coming of the Terror, The" (Machen) 220
Commonplace Book (Lovecraft) 142
Complete Fiction (Lovecraft) 250–51
Complete John Silence Stories, The (Blackwood) 193
Complete Pegāna, The (Dunsany) 199
Complete Poetry (Sterling) 288
Complete Poetry and Translations (Smith) 255
Complete Short Stories of Ambrose Bierce (Bierce) 189, 225
Concerti Grossi (Corelli) 38, 70
Concerti Grossi (Handel) 38, 57
Concerti Grossi (Joshi) 56
Concerto Grosso No. 1 in A minor (Joshi) 56
Concerto Grosso No. 3 in G major (Joshi) 56–57
Concerto in D major for 2 Trumpets, 2 Oboes, Strings and Tympani (Joshi) 57
Concerto in D major for 4 Violins and Strings (Vivaldi) 119
Concerto in F major for 3 Violins and Strings (Vivaldi) 119
Conger, Alice 148, 249
Connors, Scott 88, 232, 292, 311, 336
Conservative 97–98, 155
Conservative: Complete, The (Lovecraft) 87, 95, 97
Conspiracy of Silence (Joshi) 270
"Continuity" (Lovecraft) 332
Cook, W. Paul 248, 261
Cooke, Jon 159
Cool Air (film) 265
Cooley, John C. 38, 56–58, 70
Cooley, Marian 38–39, 56
Cooley, Peggy 56
Copper, Basil 253
Copps Hill Burying Ground 144

Core of Ramsey Campbell (Campbell–Joshi–Dziemianowicz) 166
Corelli, Arcangelo 38, 39, 57, 58, 70, 119
Cornell University 122, 239, 241, 243, 245, 256
Cosmic Meld, The 52–54, 64
Count Magnus and Other Ghost Stories (James) 223
Count of Thirty, The (Joshi) 166
Cox, Michael 223
Crane, Stephen 62, 90, 206
Crawford, Gary William 201, 292
"Crawling Chaos, The" (Lovecraft–Jackson) 86
Crimson Tome, The (Opperman) 310
Critical Essays on Lord Dunsany (Joshi) 292
Crofts, Anna Helen 275
Croning, The (Barron) 299
Cronkite, Walter 19, 32
Crowther, Pete 269, 278, 293, 312
Crypt of Cthulhu 52, 123–24, 125, 128, 144, 145, 183
Cthulhu Mythos 161, 252–53, 256, 267, 268–69, 287, 293–94, 295, 298
Cultural Correspondence 105
Curious Myths of the Middle Ages (Baring-Gould) 195
Currey, L. W. 328
Curse of the Wise Woman, The (Dunsany) 168
Curtis, Graham 331
Curtis, Margi 331
Cushing, Nicole 294
Cynick 90–91

"Dagon" (Lovecraft) 100
Dagon (fanzine) 140
Dagon and Other Macabre Tales (Lovecraft) 59, 66, 79, 126
Daily Kos 335
Dalby, Richard 193
Daniels, Les 163, 202

Dark Brotherhood and Other Pieces, The (Lovecraft et al.) 66, 117, 171
Dark Eidolon and Other Fantasies, The (Smith) 292
Dark Gods (Klein) 140
Dark of the Moon (Derleth) 287
Dark Regions Press 287, 290
Dark Renaissance Books 290, 321
Dark Shadows 22
Dark Side Mystery (TV show) 340
Darke Phantastique, A (Brock) 62
Darrow, Clarence 232, 256
Datlow, Ellen 165, 301, 314, 315
Davies, L. P. 226
Davis, Sonia H. 145, 149, 314, 323, 338, 341
Dawnward Spire, Lonely Hill (Lovecraft–Smith) 296, 313
Day of the Locust, The (West) 83
de Camp, L. Sprague 66, 73, 74, 75, 142, 143, 151, 171, 172, 179, 180, 221
de Castro, Adolphe 10
de la Mare, Walter 346
De Nardi, Claudio 158
De Rerum Natura (Lucretius) 84, 206
Dead Reckonings 251–52
Dead Titans, Waken! (Wandrei) 273
Dear Dead Women (Underwood) 272
"Death" (Rector) 63
Deathrealm 183
del Toro, Guillermo 274, 294, 347
Delderfield, R. F. 60
Delius, Frederick 120
Dell (publisher) 195
Democratic National Convention (1968) 32
Demons by Daylight (Campbell) 165–66
Dempsey, Jim 284, 303, 318
Derleth, April 195, 268–69
Derleth, August 42, 55, 66, 73, 79, 87, 89, 115, 126–27, 145, 148, 149, 150, 157, 159, 161, 172, 194, 195, 199, 248–49, 252, 253, 268, 286, 287, 289–90, 297–98, 336

Devil's Dictionary, The (Bierce) 189–90, 273
Devil's Disciple, The (Shaw) 70
Devils and Demons (Serling) 41
DeWitt, Tom 48
Diary of a Sorceress (Dioses) 310
"Diary of Alonzo Typer, The" (Lumley) 275
Dickens, Charles 60
Dikty, Thaddeus (Ted) 116–17, 154
Dillinger (film) 44
Dioses, Ashley 310
Dirda, Michael 302
Discovering Classic Fantasy Fiction (Schweitzer) 147
Discovering Classic Horror Fiction (Schweitzer) 147
Dismal Paradox and Other Poems, A (Joshi) 63
Dobson, Roger 139, 220
Documents of American Prejudice (Joshi) 204–5, 235
Doerr, Edd 257
Donnelly, Sean 248, 252
Doré, Gustave 197
Double Take 51, 64
Douglas, Drake 66
Dover Publications 132, 193, 196, 220, 232, 291
"Dover Road, The" (Machen) 220
Downfall of God, The (Joshi) 338–39
Doyle, Joe 222, 305, 307
Drake, David A. 107
Dream-Quest of Unknown Kadath, The (Lovecraft) 53, 67, 102
Dreamer and a Visionary, A (Joshi) 202
Dreams in the Witch House and Other Weird Stories, The (Lovecraft) 229
Dreams of Fear (Joshi–Mariconda) 287–88
Driven to Madness with Fright (Joshi) 312
Dublin University Magazine 199
Dunsany, Lord (18th baron) 59, 73, 104, 146, 147, 153, 167–68, 187, 193, 199, 221–23, 226, 246, 247, 276, 301, 305, 306–7, 347
Dunsany, Edward Plunkett, Lord (20th baron) 222
Dunsany, Maria Alice, Lady 222, 305, 306–7
Dunsany, Randal Plunkett, Lord (19th baron) 222
Dunsany, Randal Plunkett, Lord (21st baron) 306
"Dunwich Chimera and Others, The" (Murray) 144
"Dunwich Horror, The" (Lovecraft) 42, 53, 89, 96, 195, 197
Dunwich Horror and Others, The (Lovecraft) 42, 52, 53, 126, 127, 175
Dwyer, Bernard Austin 149, 182
Dylan, Bob 21
"Dystopia as Utopia" (Buhle) 105
Dziemianowicz, Stefan 124–25, 140, 146, 159, 163, 164, 166, 193, 200, 226, 227, 246, 250, 254, 287
Dyer, Jim 325

"Eben's Portrait" (Thomas) 259
Eckhardt, Jason C. 95–96, 102, 114, 117, 123, 128, 140, 142, 161, 166, 171, 181, 189, 269, 294
Eckhardt, Victoria 114, 181
Ecstasy of Fear, An (Pugmire) 328
Ed Sullivan Show, The 20
Eddy, C. M., Jr. 325
Edkins, Ernest A. 248
Edwards, Douglas 81
Einstein, Albert 12
Eldritch Influence, The (documentary) 265
"Eldritch Tome, The" (Joshi) 52
Elegant Nightmares (Sullivan) 107
Eleven Great Horror Stories (Owen) 42
Eliot, Charles W. 235
Eliot, George 60
Eliot, T. S. 233
Elkins, Anjeli 310, 318
Elkins, Nalini 15, 16, 18, 32, 33, 38, 40, 65, 191, 280, 309, 310, 318

Ellery Queen's Mystery Magazine 54, 222
Emerson, Ralph Waldo 157
Emperor of Dreams (Sidney-Fryer) 336
Encyclopaedia Britannica 25
Enlarged Devil's Dictionary, The (Bierce) 190
Enoch Pratt Free Library (Baltimore, Md.) 246
Epicure in the Terrible, An (Schultz–Joshi) 161
Epicurus 122
Épinal, France 329
"Error in Calculations, An" (Joshi) 52
Esoteric Order of Dagon (a.p.a.) 90, 92, 107, 123, 146, 298
Essential Solitude (Lovecraft–Derleth) 249
"Establishing the Canon of Weird Fiction" (Joshi) 236
Estro Armonico, L' (Vivaldi) 38
Etchison, Dennis 163, 202, 285–86
Euripides 287
"Events at Poroth Farm, The" (Klein) 140, 254
Everett, Justin 292
Everts, R. Alain 74–75, 88, 90, 143, 178, 179
"Evil Captain James, The" (Joshi) 62
Evolution of the Weird Tale, The (Joshi) 225–26
Exchange of Souls, An (Pain) 101
Exegesis: Lovecraft (documentary) 340
Exorcist, The (Blatty) 140
Extrapolation 183
Eyes of the God (Barlow) 230

Face That Must Die, The (Campbell) 140, 202
Fahrenheit 451 (Bradbury) 47
Faig, Kenneth W., Jr. 86, 116, 161, 179, 183, 275, 277
Fairleigh Dickinson University Press 161, 190

Fall of the Republic and Other Political Satires, The (Bierce) 189
Falwell, Jerry 233
Fantasia on a Theme of Thomas Tallis (Vaughan Williams) 120
Fantastic Fables (Bierce) 189
Fantastic Poetry, The (Lovecraft) 155, 198
Fantazius Mallare (Hecht) 226
Farmer, W. C. 310
Fatout, Paul 187
Fear of the Unknown (documentary) 265
Federlein, Suzanne 36
Fedogan & Bremer 273, 294–95, 299
Ferguson College (Poona) 12, 178
Ferris, Henry 199
"Festival, The" (Lovecraft) 114
Filippo, Joseph de 132
Finzi, Gerald 120
First Writings: Pawtuxet Valley Gleaner (Lovecraft) 87
"Fishhead" (Cobb) 290
Fitzpatrick, Fergal 297
Fitzpatrick, Vince 247
Five Jars, The (James) 224
Flack, Roberta 72
Fleurs du mal, Les (Baudelaire) 255
Floating Dragon (Straub) 140
Fly, The (film) 40
Flynn, Tom 257, 284
Fonseca, Tony 165
"For the Ahkoond" (Bierce) 189
Ford, Drew 291
Ford, Gerald 58
Former People 299
Forum 61–64, 70, 76, 82, 323
"Foulness Island" (Joshi) 54
400 Books by S. T. Joshi (Joshi) 347
Four Seasons (Vivaldi) 70
Fox, Virgil 38
France, Anatole 241
Frank, Pat 47
Frankenstein (Shelley) 278, 291, 307
Frederick Ungar Publishing Company 149

Free Inquiry 334–35
Freeman, Mary E. Wilkins 290, 321
Freud, Sigmund 235, 300
Friends of H. P. Lovecraft 159–60
Friends of the Library of Brown University 258
From Baltimore to Bohemia (Mencken–Sterling) 190
Frost, David 20
Froude, James Anthony 60
Fulwiler, William 107
Fumosa, Richard 137–38, 150, 158, 177–78, 204
Fungi from Yuggoth (Lovecraft) 53, 142, 160
Furley, David 122
Fusco, Sebastiano 158
Fuseli, Henry 229
Future Shock (Toffler) 61

Gaer, Joseph 188
Gafford, Sam 124, 220, 288–89, 338
Gailey, Cassandra 120, 121
Gailey, John 120, 121
Gaiman, Neil 347
Galloping Gourmet, The 22
Galpin, Alfred 92
Gamwell, Annie E. P. 100, 148, 181, 228, 325
Gandhi, Mahatma 13–14
Gardiner, Samuel Rawson 60
Gardner, Erle Stanley 47
Gardner cemetery 261
Garton, Ray 284
Gautier, Théophile 290, 321
Georgie (cat) 264
German, Wade 304
Ghost in the Corner and Other Stories, The (Dunsany) 307
Ghost Story (Straub) 140
Ghosts of the Heaviside Layer, The (Dunsany) 307
Gibbons, Orlando 68
Gieseker, Anne 280, 310
Gieseker, David 133
Gloria (Vivaldi) 39

Go Back at Once (Aickman) 286
God and Man at Yale (Buckley) 233
God's Defenders (Joshi) 233–34, 270
Godden, Jeff 207, 210
Goho, James 285
Goldstone, Adrian 219, 289
Gomer Pyle, U.S.M.C. 27
Gonce, John Wisdom, III 198
Goodell, Peter 48, 52
Goodstone, Tony 135
Gordon, Robert 48, 63, 81
Gordon, Stuart 196, 265
Gore Vidal: A Comprehensive Bibliography (Joshi) 256–57
Gorman, Herbert 230
Gossage, Christy 45
Gossage, Mark 45
Gossett, Thomas F. 180
Grabinski, Stefan 125, 227
Grafton, Sue 270–71, 293
Grant, Ulysses S. 49
Gray, John 302
Grayson, Perry 174, 330
Great Tales of Terror (Joshi) 232
Great Weird Tales (Joshi) 193
Great White Space, The (Copper) 253
Greek language 85, 109–10, 130, 227, 236, 281
Greek Philosophers, The (Guthrie) 110
Green Round, The (Machen) 220
"Green Tea" (Le Fanu) 278
Greene, Douglas G. 153
Greenham, Ellen 330
Greenwood Press 121, 153, 168, 226, 227, 257
Gregory, Jay 163
Grenander, Mary Elizabeth 154, 191
Gresh, Lois H. 308
Grossman, Leigh 195, 196
Grulich, Ryan 340–41
Guardian (London) 302
Gullette, Alan 236, 289
Guthrie, W. K. C. 110–11

H. L. Mencken: An Annotated Bibliography (Joshi) 271

H. L. Mencken on American Literature (Mencken) 232
H. L. Mencken on British Literature (Mencken) 247
H. L. Mencken on Religion (Mencken) 232
H. L. Mencken's America (Mencken) 233
H. P. Lovecraft (Starmont Reader's Guide) (Joshi) 116–17
H. P. Lovecraft: A Comprehensive Bibliography (Joshi) 260
H. P. Lovecraft: A Critical Analysis (Joshi) 66–67, 75, 76
H. P. Lovecraft: A Critical Study (Burleson) 157
H. P. Lovecraft: A Life (Joshi) 165, 179–83, 201, 203, 303
"H. P. Lovecraft: Consummate Prose Stylist" (Mariconda) 124
H. P. Lovecraft: Four Decades of Criticism (Joshi) 48, 74–75, 76–77, 105–6, 111, 116, 260
H. P. Lovecraft: The Decline of the West (Joshi) 154–55, 168, 206
H. P. Lovecraft and Lovecraft Criticism: An Annotated Bibliography (Joshi) 90, 91–92, 116
H. P. Lovecraft Cat Book, The (Lovecraft) 323
H. P. Lovecraft Centennial Conference 146, 155, 157–60
H. P. Lovecraft Centennial Conference: Proceedings (Joshi) 160
H. P. Lovecraft Companion, The (Shreffler) 111, 197–98
H. P. Lovecraft Encyclopedia, The (Joshi–Schultz) 197–98
H. P. Lovecraft Film Festival 265, 340
H. P. Lovecraft Forum 146, 182
H. P. Lovecraft Historical Society 328
H. P. Lovecraft in "The Eyrie" (Joshi–Michaud) 100, 276

H. P. Lovecraft's Favorite Horror Stories (Joshi) 275–76
Haefele, John D. 297–98
Haldeman, Philip 264–65
Hall, Lynn 217–18, 304, 332
Hambling, David 294
Hammett, Dashiell 55, 293
Hampton, John 44
Handel, G. F. 38, 39, 56, 57, 85, 119, 218, 305, 316, 317
Handler, Daniel 229
Haringa, Jack 251
Harksen, Henrik 308
Harms, Daniel 198
Harrall, Robert C. 94, 126, 172, 196, 258
Harris, Thomas 163
Harris, Woodburn 149
Hart, Mara Kirk 162–63
Hart, Will 104
Hartman, Forrest 126
Hartmann, J. F. 88
Hartwell, David G. 301–2
Harvard University 75–76, 108, 122
Harvard University Press 182
Harvest Home (Tryon) 52
Hashish-Eater, The (Smith) 292
Hassler, Donald M. 183
Hastur Cycle, The (Price) 199
Haunted Dolls' House and Other Ghost Stories, The (James) 223–24
"Haunter of the Dark, The" (Lovecraft) 143
Haunting of Hill House, The (Jackson) 39
Haverfordian 153
Hawaii 330
"He Who Liveth in the Depths" (Joshi) 52
Hearn, Lafcadio 290
Hearst, William Randolph 187, 224
Hecht, Ben 226
Hedren, Tippi 40
Heliogabalus (Mencken–Nathan) 272
Henry (cat) 243–44, 280, 304, 343
Henry VIII (Shakespeare) 129

"Herbert West—Reanimator" (Lovecraft) 196
Hermaphrodite and Other Poems, The (Loveman) 230
Herrera, Philip 74
Hichens, Robert 232
Higgins, Betsy 38, 69
Higgins, Kathy 38
Higgins, Patty 37–38, 55, 57, 58, 68–69, 91–92
"Higher Criticism and the *Necronomicon*" (Price) 123
Highsmith, Patricia 293
Hilger, Ron 292
Hill, Joe 315
Hinshaw, Betty 49
Hippocampus Press 142, 203–4, 223, 230–31, 248, 249, 251–52, 259, 260, 264, 275, 287–91, 321, 322, 323, 324–25, 326, 328, 333, 336, 342, 345
History of England (Macaulay) 60
History of Greek Philosophy (Guthrie) 111
Hitchcock, Alfred 40, 47, 51, 290
Hitchens, Christopher 274
Hite, Kenneth 252
Hobbs, Niels 304, 313–14
Hoboken, N.J. 158
Hodge, Julie 236
Hodgson, William Hope 276, 285, 288–89, 338
Hoffman, Charles 125
Holbach, Paul Thiry, baron d' 284
Holder, Nancy 312
Hollies, The 21
Honeymoon in Jail (Joshi) 337–38
Hopkins, Ernest Jerome 189, 190, 225
Hopper, James 232
Horizon Chorus 243
Horror! (Douglas) 66
Horror Expert, The (Long) 322
Horror Fiction Index, The (Joshi) 342

Horror in the Museum and Other Revisions, The (Lovecraft) 150, 275, 293
Horror Literature (Barron) 165
Horror on the Stair, The (Quiller-Couch) 199
"Hound, The" (Lovecraft) 326
Howard, I. M. 148, 249
Howard, Robert E. 115, 123, 125, 148–49, 248, 249–50, 329, 340
Howard Phillips Lovecraft: Dreamer on the Nightside (Long) 141–42
Howe, John 340
Huff, Glenn 19, 27, 29
Hull, Bobby 20
Hundley, Randy 35
Hurshell, Michael 118–19
Hussey, Derrick 203–4, 223, 225, 230, 231, 249, 251, 255, 258, 264, 275, 288, 291, 293, 294, 295, 297, 308, 312, 314, 321, 325, 333, 345
Huston, Emily 58
Huxley, Aldous 59
Huxley, Thomas Henry 257
"Hypnos" (Lovecraft) 176

"I Am a Murderer" (Joshi) 82–83
I Am Providence (Joshi) 275, 329–30, 346
I Am Providence (Mamatas) 313
I Am Third (Sayers) 47
I, Robot (Asimov) 47
I Saw What You Did (TV film) 40
Icons of Horror and the Supernatural (Joshi) 255–56
Icons of Unbelief (Joshi) 257–58, 272
Imp of Aether, An (Pugmire) 328
In Defence of Dagon (Lovecraft) 128
In Her Place (Joshi) 235
In the Grip of Fear (Level) 273
In the Land of Time and Other Fantasy Tales (Dunsany) 221
"In the Vault" (Lovecraft) 42
"In the Year 2525" (song) 21
Incredible Adventures (Blackwood) 221

Index to the Selected Letters of H. P. Lovecraft, An (Joshi) 99, 113
Indianapolis, Ind. 29–32
Indick, Ben 98, 246
International Conference on the Fantastic in the Arts 236
International Horror Guild Award 227
Invisible Sun (Wandrei) 273
Iran hostage crisis 114–15
Irrational Man (film) 305
Israel in Egypt (Handel) 316
Issues 82–83
It Only Comes Out at Night and Other Stories (Etchison) 285–86

Jack (cat) 280
Jackson, Shirley 39, 163
Jackson, Winifred Virginia 155
Jacobi, Carl 285
Jacobs, W. W. 291, 321
Jaffery, Sheldon 194
James, Henry 278
James, M. R. 146, 147, 153, 223–24, 276–77, 289, 341
James, P. D. 293
James, William 233
Je suis Providence (Joshi) 329–30
Jefferson Airplane/Jefferson Starship 21, 63
Jenkins, Ferguson 35
Jersey City, N.J. 133, 138, 151, 152, 154, 157, 210
"Jerusalem" (hymn) 219
John Dickson Carr: A Critical Study (Joshi) 153
John F. Blair, Publisher 63
John Hay Library (Brown University) 75, 78–79, 85–87, 90, 93, 101, 115, 142, 145, 149, 158, 160, 169–70, 172, 227, 254, 296, 308, 328
Johnson, Andrew 49
Johnson, Lyndon 32
Johnson, Robert Barbour 342
Johnson, Samuel 109
Jonathan Livingston Seagull (Bach) 60

Jones, HolliAnne 69–70, 72–73, 93, 113–14, 130, 176
Jones, Scott R. 314–15
Jones, Stephen 253
Joshi, Leslie B. *See* Boba, Leslie G.
Joshi, Nalini. *See* Elkins, Nalini
Joshi, Narayan Malhar 11
Joshi, Padmini T. 12, 13, 14–18, 23, 24, 25, 26, 27, 32, 37, 73–74, 75–76, 81, 172–73, 176–79, 207, 213, 245, 309, 318, 334, 343
Joshi, Ragini T. 12–13, 15, 16, 18, 26, 32, 65, 123, 133, 191, 280, 309, 310, 318
Joshi, S. T.: and atheism, 13–14, 17, 206, 218–19, 233–34, 257–58, 272, 283–84, 338–39; and cats, 65, 214–15, 217, 237–38, 243–45, 280–81, 343; citizenship of, 17–18, 99; and college (graduate school), 110, 122–23, 131–32; and college (undergraduate), 75–76, 81–82, 83–85, 91, 95, 109–11; and comic books, 28; and conventions, 102–5, 117–18, 142–43, 146, 149, 157–60, 166, 169, 236, 259–60, 265, 267–68, 304–6, 308, 313–15; as editor, 61, 63–64, 70–72, 96, 105–6, 140–41, 171–72, 193–94, 199–200, 202–3, 204–6, 219–25, 235, 250–51, 253–54, 268–69, 272–74, 283–88, 289–92, 293–95, 321–26, 336–37, 341–42; and elementary school, 15–16, 22–23, 30, 35–36; employment of, 131–33, 135–38, 150, 185–86; as fiction writer, 50–52, 55, 61–62, 82–83, 108–9, 200, 269–70, 276–77, 312, 323, 337–38; and films, 40, 121; health of, 27–28, 97, 283; and high school, 48–49; in India, 11–14; and junior high school, 36–40, 43, 44–45; as literary critic, 52–55, 66–67, 106–7, 116–17, 124, 146–47, 152–55, 163–66, 167–68, 183–84, 194–95, 200–202, 225–27, 252–53, 270–71, 277–79, 295,

299–300; marriages of, 152, 211, 214–17, 261–64, 266, 307–8; media work of, 329, 339–41; and music, 21, 26–27, 30–31, 37–39, 43–44, 55–58, 67–69, 70, 72, 85, 118–19, 120–21, 217–19, 243, 315–16, 332–33; as poet, 62–63; and politics, 19–20, 31–32, 58–59, 234–35, 311–12, 333–35; readings of, 25–26, 40–43, 47–48, 59–61, 66, 140; as scholar, 74–75, 76–80, 85–95, 97–102, 107–8, 111, 113, 116, 121, 126–28, 145, 148–49, 161–62, 170–71, 174–76, 179–83, 186–91, 194, 195–99, 203, 227–32, 246–50, 251–52, 254–57, 260–61, 271–72, 274–76, 288–89, 292–93, 296–97, 312–13, 336, 342; similarities to H. P. Lovecraft, 9, 38, 51, 52, 57, 60, 65, 71, 75, 93, 99, 107, 128, 130, 173, 185, 190; and sports and games, 18–19, 20, 24–25, 26–27, 31, 33–34, 59; travels of, 17–18, 69–70, 92–94, 114, 121, 128–31, 139, 144–45, 177–79, 235–37, 238–39, 246–47, 258, 304–7, 308–10, 314, 316–18, 321, 328–31; and women, 25, 44–45, 69–70, 72–73, 113–14, 129–30, 138–39, 151–52, 168–69, 191–92, 206–11, 266–67, 279–80. *See also* Lovecraft, H. P.
Joshi, Tryambak M. 11–12, 13–14, 16, 19, 30, 37, 85, 176
Joshi, Vanam Malhar 11
Journal of the Fantastic in the Arts 236
Journals (Joshi) 337
Journey into Darkness (Long) 322
Julian (Vidal) 61
Junk Fiction (Joshi) 270–71
Juvenal (D. Junius Juvenalis) 84, 122
"Juvenal and Ancient Philosophy" (Joshi) 110
Juvenilia: 1897–1905 (Lovecraft) 128

Kalem Club 338
Karajan, Herbert von 39
Keene, Brian 315
Keener, Lisa 57
Kelley, David 40
Kemelman, Harry 47
Kennedy, John F. 19
Kennedy, Robert F. 32
Kent State University Press 77, 86, 105, 106, 116, 260
Kerr, Graham 22
Kessinger, Don 35
Kiernan, Caitlín R. 252, 254, 259, 268, 269, 285, 295, 304
"Killing Me Softly" (Flack) 72
King, Mark 33, 36, 44, 64, 90
King, Martin Luther, Jr. 32
King, Matt 33
King, Stephen 163, 236, 254
King in Yellow, The (Chambers) 260
King of Elfland's Daughter, The (Dunsany) 168, 246, 347
Kipling, Rudyard 193
Kirk, George W. 162
Kirk, Russell 279
Klain, Janice 303–4, 318
Klass, David 168
Klass, Judy 168–69
Klass, Morton 168
Klass, Perri 168
Klass, Philip 168
Klein, T. E. D. 94, 118, 124, 140, 141, 163, 174, 221, 254, 285
Klinger, Leslie 302
Knox, Robert H. 140
Koontz, Dean 165
Kopacz, Mateusz 308
Koszowski, Allen 194, 312
Kramer, Erik 162
Kratzner, Mr. 49
Krueger, Ken 67, 76
Krutch, Joseph Wood 11
Ku Klux Klan 93
Kuhn, Richard 115
Kurmis, Emily 308

La Farge, Paul 296
"Lament for H.P.L." (Galpin) 92

Landow, George P. 102
Lane, Joel 166
Langan, John 269
Last Book of Jorkens, The (Dunsany) 222
Last Man, The (Shelley) 291
Last Oblivion, The (Smith0 230
Late Breakfasters, The (Aickman) 163
Latin language 84–85, 109–10, 120, 130, 170–71, 207, 227, 281
Lauck, Joe 44, 61
Lawrence, D. H. 286
Lawson, Curtis M. 339
Lazarus (Béraud) 101
Le Fanu, J. Sheridan 199, 278, 279, 286, 289
Le Guin, Ursula K. 221
Leahy, John Martin 342
Leal School (Urbana, Ill.) 15–16, 19, 24
Lee, David 29, 31
Lee, Jennifer B. 158
Leiber, Fritz 103, 105, 161, 289
Leithauser, Brad 165
Leman, Andrew 328
Let It Be (Beatles) 44
Letters from New York (Lovecraft) 228
Letters of Ambrose Bierce, The (Bierce) 190
Letters to Alfred Galpin (Lovecraft) 228
Letters to Arkham (Campbell–Derleth) 289–90
Letters to C. L. Moore and Others (Lovecraft) 313
Letters to F. Lee Baldwin, Duane W. Rimel, and Nils Frome (Lovecraft) 312–13
Letters to Family and Family Friends (Lovecraft) 325
Letters to Henry Kuttner (Lovecraft) 155
Letters to J. Vernon Shea, Carl F. Strauch, and Lee McBride White (Lovecraft) 312
Letters to James F. Morton (Lovecraft) 275

Letters to Maurice W. Moe and Others (Lovecraft) 313
Letters to Rheinhart Kleiner (Lovecraft) 228
Letters to Richard F. Searight (Lovecraft) 162
Letters to Robert Bloch (Lovecraft) 162
Letters to Samuel Loveman and Vincent Starrett (Lovecraft) 162
Letters with Frank Belknap Long (Lovecraft) 328
Lev family 113
Level, Maurice 273, 291
Levin, Ira 140
"Levitation" (Brennan) 47–48
Lévy, Maurice 91, 149
Lewis, C. S. 41, 116, 234
Lewis, M. G. 278
Lewis, Wyndham 283
Library of America 229, 250, 253, 273–74
Library of Congress 237, 247
Life Is a Hideous Thing 146
Ligotti, Thomas 163, 165
Lily (cat) 244–45, 264
Lincoln, Abraham 18
Lindahl, Thad 39
Lindsay, David 168
Lipinski, Miroslaw 125, 227
Lippi, Giuseppe 158
Listen, America! (Falwell) 233
"Literary Copernicus, A" (Leiber) 161
Literary Lapses 50
Literature of Terror, The (Punter) 277
"Little Bit o' Soul" (song) 21
"Little Sam Perkins" (Lovecraft) 332
Liverpool University Press 201–2
Lives of the Novelists (Scott) 322
Livesey, T. R. 251
Lockhart, Ross E. 315
London Evening News 220
Loneliest Continent, The (Chapman) 180
Long, Frank Belknap 72, 94, 95, 106, 141–42, 159, 174, 204, 322

Long, Lyda 141, 174
Look Behind the Derleth Mythos, A (Haefele) 297–98
Lord Dunsany: A Bibliography (Joshi–Schweitzer) 167
Lord Dunsany: Master of the Anglo-Irish Imagination (Joshi) 168
Lord of a Visible World (Lovecraft) 197
Los Angeles Times Book Review 221
"Lost City, The" (Joshi) 52
Lost Ghosts (Freeman) 290
Loucks, Donovan K. 267–68, 274
Loucks, Pamela 267
Louinet, Patrice 329
Louvre (Paris) 329
Love, Bob 20
"Love, Hate, Money and Murder" (Joshi) 50
Lovecraft, Charles (Danny) 246, 294, 330–31
Lovecraft, H. P.: influence of on STJ, 83–84, 146, 345–47; STJ's biography of, 179–83, 275, 329–30; STJ's critiques of, 64–65, 66–67, 106–7, 116–17, 123–24, 137, 143, 153, 154–55, 161, 183–84, 226–27, 252–53, 295; STJ's imitations of, 50, 54, 276–77, 326; STJ's readings of, 41–43, 59, 65–66, 73–74, 135–36; STJ's reviews of, 52–53; STJ's scholarship on, 74–78, 85–88, 90–97, 99–106, 111, 113, 116, 121, 143–45, 147–49, 162, 169–72, 195–99, 203–4, 227–30, 247–51, 260–61, 274–75, 275–76, 285, 296, 297–99, 312–13, 323, 325, 331, 335–36, 347–48; STJ's textual work on, 88–90, 97–99, 126–27, 150, 174–75, 296–97; letters of, 328; life of, 9, 60, 94–95, 323; media work on, 339–41; racism of, 14, 205, 300; recognition of, 145–46, 157–62, 265, 300–303, 313–14, 335–36, 345; and weird fiction, 83–84, 200, 221, 289, 290. *See also* Joshi, S. T.: similarities to H. P. Lovecraft
Lovecraft, Margaret 246, 331
Lovecraft: A Biography (de Camp) 66
Lovecraft: A Study in the Fantastic (Lévy) 149
"Lovecraft Criticism: A Study" (Joshi) 90
Lovecraft: Disturbing the Universe (Burleson) 157, 162
Lovecraft and a World in Transition (Joshi) 295
Lovecraft and Weird Fiction 312
Lovecraft Annual 251, 295, 299
Lovecraft Chronicles, The (Cannon) 276
Lovecraft, mon amour (Chifflot) 329
Lovecraft ou du fantastique (Lévy) 91
Lovecraft Remembered (Cannon) 323
Lovecraft Studies 107–8, 111, 116, 117, 123, 124, 127–28, 129, 140–41, 143, 144, 154, 181, 199, 251, 260
"Lovecraft's Alien Civilisations: A Political Study" (Joshi) 106–7, 124
Lovecraft's Book (Lupoff) 276
Lovecraft's Follies (Schevill) 113
Lovecraft's Legacy (Weinberg) 157
Lovecraft's Library: A Catalogue (Joshi–Michaud–Schultz) 100–101, 113, 230
"Lovecraft's Other Planets" (Joshi) 124
Lovecraftian Ramblings 52, 62, 97, 140
Loved One, The (Waugh) 47
Loveman, Samuel 162, 176, 230–31, 336
Lowney, Greg 264, 308, 318, 327, 332
Luckhurst, Roger 298–99, 305
Lucretius (T. Lucretius Carus) 84, 110, 122, 206
"*Lucretius Satiricus*" (Joshi) 122
"Lucubrations Lovecraftian" (Lovecraft) 86
Lumley, Brian 252, 253

Lumley, William 275
Lupoff, Richard A. 99, 236, 276
Lykens, Andy 44
Lykens, Randy 44

Macaulay, Thomas Babington 60
McCauley, Kirby 118
MacCulloch, Simon 166
MacDonald, Philip 293
Macdonald, Ross 55, 293
McFarland (publisher) 202
Machen, Arthur 59, 128, 129, 139, 146–47, 153, 193–94, 219–20, 226, 247, 274, 276–77, 285, 289, 292, 322–23, 338
McInnis, John L., III 158, 160
McKee, Mrs. 36
McLean, Don 72
Macleod, Fiona 193, 195
McNail, Stanley 288
McNamara, M. Eileen 170, 181
McNaughton, Brian 183
McVicker, Terence 296
Madness of Cthulhu, The (Joshi) 294
Magnificat (Pergolesi) 39
Major Literary Characters 150
Mamatas, Nick 313, 315
Man That Was Used Up, The 278
Mansfield, Lisa 44
Marblehead, Mass. 114, 142
Marblehead (Lupoff) 276
Marginalia (Lovecraft et al.) 171
Marhoefer, Jay 44, 51–52, 72
Mariconda, Steven J. 124, 142, 146, 154, 158, 163, 169, 181–82, 183, 220, 227, 229, 261, 287, 305
Mark of the Beast and Other Horror Tales, The (Kipling) 193
Marshall, Herb 96, 103
Marshall, Nancy 44
Marshall, Ron 96
Marten, Robert 144
Martin, John 196
Mass in F minor (Byrd) 218
Maturin, Charles Robert 278
Maupassant, Guy de 341–42

Maxwell, J. K. (pseud. of STJ) 270
Means to Freedom, A (Lovecraft–Howard) 249–50
Medusa and Other Poems (Lovecraft) 128
"Medusa's Coil" (Lovecraft–Bishop) 150
Menchaca, Frank 136
Mencken, H. L. 190, 232–33, 234, 237, 246–47, 256, 271–72, 323–24
Mencken on Mencken (Mencken) 271
Mendelssohn, Felix 218
Menegaldo, Gilles 329
Meng, Roderic 55
Mercier, Vivian 29
Merritt, Pearl K. 338
Mesa, Gabriel 125
Messiah (Handel) 39, 151, 218, 305, 317
Metamorphoses (Ovid) 84
Metcalfe, John 286
Metzinger, Alexis 340
Michaud, Marc A. 87–88, 90, 94, 95–101, 102, 107–8, 111, 113, 115, 117, 123, 128, 140–41, 142, 145, 155, 161, 162, 164, 166, 182, 183, 189, 198, 203, 251, 275, 323, 338, 345
Michaud, Paul R. 87, 88, 94–95
Miéville, China 230
Midnight Call and Other Stories (Thomas) 259
Midnight House 200, 232
Migliore, Andrew 265
Mikita, Stan 20
Millar, Margaret 55, 293
Millard, Ann 56, 57
Miller, John J. 229
Miller, Laura 301, 313
Millman, Michael 195–97, 221, 223, 250, 254
Mimi (cat) 244–45, 263, 280, 343
Minnesota Review 105
Miskatonic 90
Miscellaneous Writings (Joshi) 337

Miscellaneous Writings (Lovecraft) 171–72, 198, 295
Mister Rogers' Neighborhood 22
Mitchell, Stephen L. 234
Modern Language Association 304
Modern Library 229–30
Modern Weird Tale, The (Joshi) 163–64, 166, 180, 202, 225, 226, 279
Moe, Maurice W. 206
Molière, Jean-Baptiste 60
Mollie (cat). *See* Mimi (cat)
Monkees, The 21
Moonlight Sonata (Beethoven) 52
Monster Maker and Other Stories, The (Morrow) 200
Monster of Moonlight and Others, The (Joshi) 52
Moore, Bryan 265, 305
Moore, C. L. 248, 296
Moravia, N.Y. 239, 241–43, 261
More Annotated H. P. Lovecraft (Lovecraft) 196
Morey, Chris 290
Morey, Joe 290, 291, 321
Morris, Gouverneur 290, 321
Morris, Harry O., Jr. 107
Morrish, Ethel Phillips 94–95
Morrison, Michael A. 165
Morrow, W. C. 200, 205, 206, 287
Morse, Richard Ely 148
Morse, Salmi 190
Morton, James F. 9, 275, 338
Mosig, Dirk W. 75–76, 77, 86–87, 88, 90, 91–93, 96, 98, 103–5, 107, 108, 116–17, 151, 159, 160, 298
Moskowitz, Sam 139
Mother West Wind books (Burgess) 25–26
"Motives for Suicide" (Joshi) 62
Moudry, Joe 92
Moulton, Charles Wells 135–36
"Mound, The" (Lovecraft–Bishop) 106, 150
Mountain Walked, A (Joshi) 287
Mozart, Wolfgang Amadeus 57, 169, 218, 309

Mr. Cannyharme (Shea) 326
Mr. Faithful (Dunsany) 167
Much Misunderstood Man, A (Bierce) 224
Muncie, Ind. 29, 32, 35, 41, 91, 93, 99, 114, 176, 215, 245, 309, 318, 334
Muncie Evening Press 72
Muncie Public Library 40–41, 42, 66, 127, 291
Muncie Star 67
Munn, H. Warner 118
"Murder" (Joshi) 50–51
Murder of Roger Ackroyd, The (Christie) 43, 54
Murray, George Edwards 312
Murray, Will 143–44, 149, 159
Musée d'Orsay (Paris) 329
Musical Heritage Society 38, 57
"Musical Theory, A" (Joshi) 83
Musick for the Royal Fireworks (Handel) 38
My Work Is Not Yet Done (Ligotti) 165
Myers, D. L. 318
Mysore, India 177–78
Mysteries of Time and Spirit (Lovecraft–Wandrei) 227
Mystery and Horror Writers of the Twentieth Century (Joshi) 54–55, 64, 226
Mythos Books 253, 287
MythosCon 267–68, 280

"Narrative of a Murderer, The" (Joshi) 82
Narrative of Arthur Gordon Pym, The (Poe) 62
Nathan, George Jean 272
National Amateur 183
National Union Catalog of Pre-1956 Imprints 100
Naumcheff, David 33, 34, 35, 40, 45, 59
Naumcheff, Tommy 33, 40, 59
Nay, Fred 44
NECON 123, 166

Necrofile 164–65, 183, 202
Necronomicon (Alhazred) 62, 85, 104, 131, 198
Necropsy 165
Necronomicon (a.p.a.) 90
NecronomiCon (1990s) 142, 169
NecronomiCon (2010s) 295, 299, 304–5, 308, 313–15
Necronomicon Press 87, 107–8, 128, 141, 142, 145, 155, 162, 171, 182–83, 189, 198, 203, 204, 249, 251, 252, 276, 323, 338, 345
Necronomicon Suite (Sitsky) 330
Neily, Ken 52, 62, 96, 97, 102, 123
Nesbit, E. 290, 321
New Annotated Lovecraft, The (Lovecraft) 302–3
New Criterion 229
New Encyclopedia of Unbelief, The (Flynn) 257
"New England" (Lovecraft) 86
New Kalem Club 124–25, 140, 163, 192, 203, 318
New Lovecraft Collector 183
New Moulton's Library of Literary Criticism 135–36
New York, N.Y. 93–94, 131, 139, 152, 172–73, 207–11, 213–14, 215–16, 222, 228, 241, 246, 345
New York Public Library 93–94, 98, 136, 152, 163, 190, 200, 208, 220, 231
New York Review of Books 182–83, 214, 303
New York Times 132, 185, 213, 335
New York Times Book Review 127, 180, 229
New Yorker 205, 271, 301
Nicolay, Scott 299–300, 301, 313–14
Nielsen Hayden, Patrick and Teresa 150
Nietzsche, Friedrich 74
Night Gallery 22
"Night in the Bell Inn, A" (Ferris) 199
"Night Ocean, The" (Barlow–Lovecraft) 96, 150

Night of the Wolf, The (Long) 322
Night-Pieces (Burke) 290–91
Night Shade Books 198, 222, 227–28
Night with Mephistopheles, A (Ferris) 199
Night's Black Agents (Leiber) 289
Nightmare's Disciple (Pulver) 260
Nine Tailors, The (Sayers) 54
Niswander, Adam 267, 294
Nixon, Richard M. 43, 58
Noctuary (Ligotti) 165
Nolan, William F. 265, 284, 304, 342–43
Northwest Chorale 217–18, 243, 303, 316, 332, 333
Norton, W. W. (publisher) 182
Norton Book of Ghost Stories, The (Leithauser) 165
Norwescon 151
"Notes on the Prose Realism of H. P. Lovecraft" (Mariconda) 124
"Nothing Verses, The" (Joshi) 62
Nothing Verses and Other Poems, The (Joshi) 62–63
Nussbaum, Jon 44, 99
Nussbaum, Martha 122
Nyctalops 106, 107

O Fortunate Floridian (Lovecraft) 248
Oates, Joyce Carol 182–83, 303
O'Brien, Geoffrey 253, 273–74
Of Mice and Men (Steinbeck) 47
Ohio State University Press 189, 224
Ohio University Press 105–6, 107, 111, 197, 232, 233, 256
"Old Bugs" (Lovecraft) 297
Old Folk of the Centuries, The (Dunsany) 168
Older, Daniel José 300–302, 313
Olson, Dwayne 295
"On the Literary Influences Which Shaped Lovecraft's Works" (Shea) 105
Opperman, K. A. 310
Oracle 44, 61, 70–71

"Orchid of Asia, An" (Underwood) 272
Ordinary People, The (Joshi) 50, 51
O'Reilly, Bill 234–35
Original Atheists, The (Joshi) 284
Ornaments in Jade (Machen) 147, 220
Orton, Vrest 203
Orwell, George 59
Osher, Elken 188
Out of the Immortal Night (Loveman) 230
"Outsider, The" (Lovecraft) 42–43
Outsider and Others, The (Lovecraft) 90
Ovid (P. Ovidius Naso) 84
Owen, Betty 42
Owens, Shawn R. 265
Owings, Mark 76, 77, 86
Oxford University Press 223, 298–99
Oxley, Jackie 36
Ozymandias 74

PS Publishing 202, 269, 278, 312
Pain, Barry 101
Pan's Garden (Blackwood) 221
Paolo (cat) 279, 280, 310
Paradise Lost (Milton) 196
Parameters of the Weird Tale, The (Joshi) 337
Pardoe, Rosemary 223, 224
Parents of Howard Phillips Lovecraft, The (Faig) 161
Paris, France 131, 329
Parker, Scott 33
Partington, Blanche 224
"Party of Traitors, The" (Joshi) 334–35
Pasha, Qais 339–40
Pathways to Elfland (Schweitzer) 167
Paul Revere and the Raiders 21
Peake, Mervyn 168
Pelan, John 200, 285, 300
Penguin Book of Ghost Stories, The 254
Penguin Classics 195–97, 221, 223–24, 229, 235–36, 250, 253–54, 274, 292, 298–99, 302, 345

Penumbra 326
Penzoldt, Peter 66
Perkins, Jeff 216
Pet Shop Boys 169
Peter, Paul, and Mary 21
Pfaff, Chris 192, 219, 307
Pfaff, Richard William 223
Phaedrus 189
"Phantasmagoria" (Scott) 322
Phillips, Michelle 44
Phillips Exeter Academy 256
Philosophy of the Plays of Shakspere Unfolded, The (Bacon) 137
Phoebe (cat) 244, 280, 310, 343
Piccolo, Brian 20
"Pickman's Model" (Lovecraft) 42, 144–45
"Picture, The" (Joshi) 50, 51
"Picture in the House, The" (Lovecraft) 295
Pinkley (cat) 214–15, 217
Place Called Dagon, The (Gorman) 230
Planet of the Apes (film) 40
Plante, Bob 143
Playboy 54, 55
Pleasures of a Futuroscope, The (Dunsany) 222–23
Poe, Edgar Allan 38, 62, 91, 117–18, 197, 226, 278, 285, 306
Poems for Midnight (Wandrei) 141
"Poetry and the Gods" (Lovecraft–Crofts) 275
Poona, India 11–13, 177
Pope, Bertha Clark 190, 224
"Portrait of Mr. W. H., The" (Wilde) 137
Portraits in Moonlight (Jacobi) 285
Potter, J. K. 201
Pound, Ezra 283
Prawer, S. S. 111
P'rea Press 246
Presley, Elvis 21
Price, E. Hoffmann 194, 248

Price, Robert M. 52, 123–25, 142, 143, 144–45, 162, 199, 223, 234, 257, 283, 313
Primal Sources (Joshi) 230
Princeton University 122–24, 127–28, 131–32, 219–20, 345
Principles of Textual Criticism (Thorpe) 89
Private Life of H. P. Lovecraft, The (Davis) 145
Progression of the Weird Tale, The (Joshi) 337
Prometheus Books 206, 232, 233–35, 257, 272
Providence, R.I. 78–80, 81, 99, 108, 113–14, 122–23, 142, 145, 159, 160, 170, 210, 241, 258, 274, 304–5, 314, 345
Providence Evening News 86, 88
Providence Journal 183
Publishers Weekly 234, 270
Puccini, Giacomo 263
Pugmire, W. H. 253, 264, 268–69, 272, 288, 305, 308, 318, 326–29, 332
Pulliam, June 165
Pulps, The (Goodstone) 135
Pulver, Joseph S., Sr. 260, 305, 308
Punter, David 277
Purdue University 187
Putnam, Michael C. J. 84, 85, 110, 120, 122

Quebec, Canada 339
Queen, Ellery 47
Queen Anne Lutheran Church 218–19
Quest for the Well of Souls (Chalker) 76–77
Quiller-Couch, Sir Arthur 199
Quincy, Ill. 238–39
Quirk, Tom 224

Raaflaub, Hans 120–21, 122
Raaflaub, Kurt 109–10, 120–21

Race: The History of an Idea in America (Gossett) 180
Rajala, Juha-Matti 251, 268, 308
Ramsey Campbell: Master of Weird Fiction (Joshi) 336
Ramsey Campbell and Modern Horror Fiction (Joshi) 201
Ramsey Campbell, Probably (Campbell) 202–3, 269
"Rats in the Walls, The" (Lovecraft) 42, 53, 110, 195, 196
Ray, David 342
Rayner, Mindi 191–92, 205, 206–9
"'Reality' and Knowledge" (Joshi) 106
Recognition of H. P. Lovecraft, The (Joshi) 335–36
Rector, Bill 44, 49, 63
"Recurring Doom, The" (Joshi) 52
Recurring Doom, The (Joshi) 323
Recurring Doom and Others, The (Joshi) 52
Reginald, Robert 164, 183, 269–70
"Remarks on Colin Wilson's Analysis of H. P. Lovecraft in *The Strength to Dream*" (Joshi) 74–75
Remarque, Erich Maria 47
"Removal Company, The" (Morrow) 200
Removal Company, The (Joshi) 200, 270
Rendell, Ruth 293
Renshaw, Anne Tillery 296
Republican Party 334–35
Résumé with Monsters (Spencer) 253
Return of the Soul, The (Hichens) 232
Revised H. P. Lovecraft Bibliography, The (Owings–Chalker) 76
Rhode Island School of Design 91, 95, 274
Rice, Anne 163
Richard, Little 21
Rigel 90
Rimel, Duane W. 150
Rise and Fall of the Cthulhu Mythos, The (Joshi) 252–53, 256, 268, 295
Risqué Stories 145
Roberts, Dave 285

Roberts, Larry 275, 289
Rockhill, Jim 279
Rod Serling's Triple W (Serling) 41
Rodin, Auguste 117
Roe v. Wade 335
Rohmer, Sax 285
Rolling Stones, The 21
Roman Catholicism 17, 69, 171, 239
Rose, Robert C. 48, 61, 62, 63, 64, 70, 72, 337
Rosemary's Baby (Levin) 140
Rostropopvich, Mstislav 119
Rotor, Elda 254, 274
Rowman & Littlefield 292
Ruber, Peter 175, 194–95, 268, 289
Rud, Anthony M. 342
Rumsey, Digby 305
Russell, Bertrand 74, 129, 145, 206, 233, 345
Russia 335
Rutledge Hill Press 205

Sackett, Jeffrey 227
Saffel, Steve 293, 294
St. Armand, Barton L. 75, 117
St. Cloud State University 187
St. John's Catholic Church (Providence, R.I.) 143
Saler, Michael 229
Saltus, Edgar 290
San Francisco Chronicle 127, 187
San Francisco Examiner 187, 188
Santo, Ron 35
Sargent, Helen 50
Sargent, Joe 49
Sarnath Press 284, 315, 323–24, 337–38
Saturday Review (London) 167
Saturnalia and Other Poems (Lovecraft) 128
Sayers, Dorothy L. 47, 54
Sayers, Gale 20, 34, 47
Saysana, Morgane 329
Scarecrow Press 167, 257, 292
"Scherzo in D-flat" (Joshi) 62
Schevill, James 113

Schiff, Stuart David 98, 107
Schlobin, Roger 116
Schmidt, Barbara 70–71
Schow, David J. 163, 202, 268
Schrader, Richard J. 271
Schultz, David E.: editing of Lovecraft's letters, 147–48, 155, 162, 170–71, 179, 227–28, 248–50, 251, 275, 296, 312–13, 325, 347; and Hippocampus Press, 203; STJ's meetings with, 142, 169, 267; research on Ambrose Bierce, 186, 187–88, 190, 193, 224–25, 324–25; research on Lovecraft, 75, 77, 79, 101, 116, 124, 142, 143, 161, 197–98, 298; research on Clark Ashton Smith, 230, 231–32, 254–55, 296, 336–37; research on George Sterling, 186, 231–32, 288
Schultz, Gail 142
Schwader, Ann K. 288, 294
Schweitzer, Darrell 111, 147, 167, 194, 292, 307
Science Fiction Review 111
Science versus Charlatanry (Lovecraft) 88
Scopes trial 232, 256
Scott, Sir Walter 321–22
Scott, Winfield Townley 105, 145
Searchers After Horror (Joshi) 294–95, 300
Searles, A. Langley 116
Seattle, WA 138–39, 151–52, 209–11, 214–17, 238–39, 262–64, 267, 346
Selected Essays (Lovecraft) 323
Selected Letters (Howard) 249
Selected Letters (Lovecraft) 74, 99, 101, 162, 190, 197
Selected Letters of Clark Ashton Smith (Smith) 231–32
Selected Papers on Lovecraft (Joshi) 145
Selected Poems (Smith) 79
Seneca the Younger (L. Annaeus Seneca) 110

Serling, Rod 55
Sesame Street 22
Seven Deadly Pleasures (Aronovitz) 259
Seven Minutes, The (Wallace) 60
Seventh Symphony (Beethoven) 57
Shadow Coast (Haldeman) 264–65
Shadow of the Unattained, The (Sterling–Smith) 231
"Shadow out of Time, The" (Lovecraft) 174–76, 204
"Shadow over Innsmouth, The" (Lovecraft) 53, 180, 204
Shadow over Innsmouth, The (Lovecraft) 171
Shadowlands (Straub) 140
Shakespeare, William 39, 129, 136–37, 139
Shanks, Jeffrey L. 292
Shaw, George Bernard 70
Shea, J. Vernon 11, 75, 103, 105, 107, 117, 118, 296
Shea, Michael 326
Shelley, Mary 278, 291, 321
Sherman, Stuart 115
Shooting for the Butler (documentary) 305
Short Fiction of Ambrose Bierce, The (Bierce) 225
Shorter, Elliot 143
Shreffler, Philip A. 111, 197–98
Shroud Publishers 67
Shuttered Room and Other Pieces, The (Lovecraft et al.) 297
Sidney-Fryer, Donald 310, 321, 336
Sigurdson, Kirk 211
Silbert, Barbara Briggs 203
"Silver Swan, The" (Gibbons) 68
Silvers, Robert 303
Simon & Garfunkel 21, 39
Simpson, O. J. 171
Sinclair, May 321
Sitsky, Larry 330
Six Wives of Henry VIII, The (TV show) 57
"Sixteen Gargoyles, The" (Joshi) 52

Sixty Years of Arkham House (Joshi) 194
Slayer of Souls, The (Chambers) 199–200, 286
Sloan, Jerry 20
Smith, Alex 274
Smith, Carol Dorman 186, 231
Smith, Clark Ashton 79, 115–16, 125, 145, 172, 186, 224, 230, 231–32, 248, 254–55, 289, 292, 296, 329, 336–37
Smith, Michael Marshall 269
Smith, Wallace 226
Smithsonian Institution (Washington, D.C.) 237
Sneakers (cat) 217, 237, 238, 242, 244, 245
Snyder, Maryanne 264
Sole Survivor: Bits of Autobiography, A (Bierce) 189
"Some Remarks on Ghost Stories" (James) 224
Something about Cats and Other Pieces (Lovecraft et al.) 66
Something from Below (Joshi) 312
Songs from Lovecraft and Others (Joshi) 333
Songs of a Dead Dreamer (Ligotti) 163
Sonnets of the Midnight Hours (Wandrei) 141
Southern Illinois University Press 164, 202
Spectral Realms 288, 304, 318
Spectral Tales 223
Spencer, William Browning 253
Spengler, Oswald 135
Sperling, Alison 304
Spink, Mary 100
Spoor Directory (Adams) 67, 75
Spring, Darin Coehlo 329
Springsteen, Bruce 82
Squires, Roy A. 296
Stanley, John H. 79, 86, 87, 100, 160, 172, 174, 175, 204, 260
Star Trek (TV show) 168

Starmont House 116–17, 125, 147, 154, 164, 183, 201
Starr, Kevin 288
Starrett, Vincent 148, 188
Starship 99
State University of New York at Albany 191
"Statement of Randolph Carter, The" (Lovecraft) 144
Stein, Gordon 206
Steinbeck, John 47
Steinberg, Harold 135
Stepanek, Sally 136
Stephen, Leslie 206, 324
Sterling, George 186–87, 190, 224, 231, 232, 287, 288, 289, 342
Stevenson, Robert Louis 278
Stoker, Bram 193, 285
Stories from the Big Black House (Thomas) 259
Strange Adventure, A (Morrow) 200
Strange Journeys of Colonel Polders, The (Dunsany) 168
Strange Lover, The (Dunsany) 307
Straub, Peter 140, 163, 166, 229, 253, 254, 321, 343
Strength to Dream, The (Wilson) 74
Strother, Jennifer 44
"Structure of Lovecraft's Longer Narratives, The" (Joshi) 124
Studies in Supernatural Literature 292
Studies in the Fantastic 252
Studies in Weird Fiction 140–41, 147, 163, 164, 236, 252
Stuff of Dreams, The (White) 289, 291
Stump, Susan 68–69
Stumpf, Edna 127
"Stupidity Watch, The" (Joshi) 283–84, 311
Stuttman, Suzanne 130
"Style Sheet for Lovecraftian Studies, A" (Joshi) 107
Subtler Magick, A (Joshi) 183–84
"Suggestions for a Reading Guide" (Lovecraft) 136
"Suicide, The" (Joshi) 50

Sullivan, Jack 107
Sullivan, Mark 19
"Sunset" (Lovecraft) 332
"Supernatural Horror in Literature" (Lovecraft) 54, 59, 121, 146, 168, 203, 229–30, 277
Supernatural in Fiction, The (Penzoldt) 66
Supernatural Index, The (Ashley) 342
Supernatural Literature of the World (Joshi–Dziemianowicz) 226–27, 277
Swan Point Cemetery 160
Sweetser, Wesley D. 219, 289
Sydney Bulletin 331
Symphony No. 1 in C major (Joshi) 56

Taffy (cat) 237–38, 244, 245, 264
Tait, Rita 193–94
Tales (Lovecraft) 229
Tales of Horror and the Supernatural (Machen) 220
Tales of Mystery and Horror (Level) 273
Tales of Soldiers and Civilians and Other Stories (Bierce) 224
Tales of the Cthulhu Mythos (Derleth) 73, 157, 268
Tales of the Lovecraft Collectors (Faig) 277
Tangled Muse, The (Pugmire) 272
Tartarus Press 199, 272, 322
Tem, Melanie and Steve Rasnic 308
Tenn, William. *See* Klass, Philip
Terror and Other Stories, The (Machen) 220
"Testament" (Mencken) 233
Thackeray, William Makepeace 60
Thill, Christophe 329
Thing on the Doorstep and Other Weird Stories, The (Lovecraft) 197, 235
"Thinker, The" (Rodin) 117
Thirst of Satan, The (Sterling) 231
Thirty Hours with a Corpse (Level) 291
Thirty Years of Arkham House (Derleth) 194
Thomas, Jeffrey 314

Thomas, Jonathan 258–59, 268, 295, 314
Thompson, C. Hall 253, 287
Thorpe, James 89
Those Who Return (Level) 273
Three Gothic Novels 229
300 Books by S. T. Joshi (Joshi) 347
Three Impostors, The (Machen) 193–94, 220
Three Impostors and Other Stories, The (Machen) 220
Tierney, Richard L. 288, 298
Time 60, 74
"Time and Men" (Joshi) 62
Time Machine, The (Wells) 47
Times Literary Supplement 111, 221, 229, 302
Titan Books 293
To a Dreamer (Lovecraft) 323
"To Howard Phillips Lovecraft" (Smith) 79, 145
To Quebec and the Stars (Lovecraft) 171, 172
Toccata and Fugue in D minor (Bach) 38
Toffler, Alvin 61
Toldridge, Elizabeth 296
Tolkien, J. R. R. 168
"Touch of Death, The" (Joshi) 50, 51
Touponce, William F. 292
Tovatt, Anthony 47, 48, 51
Tragedy at Sarsfield Manor (Joshi) 108–9, 270
"Trap, The" (Lovecraft–Whitehead) 113, 150
"Travels in the Provinces of America" (Lovecraft) 172
Tremblay, Paul 315
Trio Sonata No. 1 in D major (Joshi) 57
Trollope, Anthony 60
Trump, Donald J. 311, 334–35
Tryon, Thomas 52, 163
Tryout 90
Turn of the Screw, The (James) 278
"Turn, Turn, Turn!" (Byrds) 21

Turner, James 99, 126–27, 141–42, 150, 157, 171–72, 175–76, 194, 198
Turner, Jeff 44, 48, 61
Turtles, The 21
Tutti i racconti (Lovecraft) 158
Twain, Mark 272
Twayne Publishers 117, 157, 191, 201
21st-Century Horror (Joshi) 279, 315
Twilight Zone, The 22
Twilights, The 68–69, 93
200 Books by S. T. Joshi (Joshi) 50, 54, 347
Tymn, Marshall 121
Tyson, Donald 253

Ukraine 335
Unabridged Devil's Dictionary, The (Bierce) 190
Unbelievers, The (Joshi) 272
Uncle Silas (Le Fanu) 278
Uncollected Letters (Lovecraft) 145
Uncollected Prose and Poetry (Lovecraft) 96, 103, 107, 113, 171
"Under the Pyramids" (Lovecraft–Houdini) 197
Underwood, Edna W. 272
United Co-operative 86
University of Georgia Press 190
University of Illinois 14, 19, 29
University of Maryland 247
University of Tampa Press 248, 252, 260, 274
University of Tennessee Press 189, 225, 324
University of Texas Press 154, 164, 180
University of Virginia 139
University of Warwick 128–29
University of Washington 130, 207, 210, 215, 237, 239, 264
"Unknown, The" (Lovecraft) 155
Unquiet 98
Unutterable Horror (Joshi) 277–79, 281, 291, 292, 346
Urbana, Ill. 14–15, 23, 28

Index 373

Vanguard 61, 70
Varieties of Crime Fiction (Joshi) 292–93
Varieties of Religious Experience (James) 233
Varieties of the Weird Tale (Joshi) 293
Vaughan Williams, Ralph 120
Verdi, Giuseppe 218
Verne, Jules 49
Vidal, Gore 32, 61, 256–57
Vietnam War 19–20, 21, 32, 43
Viking Penguin 126
Village Voice 127
Virgil (P. Vergilius Maro) 84
Vivaldi, Antonio 38, 39, 56, 70, 85, 109, 119
Vivisector 182
Voigtlander, David 19
Voltaire (François-Marie Arouet) 59, 60, 81
Voyage to Arcturus, A (Lindsay) 168

Wakeland, Leah 57
Wakeland, Ruth 39
Wakeland, William 39, 57
Walker, Alfred 19
Wall Street Journal 229
Wallace, Irving 60–61
Walters, Jerad 284–87, 308, 322, 325
Wandrei, Donald 55, 126, 141, 149, 150, 227, 248, 273, 287
Warnings to the Curious (Pardoe–Joshi) 224, 289
Washburn, Michael 312
Washington, George 95
Wasp 190
Water Music (Handel) 38
Waugh, Evelyn 47, 59
Waugh, Robert H. 146, 182, 251, 292
Wayne State University Press 149
Web of Easter Island, The (Wandrei) 273
Webb, Mila 304, 310, 318
Weinberg, Robert E. 157
Weiner, Cherry 294
Weird Fiction Review 284–85, 325

Weird House 342
Weird Tale, The (Joshi) 153–54, 163, 164, 167, 220, 223, 225, 279
Weird Tales 99–100, 102, 193, 194–95, 253, 258, 260, 296, 297
Weird Writer in Our Midst, A (Joshi) 100, 276
Wellesley Index to Victorian Periodicals 199
Wells, H. G. 47, 290
West, Nathanael 59, 83
West India Lights (Whitehead) 113
Westview School 35–36, 39, 40
Wetzel, George T. 75, 86, 105, 117
What Is Anything? 146, 321
What Is Man? and Other Irreverent Essays (Twain) 272
"What Is the Cthulhu Mythos?" (panel discussion) 143
"Whisperer in Darkness, The" (Lovecraft) 42, 53, 125
Whispers 107
White, Edward Lucas 205, 289, 291
White, Holly 327
White Album (Beatles) 20–21, 43
White Fire (Bullen) 107
White People and Other Stories, The (Machen) 220
White People and Other Weird Stories, The (Machen) 274
"White Rabbit" (Jefferson Airplane) 21
Whitechapel (Gafford) 338
Whitehead, Henry S. 113
"Who Wrote 'The Mound'?" (Joshi) 106
Whole Wide World, The (film) 340
Wilde, Oscar 137, 278
Wildside Press 269
William Hope Hodgson: Voices from the Borderland (Joshi–Gafford–Berruti) 288
Williams, Billy 35
Williams, Jason 198, 227
Williamson, Jack 104
Wilson, Colin 74
Wilson, Edmund 105, 111

Wilson, Gahan 300
Wilson, Mary Krawczak 266–67, 279–81, 283, 284, 303, 304, 307–10, 314, 316–18, 321, 326, 327, 329, 330–31, 333, 346
"Windy" (Association) 21
Winter, Douglas E. 195
Winter Wish, A (Lovecraft) 98, 108
Wodehouse, P. G. 47
Wolever, Frances 17
Wollheim, Donald A. 296
Wood, Gordon S. 109
Wood, Mary 49
Woodward, Frank H. 265
Woodworth, Stephen 294
Word, The (Wallace) 60–61
Workman, John Rowe 110
World Book Encyclopedia 25
World Fantasy Award 154, 227, 300–302, 314, 315
World Fantasy Convention 75, 108, 117, 126, 142–43, 149, 152, 154, 260, 267, 286, 296, 301, 305

World Horror Convention 304
World Science Fiction Convention (Iguanacon) 103–4
World Series 35, 311
Worlds of Fantasy & Horror 194
Worrell, Everil 342
Wrigley Field (Chicago) 331
Writings in The Tryout (Lovecraft) 90
Writings in The United Amateur (Lovecraft) 87
Wynn, David 253, 287

Yale University 75–76, 82, 122, 136, 137, 187
Year's Best Fantasy and Horror, The (Datlow–Windling) 165
Yellow Sign and Others, The (Chambers) 199–200
Yeo, Robert 55–56
"'You'll Reach There in Time'" (Joshi) 62
Yuzna, Brian 159

www.ingramcontent.com/pod-product-compliance
Lightning Source LLC
Chambersburg PA
CBHW051034160426
43193CB00010B/935